SEX & Y

The spread of sexually transm......... in the 1980s, including most spectacularly AIDS an.. ..erpes, has made everyone more aware of the fundamental relationship between sex and health. Here is the first really comprehensive account of the whole subject – a book that both informs and reassures, and disentangles the medical facts from the myths about sex and sexual problems.

Nine eminent specialists simply and authoritatively explain both the physiology and the psychology of sex-related health problems. At the heart of the book is a major survey of sexually transmitted and sex-related diseases that provides a rational path through what can be a maze of misinformation and even hysteria. Wider issues are introduced by a summary of the anatomy and physiology of sex, and the book goes on to discuss in sequence contraception, infertility, physical problems of sex, ageing and sexuality, the psychology of sex and gender, aberrant sexual behaviour and the social aspects of sexuality.

This book addresses in a human and helpful way the anxieties of a society that is trying to find the appropriate balance between the sexual inhibitions of the past and the permissiveness of the 1970s and beyond.

Sex
&
Your
Health

General Editor:
DR JAMES BEVAN

Mandarin

A Mandarin Paperback

SEX & YOUR HEALTH

First published in Great Britain 1985
by Mitchell Beazley International Limited
This edition published 1990
by Mandarin Paperbacks
Michelin House, 81 Fulham Road, London SW3 6RB

Mandarin is an imprint of the Octopus Publishing Group

A CIP catalogue record for this book
is available from the British Library
ISBN 0 7493 0046 9

Every effort has been made to ensure that the information
contained in this book was accurate at the time of going to press,
but medical research and advances in treatment
continually move forward. Each chapter is the sole work
of its author and any opinions expressed therein do not necessarily
reflect the opinions of the other contributors.

Phototypeset by Input Typesetting Ltd, London
Printed in Great Britain
by Cox & Wyman Ltd, Reading.

THE AUTHORS

THE ANATOMY & PHYSIOLOGY OF SEX Dr James Bevan MB Bchir MRCGP DRCOG, general practitioner and general editor of this book, has previously produced with Mitchell Beazley the internationally successful *Your Family Doctor* and the pocket and handbook editions of his *First Aid and Family Medical Guide* which have sold several hundred thousand copies in five languages worldwide

THE MAIN FORMS OF CONTRACEPTION Dr Jane Kilvington MB BS, Member of the Institute of Psychosexual Medicine; clinic doctor, Margaret Pyle Centre, London; and consultant, psychosexual problems, BUPA

THE CAUSES OF MALE & FEMALE INFERTILITY Mr Michael Cameron FRCS FRCOG, consultant obstetrician and gynaecologist, St Thomas' Hospital and Royal Masonic Hospital, London

PHYSICAL PROBLEMS THAT MAY AFFECT SEXUALITY Dr Alan J. Riley OStJ MSc MB BS LRCP MRCS DObst RCOG, specialist in the treatment of sexual problems; editor of the *British Journal of Sexual Medicine*; and senior research physician for a major British pharmaceutical company

THE LATER YEARS & SEXUAL SATISFACTION Pat Lloyd, marital and psychosexual counsellor, Harley Street, London; and Dr Paul Brown PhD DipPsych FBPsS, consulting clinical and occupational psychologist, Harley Street, London; and joint editor, *Sexual and Marital Therapy*

SEXUALLY TRANSMISSIBLE DISEASES & THEIR MIMICS Brian J. Ford CBiol FIBiol FRSH FLS, Fellow of Cardiff University, with a section on AIDS by Dr James Bevan.

THE PSYCHOLOGY OF SEX & HUMAN DEVELOPMENT and **DEVIATIONS FROM THE SEXUAL NORM** Dr J. G. Weir MA ChB MD FRCPsych DPM, consulting psychiatrist, St Mary's Hospital, London

SEXUALITY IN THE SOCIAL CONTEXT Dr Peter Dally MB FRCP FRCPsych DPM, consultant psychiatrist, Westminster Hospital, London

CONTENTS

INTRODUCTION

Dr James Bevan

In the past decade there has been an increasing awareness that the full enjoyment of sex has not been found despite the era of permissiveness that preceded it. The freedom from fear of pregnancy gave freedom to reassess individual morality, and this led to an increase in the spread of sexually transmissible diseases. The freedom to experiment with sexual behaviour showed that enjoyment of sex is not necessarily a matter of better technique. Gradually an awareness has developed that enjoyment also depends upon a loving relationship and an acceptance of personal responsibility for the dangers that may result.

Sex and Your Health is a book for those who may already know how to enjoy sex – it is not a manual of how to do so – and for those who are aware that they can enjoy it more with a clearer understanding of its medical aspects. Such an understanding removes the fear of the myths about sex and incorporates a knowledge of how the body is built and works, the anatomy and physiology; of how contraception works and, conversely, the problems that may cause infertility; and of what sexual difficulties may occur in those whose health is impaired and handicapped, as well as which changes result from age. Equally important is an understanding of why we react, the psychology of sex, and the problems that may arise when maturity is diverted from the main direction of psychosexual development, into ways that used to be called the perversions. Good sex most importantly requires an understanding of how to respond physically in a loving relationship.

Sex and Your Health is arranged so that chapters can be read in sequence. Approached this way it offers a logical coverage of the subject, from anatomy and physiology to the role sex plays in society. It can also be used as a 'fact-finder' – for example, sexual problems such as frotteurism and sado-masochism are arranged alphabetically. Each chapter has a brief introduction and there is a full index and glossary.

In *Sex and Your Health* I have started with a chapter on anatomy and physiology. Many readers may feel that this is something they already know. Although conception is the ultimate objective of sexual intercourse, a knowledge of the structures involved and how they work is a necessary part of the understanding of further chapters in this book. The removal of the fear of unwanted conception, contraception, and the problems of infertility need an appreciation of anatomy and physiology.

The delight and pleasure of sexual intercourse, with effective contraception, is a fundamental part of a caring heterosexual relationship. Although contraception is socially the most promising way of controlling the world's population explosion, it is an intensely personal matter to the individual concerned. Dr Jane Kilvington, who has specialized in contraception and psychosexual problems since 1964, discusses the methods currently available, from the least effective – withdrawal – to the most effective – sterilization – in the context of the person's cultural, religious and social background.

Unfortunately, one in every 10 couples wishing to conceive fails to do so. This can cause immense distress and strain. Mr Michael Cameron, consultant obstetrician and gynaecologist to St Thomas' and the Royal Masonic Hospitals, London, explains the causes and treatments of male and female infertility.

'You can only hope to succeed as a good lover if your body and your mind are in prime condition' is the approach of Dr Alan Riley, who specializes in the treatment of sexual problems. The physical problems that interfere with the enjoyment of sex can range from being too fat or too thin through hormone deficiencies to the more serious conditions, such as an amputation or a heart attack. Lack of fitness due to psychiatric illness, medically prescribed drugs as well as the social drugs of alcohol and tobacco, and the illegal drugs all cause problems with sexual intercourse.

The idea that ageing will end sexual pleasure is a common one. Pat Lloyd, a marital and psychosexual counsellor, and Dr Paul Brown, a consultant clinical and occupational psychologist, deal with this fear with sympathy and understanding, and explain that although there are physiological changes the slower tempo of life and greater relaxation may actually improve sexual enjoyment. The greater degree of privacy – freedom, perhaps, from children who have left home – and the pleasure derived from a close, loving relationship mean that there is no need for an age limit to sex.

The largest, and in some ways the most important, section of *Sex and Your Health* is about the sexually transmissible diseases. The spread of these diseases, particularly herpes and AIDS has produced its own myths, fears and, more recently, hysteria. Brian Ford, a microbiologist, approaches these diseases with the attitude of a compassionate scientist. He describes the symptoms but, much more importantly, explains how they are transmitted and treated. With this knowledge it is easy to see how they can be prevented. Sexually transmitted diseases are one facet of the social infectious diseases of mankind. AIDS, about which I have written a section, is a disease of which accurate public knowledge is particularly vital now.

The physical problems of sexual behaviour are balanced by a long section by Dr Jack Weir, until recently consultant psychiatrist to St Mary's and the Royal Masonic Hospitals, London. He writes on the psychology of sex, the reasons for how we behave and respond, and the problems of sexuality, the reasons sexual behaviour is sometimes nót as straightforward as might be expected. Dr Weir discusses the theories regarding psychosexual development and the nature of female and male sexuality. This is followed by an assessment of – and the help that can be given for – the common psychosexual aberrations.

In the final chapter of *Sex and Your Health*, Dr Peter Dally, consultant psychiatrist to Westminster Hospital, deals with sex and society. He examines the forces that lead us to a sexual partner. He considers the part that love plays in our choice, and how our desires and behaviour are moulded by our families, friends and the law.

Sex and Your Health reaches beyond the confines of one country to help all those who want to know more, or who are uncertain about their sexual health.

THE ANATOMY & PHYSIOLOGY OF SEX

Dr James Bevan

The unique approach each of us has towards our own and the opposite sex is founded on a vast and varied mixture of knowledge, half-knowledge, observations and experience, preconceived ideas, emotions and, frequently intermingled with them, the fear and guilt that arise from ignorance.

This introductory chapter on the anatomy and physiology of sex concentrates on the how and the why of our sexual functioning, the physiology, and the basic structures of the sexual organs, the anatomy. To understand fully how the body is sexually organized and works, how conception occurs and how new life begins, we should be aware that the successful reproduction of the species is the ultimate biological objective of sexual intercourse. As humans we can and do enjoy sexual intercourse simply for pleasure and as an important part of a fulfilled partnership, but biologically our prime purpose is to reproduce ourselves. So conception is the key. It is the start of a new human life, the next generation. But it is also then that gender as well as certain genetic or inherited characteristics are decided.

CONCEPTION

Conception occurs when the sperm from the man penetrates the egg of the woman. Out of the hundreds of millions of sperm in each ejaculation, only one fertilizes the egg. Most do not even enter the uterus (or womb) where the baby develops. Those that do, though, swim rapidly towards the egg and reach it generally within 15–30 minutes, their speed is faster than the sperm can actually propel themselves along because it is assisted and augmented by the propulsive effect of the uterus. An egg released from an ovary is swept into the fallopian tube, where it may then stay for as long as two days in the outer half. The sperms can survive for only three or four days, so it is there that conception is most likely, before the egg moves down the tube to the womb.

The remarkable way our bodies develop and grow, repair and replace, and gradually change from the moment of conception to the final stage of death is decided when the male sperm fertilizes the female egg. Any resemblances to our relatives, our physical dimensions, proportions and coloration can all indicate that we are part of our own family. The inheritance of lifespan, physical appearance and even marked characteristics such as the likelihood of shortsightedness or the development of diabetes result from the genetic material that is inherited equally from each of our parents.

The body is composed of a huge number of cells, each performing its own part in the working of the whole. Every cell, of whatever shape, size or function, has an outer casing like a shell surrounding an inner semi-fluid part containing a central, more solid nucleus. That 'shell' allows certain products to seep out in exchange for necessary 'food' and substances from the space between the cells. These cellular 'products' may be altered food or chemicals, such as hormones, needed for the healthy working of the body. Certain cells can destroy unwanted chemicals; others can store substances such as fats and sugars.

The nucleus of most human cells contains 23 pairs of chromosomes. Each chromosome is a thread made up of thousands of tiny segments – genes – spiralled together with its pair. And each gene is responsible for one or for part of one particular characteristic of the individual body. Such a characteristic may be affirmed or alternatively negated by the 'paired' gene on the adjacent chromosome; a gene for blue eyes on one chromosome may for example be overcome by the stronger (dominant) 'paired' gene for brown eyes. In this way, weak and harmful genes seldom cause problems. However, when not negated harmful dominant genes cause some distressing congenital disorders. Recent research has identified a number of these harmful genes, and it may soon be possible to replace them with 'good' genes using genetic engineering.

Among the 23 pairs of chromosomes is a pair of sex chromosomes. In males one of this pair, the Y chromosome, is shorter than the other, the X chromosome. In females the two chromosomes are equal in length, and are both X chromosomes. Sex cells (sperm or ova), instead of containing 23 pairs of chromosomes as in every other kind of cell, contain 23 single chromosomes. At the moment of conception, then, there is a joining together of the two sets of 23 single-chromosome cells, forming a new cell containing 23 paired chromosomes, 46 in all – half from the man and half from the woman, guaranteeing a fair share of characteristics from each. It is the sperm which contains either an X or a Y chromosome, and so in a sense it is the man who 'selects' the sex of the baby, for the egg always contains an X chromosome. If the new cell (the fertilized egg) has one shorter sex chromosome a boy will develop; if it has two full-length sex chromosomes, the baby will be a girl.

Today, abnormalities of whole chromosomes are easily distinguished by a test ordinarily carried out in early pregnancy so that a pregnancy can be terminated before a deformed baby develops. The test is carried out by extracting a little of the fluid that surrounds the fetus – a procedure known as amniocentesis. The fetal cells in the fluid are then examined to detect any abnormalities.

Very rarely, the pairing of sex chromosomes can go wrong. Then, an additional chromosome, an extra male or an extra female one, can join to produce a 'triplet' of chromosomes. This produces individuals who, in different ways, are physically or mentally abnormal.

One genetic disorder is haemophilia, due to a specific gene on the X chromosome. If this gene is not 'opposed' by a stronger, healthy gene, as it is always by a corresponding paired X chromosome – but as it may not be by a paired shorter Y chromosome – the disease will occur in the newborn child. The disease is thus sex-linked, and occurs only in males. Females simply 'carry' the gene and are themselves free from haemophilia.

This fascinating but complex process of the joining of two sex cells to form a new one is the basis of the continuation of human life on earth.

DEVELOPMENT AFTER CONCEPTION

Fertilization usually occurs in the outer half of the fallopian tube, so it is there that the fertilized egg begins to divide – first into two, then into four, and so on to form a still minute ball of cells that is swept down into the uterus. There, a week later, it begins to sink into the inner lining, the endometrium, in the process known as implantation.

Once implantation has taken place, the ball of cells (or blastocyst) continues subdividing and grows rapidly, forming first a placenta to obtain nutrition from the mother, and then the tissues that make up the organs and structures of the new body. In the first three months after conception, the developing embryo is particularly vulnerable and infections, drugs, or alcohol may prevent specific stages of development. At the end of the three months the embryo, now called the fetus, is just recognizable as a human being. In the remaining six months of pregnancy, the baby grows and matures. The mother's fitness throughout this time is very significant. If she smokes, for example, less blood flows through the placenta and this impairs the nutrition of the fetus, making the baby probably smaller than average. By mid-pregnancy, the fetus can sense the muffled sounds of the mother's voice, heart and bowel as well as noises from the outside world. Sucking, breathing and grasping movements all occur. After nine months, about 264 days after conception, the baby is ready to be born (although birth is possible well before this). The process of childbirth itself provides the stimulus for breathing to start and for the readjustments of circulation that cause blood to pass through (and no longer bypass) the lungs when the umbilical cord, from the baby's navel to the placenta, is cut.

During the nine months in the womb, then, the fetus although still physically isolated is increasingly aware of the outside world. That awareness may affect psychological development. For example, anxious mothers who have a rapid pulse during pregnancy may find that they have anxious babies.

CHILDHOOD

Although the sex of a naked baby is obvious, it is the physical similarities between the sexes that are remarkable. These remain well into childhood. At this stage the differences are less physical than cultural – imposed upon the child by clothing, hairstyle and the 'play role' encouraged by adults and friends who expect girls to look and behave like girls and the boys to look and behave like boys (see page 190).

It is not until puberty that physical sexual differences become more obvious and it is then that what are called the 'secondary sexual characteristics' develop.

Although in childhood the sexes are similar, there are responses that even then are specifically related to gender. Boys have penile erections from infancy, for example, although they are not due to sexual stimulation. As children of both sexes grow older, they may learn to get pleasure and satisfaction from masturbation, a normal and healthy part of the discovery that every child makes of how the body works; such sexual experiments are part of growing up. Obsession with them, however, can be a sign that a child is emotionally or physically deprived.

FEMALE SEXUAL ANATOMY

The two most obvious features of an adult female's anatomy that are different from a male's are the breasts and the external sexual organs. The fully developed breasts are each composed of about 20 twisting and branching tubes called ducts, the milk-producing tissue, that join under the nipple. The ducts are embedded in fatty tissue which in turn gives the breast the greatest part of its bulk and is responsible for the wide variation in the size and shape of breasts among women. However, the volume of glandular, milk-producing tissue varies relatively little, and only increases in size towards the end of pregnancy when milk is beginning to be produced.

In the adult woman, the external entrance to the vagina is partly hidden by hair covering the pubis and the outer sides of the two fleshy folds, the labia majora. These blend into the mound of tissue, the mons pubis, in the front and flatten at the back before reaching the back passage, the anus. They contain fatty tissue and some glands, like those in the man's scrotum, which produce a slightly oily secretion, sebum. Between these folds are two thinner, delicate flat folds, the labia minora. These vary considerably in size from one woman to another, and are more obvious in young girls and elderly women when there is less fatty tissue in them. In the gap between the labia minora there is, first, the clitoris, then the exit of the urethra (the tube from the bladder), both lying in front of the opening into the vagina. Behind the vagina is a ridge of tissue known as the fourchette.

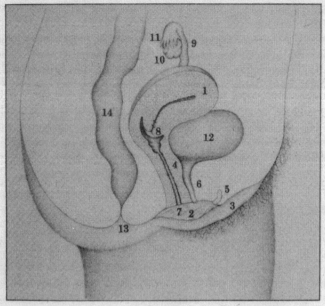

1	Uterus	6	Urethra	11	Fimbriae
2	Labia minora	7	Hymen	12	Bladder
3	Labia majora	8	Cervix	13	Anus
4	Vagina	9	Fallopian tube	14	Rectum
5	Clitoris	10	Ovary		

The vulva is the name for the labia minora and majora together with the mons pubis in front, with the clitoris and the opening into the vagina and the glands around its entrance.

The clitoris is partly covered by the labia minora, and consists of spongy tissue that stiffens and swells with blood when a woman is sexually excited. The specialized erectile tissue of the clitoris lies on either side of the front of the vagina, under the bony arch of the pubis. The clitoris is highly sensitive and when it is swollen the divided part can help grip the penis during intercourse.

In many women who have not had intercourse, the entrance to the vagina is partly closed by a thin, irregular layer of tissue, the hymen or maidenhead. Tampons or masturbation usually stretch this before the first intercourse. But if intercourse takes place without that initial stretching there may be some pain, and even bleeding, as the hymen is distended and torn by the first penile penetration. To avoid that, a woman can easily stretch the hymen herself by massaging it gently and often, with one finger. Further stretching of the hymen, reducing it to a few minor tags of skin, and tearing of the fourchette naturally occur during childbirth.

On either side of the vagina entrance are two further erectile structures, the vestibular bulbs which, like the clitoris, grip the penis during intercourse. Behind these bulbs are the two Bartholin's glands which secrete lubricating moisture over the labia minora and thus make intercourse easier.

The vagina itself is rather like a collapsible tube. Normally, the front and back walls lie against each other, but it can stretch to accommodate any size of penis. The relaxed vagina is 8–14 centimetres (3½–5½ inches) long and the walls are covered with a layer of soft, corrugated, moist skin lying in a tube of muscle. The muscle not only helps to shape the vagina but also opens and closes the vaginal opening.

The internal vaginal skin is kept moist by watery secretions that seep between the surface cells. It is responsive to the circulating female hormones, oestrogen and progesterone. This moistness increases considerably during sexual stimulation, providing further lubrication. It also contains large numbers of useful bacteria (lactobacilli) which create a slightly acid environment and help to keep the adult vagina relatively free of infection. If these secretions begin to fail, as they can in post-menopausal women, they can be stimulated again with hormonal creams containing oestrogen.

The womb, or uterus, is a muscular organ, with an internal cavity, about the size of a clenched fist. The lower third, the neck of the womb, is called the cervix and opens into the top of the vagina; the top two-thirds is the body of the uterus. In most women the uterus leans forwards, against the bladder that lies in front of it; it is then described as an anteverted uterus. But in 15 per cent of women the uterus tilts backwards, towards the rectum – a retroverted uterus. Both positions are normal. The cavity of the uterus extends from the cervix, through the body of the uterus into the fallopian tubes.

As every woman knows, at the end of each month if she is not pregnant there is the natural flow of blood from the vagina, called menstruation. A complete menstrual cycle, from the first day of one period to the first day of the next, lasts an average of 28 days – sometimes more, sometimes less. Each month's period, the four or five days when the bloody fluid from the womb flows down the vagina, is the time when the top layer of cells of the endometrium (the lining of the womb) are shed. The endometrium then regrows during the next 14 days or so, mainly under the stimulus of the hormone oestrogen. In the following 14 days, the second half of the cycle, the endometrium thickens under the stimulation of the hormone progesterone. But for most months no ovum is fertilized, and so at the end of those cycles, there is the 'period' and the whole process starts again.

The neck of the womb, the cervix, is made of tough tissue interwoven with muscle, and remains firmly closed throughout pregnancy, while the rest of the uterus grows. It is only at the end of pregnancy, during childbirth, that the cervix opens while the uterus contracts, pushing the baby into the vagina and out into the world.

The consistency of mucus secreted by the glands in the cervix varies throughout the menstrual cycle. In mid-cycle it is copious, clear, and easier for sperms to swim through. During the rest of the cycle it is thicker and more difficult for sperms to penetrate. Some women can feel this change in their cervical mucus and so assess the most fertile time of the month. A few use it as a form of birth control (the Billing's method) by avoiding intercourse at this time. Alternatively, others can use it to increase the likelihood of conception.

From either side of the top of the uterus, the two fallopian tubes bend outwards and backwards towards the ovaries. These thin tubes are muscular and lined with moist cells that are covered with hair-like surfaces which maintain a sweeping movement towards the uterus. Any interference with this delicate movement reduces the chances of conception and conversely increases the chance that a fertilized egg might remain and implant in the tube – a dangerous event called an ectopic pregnancy. Infection is a common cause of such interference. Such a pregnancy seldom lasts more than two months; usually, the fallopian tube then bursts. If the embryo is detected before the tube ruptures, it may be removed surgically. When the fallopian tube ruptures, urgent hospitalization is necessary to remove the tube.

The internal ends of the tubes have fine, finger-like tissues, the fimbriae, that surround the two ovaries. Each month the fimbriae of one or other tube 'collect' an egg as it leaves the ovary and sweep it into the tube. It is possible for the left tube to 'collect' an egg from the right ovary and vice versa, but usually the egg goes into the nearer tube.

The ovaries are about the size of walnuts and lie slightly behind and to the side of the uterus. They vary in size from woman to woman and with the time of the menstrual cycle. Each ovary has the potential to produce between 50,000 and 250,000 eggs, but of these only about 500 ever eventually mature.

During the first half of each menstrual cycle several of the eggs in one ovary mature, but usually only a single one bursts out of a little cyst of fluid, the Graafian follicle, and escapes into the abdominal cavity to be 'collected' at once by the fimbriae of the fallopian tube. Once the egg has left, the Graafian follicle changes into a hormone-secreting clump of cells (producing progesterone), the corpus luteum, that finally atrophies when menstruation occurs. If, however, an egg has been fertilized the developing embryo itself produces a hormone that stimulates the corpus luteum to go on producing progesterone until the placenta takes over this function.

The uterus, tubes and ovaries all lie within the abdominal cavity and are partly covered with the internal lining, the peritoneum, of the abdomen. There are two pairs of ligaments, acting rather like guide ropes, that support the otherwise 'mobile' uterus and ovaries and prevent undue movement.

For some months before the first period in puberty (the menarche) until some time after the cessation of menstruation (the menopause), the anterior pituitary gland under the brain maintains a rhythmic period of production of two hormones, the follicular-stimulating (FSH) and luteinizing hormones (LH), which control the menstrual cycle. In most women the cycle lasts about 28 days from the beginning of one period to the beginning of another. But considerable variation is normal: some women menstruate every three weeks, others have an interval of as long as five or even six weeks. Irregularity – a variation of more than three or four days in an individual woman's cycle – is abnormal, and if it continues a doctor should be consulted.

The FSH stimulates several Graafian follicles, but usually only one reaches maturity and produces an egg. (If two do so and each produces an egg that is then fertilized, non-identical twins result.) The cells of the Graafian follicle produce oestrogen, which has a general effect on the body: it promotes development and maintenance of the secondary sexual characteristics as well as the psychological feelings of being female. It particularly affects the breasts, vulva and vagina, and also the endometrium of the uterus, which thickens and regrows after menstruation.

The sudden increase in the LH halfway through the menstrual cycle causes ovulation, softens the cervical mucus and produces a copious, watery secretion which helps the sperm to enter the cervix. The resulting corpus luteum then produces progesterone, a hormone that acts only on tissues that have already been stimulated by oestrogen. It thickens the cervical mucus but causes secretion of a watery mucus in the fallopian tubes to ease the passage of the egg down to the uterus. Its main effect, though, is on the endometrium, which becomes thicker and fills with food substances, mainly a carbohydrate called glycogen, ready for a fertilized egg.

Progesterone also has a generally stimulating effect on the body, causing a slight rise in temperature just *after* ovulation takes place and which is maintained for the rest of the menstrual cycle. Keeping a record of body temperature first thing each morning can be used to help determine when a woman ovulates.

When fertilization occurs, the embryo itself produces another hormone, human chorionic gonadotrophin. This stimulates the corpus luteum to continue to produce progesterone and maintain the growth and health of the endometrium. Eventually, during the third month of pregnancy, the placenta itself makes the progesterone and replaces the activity of the corpus luteum. A miscarriage can occasionally occur at this time if the transition of adequate progesterone production from the corpus luteum to the placenta does not take place smoothly. During pregnancy, progesterone causes softening and relaxing of body tissues, particularly ligaments.

The rhythmic production of FSH and LH by the pituitary gland is controlled by a biological 'time clock' situated in the nearby hypothalamus, in the base of the brain, which also monitors the oestrogen and progesterone levels produced by the ovaries. If fertilization does not occur, the FSH and LH levels drop suddenly to cause a fall in oestrogen and progesterone. The endometrium no longer gets the hormonal support it needs for growth and it is 'shed', producing the discharge of blood from the uterus to the vagina, the menstruation.

As a woman grows older, particularly after the age of 30, ovulation occurs less often and the chances of conception are therefore fewer.

FEMALE SEXUAL RESPONSES

A woman's sexual responses depend partly on physical and partly on mental stimulation. Each person reacts in her own way to such stimulation. The subtleties of emotional stimulus combined with physical foreplay help to arouse sexual excitement through the local nerves activated from the brain. There is an increase in the blood supply to the clitoris and adjacent erectile tissues, causing the vaginal entrance to tighten and the clitoris to become erect. Arousal stimulates an increase in vaginal secretions which makes it easier for the man's penis to enter. The massaging effect, once the penis has entered the vagina, increases the seeping of fluid through the vaginal wall, further easing movement during intercourse.

The clitoris is the sexually most sensitive area and its stimulation, both direct and indirectly by 'messages' from stimulation of the breasts in loveplay and in intercourse, is an important factor in reaching the sexual climax, the orgasm. Vaginal stimulation is also a feature of strong sexual pleasure, but less so than through the clitoris.

The climax of sexual intercourse occurs as a rhythmic contraction of the muscles around the vaginal entrance and an increase in muscular activity within the uterus and fallopian tubes. Almost certainly, it is all designed to help the sperm to penetrate more rapidly. This involuntary physical reaction combines with a strong psychological response to produce an orgasm, which may last only a few seconds or may go on for several minutes, depending on the continuation of physical and emotional stimuli and the level of the responses of the individual woman.

Unlike the man's ejaculation, orgasm is not essential to achieve conception, although it may make it more likely. Many psychological and other factors can make it difficult for women to reach a full climax.

MALE SEXUAL ANATOMY

The male sex organs consist of the penis and prostate gland, the paired testicles and epididymi in the scrotum, and spermatic cords, seminal vesicles and bulbo-urethral (Cowper's) glands on either side.

Much of the male anatomy is external. The two testicles are surrounded by strong membrane, the tunica vaginalis, forming a protective coat. They lie in the scrotum, a bag-like structure partly hidden behind the hair in the pubis, of which the skin is wrinkled and contains specialized sweat and other glands, producing the oily secretion (sebum) that gives a characteristic odour to the adult male.

The testicles are oval, about 5 centimetres (2 inches) long and 2 centimetres (1 inch) across and have two functions: to produce spermatozoa and to produce the male hormone, testosterone. The testes are packed with 400–600 coiled tubes, the seminiferous tubules, which produce about 200 million sperm every day. These tubules are surrounded by the interstitial cells that produce testosterone. They join to form 15–20 ducts that pass from the testicles to the overlying epididymis. The production of testosterone is controlled by the luteinizing hormone LH, the same hormone as in women, from the anterior pituitary gland. The interstitial cells also produce a small amount of the female hormone oestrogen, which has little observable effect in younger men but can have a feminizing influence as the male hormone secretions decrease with age. Testosterone stimulates and maintains the physical secondary sexual characteristics in the male and also determines the level of masculinity, drive, and libido or sex-drive.

Each tiny sperm consists of a head, packed with its 23 chromosomes; a body filled with energy-producing material, and a highly mobile tail that can propel the sperm up the vagina towards the egg.

Sperm production takes place only when the testes are about 2°C (3½°F) cooler than the rest of the body. The ideal temperature is controlled by the dartos and cremaster muscles that lie within the spermatic cords and contract to pull the testicles and scrotum close to the body when chilled, or relax allowing the scrotum to hang loosely away from the body's warmth.

Each epididymis is made of 15–20 coiled ducts coming from one testicle. Sperm spend 10–15 days maturing in these ducts before passing out of the coils into a single tube, in the lower half of the epididymis, which enters the part of the spermatic cord known as the vas deferens. It takes about ten weeks from the time that they are formed for the sperm to mature fully.

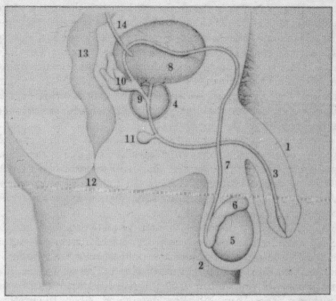

1	Penis	6	Epididymis	11	Bulbo-urethral
2	Scrotum	7	Vas deferens		gland
3	Urethra	8	Bladder	12	Anus
4	Prostate gland	9	Ejaculatory duct	13	Rectum
5	Testicle	10	Seminal vesicle	14	Ureter

Each spermatic cord, which consists of the vas deferens from the epididymis, blood vessels and nerves, as well as the cremaster muscle, leaves the scrotum and passes upwards to the side of the pubis to penetrate the muscular coat of the abdominal wall and reach the base of the bladder, within the abdomen. There, the spermatic cord enters the prostate gland and joins the ejaculatory duct. This is also joined by a tubule from the seminal vesicle on the same side. The seminal vesicles are organs that produce fluids that nourish the sperm during storage and after ejaculation. The sperm are stored in the vas deferens.

The prostate gland surrounds the urethra – the tube from the bladder – and secretes substances that also help to maintain the health and activity of the sperm during their storage in the vas deferens.

The vas deferens and duct from the seminal vesicle join to form

23

the ejaculatory duct as it enters the urethra. It is through the two ejaculatory ducts, one from each side, that sperm reach the penis when ejaculation takes place. On either side of the ejaculatory ducts are two small glands, the bulbo-urethral glands – Cowper's glands – that produce secretions that further assist in maintaining the sperm's activity after they leave the body.

Semen is the fluid produced during ejaculation. It consists of the prostatic, seminal and bulbo-urethral secretions, as well as the sperm produced by the testes. If the vas deferens are cut (as in vasectomy, for birth control reasons), semen is still produced, although about one-third less in volume because it no longer contains sperm. The normal, healthy amount of semen on ejaculation is about a teaspoonful and contains 50 million to 200 million sperm, of which 60–80 per cent are normal and the rest abnormal or dead.

The penis has two functions: to allow urine to be passed and, in the adult male, to ejaculate semen. In its flaccid state the size of the penis varies greatly between men, but when sexually aroused and the penis is firm and erect there is less difference. The urethra runs from the bladder to the penis. The two ejaculatory ducts open into it as it passes through the prostate gland. Where the urethra enters the penis, it is surrounded by the corpus spongiosum. At the tip of the penis, the corpus spongiosum enlarges to form the highly sensitive glans, which is covered with the protective flap of skin, the prepuce or foreskin. (It is this which is removed in circumcision in infancy for religious reasons – there are seldom medical reasons at this age for doing so.) There are small glands on the glans and foreskin that secrete a greasy material, smegma, that acts as a protective layer to the sensitive skin, as well as allowing the easy retraction of the prepuce. On top of the corpus spongiosum lie the pair of corpora cavernosa; all three of these structures are made of spongy erectile tissue. The stiffening of the penis, an erection, is caused by a rapid inflow of blood that distends the corpora cavernosa and at the same time this presses on the veins to make it more difficult for the blood to escape.

MALE SEXUAL RESPONSES

A man's sexual responses are usually quicker and more urgent than a woman's. The psychological and physical sexual stimuli cause an erection and increase sexual excitement. First, there is an increase of mucus secretion from the glands inside the urethra to produce moistness at the end of the penis. Then a few sperm may leak from the vas deferens into those secretions. It is this leakage of sperm that makes it possible for pregnancy to occur even if the man has not had an orgasm or ejaculated semen. (It is also why the form of birth control known as coitus interruptus, withdrawing the penis when nearing the climax, is likely to fail.) At the climax of sexual excitement there is an involuntary co-ordinated rhythmical contraction and relaxation of the vas deferens, prostate gland and bulbo-urethral glands, emptying the contents into the urethra. These are swept forward by the movement of the muscles in the pelvis, as well as the two pairs adjacent to the base of the penis. The contents of the two seminal vesicles empty behind the first part of the semen to distend the urethra and force all the semen out of the penis in a series of rapid spurts.

This moment of reflex, rhythmical activity of ejaculation is a moment of intense sexual pleasure and excitement, the orgasm.

THE CHANGES OF PUBERTY

Puberty is the period when the secondary sexual characteristics develop in girls and boys to the point where they can reproduce. The period known as adolescence, starting during puberty and ending sometime during early adult life, describes the time when a young person alters and adapts emotionally from childhood dependence to adult independence. It can be a difficult and psychologically trying time of life.

Although puberty and adolescence are different events – the first being mainly biological and the latter essentially psychological or emotional – they are interdependent; indeed the words are often used to mean the same thing.

The onset of puberty is controlled by the hypothalamus, the brain's biological time clock. The hypothalamus stimulates the anterior pituitary gland which is attached to the lower surface of the brain and connected to the hypothalamus by its own blood supply.

The anterior pituitary gland is one of the endocrine glands that secrete hormones into the blood circulation; they can reach and influence distant parts of the body which are sensitive to them. Whereas the anterior pituitary gland produces hormones that stimulate the sex glands (ovaries and testicles) and other endocrine glands, the hypothalamus also monitors the hormones these produce and regulates the amount secreted. The sex hormones in their turn affect other parts of the body, to cause changes according to gender. With the onset of puberty there is at first only gradual alteration, but after a year or two the process speeds up and brings rapid growth and sexual development. Illness, emotional disorders or too little food can all disturb the time clock of the hypothalamus and affect the crescendo of puberty, slowing down the progress or even delaying its onset.

The first signs of puberty may occur at as early an age as eight or nine in girls and a year or so later in boys.

In a girl there may be a gradual change in the body shape, a slight roundness of form characterizing the first flicker of increased hormonal activity. The timing of the onset of puberty also varies according to the nutritional state of the community as a whole, geographical factors and racial characteristics. It is earlier in children from financially better-off families than among poorer people, and it is earlier too in girls today than it was in their mothers. The onset of menstruation has advanced by about four months for each generation over the past century.

With the onset of a boy's puberty, the testicles start secreting the male hormone testosterone, and a small amount of one of the female hormones, oestrogen. Testosterone causes a variety of changes at this time: a considerable growth in the size of the penis, scrotum and testicles; alterations in body hair; effects on the skin; bloodcount and muscle development; and a deeper voice.

The penis, testicles and scrotum grow several times in size between the onset of puberty and full maturity at about the age of 20. Although sperm production starts earlier, it is only at about 13 that it is active enough for a boy to be fertile. Erections occur spontaneously from pressure of clothing, sexual thoughts and feelings; spontaneous ejaculation of semen in nocturnal emissions or 'wet dreams' may occur at night from time to time.

Testosterone causes hair growth over the pubis in an inverted V-shape – a typical male distribution – up to the navel; hair also grows on the jaw, chin and chest, and in the armpits. It may even grow over the shoulders and back as a man gets older. Hair on the arms and legs becomes thicker and longer. Hair on the scalp, too, can be affected by testosterone, but not in all men: baldness is due partly to the male hormone and partly to genetic inheritance. Many men, particularly in some racial groups, grow little body hair but never go bald, or do not start to go bald until late middle age. Clearly, hormones are only part of the reason for such hair loss.

An obvious change at male puberty is the deeper voice. The voice-box, the larynx, enlarges and produces the 'breaking voice', the discomforting alternating squeak and deep voice of the adolescent as it changes to the permanent timbre of the adult.

The whole male body is affected by testosterone. The skin becomes thicker and coarser, darkening as the sallowness of youth gradually disappears. In the late teens acne, a spotty skin condition on the face and back, is a common problem. It is a response to hormonal stimulus in some young men; research into its cause and treatment has still a long way to go, but the condition tends to improve with age. The bones thicken and the muscles become stronger as the broad shoulders, narrow hips and increasing strength of the adult male become evident. Testosterone also increases the number of red blood cells produced by the bone marrow, and the resulting increase in oxygen-carrying capacity that aids stamina.

About one in five adolescent boys experience slight breast enlargement and tenderness. This can cause anxiety, but it is just another reaction to the hormonal changes of puberty and usually disappears within six months.

All these changes take place as the boy grows rapidly to adult height, sometimes by as much as 12–17 centimetres (5–7 inches) in a year. Fatigue, changeable moods, and learning to live with these dramatic physical changes impose a strain on the pubescent youth at a time when he is also making his first tentative sexual contacts and taking academic examinations. However, a new-found strength is often shown in an increased interest in sporting and athletic skills and provides a pride in physical achievement which helps offset the emotional stresses and strains.

In the same way that a boy's genitalia increase in size, changes occur in a pubescent girl: the uterus, fallopian tubes and vagina treble in size; the lining of the vagina thickens, becomes moister and more resistant to infection and damage; the inner surface of the uterus forms the typical glandular endometrium that is shed in every menstruation; and the vulva becomes fleshier and more prominent; and there is a thickening and growth in the size of the clitoris.

At this time too the breasts develop, often accompanied by slight

27

tenderness of the nipples and a thickening of first one and then the other as each breast begins to grow. The asymmetry of breast growth is a common feature of puberty; it may cause embarrassment and anxiety, but girls can be assured that it is normal and that the breasts soon become equal in size. As the breasts grow, fat develops within them, giving the typical soft feminine appearance. The skin all over the body thickens a little but remains smooth and supple. Like boys, many girls develop acne on the face as the result of hormonal effects on the skin. One of the female hormones, oestrogen, makes the blood vessels more sensitive to bruising, a feature that affects some women more than others. There is also an increase in fat under the skin, to produce a more curvaceous appearance.

Secondary hair growth is generally confined to the armpits and above the pubic area, but not usually, as in men, up to the navel.

Oestrogen has a double effect on the growth of the bones. It causes growth but at the same time it causes the growing ends of the bones to mature more quickly, which stops the growth spurt of puberty earlier than in boys. The pelvis slowly widens to give the characteristic broad hips that so many women dislike as they lose their slim adolescent shape.

The menarche, the onset of menstruation, may not occur until the age of 16. Usually, however, it occurs between the ages of 11 and 13, yet it does not necessarily mean the beginning of ovulation. At first, periods may occur irregularly, but they generally settle down into a typical monthly pattern within a year or two. Ovulation, like menstruation, is also sporadic during the first year or so, but once a regular rhythm appears it takes place most months. Periods may vary in length, sometimes lasting for only a day or two but, more usually, for four to five days. Occasionally periods are prolonged, lasting for more than a week, with heavy bleeding and clots of blood. This is abnormal. Sometimes, women suffer painful periods (dysmenorrhoea), with pain in the back and lower abdomen. It usually occurs with the onset of menstruation, and is sometimes severe enough to cause vomiting. When it does happen a doctor should be consulted, for modern treatments are effective.

In older women a change in mood, known as pre-menstrual tension (PMT) may occur for a few days or even for as long as a week before a period. There may be an increase in irritability, or feelings of depression and tearfulness, and a physical clumsiness that may lead to accidents. PMT may be accompanied by a marked weight gain, sometimes as much as 3 kg (7 lb) or so, due to fluid retention produced by the hormonal changes before menstruation. PMT disappears with the onset of menstruation but can be helped by therapy from a doctor.

The hormonal changes in girls vary more than in boys and produce greater emotional changes, involving fluctuating moods interspersed with moments of exhilaration and sexual awareness.

Slowly, with both sexes, the turbulence and stresses of the physical and psychological changes of puberty and adolescence settle as they reach adulthood.

THE PHYSIOLOGY OF SEXUAL EXCITEMENT

The physical changes produced in the human body by sexual response are dramatic: dilated pupils, an increase in breathing and pulse rates, combined with flushing cheeks and, often, swelling of the nasal membranes with outflow of secretions, as well as a response – of course, in the sexual areas. Many women, and some men, feel tautness or tingling in the nipples, tightening muscles, particularly in the neck, and even changes in the quality of sound or light before and during the crescendo of sexual response which ends in orgasm. Each individual's experience is unique.

Because sexual excitement depends on so many factors, physical and psychological, it is clear that there must be a physical mechanism within the body to produce an orgasm.

Sexual arousal is quickest if the sexual areas – around the vagina in women and penis in men – are stimulated. The clitoris in women and the end of the penis (glans penis) in men are the most sensitive and responsive zones.

Other sensations may initiate a sexual response which prepares the partners for the closer physical contact of sexual foreplay. Sound, particularly evocative music, vision, usually more for men than women, and scent may all inaugurate sexual arousal. Touch, particularly to the sexually sensitive 'erogenous zones' maintains and increases sexual response. Not all the erogenous zones – the nape of the neck, behind the ears, the lips, the nipples, and the base of the spine, for example – cause arousal in any one individual. Some areas may be more sensitive in some individuals than in others, and some people may not respond at all to being touched in these areas.

This input of sexually arousing sensations may be added to

29

the other physical factors, less obvious ones, that increase sexual response. Around the time of ovulation or just before menstruation, women have greater sexual desire because of hormonal changes and, sometimes, as a result of feeling congestion or fullness in the vulva. A similar sensation, ill-defined but real, may occur in men if the seminal vesicles are swollen with fluid.

All these sensations are joined by the flood of psychological emotions to awaken an area deep within the brain, probably in the brain stem – a part often considered 'primitive' because it is present in the brains of all animals. This area produces a co-ordinated nervous response through the automatic nervous system that overwhelms the body at the moment of orgasm. It is little wonder that it has been likened to a 'fit', for a person can lose almost all contact with the outside world for some moments in an overpowering psychological and physical event. Part of this nervous response is similar to the way the body prepares for a physical effort, with increased breathing and heart rates and dilated pupils. But it is also like preparing for relaxation, involving flushing and an increase in sweat and oily secretions from the skin. These secretions produce substances that stimulate the sense of smell. This complex reaction combines with the swelling of the penis, clitoris and vulva, and ends with the involuntary rhythmical muscular reaction of orgasm in both sexes.

This chapter on the anatomy and physiology of sex is a foundation for the rest of this book. In an ideal world, our bodies would function in the way described and the end results of sexual activity – orgasm and conception – would be achieved with ease. But things are not always straightforward. Sometimes a variation on the biological ideal is normal, a matter of ageing. Sometimes it is acquired, through, say, sexually transmitted disease or accident. Sometimes it may be psychosomatic, the mind acting on the body in a way that is still imperfectly understood. These variations do not – as you will see – mean an end to sexual activity. The body is adaptable, and repairable, and the desire for sex is strong. The key to sexual health is knowledge and that is what this chapter – and this book – seeks to impart.

THE MAIN FORMS OF CONTRACEPTION

Dr Jane Kilvington

Contraception, or birth control, describes the ways that have been devised to enjoy sex and yet to avoid creating a new human being. Contraception may be achieved by modifying the sex act, as for example when the man withdraws his penis before ejaculation (coitus interruptus), or by using manufactured products like the contraceptive pill, French letters (also known as sheaths or condoms), caps, the coil and other methods described below. People who do not want to have more children, or even any children, may choose to be sterilized. Separating the loving part of sex from the biological, reproductive part by using contraception is of the greatest importance both for individuals and for the human race as a whole. Contraception has transformed people's lives and expectations, and may well assist in controlling the world's population explosion.

However much governments may wish to harness developments in contraception in order to reduce population growth, and however much sociologists may extol the benefits for the family, the impact of using contraceptives falls entirely on individual people, who have powerful personal feelings that determine their decisions about sex and family life. Cultural backgrounds, religious teaching, and social and family pressures are also influential, and the use of contraceptives has thus to be free of emotional conflicts and doubts on cultural or religious grounds. In addition, the contraceptives have to be regarded as reasonably safe without being intrusive or unpleasant. The decision to use them is not necessarily a simple matter – it depends on both consciously and unconsciously held attitudes as well as on wider considerations.

Separating the biological purpose of sex, producing children,

31

from the pleasures of sexual excitement and fulfilment has brought freedom from fear of pregnancy and from all the problems of having unwanted children. But it has created a sense of guilt in many people, for in some complex way sexual pleasure is often associated with guilt in Western societies. This may echo the original separation from parents involved in finding a mate, or the idea that pleasure may be at someone else's expense, or even at a deeper level, the suppressed feelings of love and seduction that were once possibly felt for the parent of the opposite sex. Whatever the cause, sexual guilt is a reality and may even extend to guilt about contraception itself. Perhaps that is why the pioneer advocates of birth control came under such bitter attack.

It is only now when new generations have grown familiar with contraception, and its usefulness has become acknowledged, that most people accept that guilt feelings can properly be set aside.

Guilt about contraception may have some bearing on the undoubted fact that the Pill is the most widely researched medication in all the pharmacopoeia. From time to time, scare stories appear which in a lurid, worrying form present the fact that the Pill can cause fatal thrombosis. We must of course be concerned when something goes wrong, but it would be more honest to point out that conception and childbirth also have their hazards. It is advisable, over the age of 35, not to continue taking the Pill if you smoke and over the age of 40 if you do not. That aside, it is probably true to say that no contraceptive holds greater dangers than childbirth.

In any case, safety is not the only consideration – quality of life counts too. Without the Pill and other contraceptive methods, the often unhappy results of unwanted pregnancies – ill health, rejection of children, shortened life for the mother – are all too obvious. The benefits of contraception are real and potentially available to every person in every country.

Religious attitudes do much to foster guilt about contraception. The Roman Catholic Church condemns the use of the Pill and other artificial contraceptive methods; some other religions share the Roman Catholics' paramount concern for the creation of children as a God-given blessing and as an essential binding force between parents. However, no doctrine is as inflexibly unyielding in its guidance as Roman Catholicism, although the Muslim religion does not encourage the use of contraceptives either. Hindus, Sikhs and Protestants are more open-minded.

Guilt is often mixed with fear. It may be general or of a more personal nature. Some contend that small families are unnatural, providing inadequate labour for the community or too few young people to support the old. Others claim that contraception causes public morals to decline, fragments family life, encourages sex outside marriage – even that promiscuity among the young is a direct result of contraceptives being too easily obtainable.

The view that birth control leads to sexual indulgence implies that fear of pregnancy is the strait-jacket which alone controls sexual behaviour. Some people fear sexuality as a destructive force and hope to confine it to marriage by penalizing extramarital partnerships in some way. Others believe that individuals should be able to choose their standards for themselves, thereby making mistakes, perhaps, but also learning to do better. No one should suppose that this dilemma is easy to resolve; there are strong and good opinions on both sides.

Fears disturb individuals too. These may be justified, as when a woman fears the long-term results of taking the Pill. They may also be irrational, causing a general, ill-defined unease. Both men and women fear that sexual pleasure may be spoilt, even that performance will be impaired. There may also be a suspicion that fertility will be compromised or that cancer can develop as a result. Such fears, however groundless, are nevertheless common. The difficulty about reassuring people lies in the fact that there is a grain of truth in what they fear. There *are* medical complications of the Pill and the coil; men do sometimes find that a sheath reduces pleasure; it has been known for women who take the Pill to lose their sexual drive. But excessive fear is misplaced – most people can work out for themselves which method suits them best at any particular point in their lives. They can accept a small medical risk or they may choose to end all chance of becoming pregnant by getting themselves sterilized.

Like so many developments in the civilized world, contraceptives can certainly be harmful as well as beneficial. Women can become unwell by using them. They can even become pregnant unexpectedly when they thought they were protected. More subtle, but important too, is the disappointment couples experience when, having avoided raising a family, they consequently find too late that childlessness is unbearable. In societies where women are traditionally subservient, and even in enlightened Western societies, men may fear or resent the freedom contraceptives give to women to be independent, to invade male preserves at work and in the professions, or even to be unfaithful without detection. But these concerns have to be set against the immeasurable support and help which contraceptives provide – the elimination of chronic ill health in mothers made prematurely old by frequent childbearing, the reduction in the number of half-starved and uncared for children.

There are more positive benefits as well. A young couple can, for instance, set out on a marriage better equipped to work together and save in order to make a better home for their family than would have been possible if their married life had been burdened by annual pregnancies. Their sexual relationship has a chance to develop and they can learn about sharing between two people before having to share their belongings and affections with more. Later, with family planning, children can be spaced out so that each is born well nourished and can grow up strong. Those parents who have had the number of children they want need not worry about further pregnancies or suffer the frustration and unhappiness of a sexually-deprived relationship in order to avoid having more. No shame should attach to a couple wanting no more children. It is quite understandable that people should feel they cannot afford a larger family or should want to lead a better social life. If the health of the mother is precarious, or there is a possibility of having a handicapped child, birth control is even more to be recommended. In a world where families are planned, mothers need not feel enslaved, nor fathers overburdened. Planned parenthood permits a happy sex life and gives couples a better chance to share their lives with more fulfilment.

FUNDAMENTAL QUESTIONS

The first question is whether contraception is acceptable at all. If it is not, a couple, or either partner, will not require information or will use contraceptives deliberately ineffectively. A man who feels he must demonstrate his fertility or virility – for instance, a Muslim man wanting to prove his love for his wife by making her pregnant again and again – may pay lip service to the exhortations of the family-planning doctor, but will not use sheaths. A woman who wants to have a child, perhaps feeling subconsciously that no one else loves her, or that she had been cheated by an earlier termination of pregnancy, may take the Pill erratically or leave her cap at home the day she goes on holiday. In such cases, clearly the contraceptive is not at fault; obviously, the forces favouring pregnancy are overwhelming.

People are often able, of course, to recognize that their motives are mixed, and it is quite possible for a woman (or a man) to say 'Part of me likes the idea of more children, but other considerations are against it.' This may help a doctor discussing available methods with them to recommend contraceptives with a higher failure rate than others so that the chances of pregnancy cannot be ignored.

For some, however, making it absolutely certain that sexual intercourse cannot result in a new baby can deaden a sexual relationship and cause loss of sexual drive. A number of contraceptive methods commend themselves precisely because they leave open a slim possibility of pregnancy.

Some find it hard to choose or use contraceptives; they feel uneasy about their sexuality, guilty and embarrassed, or even afraid of their bodies. Among them are those with unstable or uncertain partnerships – the uncertainty seems to include their inability to plan properly or to think logically. Thus, unhappy teenagers or men or women whose relationships are breaking down may be particularly vulnerable. The impediment is not in the practical measures available but in the mind.

However, suppose a couple accepts contraception genuinely and unitedly. Each partner will find different forms of contraception to their liking in different degrees. Some feel medication will disturb their bodies, others find handling articles to be worn during intercourse unacceptable. So the role of the medical adviser is crucial. In contrast to other areas of medicine in which doctors determine the treatment, with birth control it should be the patients who make the decisions. They should be prepared for a frank, unembarrassed discussion raising any fears and prejudices they have. With the choice made, a medical examination can confirm its suitability. A gynaecological examination is needed for some birth control methods; women going on the Pill or having a coil fitted must have a cervical smear first. In later years, a change of method may be needed – different circumstances call for different treatment. A woman who was happy with the Pill at first would, for instance, request a change when she wants to plan a family. It is advisable to have at least one, and preferably three menstrual cycles off the Pill before conception because it seems desirable to rid the body of unwanted hormones. That would almost certainly require the man to use a sheath for a time.

Finally, a balance is struck, and people get the information and prescription they need. The choice is their own and their partners'. They should know how to use the method they have picked, its failure rate and any possible complications that may arise, fully assured that they can seek medical help concerning any worries they may have later.

Of course, contraception also includes abstinence (the avoidance of sexual intercourse) and coitus interruptus (withdrawal). It does not, however, include termination of pregnancy.

METHODS OF CONTRACEPTION

THE CAP

The cap, like the sheath, is a 'barrier' method because a barrier – in this case a rubber or silicone cap of special design – is worn over the neck of the womb during intercourse. Caps are about 5–8 centimetres (two to three inches) wide and are used with foam, pessaries, cream or jelly spermicide. Without that, after the cap is removed, live sperm may be left in the vagina.

The choice of cap depends on the individual size and shape of the internal organs, but the most common is a diaphragm with a rim, either soft or hard. The device folds into the size of a tampon when put in and recovers its normal circular shape when inside. Women have to be taught how to use it, but it is easy enough for a well-movitated woman. A woman who is unsure of her sexuality or unable to feel inside the vagina may not like the method at first, but a sympathetic doctor can help and in this situation the cap is not only a contraceptive but also therapeutic because it encourges her to come to terms with her body. It is hard to know how many true failures there are with the cap. Many women have used it all their adult lives, planned their children with it, and used it through the uncertain menopausal years. Some women who become pregnant later admit that they forgot to take it with them on holiday or could not be bothered to fetch it once they were in bed. But there certainly are women who have become pregnant for no apparent reason, and with hindsight they might wish they had used another method. It is important not only to use the cap every time but to leave it in for six hours after intercourse. It can be inserted up to half an hour beforehand, but if it has been in position longer than that the spermicide must be brought up to strength.

Refitting is always necessary after pregnancy or if there has been a change in weight of 3 kilogrammes (7 pounds) or more. Similarly, three months after postnatal fitting the size of the cap should be checked, because the womb continues to decrease in size during this time. A cap lasts for two years at the most, and a woman should not forget that rubber perishes and holes may appear, although keeping the cap clean and dry helps. For a woman who wants a safe, non-intrusive contraceptive and is not one of the very few who are allergic to rubber or spermicide, the cap is a good method. Pregnancies are possible, but like all barrier methods it does protect against sexually transmitted diseases and may well be best for a woman whose infrequent menstrual period leads her to think she should not interrupt her ovarian function by taking the Pill.

SPERMICIDES

Chemical spermicides kill sperm. They are dispensed as pessaries, creams, foaming tablets and aerosols. Their greatest value is to reinforce another method such as IUCD (Intra-Uterine Contraceptive Devices), the sheath or withdrawal, and they should always be used with the cap. By themselves, however, they are not reliable enough. One of the latest contraceptive innovations, a soft polythene sponge containing spermicide, has come onto the market but is disappointing except for those who can accept a chance of pregnancy.

COILS AND LOOPS

Coils and loops (Intra-Uterine Contraceptive Devices) work by interfering with the implantation of the fertilized ovum in the lining of the womb. There are many types available. They are 2–5 centimetres (an inch or two) long, and the smaller ones contain copper coiled around the stem. They can be inserted at a surgery visit, and should remain in place for years. The newest devices are reliable and cause few problems.

Not all women like the idea of a foreign body permanently

inside them, but for those who do not mind, the IUCD provides a contraceptive free of care, the only requirements being an annual check and a refitting every three to five years. The larger devices, which do not contain copper, can be left in the womb indefinitely and need to be replaced only if they become uncomfortable. A thread attached to the device hangs from the cervical canal and a woman can feel this herself to check its presence after each menstrual period, for although expulsion is unlikely, it can happen. Sometimes, threads have gone up into the womb and, if they cannot be retrieved, an X-ray or a scan is needed to ensure that the device is still there. Sometimes a tampon may get entangled with the thread and dislodge the device. For these reasons, the threads should be fairly short.

There is no doubt that the IUCD is excellent for a woman who has had children. Women who have not may find a coil or loop uncomfortable and have greater period pain. Certainly all women find the IUCD causes longer, though not necessarily heavier, periods. Doctors are reluctant to fit women who have not had children because a rare complication of infection, less of a threat in mothers, may cause infertility. A new IUCD to be developed soon may dispense with threads, a promising development, for it is the threads (rather than the device itself) which are most likely to pick up any infection.

The sign of infection is unusual, severe pelvic pain. In a woman who has had no complaints for a long time, pain is significant. It may be that she has some pelvic infection or that the device is being expelled; more seriously, it may signal an ectopic pregnancy, a rare emergency which can affect women whether they have an IUCD or not.

There is no evidence that an IUCD produces cancer, but all sexually active women should have cervical smears at least every three years.

Pregnancies with an IUCD in position are, unfortunately, not unknown. But with the newest designs, if a back-up spermicidal pessary (see above) is used during the highly fertile days (days 5–17 of a 28-day cycle), the risk of pregnancy is almost nil. However, if it does happen, there is a greater than normal chance of spontaneous abortion; similarly, because it is usual to remove the device once a pregnancy is confirmed, that also slightly increases the chance of early miscarriage. However, if the device is left in position it will not interfere with the embryo's growth.

Fittings can be undertaken during or soon after a period but, except with post-coital contraception (see page 43), a woman should be sure she is not pregnant if fittings are carried out in the latter half of the cycle. There are other contra-indications to fittings: a history of pelvic infection or a history of ectopic pregnancy, a fibroid in the womb or a history of heavy, painful periods. Women with valvular heart disease must also be excluded because there is too great a risk of infection in the heart valves.

No one need feel anxious about having an IUCD. It is the doctor's responsibility to provide a friendly and confident atmosphere and help a woman to relax. Then fitting takes only a matter of minutes. The discomfort and slight bleeding which may occur during the first 28 days should, if possible, be tolerated, perhaps with painkillers, because it almost always passes.

Taking a device out after sexual intercourse earlier in the cycle may result in pregnancy. The safest way, if pregnancy is unwanted, is to wait until menstruation is in progress, or a day or two immediately after.

IUCDs which release progestogen will be available soon; with these there is hardly any risk of unwanted pregnancy and minimal problems with menstruation, or likelihood of ectopic pregnancy. Strictly speaking, this is a hormonal method of contraception but the hormone levels are very low. One such device already available has the disadvantage of having to be replaced every year – the newer model can remain for longer.

COITUS INTERRUPTUS

Coitus interruptus, or the withdrawal method, like sheaths, should ideally leave no sperm in the vagina after intercourse. It may well be the most common method in use throughout the world; some men pride themselves on being able to control ejaculation without disappointing their partners sexually. It needs no prior planning or supplies, but may not prevent pregnancy and may also be the cause of sexual disappointment because a couple have to keep thinking of self-control. A contraceptive vaginal pessary would increase contraceptive efficiency, but a couple must still not relax their self-control.

INJECTABLES

Injectables, like the mini-Pill, provide a low dose of progestogen to the woman. If administered at three-monthly intervals, medication is more continuous, a great advantage because the method works best if the chemical effect on the cervical mucus never wanes. However, side-effects such as irregular cycles and water retention, leading to headaches and breast discomfort, are a possibility with progestogen medication, and with injections these cannot be reversed.

Although there are doubts about injectables, there is no good evidence for why they should not be used, as they are, widely, in several countries. Recently, implants lasting five years have had extensive trials. They need a local anaesthetic for insertion and removal, but do overcome some of the disadvantages of the other methods.

THE PILL

The Pill has been in use for 30 years and millions of women now take it. It is preferred because of its dependability, which approaches 100 per cent, and the ease with which it can be used, enabling women themselves to control their fertility.

The Pill replaces the two natural hormones in the woman's body, oestrogen and progesterone. Although the normal cycle continues, hormone production by the ovaries falls to a minimum and, at the same time, the monthly developing of an egg-containing follicle does not occur. A total of 21 pills are taken at the same time each day on 21 consecutive days, followed by seven days clear of medication during which menstruation occurs. The exception to this rule is that when a woman is starting to take the Pill for the first time, she should take the first one on the first day of a period. Then contraceptive cover is immediate.

Irregular taking of the Pill enables the ovaries to resume normal functioning, with the possibility of egg production. If the Pill is taken more than 12 hours late on any occasion, pregnancy could result – this is important to keep in mind. Some women do forget their Pill, especially if a domestic crisis occurs; moving house or even an unusual event like a party may have the same effect.

Pills can not only get forgotten but also lost through vomiting or diarrhoea. Moreover, certain medicines such as antibiotics and anti-epileptic drugs, for instance, interfere with the Pill's action. It would be advisable on these occasions to continue taking the Pill and to take extra precautions, because the Pill cannot be expected to work until after the next menstrual period.

Some women have become pregnant when changing their brand of Pill. The best way to avoid that happening is to start the new packet as soon as the old one is finished, avoiding the seven-day break and probably a menstrual bleed that month as well.

Now that we have the lower-dose Pill, hardly anyone need suffer side-effects. For the very few who do get migraine or raised blood pressure it may be impossible to find a Pill to suit, but for most women, medically fit and keen to use the Pill, one or other variety in the large range available can usually be found. However, there are some medical contra-indications to taking the combined oral contraceptive. A history of deep-vein thrombosis, obesity, liver or endocrine disease, and sickle cell anaemia are some. More rare are otosclerosis cancer, heart disease or existing raised blood pressure. Women whose menstrual cycle is poorly established may not be acceptable; similarly, women aged over 35, particularly if they smoke, are at greater risk as well as women aged over 40, may be advised against taking the Pill.

The complication that worries people most is deep-vein thrombosis due to the oestrogen in the Pill. A clot in a vein, usually in the leg, may occur spontaneously or may be precipitated by major surgery. If practicable, the Pill should be stopped 6 weeks before any surgical operation to reduce the chance of post-operative thrombosis. The risk is negligible in those aged under 35 who do not smoke, and has been greatly reduced with modern Pills that contain much less oestrogen – but caution is still necessary during major surgery and after childbirth. If there is pain and swelling in the calf, it would be as well to stop taking the Pill and seek medical advice.

Progestogen in the Pill has been cited as a cause of cancer of the cervix, but the risk is not established, and in any case a woman can be screened with cervical smears. It has also been suggested that progestogen causes breast cancer in women aged under 25, but that too is almost certainly untrue. Cardiovascular diseases may indeed be hastened by certain progestogens, but the evidence is controversial and smoking is far more harmful. Sometimes there is a form of raised blood pressure that is reversible, so blood pressure checks are essential.

By contrast, oestrogen is thought to protect women from benign lumps in the breast and from cancer of the ovary or the endometrium (lining of the womb). Taking the Pill also has such advantages as relief from painful or heavy menstruation, making an erratic cycle more regular, relieving pre-menstrual tension, lessening pelvic infection and anaemia, and almost wholly eliminating the risk of an ectopic pregnancy. There is also a strong possibility that the Pill suppresses rheumatoid arthritis. It does not seem to make any difference how long a woman is on the Pill, and, provided that she is not too young when she starts taking it, her fertility is unaffected. But after stopping the Pill some women do take several months to start menstruating naturally again and may even need drugs to help them become pregnant. Perhaps they are the ones who would have needed such help anyway.

The modern low-dose Pill is safer than the original one, and safety is certainly an important consideration when making the decision on what form of contraception to adopt.

THE MINI-PILL

The mini-Pill is a progestogen-only pill, and a very small amount compared with the dose in the combined Pill. It is taken once in 24 hours every day without a break, preferably at about 7 pm. The idea is that it should act upon the mucus in the neck of the womb, the cervix, making it viscous and hostile to sperm. If a woman is unreliable about taking the Pill, the chemical change may fail, and if ovulation is occurring at the same moment there is the chance of a pregnancy.

It follows that women who use the mini-Pill must be conscientious and allow no more than three hours either side of their normal Pill-taking time. It also means that pregnancy could happen unexpectedly.

However, the absence of oestrogen should dispel any fear of deep-vein thrombosis, so after the age of 35 this may be a woman's choice of method.

The medication begins to take effect only after 14 days from the first day of a menstrual period. It has the same limitations as the combined Pill when other drugs are taken simultaneously.

It is a useful method especially for older women; the side-effects, if any, are slight. A few women may get a rise in blood pressure, but otherwise the worst complaint is of irregular periods, although these often regularize themselves after a few months. It there is prolonged absence of menstruation, a pregnancy test should be carried out.

Breast-feeding women tolerate the mini-Pill exceedingly well, and unlike the combined Pill it does not suppress the milk.

POST-COITAL CONTRACEPTION

Because sexual activity among young and inexperienced people can be so unplanned and unpredictable, post-coital contraception after unprotected intercourse or the failure of a contraceptive method, although not to be regarded as easy, is an alternative.

One method is a variation on the use of the higher-dose range of contraceptive Pill. Four tablets are taken: two immediately and two after twelve hours. The first two must be taken within 72 hours of intercourse. The intention is to prevent implantation of the ovum. This is followed by bleeding, probably before the period would normally arrive. The woman is at risk of remaining pregnant if the medication is delayed longer than three days and this is an important consideration if she is uncertain or untruthful about her previous sexual activity.

If the method fails there is a risk that the dose of hormone may have adversely affected the fetus. Under these circumstances termination of pregnancy is regarded as obligatory.

Higher-dose Pills can cause nausea and are contra-indicated when oestrogen might be hazardous. Another method, available up to five days after intercourse, is to insert an IUCD. This can also be done if the two pills in the first method cause vomiting (rendering them useless if it happens within three hours of taking them). Either way, pregnancy may still not be avoided and could, in rare circumstances, be ectopic.

Clearly, the emergency use of higher-dose Pills and IUCDs is upsetting, and couples are better advised to use foresight. But the chances of impregnation after rape, for instance, can be minimized by post-coital contraception and the better method is Pills; an IUCD may increase the risk of infection present in those special circumstances.

SAFE PERIOD

The safe period method derives from the fact that pregnancy depends on an ovum being in a fallopian tube when the sperm arrives. If it could be confidently predicted when the egg is in this position, then, with the knowledge that it remains there for little more than 24 hours, it should be possible for a woman to avoid pregnancy by having intercourse at a 'safe' time.

Much thought has gone into considering how a woman could recognize when she is ovulating. Temperature is one guide: it rises slightly in the second half of the cycle (although it also rises if she gets an infection). Watching the consistency of the vaginal mucus is another (Billing's method) – for a few days before ovulation it is less sticky, more fluid. If a woman has a regular 28-day cycle, she may use the fact that ovulation is thought to take place 14 days before the onset of a new menstrual period (the calendar method). Even if her cycle is sometimes longer or shorter, there are calculations she can make.

So, if ovulation could be recognized by any of these methods, or even by the slight pelvic pain that a few women have at mid-cycle, there is a chance that by avoiding intercourse from the end of the menstrual period until three days after ovulation she would avoid any risk of pregnancy.

Although the safe period is not very reliable, it is important because it is sanctioned by the Roman Catholic Church. Moreover, some women who find other methods repugnant sometimes use the safe period successfully. But largely because lengths of menstrual cycles and times of ovulation vary, it often fails, especially after childbirth and during the menopause, times when pregnancy is especially unwanted. Anyway, a couple may find that the days allowed for unrestricted love-making are not those when they want to make love.

SHEATHS

Sheaths, or condoms, or French letters, are one of the oldest methods of contraception. They are used to cover the erect penis so that at orgasm the semen is ejaculated into them leaving no sperm in the vagina after intercourse. Properly used, the method is highly effective. However, even early contact by the penis with the vagina may result in some sperm being left inside, and the man must hold the sheath in place when he withdraws. Most modern sheaths have a teat at the end for the semen which should be emptied of air – without this, or without any space at the end of a plain condom, the sheath may split. Sheaths lubricated with spermicide are probably the most reliable, also preventing any uncomfortable dryness if the woman does not readily lubricate. Alternatively, she can use a spermicidal pessary. A sheath minimizes the chance of sexual diseases being transmitted, but it should not be used more than once.

It is said that men who like to take control use sheaths more than others. Some men dislike them, either because they feel less contact or because putting them on is unpleasant. Men whose erections are uncertain also find sheaths do not suit them.

Sheaths can be bought without a prescription and can be used when other methods are not, for one reason or another, possible or reliable; they need no pre-planning. But there is often a temptation not to bother, and occasions when a couple decide to take a risk are probably responsible for many unplanned pregnancies.

STERILIZATION

Sterilization is an operation that makes a person infertile without causing serious damage. It is surgically easier with men than with women because in the male the vas deferens just below the skin on the side of the scrotum can be cut so that none of the sperm in the testicles reaches the ejaculated semen.

With a woman, sterilization usually (but not always) needs a general anaesthetic. The most common and easiest operation is to put clips across the fallopian tubes after an incision no longer than one centimetre (½ inch). Of course, female sterilization is also the result of a hysterectomy or removal of the ovaries. Some people believe that menstruation is heavier after a woman has been sterilized, so hysterectomy may then be preferred.

I know a doctor who always says 'Don't' when consulted about male or female sterilization. In this way he eliminates people who are poorly motivated, for others will ask again. It is easy for a man to do it to please his wife, and for a woman to ask for it as the only answer to her contraceptive problem, having in the past conceived unexpectedly. No one should take this step who is doubtful about it, or who acts in anger, fear, pain or bewilderment – it should never be taken at the height of a crisis like the termination of a pregnancy or a sudden family disaster, and preferably not immediately after childbirth except by very long-term intention. No one should expect to gain anything from sterilization except the removal of the fear of pregnancy. If there are exceptions to these rules, they must be seen as such – a special need must be paramount: a woman's health or signs that the children have inherited a particular disease.

All this must seem very negative. We now know that some men regret vasectomy, and that many more women (particularly if young) regret sterilization. They may have calculated wrongly about their own feelings and need to fantasize about conceiving children even if they know they never intend to do so again. But for those whose decision is well-informed, and taken against a background of security and trust, it may be the best possible answer to a universal human problem: how to use sexuality to enrich life without allowing uncontrolled fertility to spoil it.

For medically fit people, the hazards are those of any local or general anaesthetic, and the small risk involved in any surgical operation.

The effect is instant for the woman but delayed for about 16 weeks for the man, while the sperm take time to disappear from the semen. A man may suffer bruising soon after the operation, perhaps with pain and swelling, but most men find no ill effects after a day or two. It is known that vasectomy sometimes results in the formation of antibodies, but the fear that these cause coronary heart disease is groundless. The only physical long-term disadvantage is an occasional spermatocele (a small cyst) which may develop where the sperm accumulates.

However, concern about the operation is less important than the couple's feelings. The event is simple, but the decision profound. No surgeon should undertake treatment without discussing it first with each patient. For, unlike any other method of contraception, sterilization is virtually irreversible. Heroic operations to repair the tubes in either sex do take place but not more than half are successful; they would only be considered at all as a result of an unforeseen event, such as remarriage or the death of a child. Usually, the man or woman can decide, after a discussion with the doctor, whether the operation will be emotionally acceptable to them. But if there is a crisis like an unplanned pregnancy, or if the marital relationship is poor, a partner may agree to a sterilization when actually disliking the idea. When that happens, libido may be affected and sexual performance may deteriorate. Such sexual failure is not physical but in the mind – impotence has never been caused by the operation.

SPECIAL CIRCUMSTANCES

SINGLE GIRLS

It is widely accepted today that a single girl may have a sexual relationship before marriage. For some, it may be a preliminary to marriage, whereas others may choose to enjoy sex without permanent commitment to a partner as their way of life.

However, pregnancy in such circumstances is usually unwelcome, and may even rank as a disaster, like the abortion which probably ensues. So, for as long as couples are unable to support children, they should use reliable methods of preventing conception.

SPACING THE FAMILY

There is considerable need for contraception after children have been born. In prosperous countries the mother's emotional considerations are uppermost, whereas in underdeveloped countries an interval between babies may greatly improve the child's chances of survival.

Although breast-feeding partly protects a mother against quick reconception, weaning marks a return to regular ovulation, and at this time some women may be particularly fertile. A woman who does not breast-feed may ovulate only 27 days after delivery.

Certainty of contraception may not be the paramount consideration. A woman might decide not to go back to the combined Pill but ask for an IUCD or use a barrier method instead.

DIABETIC WOMEN

Diabetic women, for strong medical reasons, should be encouraged to have small families, preferably before the age of 30. When families are complete and pregnancy becomes undesirable, reliable contraception is imperative. Along with all the other considerations, diabetic women have one more – the satisfactory control of the disease.

A diabetic woman who asks for the Pill may, if she is well organized and her diabetes does not get out of control, use it for up to five years. Spacing her family is important, and in order to achieve that she may choose an IUCD, a barrier method, or even the mini-Pill. There is no doubt that sterilization, either of herself or of her husband, gives her the best chance of good health after the children are born; but there are methods other than the Pill if preferred. There is nothing to substantiate suggestions that IUCDs are less effective for women suffering from diabetes.

ASIAN COUPLES

In Hindu and Muslim cultures women are expected to be modest, chaste before marriage and, often, subservient after. The marriage is arranged by the parents, and typically a woman receives little or no sexual instruction. Her wishes are expected to be directed towards pleasing her husband and bearing his children, especially sons. Large families are the norm, for the old fears of child mortality are taking many years to fade, even in communities where they are no longer warranted.

For an unmarried girl to have a sexual relationship may ruin her chances of marriage, and consequently young Asian women seldom seek contraception before marriage (although termination of pregnancy is not unknown, despite religious precepts).

In Hindu families, contraceptives may be used to space the children, but prolonged lactation during breast-feeding often achieves this anyway. All methods are acceptable, but pills and barrier methods are preferred because menstruation may be prolonged with an IUCD in position, causing the woman to be regarded as unclean. Because a Hindu family is dominated by the male, contraception probably works better if he is involved in the choice; after his children are born, he may even consent to male or female sterilization.

More and more Muslims are using birth control although discouraged by their religion (which forbids sterilization). However, IUCDs have the same drawback for them as for Hindus and many Muslim women are often too fastidious to insert a cap and may consequently choose the Pill if their husbands sanction the choice.

ROMAN CATHOLIC COUPLES

Pope Paul VI's encyclical letter *Humanae Vitae* states that an act of mutual love without the capacity to transmit life 'contradicts the will of the Author of Life'. It forbids termination of pregnancy, even for therapeutic reasons, and condemns sterilization. However, married people may take advantage of the 'safe period' (the naturally infertile days) for making love. The method is haphazard, causing frustration and anxiety, but the promised 'dipstick' method (a simple test on a urine sample) may improve methods.

Some Roman Catholic couples ask for contraceptives like anyone else in the consulting room, and naturally their decision must be respected. Pope Paul did recognize that some organic diseases require medication which has an entirely secondary effect, namely, acting as a contraceptive. Provided it is taken solely to cure illness it is acceptable, so women who take hormones to regulate an erratic cycle are sometimes deemed to come into this category.

Although the discipline of their church is strict, many Roman Catholic women request abortions – an estimated 34 million a year in Latin America alone.

BREAST-FEEDING MOTHERS

Breast-feeding mothers may use the mini-Pill, but not one with oestrogen for that might suppress lactation. She can take the mini-Pill as soon as she likes, and should certainly be taking it within six weeks after delivery. Ovulation may not return until after she has weaned the child, but it is not certain.

However, many couples choose the sheath when they resume intercourse. Men perhaps feel this takes the responsibility off their partners. But there is no reason a cap or an IUCD should not be fitted at the six-week post-natal check: IUCDs inserted before then have a habit of being expelled. In some countries, such as Nigeria, the partners abstain from sex for as long as breast-feeding lasts. Because there this may continue for three years, it can provide the much needed interval between pregnancies; however, one would not expect it to work in a society where monogamy is the norm.

OLDER WOMEN

There is a paradox about contraceptives for women aged over 40:
although many probably could not conceive and bear a child at this
stage of their lives anyway, they should still use contraceptives,
because it is generally not possible to tell who is fertile and who
is not. Few women want to become pregnant after 40 nowadays,
not only for personal reasons but because the chance of an abnormal child at this age rises sharply.

A further paradox is that the most reliable method, the Pill, is
not medically acceptable at that age because, again, the risks
become too high. It is a pity because at this time a couple may
want to draw on the comfort and support of an untroubled sexual
relationship more than ever before. Barrier methods may not suit
them any longer. An IUCD or mini-Pill may be sufficient, particularly if reinforced by a vaginal pessary. Although these methods
are not completely effective, neither are the couple completely
fertile.

Couples should use contraception until two menstrual-free years
have elapsed, or one year if the woman is aged over 50. (The
average age for the menopause in Britain is 50 years, 1 month.)

Many couples accept with relief the freedom which male or
female sterilization brings.

FAILURE OF CONTRACEPTION

Contraception can and does fail. The Pill, used properly, is almost
always effective, but IUCDs, barrier methods and the mini-Pill
sometimes fail; coitus interruptus, the safe period, and spermicides
are still less successful. If conception occurs, often the first the
woman knows about it is that she misses her menstrual period.
Fourteen days later a urine test may prove she is pregnant. If that
is positive, she may request a termination or continue with the
pregnancy. If the latter is the case, it is usual to remove any IUCD
in position.

A woman should always report a possible pregnancy to her
doctor to make sure that the embryo is developing normally. For
a fetus to be harmed by the Pill, a coil or spermicides if conception
takes place has never been proved, although it would be advisable
to stop using the Pill or chemicals if pregnancy seems a possibility.
Sheaths are harmless. Women should not, of course, make the

mistake of stopping all contraception and then becoming pregnant in consequence, when the first suspicion was in fact groundless – they must be absolutely sure before they stop using contraceptives.

THE FUTURE

Stringent and time-consuming trials limit the marketing of new contraceptive methods. Modifications of existing methods which are in preparation include the contracap, a custom-made silicone cap fitted to the cervix for a year, which has a one-way valve to allow the menstrual flow to escape. Another new cap being considered is claimed to need no cream or chemical. Researchers are developing monthly vaginal rings, which release progestogen, as well as vaginal rings fitted for six months which contain two hormones like the combined Pill. Doctors have also thought about a twice-a-week vaginal pill and a biodegradable capsule put into the womb once a month. Most of these ideas are still a long way from being put into use. However, a 10-year IUCD with hardly any risk of pregnancy is a nearer possibility. There is also a new IUCD with catgut attachments for women after a birth. The purpose is to avoid the greater likelihood of expulsion, which often happens if the device is inserted following childbirth.

Further in the future there may be a nasal spray which would suppress pituitary activity (and, by extension, ovarian activity). Vaccines may be developed which would act against hormone production in early pregnancy or against male sperm. Indeed, other new spermicides are on trial, especially some called enzyme inhibitors.

The pill for men may be further developed (the first one ran into trouble because it proved incompatible with alcohol). A new pill is being developed from gossipol, a pigment found in cotton-seed flour. (Gossipol might also act as a local spermicide and may prove to be effective enough to be used on its own.) Anabolic steroids, which many athletes take for body-building, reduce a man's fertility and may even one day be marketed as a contraceptive pill for men.

Implants for women have had extensive trials. They act not unlike injectables but have the advantage of being effective for five years and can be removed if not wanted.

Finally, a 'dipstick' method of predicting ovulation by testing urine is an advance which may be available within a few years.

THE CAUSES OF MALE & FEMALE INFERTILITY

Mr Michael Cameron

Infertility, in medical terms, is the inability to conceive despite a year of regular sexual intercourse without contraception, and affects about one couple in 10. In one third of childless couples the difficulty rests with the man, in another third with the woman, and in the remaining third both partners have some degree of subfertility. For conception to occur, a sperm from the man must penetrate the woman's ovum so that the genetic material of the male mixes with that of the female. At that moment fertilization occurs, after which the ovum divides repeatedly and eventually produces a new, individual human being.

MALE INFERTILITY

When a couple seek medical advice about infertility the first step for the specialist is usually to make a detailed examination of a sample of the man's semen, because its 'quality' determines male fertility. The number of sperm ejaculated, their density and their motility (or degree of movement) are assessed at intervals over four hours, and the percentage with abnormal forms (for example, with two heads or two tails) is noted. More detailed examination of the sperm under the electron microscope may show other significant physical defects. The results of semen analysis can at different times vary widely in the same man. In order to achieve a reliable and consistent result, then, a couple should not have sexual intercourse for three days before the test, to avoid an abnormally low count. Because it is best that the specimen be examined immediately after ejaculation, it is usually obtained by masturbation in the laboratory.

An alternative way to examine a man's fertility is to make a post-coital test. The couple make love on about the twelfth night of the monthly cycle, when the woman's cervical mucus is most receptive to sperm. The next morning, some of the mucus from the cervix is examined under the microscope. If there are many actively swimming sperm, it shows that the man's fertility is satisfactory.

Male subfertility usually shows up in a semen analysis with a deficient sperm count, low motility or a lot of abnormal forms.

There may be no sperm at all if both testicles have not descended or have been severely affected in the past by mumps. These conditions can, unfortunately, make a man sterile. But any prolonged illness, certain drugs, failure to secrete certain hormones (gonadotrophins for example) or too high a temperature around the testicles, can affect sperm production even if the testicles are normal.

LOW SPERM COUNT

A man may have a low sperm count because he wears briefs that are too tight and hold the testicles against the body, which is warmer than the normally-positioned scrotal sac. Varicocele (varicose veins in the testicles) may have the same effect; the use of boxer shorts, cold baths twice a day, and possibly surgical treatment if the varicocele is large, may enhance fertility. If one of the testicles is missing because of injury or surgery the sperm count need not be seriously depleted, although if the man has intercourse very often there are naturally fewer sperm in each ejaculation. To improve the chances of conception, then, the couple should avoid intercourse for three days before the most fertile phase, the twelfth day of the woman's monthly cycle.

When despite simple measures a low count persists – a count of, say, less than 20 million per millilitre – hormone treatment may improve the numbers of sperm. Whether this helps very much, however, is doubtful. The intention is to stimulate the testicles either with a drug that causes the release of pituitary gonadotrophins, or with gonadotrophic hormone itself. But it is difficult to determine how effective this treatment is because greater sperm density in seminal fluid occurs only after a long delay and sperm count will still vary.

OBSTRUCTIONS

The flow of sperm from the testicles may be blocked by an obstruction in the narrow tube called the vas deferens (see page 23). Caused by scars from previous infections, or following surgery, such an obstruction may ordinarily be removed surgically, generally through the surgeon's use of an operating microscope which makes it possible for him afterwards to sew together the open ends very accurately with fine stitches. Where a blockage is the result of a previous vasectomy and the rest of the tube is healthy, about half of the operations succeed; but where a blockage follows previous infection (gonorrhoea for example), much of the tube may have been damaged by scarring and the results are poor. Sperm in the semen after an operation does not necessarily mean success, which is achieved only if the man subsequently fathers a pregnancy.

In middle-aged men who have had surgery on the prostate gland, the semen may ejaculate into the bladder. Further surgery is unlikely to correct this.

ABNORMALITIES

A few men are born with an abnormality of the penis called hypospadias, in which the urethral opening is under the shaft instead of at the end. Ejaculation of semen into the vagina then occurs at some distance from the cervix, which can cause added difficulty for the sperm to reach the egg and for one to fertilize it. Corrective surgery for hypospadias is usually carried out in childhood.

Other common causes of male infertility are impotence (when a man cannot get an erection) or premature ejaculation (when he has an orgasm too soon, before the penis enters the vagina). Impotence may result from certain diseases such as severe diabetes, hypogonadism or some drug treatments, but like premature ejaculation it is more often psychosomatic, or 'in the mind'. Both may be treated by counselling.

ARTIFICIAL INSEMINATION

When, for whatever reason, the man is unable to ejaculate high into the vagina, artificial insemination may be the answer. If the man is actually producing enough sperm, they can be collected

55

after masturbation in a rubber cap which is then placed over his partner's cervix either by a doctor or by the woman herself (artificial insemination by husband). If the man's semen contains too few sperm, his semen may be pooled with semen from a number of donors and be applied to the cervix in the same way (artificial insemination by donor). In either case, the application must take place at the right time in the woman's menstrual cycle, the day before ovulation.

A new and still experimental way, rapidly gaining ground, to overcome infertility caused by deficient sperm density is extracorporeal fertilization (outside the body altogether) through embryo transfer – the 'test-tube baby' technique. In the test-tube, a lower density of sperm than in nature can achieve fertilization of an ovum, so a man with a lower sperm count may be able to father a pregnancy.

FEMALE INFERTILITY

Infertility in women may be caused either by a physical barrier which prevents the man's sperm from reaching the ovum, or by the failure of ovulation to occur. Surgery that involves the removal of the womb, of both tubes or of both ovaries, or that requires very heavy doses of X-rays, clearly causes sterility. (The loss of just one tube or ovary does not impair fertility very much.)

TIGHT HYMENS

An unduly tight hymen or maidenhead near the entrance to the vagina may prevent intercourse. A relatively rare condition, it is easily treated by stretching the opening in the hymen under a general anaesthetic.

Anxiety about the sexual act can by itself cause a woman to tense up and involuntarily contract the muscle of the vaginal entrance. This condition is called vaginismus, and responds to prolonged and sympathetic counselling.

VAGINAL INFECTIONS

Vaginal infections, such as trichomoniasis or candidiasis (thrush), may cause so much discomfort that intercourse is impossible. Trichomoniasis (see page 179) – a generally harmless but tedious inflammation – is successfully treated with medication; the male partner should also be treated, despite a lack of symptoms. Thrush (see page 130) – an infection by a yeast fungus – is a common condition, especially in a woman who is pregnant or who has been given antibiotics for another condition. It is usually treated with antifungal pessaries.

CERVICAL INFECTIONS

Infections of the cervix which make the cervical mucus inhospitable to sperm may diminish fertility too. Such infections occur particularly in an erosion, where an area around the opening of the cervix is for one reason or another covered by a glandular mucus-producing membrane instead of the normal tough vaginal skin. The condition is easy to treat: cauterization destroys the glandular covering and should allow normal vaginal skin to replace it. Most erosions are not infected, however, so this is rarely necessary. A similar condition is a cervical polyp, a small cherry-red growth on the cervix which represents a heaping up of the glandular covering. It too is easily removed under a brief general anaesthetic.

FIBROIDS

Fibroids, benign tumours of the muscular wall of the womb, are common in childless women in the later childbearing years. They vary considerably in size and may be single or multiple; hardly ever malignant, they nevertheless often cause menstrual disturbances. If they grow into the cavity of the uterus and distort its shape, or grow beneath the fallopian tubes, they may impair fertility. More often, though, they grow outwards from the uterus and thus cannot be blamed for any failure to conceive.

A fluid which is opaque to X-rays may be syringed through the cervix and observed on a screen as it fills the uterus and tubes. This investigation (known as a hysterosalpingogram) reveals any physical distortion caused by a fibroid or by congenital malformation and should also reveal any blocked or damaged tube.

A fibroid can be removed by means of an abdominal operation (myomectomy) which, unlike the removal of the womb itself (hysterectomy), leaves a woman potentially fertile. Any operation on the pelvic organ, however, may cause adhesions, areas in which separate tissues have stuck together forming internal scars, which can cause infertility.

SALPINGITIS

Salpingitis, or inflammation of the fallopian tubes (see page 172), may also cause adhesions which commonly block the fallopian tubes or surround the ovaries, causing a mechanical barrier to fertilization. Salpingitis is caused by infection which may result from a variety of causes: sexual contact with a partner who has gonorrhoea (see page 140) or chlamydia, for instance, or following abortion or childbirth. It may also develop from infection caused when an intra-uterine contraception device (IUCD) or coil is inserted.

The initial attack of salpingitis often causes an acute illness combining fever, lower abdominal pain and a vaginal discharge. The woman clearly needs medical treatment, preferably in a hospital where antibiotics may immediately be given to kill the infection, leaving no permanent damage to the tube. If the infection is allowed to progress, on the other hand, abscesses may form in the tubes, which are then damaged beyond repair.

Unfortunately, salpingitis sometimes has a much less obvious onset, in a mild case of infection producing merely an ache in the lower abdomen and perhaps some vaginal discharge. A woman may not feel ill enough to seek medical advice and even if she does, her doctor may miss the correct diagnosis. The untreated infection then lingers on, causing inflammation and adhesions in and around the tubes which, once they have been structurally damaged, become prone to further infection. Chronic salpingitis ensues, causing recurrent attacks of a pain that is worse during menstrual periods and especially during intercourse, and which may hurt so much that ordinary life becomes impossible. At that stage, the tubes are permanently damaged, and treatment cannot restore their function.

Whether or not a woman remains fertile after salpingitis depends on the condition of the tubes – whether they are clear of obstruction – and on the condition of the cells in their lining, for it is on those that the transport of the ovum depends.

In general, doctors recommend surgery, often using micro-surgical techniques, to open blocked fallopian tubes. When the damage has not been excessive, about 10–20 per cent of women treated do become pregnant. Tubes which have been deliberately blocked by a previous sterilization operation, but are otherwise normal, may be re-opened with a 50–60 per cent chance of success.

ENDOMETRIOSIS

Endometriosis is another condition which commonly results in infertility because it causes adhesions around the ovaries and tubes, although the structure of the tubes themselves is seldom damaged. Endometriosis occurs when cells from the endometrium (the lining of the womb) gather on the ovaries and adjacent organs, carried there by some of the menstrual blood which occasionally flows backwards along the tubes. The implanted endometrial cells then undergo the normal changes of the menstrual cycle – each month they grow and then bleed – but the blood cannot escape to the outside and becomes trapped; little blood cysts are formed in and around the ovaries. The tissues react by forming adhesions which wall off the cysts – but in the process they tend to mat all the pelvic organs together, so that the egg cannot reach the opening of the fallopian tubes.

This condition most commonly affects women who have postponed having children. It causes lower abdominal and pelvic pain before periods and during intercourse, and tends to increase menstrual blood loss in many cases, both in duration and in frequency. Yet endometriosis in a pregnant woman does not affect the pregnancy, and after the birth the symptoms are likely not to be as severe as they were.

From a woman's medical history and from a clinical examination a doctor may often suspect that she has endometriosis but can confirm the diagnosis only by using laparoscopy. There is no need for treatment, however, if there are only slight symptoms (a pregnancy is the best way to prevent the condition getting worse).

More severe pain may be relieved, and subsequent fertility improved, by treatment with hormones taken for several months to damp down menstrual activity. This medication may cause weight increase. If there are large blood cysts in the ovaries, or if there are extensive adhesions, an abdominal operation to 'tidy up' the pelvic organs may improve fertility or make medical treatment more successful.

INVESTIGATIONS INTO FEMALE INFERTILITY

Doctors can examine the condition of the fallopian tubes either by laparoscopy or by an X-ray salpingogram. The former, the usually preferred method nowadays, is carried out under a general anaesthetic. The abdominal cavity between the abdominal wall and the intestines is first distended with gas; the laparoscope, a small telescope with a fibre-optic light, is then introduced through a tiny incision just below the navel. It gives an excellent view of all the pelvic organs and assists in testing whether the tubes are clear by allowing the doctor to observe the passage through them of a blue-coloured fluid injected from below into the cervix. The doctor can also inspect the ovaries to see whether there are adhesions, fibroids or signs of endometriosis. Sometimes it is possible during this procedure to divide fine adhesions or to take samples of an ovary for microscopic examination, or even to retrieve eggs for *in-vitro* fertilization. Following laparoscopy, however, many women complain of discomfort, particularly in the shoulder. This is caused by a small remaining bubble of gas pressing on a nerve which runs to both the shoulder and the diaphragm.

An X-ray salpingogram, on the other hand, may or may not be carried out under a general anaesthetic. As we have seen, it involves injecting a fluid opaque to X-rays into the cervical canal, and on into the uterus, through the fallopian tubes and out into the abdominal cavity. The information on the screen is usually a little less informative than laparoscopy, and the fluid is more likely to cause pain by inflaming the lining of the abdominal cavity – but unlike laparoscopy, which looks at the fallopian tubes, a salpingogram does show what the interior looks like.

A woman whose tubes have been removed or been damaged beyond the possibility of repair, may now consider having a test-tube baby. The method is to obtain one (or preferably more) ovum from the ovary, either through the laparoscope or using a needle inserted through the skin and guided by ultrasound into the ovarian follicle. The ova are then put in a test-tube within a specific environment and fertilized with the man's sperm, after which cell division begins. The dividing ova are then collected and transferred into the uterine cavity, where implantation and development take place just as they do when an ovum arrives in the normal way.

Of course, there are many technical difficulties that have taken years of research and endeavour to overcome, and even now expert teams of doctors expect a success rate of no more than one in four. Recovery of more than one ovum, which in any event depends on administering a fertility drug well in advance, is desirable because the transfer of two or three fertilized ova instead of one proportionately increases the chances of success.

If a woman fails to ovulate she is infertile. But why should she fail? At the top level of command in the brain, emotional upsets may block commands from the hypothalamus to the anterior pituitary gland, so inhibiting the whole system – and there is no ovulation and no menstruation. The emotional upset may be the break-up of a love affair, the death of a parent, leaving home for the first time, or even going on night duty. Women who already have irregular or infrequent menstrual periods are more likely to experience this problem. Counselling and a simple explanation of the problem is usually enough to put things right (although a doctor may sometimes prescribe clomiphene, which brings back ovulation by increasing output of the hormone gonadotrophin). However, if this is unsuccessful, a course of the gonadotrophic hormones themselves may be given by injection – but to avoid the considerable risk then of multiple pregnancy the doses must be precisely correct, which necessitates laboratory tests every day during the treatment.

It is popularly thought that a woman who has been taking the contraceptive pill risks being infertile after she stops using it. Up to a point that is true. Ovulation sometimes takes a while to start again, but the delay is seldom more than a few weeks and, after that, clomiphene can be relied on to restart it if necessary.

Some girls in their teens develop anorexia nervosa, a serious disease in which they obsessively lose weight by dieting or even starvation and self-induced vomiting. A girl can even become so thin and emaciated that she may die. The indirect cause is severe emotional disturbance, but it remains unclear exactly what causes that. Severe loss of weight, caused by this or any other illness, may cause ovulation to fail after which it seldom returns until a girl is back to her normal weight. Girls who take up very disciplined athletic pursuits, such as competitive athletics or ballet dancing, may temporarily cease to ovulate too.

A malfunctioning thyroid or adrenal gland may also interfere with the normal production of pituitary gonadotrophins and prevent ovulation. Treatment in these cases is directed at the faulty gland.

The hormone prolactin, produced in the pituitary gland, stimulates the breasts to produce milk. After childbirth, prolactin production increases immediately and lactation ensues. Prolactin also inhibits ovulation, which is why breast-feeding is a natural (though certainly not reliable) method of contraception. Sometimes, apart from childbirth, the cells that produce prolactin become overactive and the same effects naturally occur: non-ovulation and lactation. This condition, hyperprolactinaemia, is a well known cause of infertility and can be treated by a drug, bromocriptine, which restores prolactin levels to normal, allowing ovulation to resume.

Ovulation may fail because the ovary finally has no more ova. At birth the ovaries of a normal little girl contain about 250,000 ova; gradually they are used up as they mature during the woman's childbearing life. But some girls may start with a much smaller supply of eggs, and these can become exhausted after only a few years of ovulation. Such cases, often called ovarian failure, really represent a premature menopause occurring in the late teens or twenties.

Some women have ovaries which produce more male hormone, testosterone, than normal. This condition, which is known as the polycystic ovary syndrome, can show up in excessive body hair, a deeper voice, bigger muscles and obesity, with infrequent or even absent ovulation, and with infertility. It is often possible to make ovulation regular again by drug treatment, but other aspects of the condition are incurable. Women athletes who take steroids for body building to improve performance have the same condition.

Sometimes, although it is regular, ovulation is somewhat impaired. The ovum may get trapped inside the follicle and not be released, or progesterone production by the corpus luteum may be defective, and the endometrium not be receptive to the ovum.

When a doctor advises a woman who ovulates infrequently or not at all, the reason for the disorder must first be found. A physical examination provides much information, but analysing the levels of the various hormones in a blood sample establishes the precise diagnosis before treatment.

A childless couple whose fertility has been fully investigated are occasionally found to be completely normal. Perhaps there is then some other incompatibility between them, a condition that might for example be caused by tissue antibodies produced in the cervix which damage or destroy the sperm. Such tentative diagnoses remain merely theoretical.

PHYSICAL PROBLEMS THAT MAY AFFECT SEXUALITY

Dr Alan J. Riley

To get the most out of lovemaking you should stay healthy. Sex, like running, takes up energy and you cannot expect to be good at it if you are unfit. It's as simple as that – you can only hope to succeed as a good lover if your body and your mind are in prime condition. Likewise, when things go wrong with the body, your sex life will probably also be adversely affected.

Recently, a patient of mine had a minor stroke and lost the use of an arm for a time. He made a good recovery and started treatment in hospital for high blood pressure. But his main concern was that since the stroke he had lost interest in sex (although he still got erections in bed in the mornings). How many men, I wonder, would be that concerned about sex so soon after a serious illness, especially when in hospital? Sex is probably the last thing that most people would think about in the circumstances.

There are several reasons for that man to have been particularly concerned about his sexual capability at that particular time. One might have been because he really had been enjoying a good sex life before the stroke and the illness genuinely had caused him to lose interest. This is quite common and natural – just coping with illness can itself be enough to make you forget about sex. The changes that illness causes in the body may impair the sexual processes – a stroke, for example, can damage the part of the brain that generates sexual desire; moreover, there are many illnesses that have a direct effect on the sexual organs themselves. Then there are the psychological effects of physical illness – anxiety, depression, even mere worry can cause you to lose interest in sex.

Another reason for my patient to raise the matter might have been that he had had a sexual problem for a long time, from well before his stroke, and that the illness was simply the first good opportunity he had had, or the first time he had felt able to pluck

65

up the courage, to seek help over this delicate and possibly embarrassing matter. Anyway, in the circumstances, with so many intimate intrusions into his private life already – 'have you had your bowels open today?' – it was easier for him to discuss his sexual problems. That too is perfectly common and natural.

Some problems also arise from misunderstanding the basic physical mechanics of sex. For example, a man who in the past has suffered one of the fairly common complications of mumps, inflammation of the testicles (orchitis), may worry about whether it has harmed his sexual performance. He may worry so much that he does actually come to have a sexual difficulty, caused not by the mumps but by the worrying. Although orchitis may cause sterility, there is no effect on sexual desire, erection or ejaculation once the inflammation has gone.

Being ill may easily cause a patient to feel less attractive, of course, and undermines sexual self-confidence, particularly with regard to illnesses that cause permanent disability or require major surgery, like amputating a leg or an arm. In relation to diseases or surgery which affect the sexual organs themselves, the question of a patient's disturbed body image of himself becomes a critical one. Sometimes a person's self-esteem may falter so much that he or she behaves quite out of character sexually. A man may make passes at nurses, seizing opportunities to feel their breasts, perhaps, when they bend over him in bed. This is more than letting off steam due to sexual frustration. It is at a deeper level – the patient is trying to reaffirm his own sexuality, to prove to himself that he can still respond, that 'there's life in the old dog yet'. He wants and needs to reinforce his hope and belief that he is still a sexual being, not just Patient No. 25. Women may behave similarly, making passes at male doctors, with exactly the same motives.

Another possible reason for losing interest in sex is that many drugs prescribed to treat illnesses can impair sexual functioning.

Unhappily, some conditions result in permanent disability that directly affects sex. Think of the man who has cancer of the penis and has to have it amputated. Clearly, that huge physical trauma will have major psychological as well as physical repercussions. Yet even that need not be the end of his sex life, despite everything. With his partner, he can still explore ways to get the most out of the sexual feelings from what he has left. That will obviously mean a new sexual outlook and new techniques. A 62-year-old man whose penis was seriously injured found stimulation of his prostate by his wife's finger in his rectum a satisfactory substitute for penile stimulation. He introduced cunnilingus into his loveplay, which his wife enjoyed as a substitute for intercourse. These were activities they had never practised before.

Unrelated diseases can affect sexual activity in more subtle ways. Chronic lung disease, heart disease or severe anaemia can reduce a person's ability to exert himself. Again, a change in the pattern of lovemaking can overcome this. If it is the man who is afflicted, an obvious solution is for the wife to take the more active role in intercourse.

Sudden illness often causes marked disturbance to a person's social life. Patients may have to go to hospital and be separated from their sexual partners for perhaps the first time during their relationship. If the patient is the breadwinner, there will probably be financial worries as well. So, again, it is hardly surprising that thoughts about sex dwindle or disappear altogether – there are so many other pressing considerations.

Being a patient can by itself create special sexual problems. There is the embarrassment of possibly having to expose the genitals, of being prodded, of having other people's fingers and instruments inserted into various orifices. Although none of this is sexual, it is nevertheless an intrusion into the patient's sexuality. An inappropriate comment by a doctor or a nurse, especially perhaps if misinterpreted, may reinforce a patient's inner fear that he or she is sexually unusual or inadequate. One male patient overheard a woman doctor say 'It is abnormally small' when she was examining his groin. He thought the doctor was referring to the size of his penis which, unfortunately, he had always wrongly thought was smaller than average. In fact, the doctor was talking about something else. But the patient's anxiety about his imagined inadequacy was increased, and he developed a serious sexual hang-up.

Despite all this, some people – usually those who are otherwise fit but are in hospital for an injury, say – still retain their usual sexual feelings. For example, a young man with a fractured leg may have to spend weeks in a hospital bed. He may feel more and more sexually frustrated. Lacking an outlet for his sexual tensions he might seek relief in masturbation – perfectly normal. But if, given the lack of privacy that is usual in hospitals, he is found to have done this, he may, quite unnecessarily, feel guilty or

67

embarrassed, perhaps when the nurse sees semen stains on the sheets. But it is very natural to seek relief in this way.

This brief outline of the kind of physical problems that can affect sex leads us now to a more detailed account of what diseases and other conditions can do to a person's sex life, and how they may be countered or relieved. The final section of this chapter deals with drugs – including alcohol and prescribed medicines – and their relationship to sex.

ANGINA

Angina, which feels like a tight, painful constriction in the chest, is caused by insufficient blood carrying oxygen to the heart's muscles. The harder the heart works, the more oxygen it needs, which is why angina occurs during exertion, including sexual intercourse. This can be very distressing for both partners. If it happens during sexual activity, the sufferer should adopt a passive role. Many angina patients find that a tablet of nitroglycerine under the tongue or a tablet containing a drug which improves the oxygen supply to the heart reduces the likelihood of an attack.

ARTHRITIS

Arthritis is a term that describes several conditions which cause swelling, deformity, stiffness and pain in the joints. Arthritis may affect the small joints of the hand or larger, weight-bearing joints like the knees and hips. Although mild arthritis probably has little effect on sex, severe forms can cause serious sexual problems.

Arthritis, which causes deformity and reduces mobility, may cause people to lose confidence in their sexual attractiveness, which may lead them to avoid sexual encounters. The chronic pain that many arthritic patients suffer can also cause them to lose interest in sex. When the arthritis is in the hips, finding a suitable position for intercourse can be difficult and, in severe cases, impossible, especially with women, who may be unable to open their legs wide enough. Even if they can, the discomfort of maintaining the position can spoil the enjoyment of intercourse, and attempts at intercourse may even trigger bouts of pain that last for hours, if not days.

Probably as many as two-thirds of women with hip arthritis

have sexual difficulties as a direct result, and are anxious at the possibility that they may fail to please their partners.

Arthritis in the hand can also cause great difficulty in caressing, masturbation, and supporting body weight during intercourse.

At least one type of arthritis decreases vaginal lubrication and saliva production too, making the mouth uncomfortably dry and perhaps causing the patient to avoid kissing and oral–genital contact.

Unhappily, there is no easy solution to the sexual problems that arthritis can cause. Painkillers or anti-inflammatory drugs taken before lovemaking may help to relieve pain and stiffness. A cushion can support painful joints. Many women who suffer constant back pain find that a cushion in the small of the back reduces discomfort. When the hands and fingers cannot be used for caressing, a vibrator may help – there are some fairly thick ones which can be held by arthritic hands. The unaffected partner must be most understanding and considerate, and the couple should together explore ways of gaining mutual satisfaction. A counsellor can often help them towards this goal.

ASTHMA

Asthma is a disease in which spasms cause the air passages to narrow. Patients differ greatly in what triggers off their attacks – exercise and cold air do it to many; others are allergic to pollen, feathers, certain foods, perfumes or even house dust or other allergens which float off the bedclothes when they are disturbed by lovemaking.

An asthma attack at that juncture is so distressing that if it happens often a patient might prefer to avoid sexual activity completely. But there is no need for that. Some detective work might well uncover the factors that trigger the attacks, such as making love on a particular bed or in a particular room. Avoiding these factors may be all that is needed to solve the problem. If the asthma comes on because of severe exertion, less strenuous lovemaking may help. If all else fails, a medicine prescribed by the doctor that prevents narrowing of the air passages may be taken before lovemaking. Drugs that are inhaled into the lung are probably best, and a further inhaled dose can be taken if the patient feels a tightening of the chest during lovemaking or afterwards, but check with your doctor how often you can use the particular medicine prescribed for you.

BRONCHITIS AND EMPHYSEMA

Chronic bronchitis and emphysema are progressive diseases which, although they often start in middle life (perhaps as the result of too much smoking), do not usually cause disability until later. The early stages of the disease should not affect sexual functioning.

The physical effort of lovemaking may trigger bouts of coughing and wheezing, more troublesome in a cold room.

A dose of a proprietary cough medicine about half an hour before intercourse and an inhaled bronchodilator immediately beforehand should help.

As the disease gets worse, the patient becomes more and more short of breath on exertion, which can profoundly impair the ability for any exercise, lovemaking included. The general debility of the chronic illness can cause lower interest in sex, although in some men there may be a hormonal reason for this. Less interest in sex may also result from fear of reduced ability to cope with the physical effort involved. A way round the problem is to reduce the amount of effort needed – for instance if a man has difficulty, his partner can be on top during intercourse.

One feature of these chronic breathing diseases is that infections in the lungs keep recurring. That can cause bad breath, making the partner avoid kissing and close contact. Antibacterial treatment prescribed by the doctor and physiotherapy to loosen and drain the phlegm from the lungs can help, with a mouthwash just before lovemaking.

CHANGE OF LIFE

The 'change of life' is an expression that in meaning is not quite the same as the term 'menopause', which is often used to describe the change of life in women but strictly means the ending of menstruation – the last period. Change of life refers not only to that but to all the associated physical and psychological changes that failing ovarian activity creates. Another and perhaps more appropriate term for this phase is the 'climacteric'.

The menopause may be spontaneous, brought on by the natural

cessation of the ovaries' activity, or it can result from surgical removal of the ovaries. It usually occurs between the ages of 45 and 52, but climacteric symptoms can start earlier and last for several years after the last period. Occasionally, the menopause spontaneously occurs at a much younger age.

The menopause marks an important stage in a woman's life. It is the end of her capacity to have children, something which may be a great relief but which may, alternatively, fill her with dismay. Contraception is still an important consideration for a time even when a woman's periods have stopped. Before she reaches the age of 50 she would still be wise to take precautions for at least two years after the last period. Beyond that age, one year of continued contraception is advisable.

Climacteric symptoms vary in their nature and severity. One woman in five has no symptoms except her periods' stopping. Most women have occasional troubles but cope without drug treatment. About 15 per cent have symptoms that interfere with normal life and usually need treatment.

There is no reason for the menopause to herald the end of sex life. Some women feel that not having regular periods reduces their femininity, so they feel less attractive. Others become more irritable or prone to depression which can strain their relationships, perhaps seriously if there are already relationship problems.

Some women on the other hand become more interested in sex after the menopause. That may be because they do not have to worry about pregnancy or contraception any more. Also, the menopause often coincides with the lifting of family responsibilities; the children may well be in the process of leaving home, husbands now established in their careers, and the couple may enjoy more financial security than in earlier years. All these factors can help improve the sexual side of a relationship.

However, for other women the climacteric means less interest in sex and impaired function. Some use it as a scapegoat for a long-existing sexual difficulty; in others, the hormonal changes of the menopause may cause sexual problems. Less oestrogen may bring a loss of elasticity in the vagina and thinning of the lining, with decreased lubrication and less congestion of the blood vessels during sexual arousal. All these changes cause discomfort or pain during intercourse, discouraging women from sex. Furthermore, these changes may cause the base of the bladder and the urethra to bruise more easily during intercourse, giving rise to a burning

71

sensation when urine is passed. These symptoms usually respond well to oestrogen treatment.

DIGESTIVE SYSTEM

The pain of many acute diseases of the stomach and bowel usually causes a temporary loss of interest in sex. Patients with stomach ulcers tend to be quick-tempered and irritable, which may make them difficult to live with, and that in turn disrupts relationships. One drug used to treat ulcers, cimetidine, acts as a male hormone antagonist (an anti-androgen), and so can cause impotence when taken in high doses.

Heartburn may be aggravated by certain positions, particularly if the head is lower than the abdomen, as in stooping. Some positions may bring on an attack of heartburn, which can be relieved by an antacid preparation.

Chronic bowel trouble, often with diarrhoea, usually results in all round debility, with loss of interest in sex, especially when there is excessive weight loss because of the condition. Patients with coeliac disease are at extra risk of sexual problems such as impotence, but if gluten, a protein in cereals, especially wheat, is removed from the diet, these conditions can improve.

Patients with serious liver diseases such as cirrhosis often experience sexual difficulties too, and need specialist medical advice.

DIABETES

Diabetes mellitis (sugar diabetes) is the subject of a lot of popular writing which is often misinformed and may in itself disturb the sex lives of diabetic people by arousing fears of impending impotence. The disease can, it is true, make a man unable to achieve or maintain an erection, and that risk increases with time. Indeed, impotence may be the first symptom of undiagnosed diabetes, so any man who becomes impotent should get checked for diabetes. But careful control of the disease makes sexual problems less likely. Some men become impotent only when their diabetes is unstable. However, impotence often arises from physical damage caused by the diabetic process. This may be in the blood vessels (atherosclerosis) or in the nerves (a form of neuritis), and is not easily treated. Some surgeons consider that if a man cannot get an erection because of diabetes the answer may be a penile implant. However, although there have been some encouraging results with such implants, one should only be used after all other approaches, including counselling and psychotherapy, have failed.

Diabetes may also lead to inability to ejaculate, diminished sensation and retrograde ejaculation (when semen is ejected into the bladder). There are some medicines which may help some patients for these conditions, but they can cause other complications.

Diabetes may also affect sexual function in women. They may have less vaginal lubrication, although that can be helped with an artificial lubricant, and find it hard to reach orgasm. They are also prone to develop vaginal infections, especially candidiasis (thrush), which can cause discomfort in intercourse.

EJACULATION PROBLEMS

By far the most common sexual difficulty in men is premature ejaculation which describes the situation where the man comes too soon. At the other end of the spectrum is retarded ejaculation in which the man finds it difficult and sometimes impossible to ejaculate. It is difficult to define in terms of time the difference between these two extreme conditions. Obviously, when a man ejaculates during lovemaking before he penetrates the woman he has premature ejaculation. Similarly, when the man finds that he is unable to ejaculate after a long period of intercourse or during prolonged solitary or mutual masturbation he can be described as having retarded ejaculation. But what about a man who can control his ejaculation for say ten minutes in a situation where he or his partner would like intercourse to last longer? Does he have premature ejaculation? A woman who does not enjoy intercourse may find ten minutes too long and the man, from her point of view, could then be described as having retarded ejaculation. So premature ejaculation and retarded ejaculation can really only be defined in terms of the expectation and wishes of the couple concerned.

Almost all men can learn to delay their ejaculation. Being relaxed and realizing that premature ejaculation is not a physical problem does help. Special training procedures have been developed and the one most frequently used has become known as the squeeze or stop-start technique.

Men who take a longer time to ejaculate than they would like can sometimes be helped by increasing the intensity of sexual stimulation. This may be achieved by trying different methods of being sexually stimulated. For some the use of sexually explicit video recordings is helpful. Problems of retarded and absent ejaculation do sometimes have a physical cause which may be helped by appropriate treatment. It is therefore advisable for men who have difficulty in ejaculating or who experience pain at the time of ejaculation to seek medical advice.

Another form of ejaculatory problem is retrograde ejaculation in which the semen is passed into the bladder instead of being ejected to the outside. The man experiences the sensations of ejaculation but without any outward evidence that it has occurred. This condition requires medical attention.

EPILEPSY

Epilepsy is a strange condition which, in the past, many writers suggested was caused by various sexual practices, especially masturbation. The apparent similarity between epileptic fits and orgasms may have led to this idea, but there is no truth in it. There have been some cases of epileptic fits being triggered by sexual activity, but they are rare, although some patients have sexual sensations during the early phase of a fit when they feel it coming on.

Epileptic patients have more sexual difficulties than non-epileptic people, but most enjoy a normal sex life. The commonest problem is to lose interest in sex, with difficulty sometimes in maintaining erection in men or becoming sexually aroused in women. These problems may arise in part from the lack of confidence in relationships from which epileptic patients understandably sometimes suffer. Some anti-epileptic drugs may add to the sexual difficulties epileptic patients have.

A particular type of epilepsy, temporal lobe epilepsy, is more likely than others to be linked with sexual problems. Although decreased interest in sex is common, some who suffer from temporal lobe epilepsy have increased, or even abnormal, interest in sex that may lead to excessive masturbation or antisocial sexual behaviour.

EPISIOTOMY

Episiotomy is the cut that midwives and obstetricians sometimes make into the perineum, just behind the vagina's outlet, when a baby is being born, in order to ease delivery, particularly if forceps are needed, because it reduces the risk of serious tears. After the birth, this episiotomy is then easily and painlessly stitched up.

Women are usually advised not to resume intercourse until after a postnatal check, about six weeks after the delivery, although most doctors realize that many patients start regular intercourse before then.

So long as the episiotomy scar is healed there is no harm, and a longer delay than necessary could put stress on a marriage. But if the repair is too tight, a woman may have pain and difficulty in intercourse. Time, patience and adequate vaginal lubrication, artificial if necessary, usually solve the problem – only rarely is surgery needed to widen the vaginal entrance.

FORESKIN INJURIES

Foreskin injuries are painful but generally not serious. The foreskin may get hurt in lovemaking, although it does not happen often, fortunately. The commonest injury is a small tear at the frenulum, the thin piece of skin that joins the foreskin to the underside of the glans. This may bleed freely; it is seldom serious. Pressure with a cold compress may work, but if it does not, see a doctor – a stitch or two may be needed.

FRIGIDITY

At one time all sexual difficulties experienced by women were called frigidity. It is now more helpful not to use this collective term but to use words that actually say what the problem is. For example, we now classify sexual problems in women as disorders of desire, difficulty in becoming sexually aroused, lack of enjoyment, problems with experiencing orgasm and vaginismus. The last of these is a condition in which the muscles around the vagina go into spasm when penetration of the vagina is attempted or even anticipated, thus preventing intercourse from taking place. Treatment involves a programme of gradually stretching the vaginal entrance with the fingers or special 'dilators' while at the same time encouraging the woman to relax.

Loss of interest in sex in women is fairly common. It often reflects a poor non-sexual relationship, interest in sex returning when the quality of the relationship improves. Loss of sexual desire is a symptom of depression and sometimes it results from hormone imbalance. It also forms an important link in a chain of sexual difficulties that can be well recognized in some women. One link in the chain is painful or uncomfortable intercourse. This causes the woman to avoid intercourse which in turn turns off her sexual desire. At the same time, because the pain causes her to become tense, she finds that she has difficulty in becoming sexually aroused and as a consequence vaginal lubrication fails. As the vagina is then dry, intercourse becomes uncomfortable and painful and the chain of events is repeated. Some forms of hormone imbalance may also contribute to a dry vagina. Poor love play techniques in the male partner may enter the chain by not producing the right kind of sexual stimulation to make the woman aroused. Vaginal infections and diseases of the reproductive organs may also make intercourse painful. All these conditions can be readily alleviated by appropriate counselling advice or medical treatment.

Inability to experience orgasm is another problem that is described as frigidity. Some studies have suggested that as many as 50 per cent of women rarely or never experience orgasm during intercourse even though they may be orgasmic during masturbation. Few women are able to experience orgasm during intercourse without having additional clitoral stimulation either by the man using his fingers or the woman actually masturbating herself. The use of a vibrator applied to the clitorial area is also effective in providing additional stimulation. Most women can learn to achieve orgasm during intercourse by following a training programme.

HEART ATTACKS

Heart attacks have many physical, psychological and social consequences. An attack may call for a complete change of life after convalescence. Not surprisingly, a heart attack has a profoundly adverse effect on the sex life of some patients, although in many cases the men and women who have the attacks have already had more than the usual number of sexual and marital problems because of the condition in its developing stages.

The sex life of a patient after a heart attack depends greatly on the quality of the medical advice during convalescence. All too often that advice is inadequate. Patients leave hospital without knowing whether or not they should avoid sexual intercourse either in the short or long term. Many feel they ought to avoid any strenuous exercise, sex included, in case they put too much strain on the heart, risking sudden death. There is no firm evidence for this fear.

Most doctors now believe that after a heart attack it is best to be up and about again and to begin a controlled return to normal activity. Sexual intercourse is usually safe as soon as a patient can tolerate moderate exertion, like climbing two flights of stairs without breathlessness or chest pain (angina). Obviously, lovemaking at first should be gentle, the patient playing a more passive role. However, he or she can gradually increase the amount of physical effort put into the act up to the limit of tolerance. People who are recovering from heart attacks and those who have heart disease should not have intercourse immediately after a heavy meal.

Chest pain during or after intercourse, palpitations or breathlessness lasting for 15 minutes or more should be regarded as warning signs and should be reported to the doctor.

Some patients cannot manage any strenuous activity after a heart attack, but even then intercourse is not necessarily forbidden – the affected partner will just have to adopt a passive role. These patients may find masturbation exhausting too – another reason for the partner to play the active role.

HORMONE DEFICIENCY

A deficiency of male sex hormones in men is uncommon but very limiting. The hormones which make men male are the androgens, the chief of which is testosterone, secreted mainly by the testicles but also by the adrenal glands. Lack of male sex hormones impairs sexual function, but exactly how depends on when in life the deficiency occurs. If the male embryo lacks androgenic stimulation, the infant will be born with female external genitals and masculine behaviour will not be imprinted on the brain. Normally, testosterone production increases markedly at puberty, which induces the characteristic changes that occur then, but without that increase the penis and scrotum do not develop, the voice remains high-pitched, and hair does not grow on the face or elsewhere. In

77

adult life, androgen deficiency causes a loss of interest in sex, difficulty in ejaculating and inability to achieve an erection. Because androgens help muscles to grow and maintain their strength, androgen deficiency causes muscular weakness. Patients may complain that their grip is weak, particularly when undoing bottle tops. There can also be reduced beard growth and gynaeco-mastia – breast development.

Androgen deficiency has a variety of causes – for example, surgical removal of the testicles or destruction of the hormone-secreting cells in the testicles by disease or injury. The testicles sometimes fail to produce enough testosterone because there is not enough luteinizing hormone from the pituitary gland to stimulate testosterone. Hyperprolactinaemia (see page 79) also impairs testosterone production. Some patients have a normal secretion of testosterone but their cells are unresponsive to it. Certain commonly used medicines cause androgen deficiency as a side-effect.

Testosterone is carried around in the bloodstream bound to proteins which protect it from being broken down. Normally only two per cent of the circulating testosterone is 'unbound' to protein, and it is only that which exerts an effect. So if the degree of binding increases and less 'unbound' hormone circulates, androgen deficiency can result – some drugs do increase the binding of testosterone.

Men's testicles age much as women's ovaries do, but a major difference is that the ovaries cease to produce ova (eggs) around the time of the menopause whereas men continue to produce sperm. The ageing of the testicles results in reduced testosterone production which contributes to the so-called 'male menopause', a period in middle age which is a difficult time for many men but is not, of course, a true 'menopause' (for there is no menstruation to cease) but a kind of male climacteric. Not only is there less testosterone in older men, but the proportion of unbound hormone decreases with age. These changes may help to increase the sexual disorders at this time of life.

Treating androgen deficiency with testosterone often produces dramatic improvement. But it is not a cure-all. A man who takes testosterone when he is not androgen-deficient then experiences suppressed testosterone production. Excessive dosing with testosterone can cause gynaecomastia (breast development in men) because some of the testosterone is converted to oestrogen, the female sex hormone.

HYPERTENSION

Hypertension, or high blood pressure, is an increasingly common medical problem. Most patients have no symptoms and learn that their blood pressure is too high only during routine medical consultations for something else. Blood pressure and pulse rate go up, sometimes very high, during sexual intercourse, as they do during any exercise, but that need not normally cause any concern. So there is no reason for someone who has chronically high blood pressure to give up sex.

Men with untreated hypertension do tend to have more problems than others, especially in failing to get an erection. Several factors may be involved; if the arteries which supply blood to the erectile tissues of the penis are narrowed by the effects of hypertension (atherosclerosis), there may not be enough blood to stiffen the penis. Fortunately, hypertension in women does not seem to cause sexual problems for them.

Although it has no overt symptoms, high blood pressure should be treated to reduce the risk of complications. Simple measures such as stopping smoking, losing weight and meditation to induce calm are helpful, but anti-hypertensive drugs that reduce blood pressure may be needed. Unfortunately, many of these drugs affect sexual function. Some hinder ejaculation and erection or reduce sexual desire, but there is a wide individual variation in the reaction to these medicines, often depending on the dose. The doctor can deal with this either by decreasing the dose or switching to another anti-hypertensive drug.

However, some sexual problems which occur during treatment are caused neither by the medicine nor the disease. Some patients blame a newly prescribed drug for a sexual problem that they already have. Others develop an inhibition about sex once they know they have hypertension, but attribute their lower sex drive to the drugs. Whatever the problem, a patient should never be afraid of talking to the doctor about it. It is then up to the doctor to give constructive advice.

HYPERPROLACTINAEMIA

Hyperprolactinaemia is a condition involving an excess in the blood of prolactin, a hormone produced by the pituitary gland, which stimulates milk production in the breasts. Too much

79

prolactin hampers sexual behaviour and reproductive function in both men and women. Among its causes are some medicines commonly prescribed.

The condition causes men to lose interest in sex and they cannot get or keep an erection. It may also decrease sperm production or prevent ovulation, causing infertility. In women, it can impair the normal changes occurring in the lining of the womb that help the developing embryo to implant itself when the egg is fertilized.

Hyperprolactinaemia can also upset the menstrual cycle. It can reduce interest in sex and make arousal and orgasm difficult. Vaginal lubrication may dry up, making intercourse painful.

Hyperprolactinaemia is usually easy to treat and sexual function improves remarkably once prolactin returns to normal levels.

HYSTERECTOMY

Hysterectomy is the removal of the womb, generally because of gynaecological problems such as fibroids (non-malignant growths inside the womb). The uterus can be brought out either through the abdomen or vagina, depending on the reason for the operation, the practice of the surgeon and the size of the womb. Although there is no medical evidence that removing the womb physically impairs sex, some women do have difficulties afterwards. Many probably had the same problems before the operation but now find it easier to speak about them – the operation, perhaps, providing the first suitable opportunity. The loss of fertility that the operation entails can be psychologically upsetting, because for many women it is such a significant part of their sexuality. Counselling before the operation can help. Some women feel sexier afterwards, probably because anxieties about conception have now gone.

To some women, the feeling caused by the contraction of the womb during the orgasm is an important part of the experience, so the womb's absence alters the sensation. But most women notice no change.

Women should not ordinarily resume intercourse until six weeks or so after a hysterectomy, to allow time for the tissues to heal. Problems similar to those occurring after an operation for a prolapse may become evident.

Sometimes, the ovaries have to be removed, an operation called oophorectomy. This may produce symptoms like the climacteric, and some surgeons now implant pellets of oestrogen (and sometimes with a little testosterone) in the abdominal wall when they stitch up the incision, in order to reduce that risk.

IMPOTENCE

Impotence is the word usually used to describe the condition in which a man is unable to get or maintain an erection sufficient to allow him to have sexual intercourse. The condition may range from not getting an erection at all at any time to the man being able to have an erection at all times except when he tries to have intercourse. In this situation he may have an erection during love play and lose it as he penetrates the vagina. Some men find that they are impotent with one partner but not with another. This obviously points to a psychological cause (see page 89). However, not all impotence is psychological; in at least 30 per cent of cases a physical cause is identifiable. This may be inadequate blood flow to the penis, hormone imbalance, or problems with the nerves supplying the sex organs. The prevalence of impotence caused by physical factors increases with age. In one large group one quarter of all the cases of impotence was caused by the medical treatment the men were receiving (see page 94). Drugs used to lower blood pressure are particularly prone to cause impotence (see page 79).

The man who fails to get an erection on one occasion of intercourse may well become so preoccupied with that single episode of failure that he actually fails to obtain erections during future attempts. An over-demanding or non-supportive partner may also cause a man to fail to have an erection. It is sometimes very difficult for a man to overcome this fear of failure on his own, but he can usually be helped by advice given by a competent doctor or a sex therapist. With the advances made in understanding erection problems many more impotent men can be helped now than in earlier days.

LOSING A LIMB

Losing a limb, by injury or surgery, can deeply affect sex life. The mutilation may reduce a person's self-esteem, so that they feel less attractive. Patients who do not have a steady partner may worry that the disability will prevent them from finding one.

The loss of a limb can clearly cause physical problems for both partners. Few people are ambidextrous, so someone who loses their dominant hand obviously has problems, at least at first. Most people have a dominant hand in lovemaking and so find it awkward to use the other hand. Practice can nevertheless overcome these difficulties. Positions in intercourse are a further problem, but again, practice and experiment can overcome it.

KIDNEY FAILURE

When the kidneys fail to work properly, there is a build-up of toxic chemicals in the blood which can make the patient very ill. Onset of the condition is usually gradual, but it can happen suddenly. One answer to kidney failure is a transplant, but they are not available, or suitable, to every sufferer. The alternative is the use of an artificial kidney, haemodialysis, either at hospital or at home, to which patients are connected two to four times a week for up to eight hours a time. This is a disruptive routine and affects a patient's partner, so it usually takes a long time for couples to settle into it.

Sexual problems are common in both men and women kidney failure patients. Nearly all men with untreated kidney failure lose interest in sex and find it difficult to get an erection. Women, too, have less interest in sex and find it hard to become aroused or have an orgasm.

After a kidney transplant, the sexual function of women is usually better, but this is not always the case with men. Treated with haemodialysis, the patient begins to feel better generally, and interest in sex usually returns. Unfortunately, sexual function may not improve likewise, and although several different remedies for this have been tried, there is no one answer.

MASTECTOMY

Mastectomy is the removal of a breast, or worse still, both breasts, and is something every woman dreads, especially in Western countries where the breasts have strong sexual connotations for both sexes. After losing a breast, a woman may understandably feel that she has lost a vital feature of her femininity and fear that she will no longer be attractive. But careful counselling before the operation can help a lot by showing her this is not so. In fact, counselling of both partners before and after the operation is essential, doing much to reduce the psychological damage that the operation may do to both the woman and the relationship.

Most men, as it happens, do not find the absence of a breast as distasteful as women do, especially those women for whom attention to the breast is important in love play. They may even resist their partner's approaches to the remaining breast to try and divert his attention from the chest altogether. But most couples can come to terms with this, provided their relationship was all right before. Some women prefer to avoid face to face positions in sex at first as well as positions that emphasize the breasts (such as with the woman on top). As soon as the shock effect has passed, most women come to terms with their disability and resume a normal sexual relationship.

MULTIPLE SCLEROSIS

Multiple sclerosis (MS) has symptoms and features that vary enormously. The disease may cause advanced disability, confining the patient to a wheelchair, but in many patients it causes not so much disability as vague symptoms such as temporary weakness in a limb or altered sensations in parts of the body.

Sexual difficulties often occur in sufferers. MS can cause impotence and ejaculatory disturbances in men; in women it may cause a failure in lubrication of the vagina and difficulty in reaching orgasm. Loss of interest in sex may occur in either sex, too. Some patients with MS complain of decreased sensation in the penis or clitoris or, more rarely, of increased genital sensations which make contact uncomfortable or even painful. Sometimes, sexual difficulty may even be the first symptom of MS.

An important feature of MS is the way the symptoms come and go. Patients often feel them for a while and then notice improvement. This remission may last for months or even years before the same symptoms reappear or different ones arise. That happens with sexual difficulties too. Patients should continue to have sexual relationships even if they cannot complete them with intercourse or orgasm. By the nature of the disease, a spontaneous improvement in the symptoms will allow normal sexual function. People who have MS often suffer from depression, which may cause them to lose interest in any form of sexual activity, but an appropriate anti-depressant drug can bring the sexual appetite back.

In the advanced stages of the disease, spastic muscles, particularly in the thighs, may make lovemaking difficult. Patients who still have an interest in sex can try different positions to see if there is one that suits them better.

OBESITY

Obesity, or being seriously overweight, predisposes people to all kinds of medical conditions such as hypertension, heart disease and diabetes. People whose shape is not considered ideal, especially fat people, find it harder than others to find suitable sexual partners (although some people are turned on by fat people). Someone who becomes progressively overweight may also become less and less attractive to their partner, and that can result in disruption of their sexual relationship.

Obesity may also cause physical problems in the sexual relationship. Pads of fat on the lower abdomen or an enlarged abdomen itself may impede access to the genital organs. It can be hard to find a position for intercourse that is comfortable for both partners, particularly if they are both too heavy. A normal-sized person also may feel overwhelmed by an overweight partner on top.

Overweight people usually become breathless during exercise, including intercourse, making it difficult to make love. The only solution is to lose weight.

OSTOMIES

Ostomies represent the surgical result of what happens when parts of the bowel have to be removed because of disease. The surgeon may bring what remains of it to an opening on the skin surface through the abdominal wall, known as an ostomy. There are two kinds. A colostomy is where the large intestine, or colon, is brought to the opening; an ileostomy, the small intestine. A collecting bag fits over the ostomy to collect the waste matter from the intestine. Sometimes, particularly with colostomies, the procedure is just a temporary measure, and the ostomy is closed later by further surgery.

Ostomies can have severe effects on sexual activities. The patient faces psychological problems over the operation and its disfigurement, and many take a long time to come to terms with their appearance and the care of their ostomy, which they feel to be unsightly and off-putting. There is also the fear that the ostomy may leak or smell during lovemaking and, indeed, an ostomy can sometimes empty during orgasm by reflex action. Then there are the physical problems of the ostomy bag getting in the way of lovemaking; pressure on the bag must be avoided. But most people with ostomies do manage to re-establish a satisfactory sexual relationship, with support from their partners.

Sexual difficulties may arise from the physical effects of the operation itself, especially with colostomies and particularly when there has been extensive surgery to the rectum, because the nerve supply to the sexual organs may have been damaged.

PAINFUL ERECTIONS

Painful erections at night occasionally occur in some men. The penis normally undergoes a series of erections during sleep of which the man is unaware, although when he wakes up in the morning it is often with an erection. Very rarely, the erections are painful and wake him up at night. The cause is unknown but it does not seem to be related to sexual activity before sleep, so there is no need to avoid intercourse. The condition tends to disappear after a few weeks or months without treatment.

PARAPHIMOSIS

Paraphimosis describes the condition of a retracted foreskin which cannot be returned over the ridge of the glans, so that the foreskin becomes swollen. This can be alarming. Attempts to rectify it often cause still further swelling. Sometimes, an icepack applied to the engorged foreskin enables it to be returned but, failing this, surgical treatment is urgently needed.

PERIPHERAL VASCULAR DISEASE

Peripheral vascular disease is a condition, in some cases due to 'hardening of the arteries', arising from deficient blood flow. When the blood vessels which go to the erectile tissue in the penis get narrow or become blocked, a man cannot get a full, proper erection. This is because of atherosclerosis, a condition in which a fatty substance collects on the walls of the arteries. The symptoms depend upon where exactly the blood flow is obstructed. If the block is in the lower part of the aorta, the heart's largest artery, the patient may feel pain in the calf when he walks (intermittent claudication), and the legs and feet often get cold easily because insufficient blood is reaching them. He may also be unable to get an erection.

We can measure the blood flow to the penis, and that should be part of the examination of any patient who has erection inadequacy. If there is a reduced blood supply to the penis, more tests should follow to find out exactly where the blockage is. If it is in a large or medium-sized artery, unblocking it surgically often restores potency. Smoking and some drugs may also cut down the blood flow to the penis for a time.

There is very little information on how peripheral vascular disease affects sexual function in women.

PEYRONIE'S DISEASE

Peyronie's disease is a condition in which patches of fibrous tissue develop in the shaft of the penis, usually in men aged 40 to 60. The cause is not known. Because the fibrous tissue, which can be felt in the penis, is not as extendable as normal penile tissue during erection, it causes deformity of the erect penis. This abnormality may make entry to the vagina difficult and can make intercourse too painful for the man to continue.

The disease can clear up spontaneously, although that can take years. There are several treatments, including surgery.

PHIMOSIS

Phimosis describes a particularly tight foreskin. In the adult man, the foreskin can usually be retracted to expose the glans of the penis. If the foreskin is too tight it cannot be pulled back. During infancy and early childhood, it is common for the foreskin not to be retractable, and parents can do harm by pulling it back forcibly over the glans; in fact, this is one of the cases of phimosis in later life.

It is important to retract the foreskin and wash the glans regularly to remove smegma that accumulates underneath. An important consequence of phimosis is infection under the foreskin, which can be painful. Even if there is no infection, phimosis can make masturbation and intercourse uncomfortable and prevent orgasm, because the foreskin gets between the glans and the vagina.

The best treatment is circumcision, surgical removal of the foreskin.

PRIAPISM

Priapism is an uncommon condition in which a man's penis refuses to lose its erection, which becomes painful. However embarrassed the sufferer may be, he must seek medical help urgently; surgical treatment is sometimes needed.

PROLAPSE

A prolapse is what happens when the muscles and other tissues of the pelvic floor which normally support the pelvic organs become relaxed or the tissues stretch so that the organs drop from their normal positions. In extreme cases, the womb may drop right through the vagina. Minor degrees of prolapse are more common, and occur mainly in women who have borne children.

The prolapse may be restricted to either the front (anterior) or the back (posterior) wall of the vagina. Either way, the patient can usually feel a bulge, which may extend out of the vaginal opening. Anterior wall prolapse, which is the more common, is what happens when the bladder slips down to form a bulge on the front wall of the vagina known as a cystocele. It may interfere with bladder function. Sometimes, the woman has to hold the bulge back with a finger when she wants to pass urine. With a posterior prolapse the rectum is involved.

These bulges usually become more evident when a woman stands up, coughs or strains to empty the bowel. Sometimes, they are large enough to make intercourse uncomfortable and, indeed, up to four in every 10 women who have a prolapse also suffer decreased sexual activity.

Repair operations to correct the prolapse sometimes narrow the vagina and make intercourse difficult; it is best to wait at least six weeks before trying to make love again. To compound the problem, the lubrication is often inadequate too, probably because women are afraid of pain or doing harm to themselves (so an artificial lubricant helps). Some men are so concerned about hurting their partner that they may give up if they cannot penetrate the vagina on the first or second attempt, even though the woman wants intercourse. Patience and practice can usually overcome the problem. Both partners should have counselling, preferably before such operations.

Granulation tissue, which grows in the scars, is another, fortunately uncommon, problem after repair operations. As well as being uncomfortable, it may bleed, particularly on touching it; it can be put right, however, usually by cauterization.

PROSTATECTOMY

Prostatectomy is the removal of a man's prostate gland (see page 23) which lies at the outlet of the bladder: the urethra (see page 23) passes through it. In most men, the prostate gland becomes larger after they have turned 50, sometimes to such an extent that it blocks the flow of urine. This condition usually develops gradually, so that a man first notices a slower urine stream, an increased frequency of need to pass urine – he may have to get up at night – and difficulty in starting to urinate. Some men may get acute retention (when they cannot pass urine at all), and a catheter (a tube) has to be put into the bladder for the urine to drain away.

Doctors examine the prostate by putting a finger in the rectum and feeling it through the front wall. The usual treatment for an enlarged prostate is to remove the blockage by an operation called prostatectomy, performed surgically either through the abdominal wall or, more commonly now, by endoscopy through the penis. However, drugs are now being developed which, it is hoped, will shrink the prostate; at present, however, they can be used only in a few cases and tend to cause loss of interest in sex.

An enlarged prostate does not usually cause sexual problems. Sometimes, though, the semen just dribbles out instead of spurting, and there may be some reduced sensation of ejaculation. Difficulty with erection is seldom due to an enlarged prostate.

Many men who have to have a prostatectomy worry that the operation will make them impotent. It can happen, but only does so relatively rarely. Another problem may be retrograde ejaculation, when the semen ejects into the bladder rather than out through the penis.

Almost all men worry about their sexual capacity after an operation on the genitals, as is only natural. Pre-operative counselling can help to allay their fears; their partners must also understand and not be too sexually demanding. It is probably best to avoid intercourse for a while and to spend time in mutual caressing and foreplay. A man can then see that he can achieve an erection, which will give him confidence for full intercourse.

PSYCHIATRIC ILLNESSES

Over the years many incorrect ideas have been put forward about associations between sex and mental illness. At one time the experts even said that excessive masturbation led to insanity. Of course, there is no truth in that whatever. Excessive masturbation may rarely be a reflection of a psychiatric disturbance, but is certainly not the cause. But mental illness can result in altered sexual desire and function. Some patients, for example those with schizophrenia, may have hallucinations involving the sex organs, or have bizarre ideas about their sexuality. Furthermore, some of the drugs that have revolutionized treatment of psychiatric illness can themselves upset sexual functions.

Depression is a common cause of sexual problems in both men and women. Men with depression usually lose interest in sex and one in four cannot easily get an erection. About half the women who have depression lose sexual desire, find it hard to become aroused, and cannot reach orgasm. But sometimes, again rarely, depression has quite the opposite effect, causing increased sexual activity which may even lead to antisocial behaviour.

Depression may also disrupt a patient's relationships. The irritability and lack of interest in life that often accompanies depression can make someone difficult to live with and so cause further deterioration in sexual functioning.

Sometimes, loss of sexual desire is the first symptom of depression, coming on even before the patient feels low. An antidepressant often quickly revives sexual interest and brings enhanced performance.

STROKE

A stroke has long-term effects on sexual behaviour that depend on how much disability remains afterwards. In most stroke patients interest in sex remains, but in a few cases the sex centre in the brain is damaged and there is total loss of desire. Many patients have paralysis of one or more limbs and this too can obviously make intercourse difficult.

The partner's attitude is important in helping a stroke victim resume sexual activity. Some partners are afraid of inducing another stroke – but this is unlikely to happen, and there is no reason for a stroke victim not to re-establish a satisfying sexual relationship.

Some patients lose bowel and bladder control, and this can be very difficult for patients and partners to come to terms with.

THYROID HORMONE DISTURBANCE

Thyroid hormone disturbance occurs through a malfunction of the thyroid gland in the neck, which controls many of the body's chemical and physical functions. It may be overactive (hyperthyroidism) or underactive (hypothyroidism). Not surprisingly, these disorders may cause sexual problems.

An underactive thyroid causes various bodily processes to slow down, including sexual functions. There is less interest in sex and difficulty in becoming aroused for both men and women.

An overactive thyroid might be expected to have opposite effects and, indeed, a few patients do have heightened sexual desire. But other hyperthyroid patients suffer decreased sexual interest and impaired function – difficulty in getting an erection, for example. Up to half of all those with hyperthyroidism in fact feel no change in their sexual appetite or ability.

With both types of thyroid trouble, medical or surgical treatment usually resolves the sexual difficulties.

UNDERWEIGHT

Underweight, or actually being too thin, may reduce attractiveness just as being too fat may. Below a certain critical weight, too, reproductive processes stop working properly. Indeed, if a woman falls below about 45 kilogrammes (100 lb), her menstrual periods are likely to stop, by which time she will already have stopped ovulation. She usually either loses interest in sex or has great concern about her sexual adequacy.

In anorexia nervosa, young women (although it is now occurring with more young men too) diet severely in the mistaken belief that they are overweight. They become so neurotic about food intake and about a need to be slim that they may even make themselves vomit after eating. Some psychologists believe that anorexia nervosa has its roots in an unwillingness on the part of the patient to develop womanly characteristics, both physical and psychological. The condition is serious and can even cause death.

URINARY TRACT INFECTIONS

Urinary tract infections that women are particularly prone to include the unpleasant bladder infections known as cystitis. The urge to urinate is frequent, even constant, but urinating hurts. Each attack should be properly investigated by urine test, and treated to reduce the risk of recurrence and prevent chronic infections which may pass up to the kidneys. Men get cystitis too, but for them it is less common.

Because the base of the bladder and the urethra lie close to the front wall of the vagina, they may become bruised by vigorous thrusting of the penis in intercourse, which also causes symptoms like cystitis soon after intercourse, especially first intercourse (which is why such a condition then is often called honeymoon cystitis). The problem can also occur when the vaginal tissues become thin after the menopause. Intercourse aggravates cystitis and while it lasts may be bad enough to put a woman off sexual activity. A position that reduces the thrusting action of the penis on the front wall of the vagina can make intercourse less painful, and adequate lubrication with an artificial lubricant, if necessary, makes bruising of the bladder less likely. Women who keep getting cystitis can lessen the risk by emptying the bladder as soon as they can after intercourse to flush out any germs.

There is no evidence that oral sex or masturbation cause cystitis, although fondling with hands that are not clean may. A vibrator inserted into the vagina may cause bruising.

Because the bladder is sensitive to outside influences, irritation which resembles and feels like cystitis but is not an infection can occur. It is important for the hands to be clean when touching any part of the vaginal area. Sometimes, bath foams or douches may provoke an allergic reaction akin to cystitis, and even anxiety can bring on what seems like an attack.

Family doctors are notoriously unsympathetic to women with cystitis, and often not very good at suggesting how to treat it, cure it, or even make it less painful.

DRUGS AND SEX

ALCOHOL

Alcohol 'provokes the desire, but it takes away the performance', Shakespeare said. A little drink does seem to stimulate sexual desire sometimes, but alcohol is not an aphrodisiac. It stimulates only because it loosens inhibitions, allowing sexual feelings freer expression. In reality, alcohol has a depressing effect on the brain and the sex glands, reducing sex hormone production. Quite apart from the other physical damage it can do, excessive drinking can lead to serious sexual difficulties if it becomes chronic.

In men, there can be a complete loss of interest in sex, difficulty in getting an erection, and delayed or absent ejaculation and orgasm – problems which often lead to total impotence. The commonest sexual problems for women who drink too much are similar; difficulties in becoming sexually aroused, reaching orgasm, or feeling desire.

Some people turn to drink because they have a sexual problem, only to make it worse. Then they drink more, and can soon be on the slippery slide to alcoholism. Their social life is disrupted, self-esteem reduced, and marital disharmony provoked. The net result is further deterioration in sexual functioning. It must be stressed – alcohol, even in small amounts, is not a suitable treatment for any sexual problem.

Many alcoholics think that as soon as they stop drinking, their sex life will at once improve. That is not usually so. It may take months for the alcohol-induced changes in the body to be reversed. The reformed alcoholic has also to set about repairing the relationship with a partner, which may call for the help of a trained counsellor.

AMYL NITRITE

Amyl nitrite is a drug that was once used for angina but is now taken to heighten sexual sensation, particularly by homosexuals. It is usually inhaled just before an orgasm, to intensify and prolong the sensation. Severe headache is a frequent side-effect.

CANNABIS

Cannabis, like alcohol, has a reputation as a sexual stimulant. Its occasional use may, like drink, be associated with extra sexual enjoyment. Studies suggest that it reduces inhibitions and increases relaxation and sensual awareness, such as the sense of touch, rather than having a direct effect on erections, arousal or orgasm. Some people say that cannabis puts them more in tune with their partner, especially if both take the drug.

But anything more than occasional use makes sexual difficulties more likely. As with drink, regular use of cannabis leads to lower sex hormone production in both sexes. One study suggested that one man in five who uses the drug every day is impotent. Cannabis may also cause disturbances in women's menstrual cycle and cause vaginal lubrication to dry up. Long-term use also impairs fertility in both sexes.

HEROIN

Heroin addicts commonly experience sexual problems, although often the difficulties were there before they took to the drug. Many of them initially found it difficult to establish relationships. Heroin does nothing to help. On the contrary: it inhibits sexuality and may simply become a substitute for it. Some users claim that the 'high' they get from injecting heroin into the veins is like an orgasm. Coming off drugs, after the period of 'cold turkey' withdrawal symptoms, usually improves sexual functioning.

OTHER ILLICIT DRUGS

Other illicit drugs, such as amphetamines, cocaine and LSD, are sometimes said to be aphrodisiacs. They are not. They can enhance enjoyment for some people but certainly not for all. The good feelings they induce are purely subjective and probably result from the release of inhibitions and distortion of the senses and thoughts. Anything except the very occasional use of drugs such as these causes impairment of sexual functions and loss of libido.

PRESCRIBED MEDICINES

Many medicines affect sexual function, either reducing sexual desire or impairing performance, or both. Occasionally, there are reports from doctors that a particular drug, such as L-Dopa for Parkinson's Disease, raises sexual desire, but rather than being a direct effect of the drug this is more likely to occur because a patient just feels better generally. That is true for antidepressants too. A patient who has lower libido because of depression may feel a re-awakening of interest in sex after taking antidepressants: desire returns because the depression is treated, and the same drug taken by someone who is not depressed would not work as an aphrodisiac.

We know more about the effects of drugs on the sexual functions of men than on women because a man is more likely to report an obvious sexual side-effect like impotence than is a woman to complain that a drug has stopped her becoming sexually aroused. Impotence makes intercourse impossible, but a woman who does not get aroused can still have intercourse, uncomfortable though it may be.

Drugs can affect sexual activity in other ways too. For example, indoramin – used to treat high blood pressure – can interfere with ejaculation (but does not affect erection or desire). Sometimes, the sexual side-effect of a drug can help people with sexual difficulties. For example, clomipramine, used in depression and other mental illnesses, can delay ejaculation and so can be used to treat premature ejaculation.

If you think that a drug you have been prescribed is causing a sexual difficulty, discuss it with your doctor. An alternative medicine may not have the same effect. This is especially important if you have to take drugs over a long period, as with high blood pressure. It is far better to change the medicine than to stop the treatment.

SMOKING

Smoking, through clever advertisements, has been linked with sex, and cigarettes have almost become a substitute for conversation – when a couple do not know what to say, they have a cigarette. Of course, there is no evidence that smoking can have a beneficial sexual effect. On the contrary, surely, kissing a mouth that reeks of stale tobacco can hardly be pleasant.

Moreover, there is some evidence that heavy smoking can make it difficult for men to maintain an erection. It also encourages medical conditions that affect sex functions, such as bronchitis and narrowing of the blood vessels. Any man who has an erection problem and who smokes should give up the habit before he seeks any further help – that in itself can help considerably.

VITAMIN E

Vitamin E is often said to have beneficial effects on sex function and advertised to improve performance, especially in men. But there is no evidence to support this claim.

ZINC AND SELENIUM

Zinc and selenium, two metallic elements, are essential in tiny quantities for many body processes, including reproduction. Zinc deficiency is almost certainly one cause of impotence. Taking selenium is said to increase sexual activity but such claims are unfounded.

THE LATER YEARS & SEXUAL SATISFACTION

Pat Lloyd and Dr Paul Brown

As we age, we become more and more experienced and increasingly familiar with sex. But that experience may well not have been always satisfactory, and familiarity, for its part, may make sex dull and predictable. So, as we get older, we increasingly confront these two major impediments to the natural and continuing enjoyment of sex – predictable familiarity and the accumulation of unsatisfactory experiences. Added to these are the natural ageing processes of the body itself. Slack muscle tone and skin surfaces, and the blood pulsing less headily through increasingly constricted arteries, provide a depressing parallel to the lack of excitement which rocks so many relationships.

But all need not be gloom! On the contrary, in the way that we can take care of our bodies, understand the changes which are taking place and keep ourselves resilient and physically responsive, so we can take care of our relationships by investing time and trouble in them. That is true of both the emotional and sexual factors in our relationships.

In this chapter we explore how and why psychological decay may happen in relationships, how the physical ageing processes of the body may complement that decay, and how, by taking care and making the right investments in our emotional and physical well-being, we can enjoy the central, sexual side of our relationships to the end of our lives.

SEXUAL MYTHS

Anyone now over the age of 50 almost certainly began his or her adult sexual life without the benefit of readily available and socially acceptable contraception. The major methods of contraception before the middle 1960s were based largely either on fear or on abstinence.

The fear method produced all sorts of implied social instructions. 'Nice girls don't (go too far) (enjoy sex).' 'Don't get pregnant.' 'Don't bring disgrace on the family.' 'Men don't really like women who say yes to sex.' These and countless other instructions based on ignorance set up a double standard by which women were supposed to be 'pure' and brides had to be virgins, whereas men were allowed 'to sow wild oats'. A particularly wretched consequence of this myth was the cultural implication that men knew more about women than women were allowed to know about themselves – a crazy idea. Yet even today, many couples who come for help with sexual difficulties have the notion that it is the man's job to know about sex and make it work for them both. What commonly happens is that, from her own experience, a woman finds that her male partner does not know how her body works. But she is not really allowed to tell him that she knows he does not know. He, for his part, may have guessed that his partner knows that he does not know, but is not going to allow any discussion about that. So both go on, colluding in ignorance and uncertainty. It is a sure recipe for bringing sex to an end, often through the use of such excuses as 'the children growing up', a hysterectomy, the menopause, or just tiredness and 'headaches', to prevent the unwanted intrusion of an unsatisfactory experience that feels increasingly invasive. Both partners can become confused by this, feeling unwanted and rejected, a feeling that may lead either partner into affairs or into resigned, frustrated despair.

Many instances of early, unsatisfied sexual arousal may have led, for both men and women, to actual physical pain. Petting rules that decreed 'no further than the stocking tops' might have produced arousal and blood flow into the sexual tissues, but with only painful congestion rather than the relief of a climax to follow. Low pelvic pain for women and pain in the testicles for men were the common results of such unsatisfactory experiences. If a man did ejaculate, he had to do so furtively and quickly, which may well have led to problems of premature ejaculation later. It is a background of negative, destructive attitudes and events of this kind which later undermines the enjoyment of sex, and which we need to move away from.

Alas, the older we are the more likely it is that those negative attitudes were part and parcel of our upbringing. The idea that sex is dirty, to be kept furtively secret, a duty rather than a pleasure, not to be talked about, certainly not to be mentioned to the children in any way that might give them the idea that it is fun, is still widespread in our culture. In its way, this is reminiscent of attitudes in the Middle Ages, when people believed they could be possessed by demons.

Our attitudes change because our knowledge improves and, more especially, because we dare to trust and think about and share our experience.

POSITIVE ATTITUDES

Positive attitudes about sex allow us to enjoy our bodies and find in them a source of pleasure; the barriers of natural modesty and privacy can be lowered for the shared rewards of real intimacy. Each person in a sexual relationship is responsible for his or her own satisfactions, is more expert about his or her needs than anybody else in the world, uses a partner to find satisfaction, and enjoys being used in return. Sexual pleasure is essentially selfish. The mystery is that no one person can ever really know the experience of another. The excitement of sex is its reciprocity: that is, in a genuinely close sexual encounter, we get as near as it is ever possible to be to being at one with the other person. Yet that knowing is tantalizingly little, because we are never able to fully enter into the being of the loved one.

Positive attitudes about sex dispel anxieties. Anxiety, and the processes that produce it – fear, dislike of one's own body, worry about whether the other person *really* loves us, and so on – are great destroyers of truly enjoyable sex.

There are good physiological reasons for this. Sexual arousal directly affects blood flow. As our sexual interest begins to awaken blood flow increases. The body cannot respond sexually without this: erection does not happen in the man, nor does lubrication in the woman. If we are anxious, the body reserves its blood supply in the muscles for flight-or-fight responses. Positive attitudes to sex, with the consequent loss of anxiety, therefore make it much easier for our bodies to respond naturally. In keeping with that, present-day attitudes affirm that sex is for our recreation as well as for procreation.

SKILFUL SEX

The fact often is that sex is not naturally perfect. There really are such things as sexual skills.

In his book *The Joy of Sex* in the early 1970s, Dr Alex Comfort used a metaphor combining food and sex. He wrote that just as we need a regular and not too rich diet of food, so a really healthy body benefits from a regular, perhaps ordinary, diet of sex. However, even ordinary food is more enjoyable well cooked and presented. So it is with sex. Also, if someone can prepare ordinary food well they can, from time to time, produce a special meal. More effort, more thought and more planning might be necessary, but the special meal brings its own rewards. It does not just happen by accident. A good cook practises and develops the art, and enjoys lifelong experimenting.

Exactly the same holds true for sex. Good sex relies on accumulated skills, a willingness to share and experiment, getting honest responses and learning from mistakes. Unfortunately, although it is perfectly acceptable to go to cookery classes or exchange good recipes, it is not yet respectable, somehow, to be taught about sex or talk openly about experiences that have been enjoyed.

Mary and Tom are an example of this lack of communication. Because she wanted to please Tom and avoid damaging what she felt was his fragile self-confidence, Mary early in her marriage pretended to reach orgasm during intercourse and, having started along this track, couldn't face telling him the truth. So by the time they were in their fifties, there were increasing tensions in the marriage and she had lost all interest in sex. Their family doctor referred them to a sex therapist who helped them to start looking practically at their problems and their causes.

They risked discussing and showing each other how they would like to make love, they started touching each other in a relaxed way, and they set aside specific times to be together. It was almost like 'making a date' to love each other sensually. Because of what they had learned, after a few sessions Mary and Tom looked and sounded quite different. They were fitter and happier, and optimistic about continuing an active and rewarding sex life right into old age.

The sexual act has much variety attaching to it, but many people are embarrassed, too tongue-tied to describe and discuss it. Lack of open description and discussion has meant that as a society we have not really managed to benefit from the knowledge acquired over the past 15 years about how our bodies work sexually. It will take more than one generation to free ourselves of the myths, superstitions, fear and ignorance which surround this most rewarding of human encounters. The older a person is the more likely it is that his or her conditioning about sexual matters is rooted in negative attitudes and poorly constructed skills. But both can be changed. Each person must have a partner to trust or with whom to build up a trust. If you have no partner, you can still find out that pleasure lies within your body. (Later in this chapter, we answer the question 'What if I am alone?')

GETTING OLDER

One of the widely-held myths about growing old is that sex stops. People contrast the passion of youth – the excitement, the secrecy, the hopes and the innocence – with the world-weariness that can afflict them in their middle years and onwards. Family doctors and others in the caring professions have a responsibility to inform and encourage but, sadly, do not always do so. For example, Steve, aged 63, consulted his doctor because his erections were gradually becoming less reliable – only to be told 'What do you expect at your age?'. It left him feeling hopeless and finished sexually. Even until recently it was thought that little changed in adults aged between 25 and 60. But we now know that the passing years and some specific events have very identifiable phases – those, for instance, that commence when we move into our forties, reach the menopause, face redundancy perhaps, accept that the children are finally leaving home, and when we retire.

For a woman, the period from the age of 45 to 55 is likely to bring the menopause, the gradual ending – usually over two, three or four years rather than a few months – of the capacity to be the carrier of life inside her. This is a time of considerable changes in the body's hormonal balance, changes that may be detectable for some time before menstruation begins to become irregular and eventually ceases. The changes may be accompanied by marked

101

ups and downs in mood, or physical discomforts like hot flushes (hot, uncomfortable sweating) which occur at any time of the day but, perhaps, more often at night, disturbing sleep. Endocrinologists – specialists in the functioning of the chemical messengers of the body – can now alleviate many of these symptoms effectively.

One particular consequence of the menopause is that as oestrogen levels change, the tissues of the vagina may become drier and thinner, producing less lubrication in response to sexual excitement. In these circumstances, the woman may feel sexual interest but her body does not respond as it did. However, it is possible that semen has a beneficial effect on the drier and thinner lining of the vagina, keeping it 'younger' and more pliable, and there is the benefit too of penile penetration keeping it dilated. It is worth discussing hormone replacement therapy (HRT) with a doctor if a woman intends to continue an active sexual life involving intercourse and if such changes start occurring.

It is important that both partners try not to be influenced by 'old wives' tales', and that they are well informed in advance about the changes which will take place. Not all of them are physical. Keen reminders of the ageing process come from within the family: children reach sexual maturity and have their own relationships, or grandparents age, bringing increased responsibility. Other cultures, particularly in India, celebrate the passing of the menopause as a time of independence and growth. But in our society ageing tends to be regarded as 'downhill all the way'. Attitudes are so important. If a woman can think positively about her experience in the menopause, the symptoms may well be less unpleasant. The following example, from *Sexual Turning Points* by Sarrel & Sarrel (Macmillan 1984), demonstrates this:

'A 76-year-old woman who told us she never had any trouble with the menopause added: "Well, I guess it is true; I had what you call hot flushes, but I always associated that feeling with getting sexy and I liked the idea, as I was so sexy at that time in my life. So the feeling was really kind of nice." '

For many couples this is a time to drift apart physically. Yet there is so much that is life-giving in the contact and loving warmth of the proximity of a partner's body in bed. In a double bed an erection can be shared, welcomed, enjoyed. Feelings of arousal in both partners can be conveyed immediately. But crossing the divide between two single beds may discourage that sharing and, if attempted, may well cause the arousal to disappear.

Joining a partner in one of the single beds is, of course, a solution, but it means that the move is liable to only one interpretation, whereas contact in a double bed can be more relaxed and does not imply the same pressure to perform.

Good sex is not just about intercourse. It is about the experience of physical loving which can happen in all kinds of ways and which, indeed, may become increasingly important as the partners get older. The act of intercourse itself may become correspondingly less important.

For men aged 45 to 60 the hormonal changes are not so apparent, although they may exist. Life-stress changes may play a major part in men's sense of sexual well-being. It is at this time that men in particular must come to terms with their achievements – the hopes increasingly unlikely to be fulfilled, the career levels not reached or, if reached, often clung to in difficult circumstances involving interpersonal conflict; the ambitions only partly realized; the gathering sense of impending retirement. It is not uncommon nowadays for men to retire at any time from their middle fifties onwards, feeling that there may still be 30 or more years of good energy and resources, yet lacking focus for them. If energy has been invested in a relationship over the previous 30 years, it pays off at this point in redefining the future. But if that energy has been diverted entirely to work and not sufficiently into a relationship – a diversion now recognized with regret – it is worth rediscovering the person with whom one may have lived in a too casual familiarity.

There can be deliberate growth in a relationship but, like the skills which underpin good sex, it can only happen intentionally and if there is a readiness to learn from mistakes rather than to apportion blame.

WHEN CHILDREN LEAVE

When children leave home there may be a variety of effects. Some parents have a genuine sense of loss and sadness, and are left with a void that actively being a parent used to fill. Sometimes, however, the children's departure creates a sense of a task accomplished and a new-found freedom. It is easier to respond sexually in the second set of circumstances than in the first, although comfort for the first can be found in a strong relationship when sadness that is shared leads to the rediscovery of the other person and a deepening of a relationship that had tended to be taken for granted.

Sometimes, the children do not leave home and the parents wish they would. For many young people, jobs are difficult to find and accommodation is expensive, so instead of adolescence following its natural course into the life of an early adult who breaks away, the parents can be left with a sense of no ending to a task, and this can leave insufficient personal space which can overwhelm a marriage. Facing the issues and talking them out, letting the children, grown-up as they may be, see that parents have their own needs, are tasks that should be tackled — or there may be depressing consequences.

NEW HORIZONS

For most of us, life continues to be a compromise between what we have hoped for and what we have attained. The balance between aspiration and accomplishment can substantially affect our moods. If it is adverse and our mood is depressed, sex invariably suffers.

One process that women commonly experience as they move into their forties is the wish to discover themselves more. They begin to want to experiment with the pattern and substance of their lives — perhaps by taking a job, or by pursuing more seriously the things that have been no more than hobbies. This spills over into relationships too. A man who appeared strong, resourceful and striving, if rather silent, when he was in his twenties may almost have lost the art of spontaneity 25 years later, putting all his energies into work instead of finding a balance with his relationships, and he may be demandingly dull as a result. That is a recipe for a woman to want to experiment with relationships outside her marriage and discover, or rediscover, herself, leaving behind for a while the sense of being mother and wife. Many men can feel threatened — perhaps salutarily — by a partner moving into this phase. Finding a new identity, as distinct from simply continuing in a role, is difficult and a man's uncertainties may find expression in failing erections, which become part of a self-generating circle of doubt. Finding reassurance, comfort and attachment in a relationship in these circumstances can be a hard and painfully questioning process. Feelings of suppressed anger, despair, disappointment and simple confusion all adversely affect sexual function.

As a period of adjustment, in preparation for the last quarter of our lives, the forties and fifties are not unlike adolescence, the preparation period for adulthood. Turbulence, questioning, wishing to change things, sometimes dramatically, and having greater freedom, all make their demands.

Sexually, the late fifties into the sixties may be the first time couples can be certain of private time together, uninterrupted by worrying why teenagers are not yet home or expecting them any moment, untroubled by children when they, the parents, want to spend an afternoon in bed together for pleasure and to have sex, free thus of the fear that the sounds of lovemaking will be heard elsewhere in the house. This can be a time when self-indulgences can be learned – not the ones that cost money, but those to do with spending time together and re-valuing a person you have known well and with whom you have made a major life journey.

There is a foundation of knowledge which might inform this period – knowledge not only from books but shared knowledge about what one has known about oneself, the pleasures and satisfactions that there might not have been time to explore before. This period of the late fifties into the sixties can be a time of new exploration sexually. Men may be surprised to hear, perhaps for the first time, that their partners, although they enjoy actual intercourse, would like to spend more time in sensual loving which may or may not lead to intercourse. Freed from the pressure to perform, it is possible to indulge in the quality of the encounter and forget anxieties about performance and frequency.

THE PHYSICAL ASPECT

As with all skills, what is done well seems effortless. If it is done clumsily, the attempt interferes with the experience. Many men and women have never been sure if they are skilful lovers. Their partner has not felt free to express constructive appreciation of things that are enjoyed, or things that are not. This time of life is especially one where that can be put right.

We know for certain that sexual activity ending in climax for both men and women can continue, given good health, right up to the end of life. However, just like all bodily processes, the sexual process does slow down. The man may take longer to establish an erection when he is in his sixties than he did 20 years earlier; it will certainly take longer than it did in his twenties. He may find it harder to ejaculate and need more time and more persistent sensation than he used to. He may be happy not to ejaculate, but to enjoy physical intimacy, exploration, caressing and closeness without any urgency to perform. That is very natural. Unfortunately, too many couples see the loss of the man's erection as a sign that physical intimacy is coming to an end, in the mistaken way that the menopause is often taken as a signal for the ending of physical intimacy. This is one of the most important changes in the ageing process. For most of his life a man will have had spontaneous erections, sometimes at the most embarrassing and inconvenient moments, almost as if his penis had a life of its own. As he gets older that spontaneity declines: it is at that point that anxieties are understandably felt – by his partner, who may jump to the conclusion that she is no longer attractive, and by the man himself, who feels his sex drive is dwindling. He used to feel aroused by the sight of an attractive woman's legs, say, but no longer.

Jim and Jean were in their early sixties. After years of spontaneous arousal they found to their dismay that when they kissed and cuddled in bed Jim's penis remained limp. Jean was worried that he was having an affair and, after several more attempts to make love, Jim became so anxious that he avoided any situation which might be expected to lead to lovemaking. In time, they avoided sex altogether. They sought help and when they understood the changes that had occurred with age and learned that Jean could produce an erection for Jim by skilful hand and mouth stimulation, their lovemaking improved wonderfully. They learned that just as Jean had always needed a lot of foreplay to arouse her fully, Jim too now needed that kind of loving. They both accepted and enjoyed each other without pressure to achieve orgasm every time.

With skilful masturbation from his partner, an older man can achieve erection and sustain it for a long time. Because there is no fear of premature ejaculation, his partner can relax and enjoy her own orgasm(s) and not press for his ejaculation each time. There is nothing so healing to a spirit battered by the thousand stresses of life than to lie quietly against the body and in the arms of someone who creates the reassuring warmth of intimacy without necessarily any need for action. This is a marvellous time for experiment, maybe spending an afternoon in a warm room, the telephone off the hook, massaging each other with a lightly scented oil for the pleasure of being slippery together, to teach each other patterns of masturbation perhaps, or fantasize with erotic books or magazines, watch erotic video films or use body massagers.

Throughout our lives, most of us demand a lot of our bodies and tend to take them for granted. However, physical health and fitness is important to good sex. Overweight, flabby bodies make the mechanics of sex difficult at any age and it may be part of your investment in the later years of your life to spend time treating your body well. A healthy, light diet that includes not too many dairy products, not too much salt, hardly any refined sugar or white bread, but which is high in, say, fish, poultry, vegetables, home-made bread and fruit, is beneficial. Cutting down on cigarettes and alcohol also helps. If one partner smokes and drinks, it can be a sexual turn-off for the other to smell tobacco or drink-laden breath. For those who are still physically fit, gentle exercise every day such as jogging, walking or limbering up at home, all tone up muscles and make it possible, if not to make love hanging from the chandelier, at least to be agile enough to express feelings in more adventurous ways. For those not blessed with total fitness, who have aching joints, circulatory disease, the after-effects of a stroke or just the inevitable loss of muscle tone which comes with increasing age, new positions for intercourse can help. Lying side by side, facing each other or experimenting with pillows or cushions under the buttocks, legs or arms, can make things more comfortable. One couple 'discovered that they enjoyed having intercourse in a large rocking chair, she sitting on his lap as they rocked back and forth. They were convinced that the effectiveness of the technique was responsible for the lasting popularity of the rocking chair in America. To keep off the chill when they made love the wife did a little creative sewing on her flannel nightgown and designed a special movable flap at the back, so that when her husband unbuttoned the fly of his pyjamas and she moved the flap aside they could have intercourse comfortably as she sat on his lap in the rocking chair, still warmly dressed, sometimes while they watched their favourite television programme.' (*Good Sex* by Dr Ruth Westheimer, published by Warner Books, New York, in 1983.)

Sexual hygiene remains important too: a missed shave is unattractive and feels like a cheese-grater. The anxious care with which adolescents dress themselves and look after their personal cleanliness can be replaced in later years with the pleasures of warm baths, lightly scented oils, colognes and talcs. Feeling good about one's own body abolishes any anxieties about being acceptable to another person. Having time to make that happen is one of the benefits of this period in life. As the proportion of older people in the population steadily increases, we look forward to social attitudes changing to a view that sees it makes sense to enhance private and personal life in the later years and no sense simply to slip down a slope of ever-increasing boredom and depression.

NEW RELATIONSHIPS

It is inevitable that losses occur in life. Separation, divorce and death all happen, and adjustments have to be made when bodies are not as responsive as they were when younger.

One difficulty is that someone who has lost a partner in the later part of middle age may, through lack of opportunity and interest, and a remembered regard for the person who has gone, fail to engage in any sexual activity for months or years. When a new relationship begins, they may fear that sexual capabilities will not return. There is some physiological basis for this. With men, lowered frequency of sexual contact can cause testosterone levels to decline which may not return even when there is a new partner and a potentially satisfying sexual situation. A proper analysis of hormone levels from a blood sample, followed by medication, can often produce a dramatic change in function in these circumstances.

Similarly, women who have been without a male partner for some time and who have not created their own arousal, may have increasing loss of tone in the vaginal muscles and loss of vitality in the vaginal membranes. Pelvic floor exercises (called Kegel exercises, such as are used in preparation for childbirth) should help to restore the muscles there. These muscles may be identified by passing urine and stopping in mid-stream: the muscles which stop the flow are the ones to exercise. (Tensing the muscles of the buttocks and thighs has the same beneficial toning effect for men.) Local hormone cream or hormone replacement therapy may be very helpful to the environment of the vagina.

By the age of 65, an estimated 20 per cent of married men have lost their wives, and 50 per cent of women are widows. Meeting other people without partners can be daunting but, with courage, it is possible to find a social life. A good starting point is to join a club or to do voluntary work. Some people consider organizing their own groups to share interests such as bridge, wine-tasting, music or travel. Older people have the advantage of time – time to enjoy and share a relationship in a way not possible earlier in life. There will be fears – fear of the unknown, fear of the reaction of adult children, fear of sexual adjustment with someone new. However, overcoming these fears and developing a new sexual relationship can be of untold value.

BEING ALONE

How do people who have had a sexual partner all their lives cope on their own? A man who has enjoyed masturbating all his life can gain much satisfaction and relieve emotional tension by masturbating, using fantasy material such as magazines, books and video films. Perhaps a body massager or vibrator, either battery or mains, might be an enjoyable addition when used on the stomach and thighs or directly on the genitals. A woman on her own may find it very difficult to enjoy arousing herself if she has always felt it is a man's job. She too could gain much pleasure from masturbation, either with her hand or with a body massager or vibrator. The latter is to be recommended as an essential piece of equipment. In fact, many women left on their own have experienced orgasm for the first time in this way. Sadly, in many old people's homes intimacy and sexual activity between single residents are discouraged. David, aged 85, is living in such a home. He still masturbates from time to time but feels guilty and unable to relax and take time to enjoy himself because there is no lock on his door and staff may walk in at any time. If he is discovered, he may so easily be labelled 'a dirty old man'.

Indeed, there is a kind of conspiracy in our society which seeks to deny the sexuality of old people. Men who show sexual interest are referred to as dirty old men and women shelter behind the outdated myth that 'nice girls don't'. Both of these are psychological defences against expressing what is a vital part of our physical and emotional well-being.

Being alone at this time of life, particularly if there has been little or no experience of masturbation, can increase the sense of isolation enormously. The myths that have surrounded masturbation in the past – that it reduces vitality, promotes insanity or produces hair on the palms – are nonsense. Whereas in earlier years intercourse was the goal, now there is more time for lovemaking which involves prolonged sensual touching. Stroking baby-oil or lotion onto the penis and vagina to compensate for loss of natural lubrication helps towards uninhibited masturbation, either alone or with a partner. With the latter, oral sex is another enjoyable way to provide extra lubrication. It is important to be reassured that masturbation is a natural, lovely way to give one-self a treat. Only you know exactly how to best please yourself, but encouragement may be needed to show any special personal patterns of pressure and rhythm to a partner. Because sensual touching becomes more and more important in lovemaking as we grow older, the more we can teach each other and ourselves the skills of masturbation patterns and preferences the better. Go ahead, take chances, experiment and enjoy!

THE PLEASURES OF AGE

Growing older is a period for sexual reassessment. It is a time to adapt to the changes in our bodies and to welcome a more relaxed and unhurried sensuality.

Ageing is not all to do with decline and decay. It brings its particular pleasures and possibilities. It can be a time for discovering and sharing new experiences in a way which was not possible in earlier years.

There is no age limit for sex – our bodies can go on functioning sexually until the end of our lives. This is very important, because satisfying sex encourages healthy bodies and contented minds. The pleasures are of a different and gentler kind but they are still very much there to be enjoyed.

SEXUALLY TRANSMISSIBLE
DISEASES & THEIR MIMICS

Brian J. Ford,
with a section on AIDS by
Dr James Bevan

The fact that sex is sometimes associated with disease is
well known to all of us: indeed the existence of venereal
disease – as a hidden threat lying in wait for the unwary
– is part of the mythology of playground discussions about
sexuality amongst young people. Unfortunately, for all the
familiarity with the existence of these diseases, there is
a remarkable ignorance of what they are and what they
do to us. Most tragic of all is the widespread suspicion
that someone is suffering from a sexually transmitted
disease, when in fact they have nothing of the sort.

Many of us, at one time or another, believe we have
caught VD. Often this is because of a deep sense of guilt
which has become attached to a sexual encounter, or it
may be because of a symptom (a lump, a spot, or a
discharge) which the individual is certain must be due to
VD. In these cases, doctors often find that a patient simply
refuses to be reassured. A negative test, which should in
any logical world bring relief to the deluded victim, is
seen instead as an example of the fallibility of medical
practice. Sometimes a second test is done by the doctor
and that can be a serious error; in the mind of the patient,
that as good as *proves* the first test was fallible, and
makes it unlikely that satisfaction and security will ever
be found. The victim of venereophobia – those laymen
might call 'sexual hypochondriacs' – are among the saddest
and most self-deluded of people.

Medical practice is concerned with curing diseases which
people have contracted. But in the confused and

contradictory world of human sexuality, many of the people who turn up at special sexual disease clinics turn out not to have VD at all. Some have harmless conditions which they wrongly think to be VD, others have nothing detectably wrong with them. For these people, much less is done. Yet the worry and the distress can be greater for a person who is simply told: 'There is nothing the matter,' than for somebody whose test turns out to be positive. After all, the patient is receiving treatment and the satisfaction of knowing that something is being done about it. The *non*-patient simply goes home or back to work, wondering whether the medical establishment has let them down.

At least three terms are applied to sexual disease: venereal disease, sexually transmitted disease, and sexually transmissible disease. Each has its own shade of meaning. For people interested in learning about sex, there are many conditions which do not come into any of these categories (that is to say, they are not infections) but which certainly cause distress, and which can affect the appearance or the functioning of the sexual organs.

'Venereal' means 'connected with sexual intercourse' and derives from the name of the Roman goddess of love, Venus. In 1658 it emerged in its modern medical sense, when syphilis was first described as being known as venereal disease or venereal pox. The 'classic' venereal diseases are syphilis, gonorrhoea and chancroid: known popularly as pox, clap and soft sore respectively.

Sexually transmitted diseases are those that are typically spread through sexual promiscuity. These range from glandular fever, the so-called 'kissing disease', to venereal warts and herpes to pubic (crab) lice. Finally there are sexually transmissible diseases, namely those which *can* be transmitted by bodily contact. One surprising example here is hepatitis B, which is often thought of as being a 'conventional' blood-borne infection, but which is often found to be passed between male homosexuals.

The three terms are often confused (note that venereal warts, for instance, is not a venereal disease), and the modern abbreviation, preferable to VD, is STD. It covers a multitude of conditions and, even if the fringes are somewhat vague, the mainstream group of diseases which the term is intended to embrace are clear enough. In addition there are many conditions which may be spread by sexual contact, and so are strictly speaking included as STDs, but which can arise apparently spontaneously. One example is thrush, caused by a yeast known as *Candida albicans*. This organism is a frequent occupant of the environment afforded by human skin and a change of that environment can cause the organism to multiply more than usual. The contraceptive pill has been claimed to trigger this off, and so have some antibiotic treatments. The result is a whitish discharge. More than once that has raised the suspicion that 'I have caught VD', but nothing of the sort has occurred. Sometimes a particularly hardy strain of *Candida* can be spread through a towel from one sufferer to someone else to whom this organism is new, with the result that the thrush has been spread by infection; but that is not so usual. *Candida* is a normal inhabitant of our bodies and the disease arises through an upsurge in growth of the native population rather than through any 'venereal' contact.

Many people have tried to suggest that STDs are sent by heaven, or perhaps by moral destiny, to regulate our sexual appetites. You could certainly justify the view by saying that, if promiscuity ended, then so would the STDs (though that would not apply to thrush, for instance). But the fashionable view that STD is a minor price to pay for sexual liberation is dangerous. These diseases are widespread and they can be serious. Now that herpes and, more recently, AIDS have become widely known, casual promiscuous sex, for instance, is suddenly being seen as a hazardous, even life-threatening, activity.

However, you could not go further and say that STDs were *evolved* to regulate promiscuity, for one solid reason. Children, for example, suffer from a range of illnesses which vaccination can prevent – whooping cough and measles are examples. If you were to accept the moralistic argument expounded above, then you would also have to accept that the diseases of childhood were evolved to exert a sanction against children – or at least to punish people who remained unvaccinated. Those who argue that AIDS is a sanction by the Lord against homosexuality would similarly have to claim that measles is a sanction against Eskimos.

STDs are said to be the commonest infectious diseases. The number of people treated for them is steadily rising. Bearing in mind that the means available for treatment have improved dra-

113

matically over the last few decades, we might anticipate that the number of victims would by now be falling. In some instances, levels went down in the 1940s and 1950s, only to rise again in the 1970s as the sexual revolution took hold. Unfortunately, though people have heard of 'VD', they are less aware of its extent or its nature. Certainly the widely received view – namely, that sexual diseases are a minor complication of free love – will not do. They are a serious matter, and require urgent attention. But the main diseases are easy for specialists to diagnose, and can be positively cured. People owe it to themselves to undertake the steps necessary to see that both are expedited: not only to themselves, but to their partners and families too.

The most important aspect is that there are many other organisms which seem to produce diseases that mimic STDs. Most people at STD clinics who actually have an illness are victims of inflammations of the genito-urinary tract for which no specific cause can be found, but which are certainly (and demonstrably) not caused by any form of 'VD'. These conditions are unsatisfactorily grouped together as non-specific urethritis, known as NSU for short. How remarkable an indicator of ignorance it is that the commonest form of STD is one most people have never even heard of and which has no single identity.

I hope that the overview of a complicated and perplexing branch of medical science that follows will provide some insight into why the diseases are there, and where they came from. It is true that promiscuity spreads sexually transmitted diseases, and it is also true that they are not just a simple matter. But it is not that the organisms are bent on warfare against ourselves or parts of our bodies. In many cases it is our own way of living which, almost, *invites* the organisms in to places where they do not belong. Thrush may not be 'natural' to someone who is distressed by its symptoms, but then nylon tights and synthetic pants provide a thoroughly artificial environment for the parts of human bodies they are meant to protect.

The second conclusion that you should draw is that the presenting signs which people associate with VD – sores and a discharge – are more often caused by other things. Always bear in mind that the chances are you have no sexually transmitted disease at all and, if you do, then the chances are it is not gonorrhoea or syphilis. The one person who *will* know what it is is the specialist at a clinic. People are sometimes deterred from attending because they are convinced that everyone else there is riddled with disease, while they – the patient – are in a different category altogether. Not true. The other people there are, in the main, just like you.

The importance of attending is that prompt and efficient treatment is vitally necessary in the case of syphilis and gonorrhoea in order to nip seeds of later trouble in the bud. It is not good enough to feel that, well, this time it is only a little wart, or this time the discharge will go away. Even if you have one of the many other diseases mentioned in this chapter, then the sooner treatment begins, the safer is the outcome.

Above all, understand that self-diagnosis is simply impossible. It takes a trained eye to know what to look for; to spot the difference between a potentially harmful cancer and a perfectly harmless spot is not something that a non-medical individual could expect to do. If you are a chef, then you can probably tell when a steak is fried to perfection. A surveyor can tell at a glance when the corner of a room may be damp. A taxi-driver will tell by the look in the eye if he is likely to get a tip from his rider, a nanny knows just when the baby needs to be changed ... all learned indicators that to professionals seem instinctive and fairly obvious, but which are beyond the experience of the rest of us.

When it is a matter of medical diagnosis, then, why should people hesitate to go to the one person who can tell when a problem needs attention? We all know how familiarity trains us to know what to look for in the lives we lead and it is vitally important to leave diagnosis to doctors.

So often, diagnosis is quick, sure and reliable. So often, modern treatments are painless, safe and life-saving. It is up to you to benefit from the facilities made available, and to guard against dangers for loved ones, for partners, and for others in the future. If people went to STD clinics as responsibly as they could, then without any doubt at all the diseases themselves could be controlled systematically.

AIDS AND HIV INFECTION

The rapid awareness of a new and frightening disease has spread world-wide within the last few years. It is 'acquired immune deficiency syndrome', known for short as AIDS in the English speaking world, and as SIDA in the Latin communites where the order of words is subject to a different grammatical convention. The

115

syndrome results from a disorder of the body's ability to resist disease, and the symptoms are those of illnesses which the lack of immunity allows to develop.

One of the earliest indications of AIDS was a form of pneumonia caused by *Pneumocystis carinii*, a small protozoan parasite known to cause lung disease, but ordinarily a rare condition. Another was Kaposi's sarcoma, previously a rare skin disease that usually occurred in elderly people, which many doctors regard as a true cancer. These diseases often appear in communities where AIDS was common and it is the appearance of the pneumonia and skin tumour, which drew attention to the previously unrecognized presence of AIDS itself.

Where did AIDS originate?

It is probable that the disease is caused by a virus similar to one that has long existed among colonies of wild monkeys around Lake Victoria, in Africa. Outbreaks of infection in the human population may have been spread by the war and civil disorder that was rife in Zaire in the mid–1970s. By the early 1980s the virus had spread across the Atlantic to Haiti in the Caribbean. Sporadic cases of AIDS probably occurred before this. The earliest positive result was found in a blood specimen stored since 1959.

Medical authorities first became aware of the condition when doctors reported outbreaks of the associated diseases in 1981. From New York came reports of an increase in the incidence of Kaposi's sarcoma; and from Los Angeles there were increasing numbers of *Pneumocystis* pneumonia. In both places the doctors sent records and blood samples to the Infectious Diseases Center in Atlanta, Georgia, where the new epidemics were related to the gay communities in which they had been found. What was happening was a breakdown in the immune systems of these 'at risk' groups.

The nature of the syndrome gave rise to the term AIDS in 1982, and since then the condition has spread extensively across the world. Earlier theories proposed that the damage to the immune system might be a reaction to spermatozoa, introduced into the bloodstream during anal intercourse. Later it was suggested that amyl nitrite, used as a sexual stimulant, might be causing the damage. But many victims did not indulge in anal intercourse, whilst many AIDS patients had never used amyl nitrite. It soon became apparent that an infection was the most likely cause.

In 1981 a retrovirus was detected in humans, where it caused damage to some of the white cells in the bloodstream, called lymphocytes. These cells include many which provide the immune response that protects us from infections. When infected with the retrovirus, the patients were less able to resist infections. Because the virus attacked the T–cell lymphocytes, it was known as human T–cell leukaemic virus, HTLV, and was also isolated from victims of leukaemia in Japan and the Caribbean. Most forms of leukaemia in animals, unlike those that occur in man, are known to be caused by viruses, so this association was no great surprise.

In 1983 a similar retrovirus, HTLV III, was found in the blood cells of patients with AIDS, and this is now known to be the infective agent that causes the disease. Since that time the virus has been renamed the human immunodeficiency virus, HIV, which is more accurate as well as giving rise to a shorter acronym. In 1986, a second retrovirus, HIV II, was isolated, in Portugal, from patients who came from the Cape Verde Islands and from Africa. A closely related retrovirus, Simian immunovirus, SIV, is found in monkeys, and others, that cause AIDS–like illnesses, are found in sheep, goats and cats. They all invade the body's cells and alter the way in which they function so that the cell produces further new viruses.

The disease itself is not very infectious. The chances of a person catching HIV from a positive HIV partner, on one sexual encounter, without using a condom, is 1 in 500 (0.2 per cent), and with a condom, 1 in 5,000 (0.02 per cent). Heterosexuals, outside Africa, who have had no sexual contact with a bisexual male or needle-using drug addicts, have a minute chance of becoming infected with HIV. It appears to need direct blood contact with the blood or semen of an infected person to catch HIV. The virus is also found in the saliva, tears, urine and breast milk, and in the secretions from the cervix of the uterus, but it is not certain if these are truly infectious.

The normal immune system – how the body copes

The body 'recognizes' foreign substances that manage to get inside it. These substances may be an infection, material like pollen or 'foreign' tissue from another person. These are called antigens. The body reacts by attacking the antigen. There are several ways of doing this: some of the body cells 'swallow' the antigen, thus removing it from the circulation; others, special white blood cells

117

called lymphocytes, tackle the antigens in a different way. Basically, there are two kinds of lymphocyte: the T–cell lymphocyte which helps destroy any kind of infection, in a variety of ways, and starts acting as soon as it detects the antigen; and the B–cell lymphocyte that 'learns' about the antigen so that it can be recognized in the future. The B–cells produce antibodies that are unique to the particular antigen. These antibodies are the true and precise immunity to each infection; they remain in the circulation for many years and reappear as soon as the specific antigen is encountered again. This can be seen in the seasonal attacks of hay fever, when a specific pollen (antigen) triggers off a marked response in the nose with the combination of the body's specific antibody.

Defects in the immune system

Although there are illnesses that can be caused by over-production of antibodies, such as acute allergic reactions to drugs and the inherited condition of eczema, these are not of concern when considering AIDS. There are, however, conditions in which defects of the immune system can occur. The problems that arise are similar to those occurring in AIDS. These patients are usually called 'immunocompromised'. This condition is commonly seen in those who have had organ transplants, when the treatment given to the body prevents it 'recognizing' foreign tissue, in chemotherapy for cancer and when large doses of cortisone are used to treat diseases. Some children are born with defects in their immune systems, young babies and the elderly have poorly developed or impaired immune systems, and many forms of cancer have disorganized immunity.

The knowledge of how to treat immunocompromised patients has helped in dealing with those who have HIV infection and AIDS.

How does HIV infection affect immunity?

Although a great deal is now known about the HIV virus, and how it infects the body, not enough is known about the way it becomes active after infecting the body cells. The HIV virus primarily infects the T–cell lymphocytes, enters the cell's genetic code and alters its normal function. It is not known what factors make the disorganized cell become 'active' and produce further viruses that spread to other T–cells and, eventually, disorganize the whole immune system. Once this starts to happen, sometimes after many months or years, there is steady progress towards AIDS.

What tests are there for HIV?

Unless the amount of infection is known, such as that occurring with a blood transfusion, the length of the time of incubation of the virus is not precisely known. It usually takes 1 to 2 months for HIV antibodies to appear but, occasionally, it can be as long as a year, if the initial amount of infecting virus was very small. During this initial incubation phase the individual may be infectious to some degree. It is now known that, a week or so before the HIV test becomes positive, a large amount of the virus is released into the blood stream and the person is highly infectious.

Although there is a test for the virus itself, an antigen test, this is complicated to use and may, in some parts of the world, produce positive results due to other non–HIV viruses. The commonest tests rely on detecting the development of antibodies in the blood. These tests are the ones that give what is often called an HIV positive test. These tests may, ultimately, become negative when the person has developed such severe AIDS that very few antibodies are produced. If a test is found to be positive the laboratory will always check it, using a different method, to ensure that a 'false positive' has not occurred. In fact the tests are about 99 per cent accurate.

HIV testing is used on those who may request it, either as a method of diagnosis or, increasingly for medico-legal reasons; for insurance companies; for screening of blood and organ donors, and for the follow-up of those who have had positive results. Until now, in this country, blood tests could not be done on people without their permission and after counselling about the effects of an unexpected positive result. Anonymous HIV tests will now be introduced to study the spread of the infection in the community. In this situation permission will not be needed, as the individual will not be told the result and the researcher will not know from whom the blood has come.

It is important not to do an HIV test too soon after a possible time of infection. A negative result, within 3 months, may give false hope. The person must be counselled to wait, to learn about 'safe sex' and to tell their partner of the fear.

Now that HIV II infection has appeared, it is necessary to consider this as a separate test in suspected people. It may have to be used,

119

on a regular basis, on blood and organ donors as the usual HIV I test will only be positive in about 80 per cent of HIV II infections.

Who are the people most likely to become infected with HIV?

In the United Kingdom over 80 per cent of HIV positive victims are homosexual men with the next largest group (8 per cent) being haemophiliacs and others infected by blood products or blood transfusion. Present screening methods have virtually eliminated the chances of catching HIV from a blood transfusion and the treatment now of other blood products, such as those used for haemophiliacs, kills the HIV virus so that infection is no longer possible. In some parts of the country, such as Edinburgh, intra-venous drug users have a high incidence of infection but, overall drug users make up only 2 per cent of the total. Heterosexual infection, usually from intravenous drug users and bisexual males, is about 4 per cent.

In Africa the incidence of HIV infection is nearly the same in women as in men. It is thought that this may be due to frequency of ulcers on the genitalia, either from other sexually transmitted diseases or other forms of infection, causing slight bleeding and therefore easier access for the HIV infection. Nearly 90 per cent of prostitutes, in some areas, have positive tests.

As anonymous testing has not yet started in the United Kingdom, it is difficult to know the overall incidence of infection. The Government has now given permission for this to start so, hopefully, useful statistics will become available within the next year, by 1990. However, there has been a rapid increase in positive tests in homosexual men attending clinics dealing with sexual diseases and a slower increase amongst other patients. In the United States the incidence of infection is better known: overall about 140 people in a million are HIV positive but this may be nearly 1,000 in a million in New York and San Francisco.

How certain is an HIV positive person to develop AIDS?

It is not certain that everyone with a positive HIV test will develop AIDS. The rate of development seems to vary from one country to another. It is not clear why this should be. In Denmark 8 per cent of men tested as positive developed AIDS in 3 years while in New York over 30 per cent of intravenous drug users tested as positive developed AIDS in the same time. It is likely that 1 in 20 (5 per cent) of those who are HIV positive will develop AIDS each year. Other factors, such as malnutrition, other infections like Hepatitis B, and the effects of the drugs themselves probably further reduce the body's ability to cope with the HIV infection.

How is HIV Infection Transmitted?

The HIV virus is usually carried in the blood. Sexual intercourse may cause minor bleeding and this is much more likely to occur with anal than vaginal intercourse, hence the prevalence in the homosexual population. The virus is found in the tissues used in transplantation, such as cornea, kidney and liver and from the mother to child, both in the womb before birth and afterwards through breast milk. Although HIV infection has occurred in all these ways it is now much less likely with the adequate testing of donors. Small amounts of blood adhere to needles and this causes transmission in the shared needles of drug addicts and, unfortunately, on the rare occasion when a nurse or doctor accidentally sticks an infected needle into themselves. Luckily these needle-stick injuries rarely (less than 1 per cent) produce a positive result. Occasionally, infection has occurred when a nurse has a skin wound and has been exposed to a victim's blood. There have been no cases of infection occurring in people who simply share the same environment, using the same bathing and cooking equipment. Theoretically it is possible to catch HIV from kissing, particularly deep, so-called French kissing, as minor bleeding may result from infection of the gums. So far this has not been known to occur.

How can HIV infection be prevented?

The safest way to prevent infection, short of avoiding sexual intercourse altogether, is to remain within a single partner relationship. If this is not possible confine contacts to as few people as possible, use a condom and know about your partner's past sexual and drug history. The chances of infection are greatly reduced if your partner comes from a low risk group. High risk partners are homosexual or bisexual men, drug users by injection and haemophiliacs – or their partners – and, also, anyone who has had casual

121

sexual intercourse in Africa. The more partners you have the more likely you are to catch HIV.

Guidelines to safer sex

Outside a known, safe sexual relationship, the likelihood of catching HIV depends on the way you have sex. The so-called 'Guidelines to Safer Sex' are only a help in reducing the chances of HIV infection:

Low risk Close physical contact, including fondling and rubbing with mutual masturbation and soft, dry kissing.

Medium risk Deep, French kissing; the so-called 'rimming' of the anal region with tongue and lips; fellatio (sucking or licking the genitalia) before the man reaches an orgasm.

High risk Anal and vaginal intercourse (the risk is greatly reduced if a condom, male or female type, is used); any sexual activity that causes bleeding, such as biting, sharing of various forms of stimulating sexual equipment and 'fisting' (pushing the fingers, or fist, into the anus); fellatio to orgasm.

Those who are known to be HIV positive must be told about safe sex for their partners. Drug users can be given sterile syringes for single use and told how to dispose of them without risking others who may either use them or receive needle-stick injury while dumping them. Those who are HIV positive should tell their general practitioner and dentist about their condition. This is sensible as it will enable particular care to be taken when treating them, not only for the carer's sake but, also, to ensure that the correct treatments are given to the victim. Pregnant women, who are HIV positive, may want a termination of pregnancy and should be advised not to breastfeed if the baby is found to be HIV negative at birth. There is a 1 in 4 (25 per cent) chance of the baby being born HIV positive, in Europe, and nearly 1 in 2 (50 per cent), in New York. The chances of the baby becoming infected by an HIV positive mother increase if the baby is breastfed.

How does HIV infection progress?

After a person has become infected with HIV the virus grows within the body, mainly in the T–cell lymphocytes, and, after 1 or 2 months, causes the production of antibodies. When this occurs there may be an illness similar to glandular fever. This is called the sero–conversion illness and is accompanied by a fever, vomiting and diarrhoea, severe headache, swelling of the lymph glands and a diffuse rash over the body. In a few people there is brain infection (encephalitis) causing coma and even temporary paralysis. This can last some weeks before settling slowly. Most people with HIV infection do not at first exhibit any form of illness but they are still infectious. The degree of infectivity may vary from time to time. During this phase of apparent good health, various blood tests will show that the individual is not entirely normal.

Although the period of chronic infection may last months or years, before AIDS develops, there are two types of intermediate illness that may occur. About one-third develop generalized enlargement of the lymph glands, this is known as Persistent Generalized Lymphadenopathy, PGL, without any sign of other illness. Another condition, known as AIDS–related complex, ARC, is a form of pre–AIDS in which the victim has some of the characteristics of the full-blown AIDS, such as prolonged fever or more usually an illness, from which temporary recovery is made, before progress to AIDS. ARC is not so commonly diagnosed now that there are better tests for HIV infection and the illness can be followed more closely than in the past. One of the problems with ARC is the difficulty in defining it. The patient may feel vaguely unwell with intermittent diarrhoea and gradual weight loss and, sometimes, slight fever with profound sweating at night. If no other cause can be found HIV may be the reason. In addition various skin rashes, often due to fungus infection, occur and a sore mouth, a sign of thrush infection, *Monilia (Candida)*. Impetigo, cold sores (*herpes simplex*) with warts on the hands and genitals may occur. An attack of shingles, *herpes zoster*, can develop and be unusually severe. Herpes infection of the genitals often reappears for the first time in many years. There are several blood tests that can be done to show that HIV infection has been progressing. The doctor diagnoses ARC on a combination of two symptoms, two signs on physical examination and two abnormal blood tests.

How is AIDS defined?

Since 1986 AIDS has been defined according to the classification of the Center for Disease Control, Atlanta, USA, which tries to take into account the various ways that HIV infection can produce illness: *Group 1*: Acute infection, the sero–conversion illness; *Group 2*: Chronic infection, without signs of illness; *Group 3*: Persistent Generalized Lymphadenopathy.

Group 4 is divided into sub-groups according to the type of illness and is independent of PGL: A: Persistent fever and weight loss for more than 1 month; B: Brain and Nerve Infections; C: Infection with one of the known AIDS-associated infections, such as *Pneumocystis carinii*, or recurrent infections of other diseases; D: Cancers, such as Kaposi's sarcoma.

Although it is usual, nowadays, to obtain a positive HIV test, as a means of confirmation, the diagnosis of AIDS is made, by the doctor, on the type of illness that the victim is suffering from, the way it has developed and the fact that there is no other cause, such as depressed immunity due to an organ transplant or cancer.

AIDS is the final development of HIV infection and is one of a collection of the various illnesses that occur in a person whose immunity is fatally damaged.

What are the Symptoms of a Person with AIDS?

As there are so many illnesses that can afflict a person with the end stage of HIV infection there is no single symptom that makes the diagnosis clear. At some time pneumonia is likely to occur and this is commonly due to the protozoan germ, *Pneumocystis carinii*, which appears in 50 per cent of AIDS cases. In healthy people, with normal immune systems, the most it may cause is a mild cold-like illness. However, in those who are receiving treatment for cancer or organ transplant it has long been known to cause life-threatening pneumonia of slow onset with increasing breathlessness, cough and fever. Other forms of pneumonia, due to bacteria, viruses or fungi, and tuberculosis often occur.

Kaposi's sarcoma has been known for many years and, until AIDS appeared, most commonly affected elderly men who lived near the Mediterranean, or who were of Jewish origin. It was also seen in young Africans. Violet coloured lumps appeared on the skin of the legs and grew slowly. In patients with AIDS, the disease is different; it develops rapidly with lumps appearing anywhere on the skin as well as internally, where they cause symptoms of obstruction to breathing or the intestine.

Various forms of cancer, particularly those of the lymph gland system known as lymphomas, commonly appear and complicate the treatment of the infections associated with AIDS. These can appear anywhere within the body.

Involvement of the intestine stops the normal absorption of food and causes diarrhoea, so rapid weight loss results. This is frequently seen in Africans where it is known as 'slim disease'. This intestinal involvement is usually due to various infections, again viral or bacterial, and forms of cancer, particularly the lymphomas.

Infection of the brain and the nervous system results in dementia with loss of memory for recent events, slowing of the mind and, just to make a bad situation worse, moments of confused mental overactivity, a kind of mania, with hallucinations. Other problems lead to neuritis in which weakness of the limbs and even paralysis may result.

The AIDS patient may have some of these diseases appearing in different parts of the body at the same time and further complicated by the illnesses that have already occurred in the early AIDS–related complex. Shingles and various fungus infections make the life of the AIDS sufferer even worse.

Although many of the infections of AIDS can now be treated, the respite from the onslaught of the infections is merely reduced as one infection follows another with increasingly shorter times of relief in between. The increasing debility, fever, loss of weight and diarrhoea finally leads to death.

How can AIDS be treated?

There are two aspects to the treatment of AIDS. The first is to try to prevent the progress of the infection and the second is to treat the infections and complications that result from loss of immunity.

An immense amount of research and money is being spent on AIDS. So far there is no immediate prospect of treatment curing AIDS or of any effective vaccine to prevent people catching the virus. Some drugs seem to reduce the speed with which HIV infection progresses; the one that is presently used, Zidovudine, AZT, seems to help prevent recurrences of illnesses when given to patients who have had one episode of ARC. Unfortunately, it makes many patients very nauseated, at the beginning of treatment, and in nearly half damages the bone marrow so that anaemia and a bleeding tendency occur. These severe side-effects mean that only about 50 per cent of patients can persevere with the drug. Newer drugs may have fewer problems and, hopefully, be more effective. A group of drugs, the Interferons, are similar to antiviral substances produced by the body and could be another form of therapy but, again, the side-effects have been very severe and the treatment not as effective as hoped.

Considerable research is directed at making a vaccine. This is theoretically possible but the HIV virus seems to change in minor ways, from time to time, and this makes an effective vaccine even more difficult to manufacture.

At present, antiviral treatment is kept for those with ARC or AIDS but it is hoped that earlier treatment, with an effective antiviral drug, might slow or prevent ARC developing.

With a disease that is so frightening and that has received so much publicity any small advance in treatment, or suggestion that a new drug has been found to be effective, tends to bring new hope to those with AIDS, only to be destroyed when the deaths from the disease continue unabated. It is difficult to maintain a balanced view when dealing with an infection that has so many ways of producing illness.

A patient with ARC or AIDS needs to have each illness treated at once and as effectively as possible. Each infection seems to damage the immune system and make the progress towards ARC and AIDS that much faster. There are as many treatments as there are diseases. Some of these treatments can cure the infection and, with *Pneumocystis carinii*, continued antibiotic treatment may prevent a recurrence. Radiotherapy is often helpful with Kaposi's sarcoma and will certainly give considerable, temporary relief when the swelling occurs in an area, like the lungs, that is producing serious symptoms.

On an optimistic note it has been helpful to find that HIV positive people who maintain excellent health are slower to progress on a downward course. They should take active steps to keep fit, mentally and psychologically. Regular exercise and a healthy, nutritious diet with an occupation that is interesting and one that may help other people, even if it is counselling other HIV positive individuals, is essential.

How can a person who is fearful of AIDS be helped?

Skilled counselling is an essential part of treatment. Many people, the so-called 'worried well', exhibit fear of having caught the infec-

126

tion as a sign of guilt for some illicit sexual act. In fact the chances of catching HIV from one sexual encounter, with a person not already proven to be infected, has been calculated as 1 in 5 million, if a condom is not used, and 1 in 50 million, if a condom is used. Fear of AIDS may be a symptom of an underlying insecurity in sexual and other relationships, or of ignorance about the ways of catching HIV. A discussion with a counsellor before having an HIV test is essential; this gives a chance to bring realistic and unrealistic fears to the surface before facing the result. Sometimes the anxiety is justified but, more often, it is simply fear itself that is the problem.

Inevitably some of those who have HIV tests will be positive. These people must have a chance to discuss their position, before the test is done, so that they can anticipate what their reaction will be. The counsellor will need tact and sympathy. Many of the questions that are asked, like 'When will I develop AIDS?' and 'How long will I live?', are impossible to answer. Often the immediate response to a positive test is one of disbelief mixed with anger and shock. This is followed by a time of remorse and guilt which may produce moments of wanting to 'take it out on the world' in a form of revenge, by attempting to destroy healthy people of whom the victim is jealous. This may take the form of indiscriminate, promiscuous sexual behaviour. These mixed emotions need skilful help to overcome and achieve a more level state of reality. It can be explained that every minor illness is not a sign of AIDS and that a normal life is to be expected for a considerable time to come. Sexual adjustments have to be made and the realities of living in a world where HIV sufferers are considered to have a modern form of leprosy need to be considered.

Often severe depression occurs and this may need medication to produce recovery; less frequently there is a complete psychiatric breakdown needing in-patient hospital treatment.

It is important to try and involve the partner in helping the HIV-positive person. This is necessary not only for the partner's health but also for the stability of the relationship which needs the strength to cope with the bad news. Both need to know the difference between HIV positive and AIDS, how to cope with 'safer sex' and to know where they can find help when it is needed, both physically and psychologically.

THE FUTURE

In January 1989 there had been over 2,000 victims of AIDS, many of whom have died, in the United Kingdom. The number of people who are HIV positive is not known but is estimated to be 50,000 to 100,000. These figures are probably doubling every 6 to 9 months, although the rate of increase is now thought to be slowing down. We are at the beginning of a major epidemic of a still untreatable infection. In some parts of the United States, AIDS is already the major cause of death in males aged 20 to 40. This may soon become the situation in the United Kingdom.

Although, at present, there is no effective treatment or immunization against AIDS, there is the hope, within the next 5 to 10 years, that these may be available. In the meantime the best protection is effective publicity to all sexually active groups in the population, to explain that 'safer sex' is sex with only one partner and that the danger groups, homosexuals, bisexual men and drug addicts using needles, must modify their behaviour to reduce the chances of catching the HIV infection.

BARTHOLIN'S ABSCESS OR CYST

A Bartholin's gland is one of a pair of lubricating glands at the entrance to the vagina. If the duct from the gland is blocked, and the secretions continue to be produced, it will swell, forming a cyst. A cyst by itself may cause discomfort, a feeling of stretching, and also awkwardness when walking. It may also cause discomfort or pain during intercourse.

If infection caused the blockage, an abscess may form. This is extremely painful and may be accompanied by a temperature. Any woman with vaginitis (see page 184), a common condition, may develop a Bartholin's abscess. It is a common complication of gonorrhoea.

Antibiotics may help to control the symptoms of an abscess but it is likely that it will have to be cut open under a general anaesthetic. If a cyst, or further abscess, forms then it is advisable to have an operation to remove the damaged gland so that it cannot cause further problems.

CANCER

Though any lump on the external genitals may cause anxiety about the possibility of cancer (see MIMICS, LUMPS and BUMPS, page 159), it rarely occurs. Most forms of genital cancer are not related to any form of sexually transmitted disease.

Cancer of the uterus and ovary are relatively common, cancer of the vulva is rare. Cancer of the cervix is rare in women who have not had intercourse and is most common in women who started intercourse when very young, who have had several partners, do not use a physical form of contraception (the sheath or cap) and do not have a high standard of personal cleanliness. It has been suggested that smegma from the man's penis is a cause of cervical cancer, but there is little evidence to support this. Probably of greater significance is a virus infection, and both herpes (see page 151) and the genital wart (see page 138) have been suggested as possible causes. Both viruses have been seen, using an electron microscope, in the cervical cells. However, the presence of a virus is not conclusive evidence of the cause of the problem. It is possible that one of these viruses with some other agent, perhaps smegma, combine together to produce a cancer-causing substance.

Until a cause, if there is one, for cervical cancer is found, all sexually active women should have regular smear tests. There has been controversy over these tests. Even when they were introduced, they had a far greater effect on the incidence of cervical cancer (which went down) than they did on the death rates from the disease (which were much the same). Secondly, when clinics began to administer the tests there were cases where a patient was never told of a positive result and death resulted.

The first problem is related to the variety of forms in which cervical cancer presents itself. Some of the forms develop slowly and seem not to be particularly threatening. These are the kinds that are most easily picked up during routine screening of a population. Others which may have a virus cause can have a much more rapid course. Some specialists in venereal medicine now believe that these forms can be transmitted through promiscuous sexual contact.

The second problem can be solved only by adopting a 'fail-safe' system of notification for women at risk after a positive cervical smear.

Apart from cervical cancer, other cancers of the genital area are uncommon. Some diseases, such as leukoplakia, can develop later into cancer, but are usually recognized beforehand and treated in time. Even these are rare.

Cancer of the penis is thought to be due to smegma, the greasy secretion over the glans. Penile cancer is virtually unknown in those who have been circumcised and very rare in men who maintain a high standard of personal hygiene. It seems that smegma acts as an irritant, in those who do not wash thoroughly under the foreskin. However, penile cancer usually occurs in the elderly and, since it can be seen easily, can be effectively treated if shown early enough to a doctor. Cancer of the testis, of which there are two kinds, occurs now more frequently than it has in previous decades but the reason for this is not known.

CANDIDIASIS

Candidiasis is caused by a yeast-like fungus now known as *Candida albicans*. It used to be called *Monilia*, and the disease it produces is still sometimes referred to as moniliasis. Candidosis is an alternative medical term used for the condition. Colloquially it is referred to as thrush. *C. albicans* is the commonest species to infect mankind, but there are several others which cause distinct diseases of their own, including *C. tropicalis*.

Origins

The fungus is a common resident of the human skin and the organism, or the spores it forms, can easily be found in the nose, mouth, intestine and on the skin of people of both sexes and of all ages.

If candidiasis is diagnosed in a man, he probably acquired it from a female with genital thrush, since males do not have the recesses in which the organism can take hold. If it occurs in a woman, then it is not such an easy matter. Here the question is not so much 'where did it come from?' but 'why has this ubiquitous fungus suddenly multiplied?'.

Some factors are known to be involved, such as an acidic environment (a lowering of the vaginal pH 3.5–4.5 in healthy women who are still capable of menstruating) which can come about through some unrelated bodily change. A warm and moist environment helps the organisms to reproduce in an otherwise difficult situation, so the wearing of tight confining undergarments may be involved. If some of the normal bacterial inhabitants of the vagina are killed off, perhaps by antibiotic treatment for some separate complaint, then the thrush organism can get out of control; in people taking chemotherapeutic agents or even steroids there is a chance for the balance to shift and for the *Candida* to get out of hand. Sometimes going on the contraceptive pill for the first time will bring in its wake an outbreak of genital thrush.

Symptoms

The symptoms vary from case to case and from person to person – in many instances the condition exists (notably in women) without being detected at all, and in a sense the organism is very widespread.

Men A man often reacts as though allergic to the overgrown yeast population in his female partner. He may experience a strong burning sensation on the penis, either immediately after intercourse or after a week or two's delay. A rash may form on the penis, sometimes with small spots or blister-like eruptions – which need to be distinguished from other diseases – and occasionally a cheesy build-up of the fungus cells occurs under the foreskin, looking rather like smegma. From time to time a rash will extend to cover the scrotum and there are rare cases where the organisms penetrate the urethra and produce symptoms like those of early gonorrhoea.

Women Though symptoms may well be absent altogether, even when there is a considerable overgrowth of the yeast cells, burning or intense itching of the vulva is a common symptom of thrush. The degree of itching varies, but it can become intolerable. There may be burning sensations in the vagina triggered by intercourse, and passing urine can be painful if it comes into contact with inflamed and raw tissues.

The vagina may produce a discharge that has the appearance of cottage cheese, but it is important to understand that many women complain of vaginal dryness and experience no discharge at all. A discharge is not a reliable sign of candidiasis, even though many people think that it is the cardinal symptom. Sometimes a thin discharge is produced. A laboratory test is needed to establish what the condition really is.

131

Children In young children thrush usually appears in the mouth, when the yeast cells multiply and produce whitish patches inside the cheeks. The disease can be picked up by newborn babies from a virulent strain of the organism present in the mother's vagina, but a constitutional upset may well lead to an attack of thrush from organisms normally quietly resident in the mouth. But this is not certain: more than one microbiologist has concluded that the disease-causing varieties of the fungus are *always* disease-causing. If that is so then a child with thrush must have caught it. As yet scientific knowledge is insufficient to draw firm conclusions.

Treatment

For most cases, treatment is by creams and pessaries containing antifungal substances. There are two groups of antibiotic in use at present, the polyene drugs and the imidazole group. Both are said to produce high rates of cure. Pessaries alone are not as effective as pessaries and cream used together, and treatment of the partner is always important. The cure rates are higher if the treatment is kept up for a fortnight. But many patients (about half of them, says one report) discontinue the treatment once the symptoms have disappeared, and they may relapse in time.

You do not have to rely on medicines. Boric acid wash can help to relieve the condition, so can potassium sorbate. There are even reports that ultrafine aluminium powder or a liberal application of natural yoghourt can provide satisfactory treatment.

The main way to avoid thrush is to allow the genitals to have a light and airy environment. The future may bring perfection of a pill that can be swallowed. One has been tried with success. It is Ketoconazole and a three-day course of five tablets a day seems enough to cure candidiasis in more than 90 per cent of cases. Another possibility is the use of pessaries of the Clotrimazole type, which prevents thrush from appearing.

In a small number of women patients the disease recurs after treatment. Some put up with the itching for years. One thing a doctor can do is to find out if reinfection is taking place. The yeasts can live under the nails, in the mouth, or in the intestines. Are they being picked up from recycled underwear? Cotton undergarments should be used and must be boiled. The sexual partner needs investigation and towels should be properly sterilized during the washing cycle.

In these difficult cases a sympathetic and committed doctor is the prime requisite for any women. The feeling of being 'fobbed off' can be exceedingly damaging and the fact that the disease is not life-threatening can never be a reason for dismissing the sufferer as though it did not matter.

Candida albicans is not the only cause of thrush, even though it is the commonest one. A proportion of cases (less than 10 per cent in a typical STD clinic) are caused by a different yeast, *Torulopsis glabrata*. The symptoms are similar, however, and the treatment is the same. Together, these organisms are responsible for the greatest number of vaginal infections out of all the sex-related diseases, so they have to be taken seriously.

CHANCROID

This disease, known also as *ulcus molle* and more popularly as soft chancre (soft sore) is now rare in temperate countries. It is caused by a bacterium discovered in 1889 by a microbiologist named Ducrey and was named in commemoration of his observations *Haemophilus ducreyi*. In the East and in tropical and subtropical countries it is far commoner and in some places is the most common disease causing genital ulceration.

Symptoms

The disease has an unusually short incubation period for such illnesses, often just a few days, and perhaps just one. Occasional cases complicate the picture by taking as long as a month to appear. Like syphilis, there may be a single sore, but there can be several. The sore is usually found on the genitals; there is not the wide geographical spread of syphilitic lesions. The initial lesion erupts into a painful sore with ragged edges, quite unlike the chancre of a syphilis which is hard, regular and painless. Also, in chancroid the sores bleed easily when picked or disturbed.

In women the commonest areas for the infection are the vulva, around the anus and on the thighs; in men the ulcer is almost always on the penis. If anal intercourse has taken place, the ulcers may be around the anus and cause great pain on defecation. Usually more than one ulcer is present.

In most patients, the lymph glands, on the side of the ulcers, rapidly enlarge, becoming tender and finally forming a painful

133

abscess (called a bubo), which will usually burst, producing purulent fluid.

Healing takes place gradually with a considerable amount of scarring that deforms the shape of the penis or vulva.

Causes

It is true that the ducreyi bacillus causes chancroid, but there are difficulties. The bacteria can be isolated in many cases, but it is not always possible to be absolutely certain that the disease has been caused by the germ. In some cases other organisms are present too, as in the unusual *phagedenic chancroid*, when organisms known as Vincent's bacteria (see page 146) are found. This disease can be so serious that it destroys the genitals entirely in a relatively short time. It is the Vincent's bacteria, rather than the true ducreyi bacillus of classical chancroid, which produces the serious effects.

Treatment

As might be expected when the exact cause of the disease is not certain, there have been varied reports about the best means of treatment. Sulphonamide has been the drug of choice since before World War II, though in countries ranging from Singapore to Zimbabwe come reports that a percentage of patients fail to respond to the drugs. Tetracycline seemed promising when it was introduced, though some trials in Vietnam showed that it had a proportion of failures. Doxycycline has proved to be effective, but it apparently masks the existence of a concurrent infection with syphilis and that could be dangerous in the long term, so the use of this drug is carefully limited.

Penicillin has been used, though a strain of *H. ducreyi* which can produce ß-lactamase has been isolated. This enzyme destroys the penicillin, allowing the bacteria to survive. Perhaps the best results have been obtained by using streptomycin. Another approach is the application of a combination of tetracycline and sulphonamide.

There are many possible treatments for the condition. This in itself suggestive that in chancroid we may have not a single disease, but rather a group of diseases caused by different organisms. If that proves to be so, then it would be best if the term chancroid was restricted only to those cases where an infection with *H. ducreyi* has been proved beyond doubt. The rest would be better known as *chancroidal ulcers*.

Victims should not be discouraged if the doctors admit they cannot be definitively sure about the cause of a specific case. If one treatment fails, there is likely to be an alternative that will work.

At least 25 per cent of patients with chancroid will have some type of STD, most commonly gonorrhoea or syphilis, so it is essential that these should be looked for and a definite diagnosis made. If an additional STD is found, it must be treated independently of the treatment for chancroid.

CLAP

A lay term for gonorrhoea (see page 140). There are similar words in old French (*clapoir*) and early Dutch (*klapoore*), meaning a sexual sore; it may be that they are the source of the slang term in English.

CRABS

The crab louse, *Phthirius pubis*, is a tiny insect with a tapering rounded body and stubby legs which in an adult span 2mm. The adult lice have a body the size of a large full stop and the claws on the appendages are evolved to attach firmly to the crinkled hair of the pubis, the armpit and even, sometimes, the eyebrows. They never seem to infest the scalp, apparently because head hair grows too closely for the lice to have room to mate.

Crabs can be picked up from lavatory seats, and from bedding or infested towels. Nurses, ambulancemen and police officers can catch the lice when attending accident victims. Usually, however, the lice are acquired directly through sexual contact. As with scabies (see page 172), the itching that is often the first sign of an attack is produced not by the mechanical action of the lice, but through the development of sensitivity. For this reason, the creatures are often well established before the symptoms begin to manifest themselves.

The life-cycle of the louse begins when eggs are laid by the female adult at or near the base of the (pubic) hair. These, the nits, take more than a week to mature and they then hatch out into minute versions of the adult. They feed exclusively on human blood which they drink through a small puncture wound. The adult lice are a steely grey colour and look rather like little pinheads.

Treatment usually involves dicophane, painted over the skin. If the pubic hair is all that is affected, then the region of the body covered by the treatment emulsion should extend up as far as the waist and down as far as the knees, with particular attention being paid to the hair around the anus and the pubis. Malathion preparations are also used and may be an improvement, since malathion is able to penetrate the egg case of the nit and kill the embryonic lice before they develop fully and hatch.

CYTO-MEGALOVIRUS (CMV)

A member of the HERPES family of viruses that can produce symptoms like those of GLANDULAR FEVER (see pages 139, 151).

CYSTITIS

Cystitis is an acute or chronic inflammation of the female bladder, causing frequent and painful urination. It varies in severity from a slight increase in the need to urinate accompanied by a burning sensation, to severe pain with blood in the urine, fever and backache. It is more likely to recur in those who have had previous attacks of cystitis, or affect those who have got some structural abnormality of the bladder, or those who have some form of genital infection.

'Honeymoon cystitis' is a common expression for the cystitis that occurs when a woman first starts having sexual intercourse. Usually this is due not to a genital infection, but to the frictional effect of intercourse forcing germs, from the skin, up the urethra and into the bladder.

Fortunately, most cases of cystitis are easy to treat with antibiotics. Recurring cases, however, should be investigated fully to discover if there is some underlying area of infection that may precipitate the attacks.

DISCHARGE

Discharge is normal, but abnormally may indicate a problem (see pages 182, 183).

GAY BOWEL SYNDROME

In the last 10 years the name 'gay bowel syndrome' has been given to a variety of abdominal symptoms occurring in gays. These symptoms are the result of infections transmitted during sexual activity that involves the anus. If the person to whom this is happening has an intestinal infection, the infection can be transmitted to the active partner. Though these activities are mainly carried out by male homosexuals, they can, of course, be carried out by heterosexual partners, with the same risk of infection. In countries with high standards of hygiene, where the water is pure and the population is unlikely to have many intestinal infections, gay bowel syndrome is relatively rare. Its spread in countries like the United States may be due to immigrants from parts of the world with lower levels of sanitation.

Amoebiasis is caused by a form of amoeba called *Entamoeba histolytica*, most frequently found in hot countries. It is one cause of gay bowel syndrome. The normal symptom is bloody diarrhoea.
Giardiasis is a form of the disease caused by a protozoan parasite called *Giardia*.

Other causes include threadworms and, most commonly, the dysentery organisms *Salmonella* and *Shigella*.

Symptoms

Gay bowel syndrome displays a variety of symptoms in varying degrees, depending on its severity, but they usually consist of diarrhoea, flatulence and abdominal distension.

Treatment

Treatment is seldom easy as it requires not only a definite diagnosis but a change in the individual's sexual habits. Even when the diagnosis has been made, and appropriate treatment given, there is a tendency for some of the symptoms to continue. This may be due, in part, to a change in the microbial content of the intestine. Unfortunately, a person with gay bowel syndrome is a hazard to other members of his community, particularly if food handling is part of his job. Faecal contamination of the fingers will transmit the disease to food and thus to others. Inquiries into a person's sexual activities by public health authorities have to be accepted as part and parcel of controlling the spread of the syndrome.

GENITAL WARTS

Warts anywhere on the body are probably caused by the same agent – the papilloma virus. There are at least five different forms of papilloma virus, each form tending to confine itself to its particular area on the body, for example, hands, feet or genitals. It is possible that a person can transfer the virus from a wart on the hand to the genitals and in that way give themselves genital warts. But there are clear reasons to assume that the condition is more usually spread sexually. Most of the people who develop warts on the hands never have genital warts, but most of those who do share the problem with their sexual partners.

The incubation period is typically about two months, though it ranges from one to nine months. The warts usually form on moist surfaces, behind the foreskin or inside the meatus (the opening at the end of the penis), and on the vulva or in the vagina. Warts are also found around the anus and in this site they are believed to be spread from the vulva or by male homosexual contact.

Symptoms

The wart starts as a small red lump that grows until it is stalked. The warts may be multiple and can form small clumps which in some cases even look like a cauliflower. Some can be several inches across, if they are left unattended. Small warts occasionally grow rapidly during pregnancy, though no one knows why.

It is important that the warts are seen by a doctor, as warty growths are also produced in secondary syphilis. The medical terms for genital or venereal warts is *condylomata acuminata*, and for the warty growths in syphilis *condylomata lata*, and it takes laboratory tests to distinguish between the two. Clearly, treatment for genital warts would be dangerous if it was actually syphilis which was causing the trouble.

Treatment

The main treatment (apart from surgical removal of giant warty masses) is podophyllin in the form of a tincture. But it has to be used carefully; it is possible to become unwell if a strong solution is overused and one case is on record of a patient becoming seriously ill through painting on a strong solution immediately after the warts had been surgically removed. Injections of bleomycin have been tried, though that drug can cause side-effects, and 5-fluoracil cream seems effective against warts that grow inside the opening of the urethra. Finally, the warts can be treated using cryosurgery, a term meaning that they are frozen off. Burying a potato in the garden, or any of the other folk remedies for warts elsewhere on the body, remain unproven remedies for genital warts . . .

GLANDULAR FEVER

Glandular fever occurs when the lymph glands enlarge, the temperature rises, and the blood reveals an unusual number of lymphocytes (a type of white cell). This is known as *mononucleosis*. However, several different causes can give rise to this condition, and the illness known as *infectious mononucleosis* (IM) is strictly confined to a single causative agent. This is the Epstein-Barr virus (EBV), a member of the herpes family. Its presence is detected by means of an agglutination test on a blood sample from the suspect. This, the Paul-Bunnell test, was evolved before the virus itself had been identified. So if you have a Paul-Bunnell test, it is infectious mononucleosis (IM) the doctor is looking for, and if you are positive then it is IM from which you are suffering, or which you have suffered in the past. There are now some rapid screening tests available which are of value in outbreaks.

Tests of this sort are important since there are many agents that can give rise to glandular fever, in the loose sense of the term, including brucellosis, toxoplasmosis and cytomegalovirus infection.

Symptoms

Symptoms of glandular fever usually start with a period of increasing fatigue and lethargy, lasting for a week, and then there is an onset of an acutely sore throat, like that of tonsillitis, with a high fever and generalized enlargement of the lymph glands throughout the body, but most noticeable in the neck. There may also be a faint pink rash over the body. This acute phase of the illness lasts

139

for seven to 10 days before gradually improving. The victim may feel exhausted and tired for some weeks or months after it. A relapse may occur if the victim tries to do too much too quickly. Sometimes the illness is confined to a high temperature without any throat or gland involvement.

Conversely, the IM virus can give rise to tonsillitis, neuritis, even a form of meningitis, and to hepatitis (see page 146) much like that caused by the true hepatitis viruses.

The incubation period is between one and two months (so a bout that arises at the weekend has nothing to do with a partner you met during the previous week or two) and in children the disease is usually like week-long, 'flu-like illnesses so the diagnosis is often not made. The main means of transmission in the teens and later life is through saliva: hence the term 'kissing disease' (see page 156) which has been attached to glandular fever. It is for this reason that it is included in a survey on 'sexually' transmitted diseases, though not much in the way of sexual activity is necessary.

As a rule the disease clears up after a few weeks, and only in exceptional cases are drugs such as steroids necessary. The peak of incidence, at least so far as glandular symptoms are concerned, is the late teens and early twenties.

GONORRHOEA

Gonorrhoea has been with us since pre-history. It is said that a reference to a 'running issue out of his flesh' in the Old Testament, Leviticus chapter XV, referred to the disease. The organism is a small bacterium which always grows in pairs. Originally known as *Diplococcus*, it was subsequently renamed *Neisseria* to honour Albert Neisser, the bacteriologist who first recognized it as the cause of the disease in 1879. The genus *Neisseria* contains many other species, including *N. meningitidis*, the causative agent of classical meningitis, and a number of harmless organisms normally found growing in the human mouth, such as *N. catarrhalis* and *N. pharyngis*.

There are several strains of gonorrhoea bacteria, and they vary both in their liability to cause serious symptoms and in their susceptibility to treatment with different antibiotics. Like the treponema of syphilis (see page 175), they are quickly killed by drying and so sexual transmission is ideal for their spread. It is this factor that makes it difficult to believe that gonorrhoea has been, or can be, picked up from a lavatory seat.

There are far more cases of gonorrhoea, colloquially known as the clap, than of syphilis. Levels of 200 to 300 per 100,000 population are common in Western countries, though the extent of the problem is uncertain. In the same year, for instance, two authorities estimated the global total of cases to be 70 million and in excess of 200 million.

The era of sexual liberation has given rise to much of the mushrooming growth in gonorrhoea that was witnessed in the 1960s. Between 1966 and 1970, the number of cases in England rose by 42 per cent, for instance; but, following a nationwide campaign using television, the levels in the United States – which were increasing at 12.7 per cent per annum in 1973 – slowed to an increase of 6.9 per cent in 1976. There has been a measurable increase in the number of homosexual males contracting the disease, as a proportion of the total, and much of the spread of gonorrhoea elsewhere has principally involved the age groups between the late teens and early twenties. Currently there is roughly one case per 1,000 of the British population, (and several times as many per 1,000 in the United States). New cases in the age group 16–24, however, amount to 400 to 500 per 100,000 a year (ie, four or five times as much).

It is important to understand that about a quarter of all cases are due to reinfection and a study in the United States suggested that a relatively small number of people acting as an infective source were responsible for nearly a third of new cases. There seems to be evidence that the level of gonorrhoea in the population results from persistent reinfection through a relatively small number of persistent offenders. There are no natural reservoirs in other species and it is clear that adequate self-awareness and attendance to public health could greatly reduce the levels in society.

Symptoms

The first sign of gonorrhoea is pain on passing urine. The patient notices a pronounced burning sensation. This is not an invariable symptom, however; in many women *and also in some men* (though this latter fact is much less well known) the burning sensation never appears. Usually about five days, but sometimes as long as

141

a fortnight after infection pus may be produced through the urinary duct, the urethra. This is easier to see in men than in women, and it is for this reason that female sufferers may miss the first sign. The gonococcus can also infect other sites besides the urethra in men and women: in the mouth where it can cause a sore throat or tonsillitis; in the rectum, where it will often pass unnoticed, as also happens when it infects the cervix in women; and the Bartholin's glands producing an abscess (see page 128).

As the discharge dries up, and the discomfort on passing urine goes away, scarring gradually takes place. The subsequent narrowing of the urethra can sometimes cause further problems with urination.

The bacteria settle into the ducts and glands that lie within the genitals and can produce a variety of conditions, some of them bizarre (like the aptly named 'watering-can fistulae' of the glans penis, in which urine emerges from several separate openings, the result of erosion and the formation of new pathways through the action of the bacteria on the tissues within). The effects can produce sterility, and one of the commonest complications of undiagnosed gonorrhoea in women is its spread into the uterus and the fallopian tubes. The result is what is known as Pelvic Inflammatory Disease (PID) (see page 166), which is usually accompanied by fever and pain in the lower abdomen that can be mistaken for acute appendicitis.

The bacteria can also affect other areas of the body in time. The spread of the disease from its original site, known as *metastasis*, can give rise to *gonococcal arthritis*, when it affects the joints; septicaemia, when it spreads into the bloodstream, and occasionally other tissues throughout the body.

An increase in sexual adventurousness has led to an increase in the number of cases of gonorrhoea in the throat or tonsils, and infections in the region of the anus are increasingly reported in passive male homosexuals.

It is very unusual for gonorrhoea to infect young children; in boys it is a rare condition, in girls slightly less so. Gone are the days when gonorrhoea from an infected mother led to frequent cases of eye infection and even blindness. Before World War I *ophthalmia neonatorum* (which means, literally, eye disease of the newborn) was such a major problem of child health that the disease was in 1914, in Britain, made into a Notifiable Disease under the Public Health regulations.

Diagnosis

The main on-site method of diagnosing the condition relies on examination of the pus with a microscope. The white blood cells that control the infection (and which make the urine cloudy when they are present in large numbers) can clearly be seen, and amongst them lie the paired round bacterial cells. The organisms can be cultured on special media which contain factors which repress competitors, and they can then be recognized with 98 per cent accuracy. And finally there are, of course, agglutination tests from blood samples which have limited application when the standard methods are so reliable.

The only further procedure which is now being used on a wide scale is the test to see if the organism is sensitive to penicillin. The newer ß-lactamase penicillin-resistant strain is being carefully monitored in many countries, and sensitivity testing is the first step to identifying this troublesome microbe.

Treatment

Earlier this century sulphonamides were used to treat gonorrhoea with considerable success, but during World War II cases of resistance began to occur. Penicillin then came onto the scene with dramatic results. In 1943 a trial showed that all but one of a group of patients were cured with a very short course of what would now look like a low dosage of the drug and since that time penicillin has become, world-wide, the drug of choice. 95 per cent of sufferers will be cured with a simple injection of penicillin, and other antibiotics are used for those who are resistant, and longer courses of penicillin will be used when the infection is severe. In babies, penicillin eyedrops as well as injections cure without complications.

However, a more recent trend has been the emergence of a new strain of the bacterium which produces an enzyme which destroys penicillin. This enzyme, originally known as penicillinase, is more accurately known as ß-lactamase. Strains of ß-lactamase-producing bacteria have appeared in several countries. The first reports were from the Far East at the end of 1975, or the beginning of 1976, and examples from the United States were reported at about the same time – in each case a strain of the bacterium that seemed identical in all respects to the traditional cause of gonorrhoea, but which produced the enzyme.

By October 1977 the ß-lactamase strains had been reported from many countries in Europe and the Far East, including Australasia (though excluding, for the time, the countries of South America). Since penicillin was of no value in treating these cases, tetracycline was tried instead. But it gave higher failure rates than expected, notably in the treatment of gonorrhoea of the rectum and in women, and so two different antibiotics were brought in: spectinomycin and cefuroxime. These seemed to bring the outbreak under control.

The question of further resistance developing is one on which it is disturbing to speculate. As it is, the most systematic and enthusiastic cooperation amongst public health authorities cannot prevent strains of the penicillin-resistant organisms emerging from less developed countries even if – in some idealized society – the organisms were entirely controlled in a single nation state like Britain or the United States. More threatening than that is the possibility that strains resistant to all known antibiotics may emerge, although there is no immediate likelihood of that occurring. But it is possible that the bacteria of gonorrhoea might transfer the portion of DNA (deoxyribonucleic acid) coding for the production of ß-lactamase from *Neisseria gonorrhoeae* to its close relative, *N. meningitidis*. This would make bacterial meningitis untreatable with penicillin. Meningitis is a more difficult disease to treat, using other antibiotics, and it is far more immediately life-threatening than gonorrhoea. If that happens, then there could be a resurgence of a potentially dangerous disease which most of the public imagine had all but disappeared.

Avoiding Gonorrhoea

If the disease really does spread from foci of infection, as now seems to be so, then avoiding likely sources of the disease would help to stop its spread. It is not so difficult to tell who is likely to be infected, and who may not be; and though this does not guarantee safety it at least helps one avoid unnecessarily high risks. Secondly, treatment, if the need arises, should remain a high priority. Treatment is effective and a cure is still easily obtained. But the condition can exist without producing significant symptoms, most particularly in women but also (to a greater extent than many realize) in males.

Do condoms keep the infection at bay? They certainly prevent direct genital transmission, unless there is a larger than normal perforation in the rubber, but cases still occur even in assiduous users of condoms. These seem to come from genital contact before or after copulation, and perhaps from the manual transfer of infectious organisms from one partner to another. Strict personal hygiene – avoiding manual contact with possibly infected areas – would be necessary in addition to the use of a condom if the transfer of infection was to be avoided altogether.

Finally, what about the fabled lavatory seat? The bacteria are less liable to destruction by drying than are the fine and tenuous organisms of syphilis and it has been shown that gonorrhoea germs can – just – survive in paper waste and towels. But there is no reliable record that transfer of the germs in this way has ever occurred in normal circumstances.

GRANULOMA INGUINALE

Granuloma inguinale is a disease of dark-skinned people and is found across the tropics, in West Africa, northern Australia, China and the southern States of the United States; it is common in India, Indonesia and the Pacific islands, South America and the Caribbean. The organism is correcly known as *Calymmatobacterium granulomatis*, but it was originally named after Donovan, its discoverer, as *Donovania granulomatis* and this is the more popular name. The strange small bacteria which can be seen inside the cells from victims of the disease were known as Donovan bodies, since for some time their exact nature could not be decided. The incubation period is not known and may be as long as several months.

Symptoms

The disease is sexually transmitted and the first complaint is of a deep red painless spot which forms an ulcer on the genitals or nearby (in homosexual males on or around the anus). The spot spreads partly by expansion but also by inoculation of the surrounding skin by Donovan bodies from the original site of infection. The lesions spread only slowly, but can eventually cover the genitals and extend into the groin. In women the disease spreads to the cervix, involving the vagina. In unusually severe cases there is a loss of tissue, with the production of offensive deep sores,

145

particularly when other organisms (such as Vincent's organisms) colonize the area.

The disease is diagnosed chiefly by the staining of smears taken from sores using microspical stains. The characteristic Donovan bacteria have a strange appearance, looking rounded and elongated and with a pale centre. The two densely staining ends of the cell make each one look rather like a safety pin. The diagnosis is quite certain.

Treatment

The main drugs used to treat this condition are tetracycline, chlortetracycline and oxytetracyline, though some other antibiotics (gentamycin and lincomycin) are used and sulphonamide and the penicillin group are both employed to control simultaneous infections with other organisms.

HEPATITIS

The condition of viral hepatitis is produced when a virus invades the liver and interferes with its normal function. A number of viruses can be responsible, some of them not normally thought of as 'hepatitis viruses' at all. The Epstein-Barr virus (EBV) which causes GLANDULAR FEVER can bring on hepatitis, as can cytomegalovirus (CMV). The hepatitis viruses themselves are at least three in number, and are known as hepatitis A virus (HAV), B virus (HBV) and a third category which can be shown in laboratory tests to be neither – and which has been poetically named non-A: non-B (NANB). It remains to be seen whether this should eventually be termed 'hepatitis C' since there is no reason yet to be sure that this is a single virus we are dealing with: it may yet turn out that NANB hepatitis is due to several distinct viruses. Until we can be sure, we are stuck with this negative definition.

Infectious hepatitis It is by this familiar name that hepatitis A became generally known. In primitive communities the virus infects children much like any other 'disease of childhood' and after causing an illness (usually mild, though sometimes severe) it resolves, leaving the patient protected for life by the resultant antibodies that remain in the bloodstream. One attack of HAV confers long-lasting immunity. Second attacks are unusual.

The virus spreads mainly through faeces, so it can be transferred by poor hygiene within a community. It also occurs in water supplies. The feeding habit of shellfish which filter particles from water for food has led to a number of epidemics of HAV, since the shellfish concentrate the virus which is then consumed by the unwitting victim. In other cases the virus is spread from a small number of carriers through a water supply system until a whole area becomes infected with the virus. One example in India involved a community in which a high level of natural immunity to HAV was certain, but in spite of that, there was a large outbreak of virus carried by tapwater. It eventually infected 30,000 people – and there had been no apparent breakdown in the water purification system.

It will not do to suggest that hepatitis A is a natural disorder which people simply have to accept. Even in the communities where the virus is a normal part of daily life, it can still produce devastating effects and it requires a considerable public health effort to ensure that the population enjoy the health they deserve.

Symptoms

The normal incubation period ranges from two to six weeks. Even after that, most people seem to show few signs of being infected. For those that do, the classical signs are a loss of appetite, a feeling of listless ill-health and a fever. As these symptoms fade, the jaundice begins to appear. The skin becomes increasingly yellow and the urine becomes progressively darker. At the same time, the faeces begin to show a paler colour. After two or three weeks, the jaundice fades, but full recovery may take some months. The liver, which was painfully enlarged, returns to its normal size and the patient is usually left without any after-effects.

In a few cases, the virus produces devastating effects on the liver cells, and the patient succumbs to the massive liver disorder that results. The liver is the organ which does just that – it makes you 'live'. The breakdown in its normal function is incompatible with survival, and for those occasional victims of HAV the outcome is too often fatal.

Hepatitis A is not usually spread sexually. Since the virus is found in the intestinal tract and is excreted through the faeces, the patient is infectious for a week or two before the hepatitis appears until a few weeks after it resolves. The occurrence of the

147

virus in the faeces means that it is sometimes spread through homosexual oral contact and, rarely perhaps, via the fingers of heterosexual couples. So the transmission of HAV via sexual contact, though now recognized, is not a serious problem. HBV, as we shall see in the following section, is a different matter.

Serum hepatitis is the name by which hepatitis B has become generally known. The virus is quite different from the virus of type A hepatitis and acts in a different way. Instead of being shed into the intestine, and from there leaving the body in the faeces, serum hepatitis caused by HBV is shed from the cells of the liver into the blood plasma. It is not even found within the circulating blood cells, only in the liquid in which they are borne.

The patient's view of the disease is that it is much the same as hepatitis A. The main differences are that the incubation period for HBV can vary from a few days to several months (up to 26 weeks). In addition, there is a rather greater tendency for rashes and arthritis to occur in the early stages of hepatitis B. Finally long-term chronic liver disorders, such as cirrhosis, may occur following an infection with HBV, but are virtually unheard of with its type A counterpart. As in HAV, HBV carries the risk of rapid and serious liver failure with a fatal outcome.

Although HBV is mainly spread through blood and blood products, or by a poorly sterilized needle – such as occurred during the war when many people were immunized without changing the needle, and now happens with drug addicts – it has also been shown that the virus can be found in various body fluids such as semen, breast milk, saliva, vaginal discharges and even menstrual blood. Infection may occur accidentally among dentists who work on infected patients or be transferred by infected tattooing needles, ear piercing and acupuncture.

Many workers in the past have concluded that HBV can be spread by being swallowed in a similar way to one of the modes of transmission accepted as applying to HAV. In all probability the conclusion was wrong. It is more likely that the 'swallowed' virus was actually gaining access to the new host's blood supply through tiny wounds in the mouth or throat or, even more likely, through the area where the gum meets the teeth. This is rarely a good seal. Not only is the gum disease gingivitis a common condition, causing obviously raw edges to the gum margin, but even in healthy people a simple act like toothbrushing can reveal bleeding edges to the naked eye, while red blood cells are often found in scrapings from around the teeth.

Traumas to the sex organs are not usual in heterosexual intercourse, but rectal traumas – which can be severe – are common in male homosexuals and provide a clear route for the transference of the virus.

Unfortunately the infective carrier state of HBV is very common and though the victim may not have any signs of the disease, unless detected by laboratory tests, there is always a potential source of infection. In many tropical countries where a standard of hygiene is low, HBV is found in a much younger age group. It is likely that some of those infected were infected before birth, across the placenta from a mother who is a carrier, or during early childhood when minor abrasions are common and close physical proximity to other children and adults makes the transmission much easier.

How widespread the problem really is can be debated. A high level reported in a group of prostitutes by one worker will bring another report that similarly high levels have been found in celibate communities in religious orders. But what cannot be denied is that levels of virus in homosexual communities seem to be very much higher than the levels found in volunteer blood donors undergoing routine blood tests. That, coupled with the fact that a blood route for the spread of the virus is easily demonstrated in homosexual practices, makes a sexual route for dissemination of HBV obviously possible. For that reason, any person who is a victim of the disease should realise that they run a risk of infecting sexual partners.

Treatment

There is no specific cure for virus hepatitis. The mainstay of management is caring for the patient while the disease takes its course. However, there are measures that can be taken to limit the extent of the symptoms, to reduce the likelihood that a contact will develop the disease, and to protect people around patients from catching it themselves.

The victim of hepatitis A usually suffers 'a bout of hepatitis' and recovers. It is cases of type B that require more by way of management. High on the list of measures that minimise the effects of hepatitis in both groups is avoiding the intake of

149

substances such as drugs or alcohol that themselves place a strain on the liver.

Alcohol must be avoided for six months. The molecule of ethanol (the kind of alcohol we drink), places a load on the liver cells, which is why excessive consumption can cause severe damage to the liver in an otherwise healthy person. Eliminating ethanol from the daily intake relieves the liver of one great source of metabolic stress. But the avoidance must be total.

There are drugs which may have an application in the management of hepatitis, including some steroids, and azathioprine which is an immunosuppressant and is also employed in the management of transplant patients. However, these are usually tried in chronically ill patients and the results have not been reliable.

Transmission

The fact that the virus is present in serum and in many of the body's secretions (that may actually be 'all', not 'many') makes victims of hepatitis B a highly infective source of the disease if they are careless. Blood from a wound or serum from a spot or a scratch will contain virus, so care must be taken if a person has a cut – and medical attendants after blood samples should be aware of the fact, as should the patient's dentist.

All needles are a source of danger. The disease is spread amongst junkies who share a needle and has been a source of risk to technicians, nurses and people in blood transfusion centres. There is no risk to the volunteers who donate blood. They are given a new sterilized set each time and from the viewpoint of infection this is much safer than any of the daily activities in the home or the street that we all undertake without demur. The hazard is only from hepatitis sufferers to staff, who may then be handling infectious products. If you are, or may be, a victim then it is important not to attend such a centre. And attendants should always be made aware of your condition, in fairness to them.

Prevention

Gamma globulins are the fraction of the blood which contains many of the body's defences against infection. It is possible to obtain gamma globulin that will give temporary protection against HAV and HBV. It is common for people going to parts of the world where HAV is prevalent to be given injections before they set off. Gamma globulin against HBV is more difficult to obtain, but can be used for those who are at more serious risk, such as those working with blood products in transplant centres or laboratories. It can also be used for those who have been at particular risk at a single exposure, such as male homosexuals, and those who have inadvertently had blood injected into them. This may happen in laboratory accidents.

Unfortunately, gamma globulin does not give complete protection and the protection that it gives is temporary, lasting only three or four months.

In the last couple of years a vaccine against HBV has become available. It is expensive and requires three injections at one month and then at six-monthly intervals. It gives almost complete protection and can be used for those in highly vulnerable groups and particularly for active gays who have been shown not to be infected with HBV.

Non-A: non-B hepatitis is probably transmitted only by blood products and is a common cause of post-blood-transfusion hepatitis. There is no evidence that it is particularly prevalent in the gay population and it would seem that its level of infectivity is rather low. It is treated in the same way as HAV and, at present, there is no known way of preventing infection occurring.

HERPES

Though herpes has recently become a household word for a frightening, sexually transmitted disease, it is in fact a family of closely related viruses of which only one (*herpesvirus hominis* type II) causes the genital infection.

There are four main groups of herpes virus. The varicella virus causes chicken-pox in children and shingles (herpes zoster) in an older age group. In shingles it is probably an alteration in the body's immune state that allows the varicella virus to reactivate after remaining in the nerves for many years.

Another group, the cytomegaloviruses (CMV), can produce an illness similar to that of infectious mononucleosis, but without the positive Paul-Bunnell blood test. These viruses can cause congenital abnormalities in a baby if the mother is infected during pregnancy.

The third group is the Epstein-Barr virus (EBV), which causes

151

the well-known illness infectious mononucleosis or glandular fever.

Finally herpes simplex, herpesvirus hominis, are two similar but different viruses. A person can be infected with both at the same time. Type I virus produces 'fever' or 'cold' sores and type II the sexually transmitted disease.

The presence of herpes can be discovered by blood tests to detect the antibodies. In some populations everyone has had the type I virus in early childhood, while in other groups less than half of all adolescents have caught it. Most of those who have been infected will not remember developing a 'fever' sore and do not have recurrences. The virus can be cultured from the 'fever' sore when it appears and in between attacks may be secreted in saliva and tears. The virus of both types of herpes simplex retreats into the local nerves between attacks, type I into the nerves of sensation in the face and type II into those from the sacrum, where it lingers, long after the attacks have seemingly stopped. With type II (genital herpes) the primary infection is from close body contact, either sexual activity or by kissing, and not from talking to or meeting someone who has it. There is, however, increasing evidence that the virus can survive for a short time – half an hour or so – on cups, lavatory seats, etc.

Here we are concerned with the type II sexually transmitted herpes virus but it is possible for the 'fever' sores of the type I to occur on the genitals and sometimes for type II herpes to appear on the lips if oral sexual activity takes place.

Symptoms

Though the first attack of sexual herpes is usually the most severe, and recurrent attacks are milder, they all follow the same pattern. After infection there is a lapse of four to five days (the incubation period) while the virus grows in the body and spreads into the nerves. At the end of the incubation period there is a characteristic local irritation and soreness, which on the first occasion may puzzle the victims, who will not be able to find any reason for the symptoms. Within a matter of hours or, at the most a day or so, local redness appears which rapidly turns into typical small, pale blisters of genital herpes. These grow and burst, forming painful, irritating ulcers covered with straw-coloured crusts. The underlying tissues become swollen, inflamed and sore. In the first attack the lymph nodes in the groins are enlarged and tender, and there is frequently a headache with slight fever which may last for three to five days.

The affected area varies from patient to patient. In women the vulva is usually involved and blisters may spread forward onto the firm, fleshy area of the pubis or backwards around the anus. Often the external blistering is minimal and the complaint may be of vaginal discharge, from infection of the neck of the womb, the cervix. In addition there is frequently a burning urgency on passing urine which may sometimes be so severe and painful that acute retention can occur.

In men the whole penis is usually involved, with spread onto the pubis or scrotum commonly occurring. Sometimes urination is painful and frequent, with an accompanying pale discharge from the penis due to an infection of the urethra (urethritis). In passive homosexuals the rectum is the area of blistering and may produce severe rectal pain with a mucus discharge and anal spasm. The skin around the anus is frequently infected, causing additional pain from the ulcerating blisters.

The severity and area involved varies greatly from one person to another. The infection may be only one or two small blisters that last three or four days, cause little discomfort and never recur, to the other extreme of a very severe, painful local ulceration accompanied by a fever and generalized illness lasting as long as 10 days.

With the first infection there may be a spread to other parts of the body, particularly the fingers, if the genital areas are touched or scratched. If oral sex has taken place, then the mouth, lips and face can be infected.

The lesions of herpes are infectious. The virus is carried in the secretions from the ulcers and in the skin as it peels during the two-week healing phase. Once the skin returns to normal, the pain disappears and the virus 'retreats' into the sacral nerves of the pelvis. Reports about the likelihood of a recurrence vary greatly; some physicians find that only one-third of people have recurrences while others report that three-quarters of those who have had one attack will, sooner or later, have another. Fortunately, subsequent attacks tend to be less severe and less frequent as time passes.

Recurrent attacks can be caused by a great variety of stimuli. Unfortunately sexual intercourse is a common and frequent reason and women may find that menstruation produces a crop of ulcers. This may be partly due to hormonal changes or to the physical presence of internal tampons or external pads. In the same way that 'fever' sores of type I recur, other illnesses, particularly if feverish, may trigger off an attack of genital herpes. Prolonged psychological stress or physical fatigue may also stimulate an attack. Finally, medical treatments involving the use of steroids, or other drugs, will allow the herpes virus to reactivate.

Many people who have had recurrent attacks of herpes recognize the 'trigger' that starts one off and quickly realize that avoidance of the cause, or early treatment, will prevent the full-blown infection occurring.

The patient taking steroid drugs, or having immunosuppressive treatment, is particularly likely to develop the complications of herpes, and in this case the generalized infection can lead to the serious complications of encephalitis or meningitis. These patients need particular medical care and immediate treatment to prevent this happening. In women, for instance, recurrent attacks of herpes in the cervix are frequently not noticed, but they are infectious and she is liable to transmit it to her partner already undergoing treatment.

Unfortunately, pregnant women who catch herpes for the first time, during pregnancy, may even infect their babies. In early pregnancy this increases the chance of miscarriage or can produce congenital abnormalities. If a pregnant woman is known to have recurrent attacks of herpes viral cultures must be taken from the cervix and vulva. If they are positive within two weeks of the date of the expected delivery, most obstetricians will do a Caesarean section to prevent the baby becoming infected during the labour.

There is evidence that herpes infections are associated with cancer of the cervix. It is not clear whether the virus itself causes the cancer or whether it has to combine with some other unknown factor, or factors, to do so. (See page 129 CANCER).

Not all painful ulceration of the genitals is due to herpes. There are other causes and it is essential therefore to seek specialist advice.

Herpes is also common in gay communities where promiscuity greatly increases the probability of infection. The frankness with which the infection is discussed seems to be greater in gay communities and a consideration for others – gay or not – who may not be infected is of paramount importance. Even if it is known that someone has herpes it is essential to realize that other infections can be present, so it is vital that a physician is consulted.

It is difficult to estimate the number of people needing treatment. It is estimated that there are 10 to 20 million people in the United States who have herpes and that there may be as many as 500,000 people each year with an initial attack. This is at least a 10-fold increase in the past 15 to 20 years. In the United Kingdom the increase is much less with only about 12,000 new patients each year.

Treatment

Until recently effective treatment of herpes was not possible. Treatment was directed towards the symptoms and not the cause. These treatments are still necessary as they reduce the suffering, even though the progress of the illness is unaffected. Pain-killers accompanied by cold compresses or ice packs will reduce local pain and swelling, and as the ulcers can become infected the use of mild antiseptic solutions is not only soothing but also prevents the pain increasing from additional infection.

In recent years Acyclovir, an antiviral drug, has been found to reduce the length and severity of an attack and the length of time the virus continues to be 'shed' in the infected cells. Unfortunately, it is not a cure and it does not prevent recurrences unless taken continuously, which is both very expensive and may produce side-effects that are hazardous. Continuous use is probably justified in patients with suppressed immunity, such as those taking cortico-sterol drugs and those who are infected with herpes.

Another drug, Idoxuridine, is also an antiviral agent. It has been applied in a special solution, DMSO (dimethylsulphoxide), to penetrate the skin. (It is too dangerous to give intravenously or by mouth.) Ideally, the skin is treated as soon as the first tingling and pain occurs, and rapid and frequent treatment may stop an attack developing. Herpes infections of the fingers are common and painful but fortunately respond well to Idoxuridine. The likelihood of finger infections can be greatly reduced by using rubber gloves when applying creams and lotions.

Recently, reports of Acyclovir-resistant herpes infections have appeared, but these have been in patients who already have damaged immune systems.

The hunt for a herpes vaccine continues. Though there have been reports that a vaccine is being used, it has not been shown to be of significant benefit. A great deal of research remains to be done before a safe and effective vaccine will be available.

155

INFECTIOUS MONONUCLEOSIS

Like mono, or mononucleosis, this is common usage in North America for glandular fever (see page 139).

ITCHING

Itching is medically called pruritis and is a common symptom of many diseases, when it may occur all over the body or locally in the genital region. If the sufferer is also anxious about veneral infection, it can be a most unpleasant and frightening symptom. The very anxiety and focus of conscious and unconscious attention on the genitals may cause itching. The sufferer then scratches the itch and the skin becomes roughened and infected, thus perpetuating the symptoms. The proper course of action is to consult a doctor.

Candidiasis (see page 130), particularly following antibiotic treatment for some other infection, may spread around the anus and vulva and cause intense itching. This is probably the cause of itching that occurs when a person has diabetes. A vaginal or rectal discharge, for whatever reason, creates a moist, warm area that will produce minor local irritation. Any of the skin rashes (see page 170) may cause itching.

Rarely, a generalized illness, such as cancer or Hodgkin's disease, may cause itching, though this is more likely to be generalized than merely local. Whatever the cause of itching, the treatment is to keep the genital area clean and dry while appropriate treatment is given.

KISSING DISEASE

Kissing disease is a lay term for glandular fever (see page 139) – it is thought that this illness is commonly transmitted by teenagers kissing each other, thus explaining outbreaks in that age group.

LICE

The human body louse is *Pediculus corporis* and it is adapted to life amongst the body hair. The head louse is known as *P. capitis*, but though it has its own specific name it is probable that the two are merely strains of the same species, *Pediculus humanus*. They

156

may carry the infections of relapsing fever and typhus from one person to another, thus causing epidemics in areas of poor sanitation and housing. (See also CRABS page 135)

The lice are pale brown or straw-coloured and look rather like tiny flattened ants. They can in this way be clearly distinguished from the appearance of crab lice. Body lice in the pubic hair are often the result of sexual transmission. The condition is easily treated with a commercially available shampoo made for use on louse-infected children in outbreaks contracted in school. After the hair has been shampooed thoroughly, it is left to dry and is then combed through thoroughly the next day to remove dead lice. A second application is made a week later to ensure that the parasites are eliminated altogether.

LYMPHO-GRANULOMA VENEREUM

Lymphogranuloma venereum is known for short as LGV. Over the centuries it has had many other names: panniculus, struma, althaum and inguen among them. It has been known for countless years, and was documented by ancient Greek, Roman and Arabian physicians. In more modern times names such as climatic bubo and esthiomene were attached to the disease. But in 1925 a skin test was developed which enabled the various forms LGV takes to be grouped under a single heading.

Causes

The causative agent called *Chlamydia* is a tiny organism, so small that it was originally thought to be a virus. But in spite of its diminutive size (less than a two-thousandth of a millimetre in length, so you could lie 20 of them alongside a single treponeme of syphilis) it cannot be a true virus. Modern research has shown that the germs contain both DNA and RNA (ribonucleic acid) (viruses contain only one or the other), they divide in half like bacteria (viruses undergo a process called replication, which takes place within other living cells), and they possess a true cell wall (viruses are simpler structures by far, more like complex chemicals than minute living organisms).

There are two main types of chlamydia and each is divided into several sub-groups. *Chlamydia psittaci* causes infection of parrots which can be transmitted to humans and cause a type of

157

pneumonia. There are at least fifteen types of *Chlamydia trachomatis*: three of them cause LGV; at least four cause the tropical eye disease, trachoma; and many of the others will cause infections of the bladder or genital organs producing urethritis, pelvic inflammatory disease, and at least 30 per cent of those patients who have Reiter's disease (see page 171).

Symptoms

The symptoms and signs of LGV usually appears in three stages. An incubation period of between one and three weeks is followed by the appearance of a small spot, rather like a cold sore of herpes, in about 25 per cent of patients. In the rest the spot may not appear at all or be so small that the patient does not see it. It is found on the penis or vulva: if it appears in the vagina or cervix it cannot be seen. It may ulcerate, but is seldom painful. This primary stage is accompanied by tender swelling of the lymph glands in the groin.

The secondary stage may last for several weeks or months. The lymph glands in the groin become extremely swollen, painful and inflamed. There is fever, shivering attacks, aching joints and headaches. The swollen glands (buboes) usually burst and discharge, producing a suppurating mass. It is common for men to experience pain when passing urine and in women infection of the cervix can be seen on examination.

In many victims of LGV inflammation of the rectum will cause pain and bleeding, as well as fever, aching joints and headache. Diarrhoea, and pain on passing faeces, will often cause great distress. Occasionally rectal abscesses and false passages (fistulae) may form, allowing faeces to seep through them to the skin around the anus. In rare cases, LGV can spread to cause a serious form of meningitis or eye infection.

The tertiary stage of LGV occurs several years later when the secondary lesions have healed, forming scars. These scars obstruct the return of fluid from the tissues, due to blockage of the lymphatic vessels, and this produces swelling of the genitals, rather like elephantiasis. Unfortunately, these swellings are liable to infection and the formation of fistulae. Scarring within the rectum may cause a stricture and difficulty in defecation. These lesions tend to be painful and cause extreme distress.

Treatment

In the tropical areas, where the disease originates, little is known about its exact extent. Another question is how widespread the organism is in nature. It could be, for example, that it occurs on the genitals of apparently healthy, uninfected persons and is 'triggered' by some separate mechanism. And there remains the possibility that there are different strains of the organism, perhaps with differing levels of danger to the host and possibly with individual characteristics of epidemiological behaviour.

Fortunately, there are now various tests that indicate whether a patient is infected with LGV and detect the type of chlamydia that is causing the infection. It is a difficult organism to culture but, with modern techniques, this is now possible.

Though treatment with sulphonamides or tetracycline is usual, there is not much evidence that they are very effective. It is therefore lucky that most people with LGV do not progress to the tertiary stage. Usually the fever and buboes start to improve with antibiotic treatment and, if the buboes are also aspirated (the contents sucked out with a syringe and needle), the complications of fistulae may be avoided.

If an individual is unfortunate enough to progress to the tertiary stage complicated plastic surgery may be necessary to restore the tissues to something near normal.

There is no sign on the horizon of a vaccine against the disease. The organism was first cultured experimentally outside a human host as long ago as 1930, when it was shown to be capable of transmission to monkeys. But for the moment, public health research coupled with antibiotic therapy for victims of the disease seems the best answer.

MIMICS, LUMPS & BUMPS

Anxiety about sexually transmitted disease frequently persuades people to put the worst possible diagnosis on genital abnormalities – or even upon what is normal but had not, until the anxiety arose, been noticed. A case in point is cutis anserina (goose skin), a term sometimes applied to the wrinkled, bumpy skin of the scrotum. It is normal for the skin of the scrotum to develop in that way, but when it is first noticed by an adolescent he may worry that he has caught something. Others are convinced that a lump, if it does not mean veneral disease, must mean cancer. And there are rashes and other skin disorders which, while their mimicry of true STDS is not precise, may be interpreted through a mist of ignorance as STDS.

Normal variations in the skin around the genitals, which may be seen only for the first time by a person searching for disease, are hair follicles, Fordyce spots, papillae of the glans penis, smegma, normal vaginal and urethral discharges, and the effect of sea water from damp swimsuits. Details of some of these conditions are given below. In addition, there are various lumps and tumours which may be felt, some of which are of little or no significance. Anyone in doubt, however, should seek professional diagnosis.

There are, however, one or two conditions not due to sexual disease that may cause realistic concern. In a man balanitis, inflammation of the head of the penis (glans penis), and in a woman vulvitis or vulvovaginitis, may simulate real disease. There are one or two relatively rare skin diseases, such as pemphigus and pemphigoid, Behçet's disease, and erythema multiforme, which, while generalized skin disorders, may affect the genital organs with blisters that may be mistaken for herpes.

Balanitis Inflammation of the foreskin is known as posthitis, that of the glans penis as balanitis. The term balanoposthitis can be used for both conditions. The list of conditions that cause this painful symptom is almost endless. Among the infections that can produce it are CANDIDIASIS (see page 130) and TRICHOMONIASIS (see page 179), bacteria of many kinds and fungi. Contact dermatitis and reaction to drugs can cause allergic reaction, as well as various skin conditions such as psoriasis and lichen planus. Both syphilis and gonorrhoea can produce symptoms of inflammation.

The glans becomes itchy, often painful and appears red with, frequently, a discharge of pus from under the foreskin. This is usually due to a mixed infection resulting from poor personal hygiene.

Treatment is directed at the cause, but in some men circumcision is necessary. Balanitis is seldom a problem in those who are circumcised.

Two rare afflictions of the glans are, first, the plasma cell balanitis of Zoon which produces shiny, reddish-coloured moist sores at the end of the penis. It is not clear what the cause is, but treatment with steroid creams and keeping the end of the penis dry seems to cure it. The second rare condition is balanitis xerotica obliterans, in which shallow patches of dead skin are seen at the end of the penis and which, occasionally, extends to the rest of the genitals. It is not an infection, but seems to be due to the loss of the elastic fibres in the skin. It may be helped by treating with steroid creams.

Boils Boils of the genitalia are quite common. They may occur in the perineum, on the vulva, in the scrotum or at the base of the penis as well as around the anus. They probably occur because the area is moist and warm and the grease glands can become blocked with stagnant secretions. They are treated with high standards of hygiene and local treatment of the boil, which will usually discharge. If it does not discharge, a firm lump may be left for some time.

Epididymal cyst see **Spermatocele** page 162.

Fibroma Small, lumpy painless growths may be felt in the labia or scrotum. These are made of scar-like tissue and may be a reaction to previous areas of infection or trauma.

Fordyce spots Minute spots seen under the foreskin in men and within the labia of women. They may also be seen on the lips of both sexes. They are, in fact, sebaceous glands that secrete sebum, a slightly greasy material that protects the skin.

Glands The lymph glands, in the groins, are frequently swollen and slightly tender, due not to genital infection but because they are the first glands that deal with infection that arises in the feet. Athlete's foot (tinea pedis) can cause infection which spreads to the glands in the groin and may cause anxiety in someone fearful of a sexual disease.

Haematocele A blood clot caused by deep bruising in the tissues of the genitals. The clot will, initially, feel soft and spongy, but as it heals up becomes firmer, forming a lump.

Hair follicles Both the scrotum and vulva are surrounded with hair. The hair roots may sometimes feel swollen and, if infected, form little lumps. These may be felt most easily if the skin is stretched and will sometimes cause anxiety.

161

Hydrocele This is caused by an excess of fluid in the *tunica vaginalis* of the testicle. A primary hydrocele, which has no known cause, may make the testicle appear to be several times its normal size. The treatment is to remove the fluid with a needle, under local anaesthesia, or to operate and remove the bag that forms the fluid. A secondary hydrocele occurs as a reaction to underlying infection or disease of the testis. It is then necessary to treat the cause. The appearance of a hydrocele may cause alarm and, if it increases in size, can cause discomfort when a man is walking.

Lymphocele Caused by a blockage of the lymphatic vessels. It forms a firm lump under the skin, near the tip of the penis. It is not painful and does not need treatment.

Papillae These are minute, pointed protruberances on the surface of the glans. They are a normal finding most commonly present near the edge where the foreskin joins the penis. If they are slightly larger than usual they may be mistaken for warts.

Paraphimosis See page 85.

Peyronie's disease See page 86.

Phimosis See page 86.

Sebaceous cyst The sebaceous glands form the grease that protects and moistens the genitals. If the gland exit blocks, the gland may swell, forming a hard, mobile lump. This is not a serious condition, but may cause anxiety to the person who finds one or several under the skin. Rarely, they become infected, forming a small abscess. It is best to leave them alone, though they can be easily removed under a local anaesthetic.

Spermatocele An abnormal swelling of part of the sperm storage sacs within the scrotum. A cyst forms, of considerable variation in size, which may be felt by the man. This is not a serious problem and only needs to be treated, surgically, if it becomes inconvenient.

Tumours Tumours of the genital skin may be benign or, rarely, cancerous. A medical opinion must be obtained.

Varicocele A collection of varicose veins may occur within the scrotum or vulva. They are seldom a problem to women, but in men may cause low sperm count, due to increased warmth of the testis, and thus lead to subfertility. They can be cured only by surgery; if a dragging sensation is felt in the scrotum, a support will give comfort.

MOLLUSCUM CONTAGIOSUM

Molluscum contagiosum is a contagious condition in which spots appear on the skin. They can be anything from the size of a pinhead to the size of a pea and are often a pearly colour with a depressed centre containing a white, waxy semi-solid mass which can be expressed by pressure.

The spots may well occur on the body or the arms and legs, and in this siting they have probably resulted from virus picked up from a towel, perhaps in a sauna. Sexual transmission of the virus gives rise to spots on the genitals and around the tops of the thighs, with sites around the anus in homosexuals. The disease can be spread at the same time as syphilis, and that is why the tracing of contacts and careful testing of the patient may be found even though molluscum contagiosum itself is a relatively harmless complaint.

Self-treatment is possible, though unwise. But self-diagnosis would be impossible and could be foolhardy. Unless you have gained much experience through managing countless cases you would not know what you were looking for and it is perfectly possible to think that you have contracted molluscum contagiosum when it is actually something much more sinister. As in all these cases, it is the advice of a doctor which is required.

MONILIASIS

Until the past few years monilia or moniliasis was used in preference to candida or candidiasis. However, it is now considered that candidiasis (see page 130) is the appropriate name.

MONONUCLEOSIS OR MONO

Mononucleosis (or Mono) is a term commonly used in North America for glandular fever (see page 139).

NGU

Non-gonococcal urethritis. See NSU below.

NSU

Non-specific urethritis may not seem a familiar term of topical conversation, but in the field of diseases of the sex organs it should be more familiar. NSU is the most common disease of this part of the body. As the name implies, there are many causes of this disease. Over seventy are already known.

The characteristic symptom is pain on passing water, often described as 'burning' or 'scalding'. This is a presenting sign of gonorrhoea, of course, and many sufferers of NSU draw the conclusion that they are suffering from gonorrhoea instead. That disease is often characterized by a discharge of pus, a symptom less marked in cases of NSU.

There are many causes of NSU. The commonest, at least 50 per cent, is now known to be *Chlamydia trachomatis* with *Trichomonas vaginalis* as the next most frequent organism. A great number of other organisms, including *Gardnerella vaginalis*, *Herpes simplex*, *Bacillus coli*, and *Candida albicans*, have been found to cause NSU. Occasionally, allergy, chemicals and even growths within the penis can cause the symptoms. Obviously not all of these are sexually transmitted.

Symptoms

As you would expect with a condition with many causes, the incubation period varies from 2 days to 2 months. There may be a discharge, though this is often so slight that it is only noticed during the passing of morning urine, when the amount has built up overnight. In some cases the discharge is as heavy as in classical gonorrhoea. The degree of discomfort varies considerably. In males there may be pain on ejaculation, and sometimes a drying discharge sticks to the opening of the urethra. On occasions a trace of blood in the urine can give rise to a patient's suspicion that they are suffering from kidney failure or cancer, quite without cause.

Diagnosis

Doctors take samples from an infected urethra by means of a swab – a bud of cotton wool on the end of a stick. This enables them to culture many of the bacteria which might be found, and identify them. A smear is another method of preparation, in which a minute portion of discharge is spread across a microscope slide and examined under a high power lens. Some of the parasite infections can be identified by this means. But the difficulty many cases pose is that no causative organism can be found. One technique, which is now being exhaustively studied for the first time, allows us to 'amplify' the number of microbes in urine samples. This method, a version of a test known as ELISA, is already showing that many male patients may be suffering from a *Chlamydia* infection without knowing it. The use of an early-morning urine sample (which has built up the numbers of organisms overnight) is providing a useful guide as to how widespread the condition might be. This is examined by passing urine into 2 glasses, known as the 2 glass test; the first contains most of the infection and is cloudier than the second.

We may be experiencing an undetected epidemic of a disease few people recognize. And it is important, too; *Chlamydia* infections in females can cause sterility.

Treatment

The drug depends on the organisms causing the condition in each individual case. Erythromycin is an important antibiotic as it acts against *Chlamydia* and also against a T–strain mycoplasma germ, *Ureaplasma urealyticm*, which occasionally causes NSU. Tetracyclines are also used, and it is important to remember that dairy products can interfere with the absorption of such drugs. Milk and cheese should be avoided when a tablet is due to be taken. Pulling the penis, or milking the urethra, can make the inflammation worse, and intercourse should be avoided during treatment for NSU. It is important that sexual partners be examined. The female partner, of a man with NSU, should be treated even if she does not have any symptoms and the infection cannot be discovered.

Complications

These may include prostatis (see Prostate Problems page 169), epididymitis (an infection of the fine tubes leaving the testes), and Reiter's disease (see page 171).

The need to avoid alcohol has been over-estimated. It does seem to be the case that excessive indulgence can exacerbate the problem in certain individuals, but in many people a small intake has no effect at all. It seems an unnecessary additional privation at a time when the patients need all the moral support they can obtain.

The incidence of all NSU together continues to rise. Until the mid 1960s in Britain there were approximately equal numbers of cases of gonorrhoea diagnosed in men as there were of NSU, but since that time the number has increased, until by the late 1970s there were more than twice as many NSU victims than there were of gonorrhoea.

As the figures are collected and our knowledge of these diseases increases, it is important to remember *firstly* that much NSU is not sexually transmitted and *secondly* that this is by far the commonest form of disease of the genitalia. I believe we need a new term, *Chlamydiasis* perhaps, to designate cases of *Chlamydia* infection. After all, where we know the identity of the culprit then 'nonspecific' no longer applies.

PAINFUL PENIS

A painful penis may be a symptom of local infection of the tip, such as balanitis (see page 160), or urethritis (see page 182), or externally with a variety of sexually transmitted diseases. Skin conditions may occasionally cause pain or discomfort during an erection. For a number of conditions that affect the penis, see pages 85–87.

PELVIC INFLAMMATORY DISEASE

Pelvic inflammatory disease (PID) is a term that has recently been used, with greater frequency, to describe infection of the uterus, fallopian tubes and ovaries. Infections of one part seldom occur without involving others to some degree, so infections of the uterus (endometritis), fallopian tubes (salpingitis) and the ovary (oophoritis) are often considered as pelvic inflammatory disease.

Though PID can occur without sexual involvement, it is a

common complication of sexually transmitted diseases. It is a frequent cause of sterility (see pages 56–58), pain during intercourse (known medically as dyspareunia), or painful periods (often called dysmenorrhoea).

An intra-uterine contraceptive device (IUCD) (see page 37) can encourage germs to ascend into the uterus and fallopian tubes. This can occur without any obvious vaginitis (see page 184), but is common if infection is already present and even more common if the neck of the womb is also infected (cervicitis).

PID can occur suddenly. It causes severe lower abdominal pain, with spasm of the overlying muscles, fever, backache, and vaginal discharge with symptoms suggestive of cystitis.

The symptoms may be so acute and severe that appendicitis will be suspected. On vaginal examination by the doctor there will be pain if the uterus and pelvic organs are touched or moved.

If the infection is less severe, or the acute symptoms are decreasing, the woman will feel unwell with generalized lower abdominal aching, backache and vaginal discharge. Intercourse is usually painful and leaves a prolonged dull ache for some time afterwards. Menstruation is frequently heavier than normal and accompanied by dysmenorrhoea.

In women with these symptoms some form of sexual disease – often gonorrhoea – should be suspected and a definite diagnosis must be made before treatment with antibiotics is given. If an IUCD is still in place it may be necessary to remove it before the infection can be cured completely. In those with prolonged low grade symptoms, antibiotic treatment will have to be continued for some weeks and accompanied by a form of therapeutic electrical treatment (short-wave diathermy).

Sometimes pain and discomfort continue and it may be then necessary to operate and remove a fallopian tube or ovary which will never be of any use due to the damage from the infection.

Though PID may occur after abortions, and with an IUCD in place, it is the problems with the STDs that need the most careful assessment to avoid further or recurring infections from an untreated partner.

PILES (HAEMORRHOIDS)

Piles, a common problem generally, can be caused by anal intercourse. Sexually transmitted diseases, such as gonorrhoea and chancroid, will make the anal region infected and sore, and piles will greatly increase the discomfort.

POX

A lay term for SYPHILIS (see page 173).

PRIAPISM

A condition in which the penis becomes permanently erect (see page 87).

PROCTALGIA FUGAX

Proctalgia fugax is a medical name for intermittent severe pain occurring in the anal region. This commonly occurs at night and, if there is no serious physical cause for it, is usually a sign of underlying anxiety. Individuals who are fearful that they may have some form of sexually transmitted disease, particularly of the rectum, may unconsciously simulate the symptoms of the disease that they fear they have caught. The diagnosis of proctalgia fugax has to be made by a doctor, who excludes any physical cause for the pain and is then able to reassure the patient that disease is absent but that fear of the disease is the cause of the problem.

PROCTITIS

Proctitis is an inflammation of the last part of the intestine, the rectum. There are many different causes and it may be part of a general intestine disorder, such as ulcerative colitis or amoebic dysentery. Less frequently, it can be associated with sexually transmitted diseases and damaging sexual activity. Local infection may result from those, of either sex, who have had anal intercourse, though it is commoner with gays.

Symptoms of diarrhoea, often with pain, sometimes accompanied by blood and mucus, are frequent complaints. In severe infections the person may have a fever and feel generally ill.

Sexually transmitted diseases, such as gonorrhoea and chancroid, may produce these symptoms, but in recent years it has become commoner for other organisms to be involved as part of the gay bowel syndrome (see page 137).

Proctitis may be aggravated by piles and inflammation around the anus with candidiasis. In gays, herpes infection and the spread of genital warts into and around the anus will cause immense distress.

In those who use instruments such as vibrators, or fingers, damage to the rectal lining with subsequent infection and abscess formation may occur.

A definite diagnosis must be made before appropriate treatment is given. It is clearly essential that sexual activity should stop while treatment is being given and, if sexual disease is found, the partner must also be treated.

PROSTATE PROBLEMS

A gradual enlargement of the prostate gland, known as benign prostatomegaly, usually occurs with increasing age. Sometimes an enlargement may be caused by cancer of the prostate. As the prostate enlarges, the urethra, passing through it, is distorted and this may cause problems with passing urine. The symptoms are usually of increased frequency of urination, with less force than when younger, and a tendency to dribble or difficulty in starting. Rarely, an acute blockage can occur. These symptoms tend to appear in the older man. Constant urinary stimulation may increase sexual awareness and, if there had been a chance of infection, cause anxieties about having caught an STD.

True infection of the prostate (prostatitis) may result from gonorrhoea, non-specific urethritis (NSU) or infection spreading from the intestine. Prostatitis causes painful passing of urine, similar to cystitis, and sometimes the infection will spread backwards towards the testicles producing an inflammation of the epididymis (epididymitis), an occurrence that commonly happens with gonorrhoea.

To a certain degree the symptoms of prostatitis and prostatomegaly are similar, but they tend to occur in different age groups. Prostatitis should be treated with prolonged courses of antibiotics to ensure that the infection is finally conquered. Prostatomegaly, on the other hand, can be treated only by surgery in which the gland is removed. Nowadays this is usually done through the penis; the gland is removed a little at a time. This is known as a trans-urethral prostatectomy.

If a prostatitis remains untreated, complications such as Reiter's

169

disease (see page 171) may occur. The man also remains a potential source of infection to his partner (see also page 88).

PRURITIS

A condition which can affect the vulva or the anus. (See ITCHING page 156).

RASHES

Any rash that involves the genitals may cause anxiety and distress. It is not that the disease itself mimics a sexual disease but, in the imagination of the victim, will appear to do so. In many people the diagnosis may easily be made by examining the rest of the skin, where other signs of the disorder may be seen. Psoriasis, a common, frequently inherited skin condition, may particularly affect the genitals but lesions will usually be seen elsewhere on the body.

An itching rash may appear from scratching as a reaction to crabs (see page 135) or candidiasis (see page 130). Lichen planus, a common skin condition, may produce purplish areas on the skin which will frighten an anxious person. Even shingles will cause blistering suggestive of herpes (they are closely related diseases, one is herpes zoster and the other herpes simplex) if the infection involves only nerve endings in the groin and over one side of the genitals. Fungal infection with tinea cruris will cause soreness, redness and swelling around the genitals. Sometimes rashes are caused by contact allergy with scents used as deodorants, detergents used in washing clothes and, occasionally, by a direct reaction to dyes – classically seen in Dhobi's Itch where the skin reacts to the dye (bhilawanol oil) used as a laundry mark in India. Occasionally the allergy is to something used at work, which settles in the clothing, producing skin sensitivity in warm, moist areas such as those around the genitals.

There are many rarer skin disorders that can produce blisters and rashes in the genital area. It is the possibility of sexual disease that frightens the afflicted person. Once the fear has been dealt with, the problems of the skin disorder or infection can be treated correctly and without undue emotion. The important thing to realize is that even though the skin disease may appear to be confined to the genitals, a careful search for other lesions may help the correct diagnosis of a generalized skin problem. See also MIMICS, LUMPS and BUMPS (page 159).

REITER'S DISEASE

Reiter's disease is a combination of symptoms that commonly occur together and are frequently associated with non-specific urethritis (NSU) (see page 164). Reiter's disease, or syndrome as it is often called, consists of some or all of the following symptoms: urethral discharge in men or cervicitis in women; conjunctivitis or other eye inflammations; a varying degree of arthritis; balanitis (see page 160); various skin rashes or lesions; and tendon inflammation, often of the foot or Achilles' tendon. These symptoms vary greatly in intensity and the length of time that they are present: the disease may be so mild that the patient makes little or no complaint or so severe that treatment is required in hospital. Reiter's disease is commonest in young men and there is evidence that some have an inherited tendency to develop the disease if NSU is caught. In the United States and Europe, NSU is the most common reason for developing Reiter's disease, but in Asia and Africa shigellosis dysentery seems to be the usual cause. There are various infections that are suspected of being the cause of Reiter's disease: these include *Shigella*, *Salmonella*, *Chlamydia trachomatis* (a common cause of NSU) and various other organisms. It is often not possible to find any form of infection when a person has developed Reiter's disease.

There are no tests with which Reiter's disease can be confidently diagnosed and the best way of assessing the cause of the illness, which may last some weeks or months before getting better, is to use the erythrocyte sedimentation rate (ESR). This is a commonly used test that measures the speed at which red blood cells (erythrocytes) settle in a vertical tube of blood. A rapid rate suggests active infection or disease.

Though most patients with Reiter's disease lose it completely within a few months, there are a few who experience recurrent attacks for many years.

Unfortunately there is no easy treatment. The NSU must be treated with antibiotics (see NSU) and, if the arthritis is severe, rest in hospital may be needed. Antiarthritic drugs are used and physiotherapy given as soon as pain is decreasing. An important aspect is to maintain morale through an illness that can be pro-

171

longed and cause great distress if it is felt it is some kind of retribution for sexual misbehaviour.

Counselling and discussion about the disease, its causes and its outlook are needed at the onset. Sexual intercourse must be avoided until the urethral discharge has gone and the physician advises that it is safe to start again.

SALMONELLOSIS

Bacterial infection of the bowel (see GAY BOWEL SYNDROME page 137).

SALPINGITIS

Salpingitis is an infection of the fallopian tubes. As the infection is seldom confined to the fallopian tubes alone, it is now much more commonly called pelvic inflammatory disease (see page 166). See also page 58.

SCABIES

The tiny mite known as *Sarcoptes scabiei*, which is responsible for scabies, lives by burrowing beneath the skin, producing symptoms that give rise to the old colloquial name for the disease: the Itch. People are infested through close bodily contact and cases often occur through a single family. Sufferers can then infect other areas of their own bodies by scratching, which transfers the mites. However, it is not the mite itself that produces the itching: the body develops a sensitivity to it, rather like an allergy, and it is this that causes the symptoms. In people infested for the first time there is no itching for a month or so, during which the sensitivity develops and then itching begins to appear.

The irritation produced by the sensitivity is usually worse at night and the usual sites where burrows are found are between the fingers, on the wrists and elbows, or around the umbilicus 'belly-button', the anus and the feet. There may be a single burrow or up to a dozen. Lesions rarely occur on the female genitals, but they are often seen on the shaft of the penis or in the scrotum. The burrows produced by the mites look like dark-coloured wavy lines (rather different from the scaly skin that covers burrows in non-genital areas of the body).

Scratching of the sites on the male genitals can lift the lid off the burrow, leaving behind a long, thin, shallow ulcer. By this time there are often lesions elsewhere on the body (the head is usually unaffected, except in very young children) and the doctor finds it easy to locate the mites in the scrapings from them.

It has been claimed that scabies occurs in 30-year cycles. The last major outbreak began in 1964 and – if this 'rule' holds good in practice – we should expect the next upsurge to start in the mid-1990s.

Treatment

Scabies is controlled by painting the skin with preparations designed to kill the organisms. Obviously though, the itching does not finish immediately, for the body still contains the proteins to which it has developed sensitivity. However, the drugs are reliable and just because the symptoms persist it does not mean that the treatment has failed. It takes a little time, that is all. Even in the worst cases (one or two examples are on record in which there were thousands of mites infesting a patient, rather than the less-than-a-dozen which is normal) recovery is usual.

SHIGELLOSIS

Intestinal disease caused by *Shigella* bacteria (see GAY BOWEL SYNDROME page 137).

SIDA

SIDA is the acronym in many Continental countries for AIDS.

SOFT SORE

Soft sore is a lay term for CHANCROID (see page 133).

SYPHILIS

The story of syphilis provides one example of the way in which the STDs may have arisen from earlier diseases. There exists in the tropics a disease known as yaws (and in South America a variety known as pinta). Patients show lesions on the skin rather like giant chicken-pox spots, which sometimes form ulcers. The initial lesion seems to correspond to the site where the organism originally gains entry, following an incubation period of about a month. Sometimes the lesion becomes secondarily infected. If it exists on the foot it can alter the way the patient walks and that can often be the first diagnostic sign of the development of yaws. After another month or two, further spots appear on the body, though the patient still feels relatively normal and a generalized feeling of being unwell seems to be rare.

Later on – often many years after the initial phases of the illness have come and gone – there may be lesions of the skin and in the bone. Sometimes the bones of the nose are attacked, causing disfigurement; sometimes the fingers are attacked and the destruction of areas of bone in the digits can cause them physically to shorten. There have been attempts to eradicate yaws and the organism seems to be well controlled by the use of drugs like penicillin.

And what is the germ that causes yaws? It is a strange corkscrew-like organism, hard to see by using conventional optical microscopes because it is so tenuous. Brought into view by the use of dark-ground microscopy, in which the organism shines out against a black background, it can be seen as a tiny spiral, like a spring from the mechanism of a retractable pen. It spins around as it swims, darting backwards and forwards at a speed which – size for size – a human swimmer would be unable to emulate.

It needs a liquid medium in which to swim and if dried out it dies instantly. So this delicate organism is transferred from one person to another through the film of moisture that passes between people when they have close contact. It can be spread in a kiss, even by being left on the ground in a water droplet. The conditions in the tropics are ideal – temperatures are often around body heat and the high humidity helps ensure that the organism survives.

But this tiny organism, about one-hundredth of a millimetre from end to end, seems to have evolved another way of transmission that enables it to pass from one person to another even when tropical conditions are absent. The need for moist environmental conditions at around blood heat is paramount. In northern latitudes, we wear clothes that insulate our bodies from each other as much as from the cold. There is no medium of transmission which the tiny spiral germ of yaws could utilize – except one. That is the warm, moist fluid connection that results from sexual intercourse or from kissing. A strain of the yaws germ, *Treponema pertenue*, seems to have made that adaptation and specialized for transmission through the fluids people produce, in substitution for the normal 'home' of the organism in the tropics.

This strain is now known to us as *Treponema pallidum*, and the illness it causes (quite like yaws) is now called syphilis. As far as we can tell, syphilis as we now know it was absent from the northern countries until the late 15th century. It may then have been picked up by sailors with Christopher Columbus who reached the West Indies in 1492 and returned with a strain of yaws the following year. It is said that during the voyage home to Palos in Spain, many of them developed 'Indian measles'. After they were paid off, some became soldiers under Charles VIII of France at the siege of Naples, Italy. An epidemic of syphilis which occured in 1494 caused so much morbidity amongst the forces that the French army was disbanded; the mercenaries spread across Europe, looking for employment and taking the disease with them wherever they went.

By 1495 it was in France, Switzerland and Germany; it spread to the Netherlands and the Balkans the year following, reached Britain in 1497, and spread across Hungary to reach Russia in 1499. It then travelled with Vasco da Gama's explorers to reach India in 1498 and was in China by 1505. During this time it was known widely as the pox – the French forces called it the Italian disease (or Italian pox); the Italians and the English called it after the French.

The modern term 'syphilis' was first used by a Veronese poet, Fracostoro. In a narrative poem published in 1530, he coined the name for the anti-hero (a shepherd) of the story: 'Syphilis, sive Morbus Gallicus', and in that way the disease acquired the name by which it is known to this day. It was not until the 17th century, however, that the relationship between the disease and promiscuity was understood. Until then it was seen as a disease in the general group of poxes – smallpox, chicken-pox and the rest. But in 1658 it was first suggested that 'venereal disease is vulgarly called the French Pox' and so the sexual mode of transmission received recognition.

Syphilis is thus probably a descendant of yaws, possibly brought to Europe by the first explorers of tropical America and subsequently adapted to transmission as a sexual disease. The organism – this tiny spiral of life – is able to penetrate tiny gaps between the cells that make up our tissues, which explains its ability to end up deep inside the body, even into the nerve tissue.

175

Symptoms

After infection, through one of the mucous membranes, such as the vagina or the male urethra or, occasionally, through grazes in the skin, there is an incubation period before any symptoms appear. This varies in length, from as short as a week to as long as three months but is usually just under a month. The disease then progresses through three stages, known as primary, secondary and tertiary syphilis.

The first sign of primary syphilis is a small, painless red spot which appears at the original site of infection. After a few days it ulcerates, producing a chancre, usually a painless lesion with a firm base. It does not bleed, but commonly exudes a clear fluid containing the spirochaete – or the germ – of syphilis. The local lymph glands may also become painful and slightly swollen, but most people experience no symptoms at all. The site of infection is usually the penis or vulva. However it may be found in the vagina or around the anus or in the rectum, particularly in gays, or on the lips, tongue or even tonsils.

The chancre is highly infectious, but heals gradually in a period of weeks, usually leaving a thin scar within a couple of months. In some people the chancre does not appear and the disease progresses to the secondary stage.

Diagnosis

You cannot hope to diagnose syphilis for yourself. The skin spots and rash of primary and secondary syphilis are similar in some cases to the symptoms of dermatitis, psoriasis, measles and scarlet fever; they can look like the spots produced by a range of diseases and disorders ranging from leprosy to flea-bites. Before treatment is undertaken, a definite diagnosis must be made. This can be done only by specialists who have the specialist skills and proper equipment. The living spirochaete can be seen, under the microscope, if fresh fluid is obtained from a chancre or skin lesion of secondary syphilis. In later forms of syphilis diagnosis is made on the knowledge of the type of illness and on positive blood tests. Modern forms of these tests, which depend on the body's reaction to the infection – the production of antibodies – are extremely sensitive and accurate.

It is essential to be certain of the diagnosis as other conditions may mimic the infection or cause confusion. As most people presented with what they believe to be syphilis turn out not to suffer from the disease, the diagnosis that they have *not* got it is of vital importance.

It would be a fundamental error if you were to imagine that a hard spot meant you had VD. There are many other causes of this common sign. Sebaceous cysts can produce hard rounded lumps within the skin of the labia or the scrotum. They are ordinarily harmless. Genital herpes produces small open spots, often in clusters, which some people mistake for chancres, and soft chancres occur in chancroid, a condition rare in temperate countries but common in the tropics. The chancroid sores are often multiple, not single; they are painful, not symptomless; and they bleed easily which the chancre of syphilis does not. Multiple sores are also found in Behçet's disease and a condition that is a form of balanitis.

Two other diseases that produce similar signs are granuloma inguinale and lympho-granuloma venereum, and there are even some rare forms of tumour that produce lumps which people mistake for the manifestations of syphilis. It is important that any possible sufferer seeks prompt medical advice.

Secondary syphilis is the stage in which the organism spreads around the body and usually appears about two months after the initial infection. It causes a general 'flu-like illness with fever, headache and aching of the limbs before a generalized reddish rash appears all over the body. Flat ulcers, with slightly raised edges, frequently appear in those parts of the body with mucous membranes, such as the mouth, vulva and end of the penis, as well as around the anus. These ulcers are extremely infectious. In more moist places on the body, such as the areas around the genitals, around the anus and under the breasts, the skin rash may thicken and form lumpy lesions called condylomata lata, which are filled with organisms and are therefore very infectious. A form of mild meningitis with severe headache may also occur.

The rash and all the signs of secondary syphilis clear completely within a matter of a few weeks and leave no sign of the infection.

About two-thirds of patients with syphilis will not develop further signs of the disease, though a blood test will show that a low-grade infection is still present. In the one-third who develop signs of tertiary syphilis the problems may take many years, often as long as 20, before they appear. Tertiary syphilis may affect the blood vessels (cardiovascular syphilis), produce swellings in the

177

skin, bones and intestinal organs (benign tertiary syphilis) or the central nervous system (neurosyphilis).

Cardiovascular syphilis typically damages the main blood vessel of the body, the aorta, causing it to become dilated. This aneurysm may be sufficiently gross to compress the adjacent organs, resulting in difficulty in swallowing or the collapse of part of the lungs. The danger of aneurysm is that it may rupture, suddenly and fatally. Heart valves may also be affected, causing angina pectoris or heart failure.

Benign tertiary syphilis is characterized by swollen areas of firm, scar-like tissue, known as gummas. These may affect any part of the body, but usually only produce minor symptoms caused by the local swelling. They heal by scarring and if this occurs on the skin the scars remain visible. They may also cause deformity of bones. Any tissue in the body may be involved, and if the vital organs are affected then the results can be disabling.

Neurosyphilis may first develop in the membranes surrounding the brain, thus causing a slow form of meningitis that paralyzes nerves as well as causing mental disorders. It may spread into the spinal area, causing a variety of weaknesses or paralysis. The more generally known forms of neurosyphilis are General Paralysis of the Insane, now a very rare condition, where there is a gradual deterioration in the mental state, sometimes producing delusions of grandeur. This will be accompanied by increasing weakness and lack of coordination, often complicated by epileptic fits. A final symptom is tabes dorsalis, which affects men more than women, and is a very gradual onset of paralysis. It is typified initially by a slight change in gait accompanied by shooting pains down the legs or across the stomach.

Unfortunately, syphilis can be transmitted by the mother during pregnancy to the unborn fetus. Some infants with congenital syphilis will never develop symptoms, while others will, shortly after birth, produce a great number of serious signs, such as characteristic patches around the mouth and nappy area, blood-stained nasal discharge followed by symptoms of meningitis, epilepsy or mental retardation. Other children do not develop problems for some months or even years and there may then be abnormalities of the incisor teeth, infections of the eyes and gradual deafness with neurosyphilis.

Treatment

Fortunately, the treatment of syphilis, once diagnosed, is simple and very effective. Penicillin, in various forms, is the mainstay of treatment. If the patient is allergic to it, alternative antibiotics can be used. Occasionally a severe fever occurs soon after the start of treatment. This, the Jarisch-Herxheimer reaction, is probably due to a large number of spirochaetes being killed at once. The severity of the reaction can sometimes be reduced by giving cortisone-like drugs to patients prior to treatment.

The length of treatment depends on the stage of the disease. It is essential that cases of early syphilis should be followed up at fairly frequent intervals for at least a year. Those patients who are found to have later stages of syphilis need to be monitored for the rest of their lives.

Congenital syphilis is also treated with penicillin. If the mother is treated before the fourth month of pregnancy, the fetus is not affected, but if treatment is delayed until later in pregnancy there may be some signs of damage to it. The amount of damage varies. In all cases both mother and infant must be closely observed for a year or two after birth.

Syphilis is relatively uncommon in Western Europe today, largely due to effective treatment combined with fast follow-up on the chain of contacts as soon as the disease is diagnosed. Syphilis remains highly infectious and until an effective vaccine is discovered – and despite years of intensive research there is none yet – the spread of the disease can be controlled only by health authorities. Sufferers have a real responsibility not only to their partners – with whom there should be no sexual activity of any kind during treatment – but also to society at large.

THRUSH

Thrush is the colloquial word for CANDIDIASIS (see page 130).

TRICHOMONIASIS

Trichomoniasis is a disease that is usually spread by sexual contact, though it can be congenitally transmitted to newborn babies and is sometimes passed on through towels or unhygienic contact. It is a common disease and, in women, one-fifth of whom are

179

affected at some time during their lives, probably the most widespread of all diseases caused by parasites.

Cause

Of the three species of *Trichomonas* that infect mankind, *T. buccalis* is found in the mouth and *T. hominis* in the lower part of the intestine. *Trichomonas vaginalis*, which was discovered in 1836, is the species that causes genital infections. In Britain there may be something like 20,000 cases at any one time, about a tenth of them in men, though one survey suggested that 16 per cent of children in the first year of life showed the parasite. As it can exist in a symptom-free form (and there may even be relatively harmless strains of the organism) the exact extent is hard to ascertain. However, as it is amenable to treatment, and does not usually cause pronounced illness, it is regarded as less of a problem than other STDs.

There is evidence that people vary greatly in their liability to develop the disease: some seem to act as passive carriers. It occurs frequently in people who are liable to other sexual illnesses because of promiscuity. Thus it is found to co-exist with gonorrhoea and the discharge produced by the trichomoniasis masks the much more insidious manifestations of the venereal disease. Though most women catch the disease through sexual contact, it seems that in men sexual transmission is the only way to catch it. Newborn boys do not have the illness, largely because there are limited sites for the organisms to survive on the male genitals, but it is believed girls can harbour the parasites – without suffering symptoms – from birth until adulthood and then develop trichomoniasis.

Symptoms

Men As a rule there are no particular symptoms, though a few patients may notice a slight discharge and a passing tenderness on passing urine. It is a cause of non-specific urethritis (NSU). Occasionally, however, the disease can lead to an easily visible discharge and to pain in the urethra, which can make it impossible to maintain an erection. Men with a long foreskin will tend to harbour the organism more than men without and there can be irritation, while in severe cases the organisms can penetrate into the structures of the scrotum and even the prostate gland, causing chronic symptoms.

Women Many women suffer virtually no symptoms at all and in others the only sign is a slight vaginal discharge which requires little special attention. In more severe cases the discharge becomes heavy and offensive. The greenish-yellow fluid carrying the organisms across the skin around the genitals can produce a rash that can become painful and make walking uncomfortable. The discharge, if heavy enough, may have a characteristic odour of hay. In these instances, the mucous membranes that line the genitals can become inflamed and tender. Occasionally the organisms spread deeper within, producing cystitis, for example.

The diagnosis can often be made by examining a drop of the vaginal discharge under a microscope and seeing the moving organism or by cultivating it in the laboratory.

Children Sampling suggests that far more babies may carry the organism than is generally suspected, but in little girls the condition does not usually produce symptoms. When it does, the discharge will be examined by a doctor or at a clinic, so that treatment can be instituted. But the extent to which children are unwitting carriers remains to be measured.

Treatment

Several drugs are available and each has a high rate of success. Local treatment, by inserting a pessary, would seem to be the obvious route of administration, but that is usually painful because of the inflamed tissues in the vaginal area. However the old traditional stand-by gentian violet, painted on the inflamed areas, is very soothing, and this is a clear indication to a partner that treatment is under way and abstinence required until the tissues are safely healed.

The drugs to be taken by mouth are tinidazole and nimorazole, both of which are rapidly effective, and metronidazole, which should not be taken without the patient being aware of the need to avoid alcohol during the treatment. Although the drug dosages are rather high, side-effects are rare and the occasional sensitive patient should develop nothing worse, as a rule, than headache, mild stomach upset or a temporary rash. Compared with many drugs that people take haphazardly, those for the treatment of trichomoniasis are extremely safe and reliable.

181

Many doctors say they now treat patients – and their partners, wherever possible, to avoid reinfection – with single large doses, with effective cures in more than 95 per cent of cases. The introduction of other drugs in the metronidazole group means that the range of possible treatments is now impressively wide. The single dose, usually of 2gm of the drug, seems to be the correct answer to this irritating and sometimes distressing condition.

URETHRAL DISCHARGE

Urethral discharge is a symptom, not a disease. It may not even be a sign of infection. The lining of the healthy urethra is covered with tiny glands that secrete clear mucus to protect the membrane against infection. This mucus is washed out every time urine is passed but, overnight, enough may have formed to leave a slight sticky 'discharge' at the tip of the penis. This is normal and healthy.

The amount of mucus formed is greatly increased during sexual excitement (it acts as a lubricant for intercourse) and may cause sufficient moistness to cause embarrassment. If the man is fearful that he has a sexual disease, this moistness may seem to be a sign of infection. Self-examination of the penis and massaging it to see if more discharge occurs will, by irritating the urethra, produce the 'discharge' that is feared.

Occasionally constipation in young men, causing straining during defecation, will produce a very small amount of milky fluid from the penis. This is semen, and it is more likely to occur if ejaculation has not recently taken place. It is produced by pressure on the prostate gland and seminal vesicles during forced defecation. These are normal, healthy forms of urethral discharge. An abnormal discharge frequently causes discomfort, is discoloured (often yellow or grey-white) and will be found staining the underclothing. See URETHRITIS, NSU (page 164), PROSTATE PROBLEMS (page 169), GONORRHOEA (page 140).

URETHRITIS

Urethritis is an inflammation or infection of the urethra. In women urethritis produces a discharge but, because the urethra is much shorter than in men, it may be more difficult to see and, since it mixes with the vaginal secretions, may not be noticed. Pain and frequency of micturition are suggestive of cystitis, but the urine may be clear of infection before it enters the urethra. In women urethritis is sometimes called the urethral syndrome, a term that is not very helpful and may confuse the patient.

In men urethritis is always a serious symptom but in women it may sometimes be associated with vaginitis or over-vigorous sexual intercourse that temporarily bruises and damages the urethra, allowing a mild infection to take place. This is a common cause of the so-called 'honeymoon cystitis' and is usually due to an organism found in the intestine, *E. coli*.

Urethritis, in either sex, can be due to any of the sexually transmitted diseases. In men it may be associated with infection of the prostate gland (prostatitis). It is essential that a definite diagnosis of the cause is made by examining the discharge under the microscope, when the organisms of gonorrhoea or syphilis may be seen, and by culturing it in the laboratory – not only to discover the cause, but also to find out which are the best antibiotics to be used for treatment. Gonorrhoea and syphilis are specific causes of urethritis. If they are not present the discharge is called non-specific urethritis (NSU).

Occasionally urethritis can occur from self-treatment with anti-septics when the person is fearful of having caught a sexual disease. Injection of antiseptics, in cream or fluid form, into the urethra will confirm the person's worst fears by apparently creating a discharge.

VAGINAL DISCHARGE

Some degree of vaginal discharge is normal and healthy. The amount will vary from time to time. A newborn baby girl may have a considerable amount of vaginal moistness, in response to its mother's hormones, which circulate in its body for some time after childbirth. Young girls and women past the menopause will have only a slight dampness. At puberty there is an increase in healthy, normal, clear, slightly sticky discharge, but it may be sufficient to cause concern if the pants are dampened. Within the normal menstrual cycle most women will notice a fluctuation in their vaginal secretions, often increasing mid-cycle and just before a period. Indeed, a few women can detect changes in the stickiness of secretions from the cervix that indicate the time of ovulation (known as Billing's method of detecting the 'dangerous days').

Sexual stimulation, either emotional or physical, will cause a rapid increase in vaginal secretions, which act as a lubricant during intercourse. It must be remembered that contraceptive foams, jellies and creams will also appear to be a vaginal discharge when, in fact, they are nothing to do with the body.

There is always an increase in vaginal secretions throughout pregnancy and this may be sufficient to cause discomfort during the last few weeks. There is nothing that can be done to control it.

A vaginal discharge is abnormal when it is irritating, changes colour or smell, and is increased in amount. It may cause pain on intercourse or passing urine. See VAGINITIS, VULVITIS, PELVIC INFLAMMATORY DISEASE (see page 166).

VAGINITIS

Vaginitis is an inflammation or infection of the vagina. Symptoms of soreness, irritation, and an unpleasant, smelly, increased vaginal discharge are common. The vulva is usually involved (VULVITIS).

Vaginal inflammation may be produced by local irritants, such as excessive douching with antiseptic solutions, or, rarely, by allergy to contraceptive foam and creams. More commonly, vaginitis is due to an infection and will involve the cervix (the neck of the uterus). It is sometimes associated with pelvic inflammatory disease. Candidiasis and trichomoniasis are the commonest causes, but any of the sexually transmitted diseases may produce vaginitis. Often a definite cause for the infection is not found. Minor damage to the vaginal wall, by intercourse or chemicals, may allow other germs to encroach, giving a kind of 'catarrhal' infection. This is most commonly seen in the elderly, in whom the vaginal lining is less resistant to infections. Sometimes a bacterium, known as *Gardnerella vaginalis*, is found. This does not cause a true infection, but is a germ that normally lives in the intestine. It is not true vaginitis, but sometimes can give an unpleasant, fish-like smell which can be distasteful to both the woman and her partner. It is not clear why this organism should replace the normal beneficial organisms, or salugens, in the vagina. It is possible that sexual intercourse is a cause. However, if it is found, it is very easily removed by a course of metronidazole.

In general, the treatment is directed at the cause once this has been diagnosed. This is done by careful examination and culture of the specimens of abnormal discharge. See also VAGINAL DISCHARGE.

VULVITIS

Vulvitis is an inflammation or infection of the vulva causing soreness and, frequently, itching. This may be the result of tight clothing rubbing against the area; itching from psychological causes, such as anxiety, and then scratching, which damages the skin and allows infection to occur; or to a variety of infections. These infections are most commonly due to candidiasis or trichomoniasis but any of the sexually transmitted diseases, including warts, scabies and herpes, as well as local vulval skin disorders, such as lichen planus and leukoplakia, may cause vulvitis.

The treatment is to find the cause of the problem and then give appropriate therapy. Until the correct treatment is given, symptoms of severe vulvitis, which can be extremely painful and sore, may be calmed by using cold compresses, painkilling drugs and the local application of steroid creams. See also RASHES (page 170); MIMICS, LUMPS and BUMPS (page 159).

VULVO-VAGINITIS

Vulvo-vaginitis is a term describing inflammation or infection of the vulva and vagina at the same time. Vaginitis is usually accompanied by some degree of vulvitis, but vulvitis may occur on its own. See VAGINITIS, VULVITIS, VAGINAL DISCHARGE.

THE PSYCHOLOGY OF SEX & HUMAN DEVELOPMENT

Dr Jack G. Weir

Our perception of sex, and our attitudes towards its expression, colour a large part of our everyday lives. Indeed some psychologists – Freud is the classic example – have found in our sexual natures the inspiration for almost all our actions. Unlike the anatomy and physiology of sex, which can be examined and measured in precise physical units, the psychology of sex is uncertain, a field in which the hundreds of thousands of case histories available may still offer only uncertain clues to the motives that produced them. A unified field theory remains as elusive as ever.

But, even if there is no one theory that satisfies all tests, the wealth of observational evidence available does allow us to construct coherent, even if sometimes mutually exclusive, theories and does allow us to demonstrate that sometimes society's views are based on misinformation.

SEX AND GENDER

Becoming sexually mature is a complicated process that is still only partly understood. It is, clearly, founded on such physical factors as genital organs and hormones, but there are also cultural factors which we take in through the pores, as it were, by following the instructions and behaviour of our parents, teachers and friends, and which vary between societies and at different times in any one society. Together, these sexual and cultural factors determine an individual's gender. Gender, then, is a wider term than sex even though the two terms are often interchanged. Sex relates to male and female; gender to masculine and feminine.

At birth, anatomical differences obviously dictate whether the baby is a boy or a girl. The parents-to-be may have been secretly

187

wishing for one or the other – more likely it seems, a son, for surveys have shown that almost all men and most women would prefer a boy if they were to have only one child. However, as soon as the baby arrives, the hoping and wishing are over. The evidence is clear; the tiny penis and scrotum, or the little vulval slit are well formed and unmistakable. Sex-assignment, as it is called, is usually a straightforward matter.

However, occasionally a baby is born whose sex is not clear. Such a baby is called a pseudo-hermaphrodite. It may look like a boy whose testicles have not descended and who has a small, guttered penis. Or it may look like a girl with an enlarged clitoris and partly fused labia. In either case, the baby may be a boy or a girl, and an expert is needed to establish the true sex and to advise whether minor plastic surgery or hormone therapy is necessary. Where expert advice is unavailable, or not asked for, and a guess is made about the baby's sex which turns out to be wrong, psychological trouble is in store. For example, a female who is labelled male at birth and brought up as a male could be embarrassed later on by an undersized 'penis' and apparently undescended testicles. Swelling breasts at puberty will then cause even greater anxiety. The cat is out of the bag, but it is far too late to tell 'him' that 'he' is a 'she', although some doctors have been foolish enough to try. It is far too late because gender identity is securely established long before puberty.

Similar problems await the male labelled female at birth and brought up as a girl. Only experienced, sympathetic counselling can obviate the catastrophes which arise from the wrong guess at birth, but only partially, and only when these scarce services are available.

Gender identity usually becomes apparent between the ages of three and four, when the child comes to recognize 'I'm a boy' or 'I'm a girl'. A year or so later they recognize other people's gender – not on the basis of a person's having or not having a penis, but mainly because of clothing and hairstyle. Several investigators have shown that pre-school children, when asked to match pictures of the upper and lower halves of naked and clothed bodies, make many errors when the matching depends on genital recognition, and even at the age of five the average level of error is reduced only by a half. Not until they are seven can children be expected to do this correctly, and it is not until they are as old as 11 that they are fully aware that the essential difference between boys and girls is the genital difference.

Once a person's gender identity is established, it is well-nigh impossible to change the sex assignment: there is no going back and the individual has an unalterable conviction of being male or female. However, until the gender identity is established, it is possible to go back and reverse the sex assigned to an individual at birth: the sex assignment can also be changed, even when it has been properly assigned at birth. The classic example of this was the boy brought up as a girl after his penis was burnt when he was seven months old. He had been taken, along with identical twin brother, to be circumcised. The doctor used electrocautery to remove the foreskin but the cautery needle became too hot and the penis sloughed off completely a few days later.

The parents did not know what to do and there seemed no one who could advise. One surgeon suggested sex reassignment, but the idea did not appeal to them. However, they happened to see a television programme about sex-change work at John Hopkins Hospital, Baltimore, and asked the hospital to help. Its gender clinic is the most famous of its kind. It opted for sex reversal. The alternative, a penis made from the skin of the abdomen, would have been apt to leak, prone to infection, inclined to ulcerate, and unable to erect. So, from the clinic's point of view, here was a golden opportunity to show what could be done with skilled gender rearing. Here was a baby boy, normal until the surgical accident, whose parents rightly thought he should have his sex reversed and be brought up as a girl. And there was his identical twin, who of course was going to be brought up as a boy, with whom to compare and contrast the gender development.

The accidentally mutilated twin was given a girl's name and the hair was allowed to grow. When 'she' – for 'she' she now was – was 21 months old, the testicles were removed and feminine genitals constructed. At 17 months, the parents had had to decide firmly not only about the operation but about rearing the child as a girl. That would have to be done thenceforward unswervingly. Relatives and friends were given as many details as they needed and over the years the twins were told, little by little. Parents and twins visited the clinic annually for checks and counselling. By the time the twins were four years old they were behaving as a boy and a girl, and there was no mistaking. At five years old, the little girl preferred dresses to trousers, liked frilly blouses, was neat and dainty in contrast to her brother, liked to help her mother in the kitchen and asked for dolls and a doll's pram for Christmas. In the last report at hand, made when she was nine years old, she was tomboyish but very much a girl. She was due to have female hormones when she was 11 or 12 years which would feminize her body for the rest of her life. Later, perhaps, if she fell in love and wanted to get married, she could have a vaginal canal constructed which would allow sexual intercourse. Professor John Money gives a first-hand account of it all in *Love and Love Sickness* (1980).

That story graphically illustrates how a child's environment influences it to think it is a boy or a girl and to behave accordingly. Society subtly imposes masculinity and femininity on the individual from the time of birth until death. It begins in the delivery room when the midwife, on ascertaining the sex, handles the girl a trifle more gently, the boy a little more firmly. Parents do, of course, ascribe differences to the newborn infant but they are differences which at that stage are not there. When some American psychologists interviewed first-time parents about their babies within 24 hours of the birth, the 15 baby girls (according to their parents) were softer, weaker and more inattentive than the 15 baby boys (as judged by theirs). Yet there was no difference between the baby boys and girls in muscle tone, reflexes or weight.

Parents also quite early on begin to treat their child according to its sex. First-born boys three weeks old thus have their limbs exercised and stretched more than first-born girls of the same age. When they are three months old, first-born girls are more likely to have their infant sounds repeated by their mother than are boys of the same age. Mothers nurse their infant daughters more closely than their sons and for longer at a time.

Consciously, and unconsciously, parents treat their baby sons differently from daughters. After a few weeks of neutral white they are dressed in pink or blue. Strangers can then instantly recognize their sex and treat them appropriately. Neutral toys are replaced by gender-appropriate ones, so that by the time they are 12 months old boys are into trains and girls are settled with dolls. Parents allow, approve, encourage or praise behaviour that is gender-appropriate, and ignore or discourage behaviour that seems inappropriate. Gender-typed clothing, toys and behaviour are seen as more important in boys than in girls: parents do not particularly want a tomboy for a daughter – but having a cissy for a son is unacceptable. Fathers, especially, play more roughly with their sons and use tougher punishments. They want their boys to stand up for themselves, not to show emotion, not to cry, and to interest themselves in manly things rather than sewing, knitting, cooking or cleaning the house. In this way, children develop into society's moulds. Their behaviour, particularly that of the boys, is clearly sex-typed well before they recognize their gender identity. For instance, when previously unacquainted children under three years are paired off, play is more active in same-sex pairs than in mixed pairs. That is to say, before they realize 'I'm a boy' or 'I'm a girl' they sense something about their partner's sex and prefer playing with same-sex partners.

Nonetheless, masculine and feminine ways of behaving and thinking may not arise entirely from cultural influences. The new-born infant mind may not be a totally blank screen on which experience writes whatever it will. Some differences in behaviour in newborn infants cannot possibly be the result of culture. Within the first days of life, for instance, girls react to smaller degrees of touch and pain. They sleep longer and they are more responsive to sweetener. There may be many other inborn differences between the sexes which are not so easily observed, differences between the male and female brain – for what else can explain them? But so far, examination of the human brain has not revealed any difference, although in rats and other lower animals there are distinctions between the male and female brains, some of which may be seen with the naked eye and which are produced by sex hormones. Adding male hormones shortly after a rat is born makes its brain more male, less female. If monkeys' mothers are given male hormones before giving birth, the offspring are more male (but not less female) in behaviour. Human mothers who have large amounts of male hormones in their blood from disease or drug treatment give birth to baby girls with vulvas which may be mistaken for male genitals and who became tomboys during child-hood. This leads to the view that hormonal balance sets off the development of differences between the male and female human brain and that that difference, in turn, is responsible for certain male and female behavioural patterns.

How much these inborn factors determine the different ways men and women think, feel and behave is a matter of continued controversy. Which side of this nature-versus-nurture debate you take depends in part on what you want to prove, but the nurture side has surely gained more points in recent years. If women have been seen as inferior to men, it is because society has made them appear so. In *The Psychology of Sex Differences*, the authoritative book on the subject, E. A. Maccoby and C. N. Jacklin showed that many of the differences are illusory and others are socially determined. But a few interesting differences remain which might not be. Most of these could well be the result of subtle differences in rearing – for example, girls after the age of 10 or 11 are superior in verbal ability, whereas boys are better at mathematics. As we might expect, the authors could find nothing to show that girls are less intelligent than boys, or boys more than girls, but they found nothing to show either that girs are inherently more sociable, more helpful towards others, more dependent, more suggestible, or lower in self-esteem, as we might have thought would be the case from what we know of our young people's upbringing. Nor are girls 'auditory' and boys 'visual' learners, as many people think.

The only clear psychological difference that emerged from the study was greater aggressiveness among males. Females are more likely to express their aggression verbally than physically, but are still less verbally aggressive than males. Society encourages this difference, which affects all ages in all cultures, stigmatizing aggressive woman as masculine, and – with less tolerance – a tender man as effeminate. Even so, there is not that much difference in our society between the aggressiveness of the two sexes. An observer has to spend a long time watching pre-school children before being able to assess the differences in male and female aggression, and displays of aggression are less frequent as children grow older.

Men are also stronger, by and large, like most males in the animal kingdom (except for a few species, such as the hamster). Our culture encourages boys to develop this as an attribute, and so enlarges the difference. Primitive man, strong and aggressive, is thus thought to have employed himself in hunting and warfare while the woman looked after home and children. It is a division of labour that exists in many primitive societies although, despite it, the women have often to exert more physical strength than the men – carrying heavy loads or children for many hours, for example.

Obviously, little in normal daily life in Western society depends on strength or aggression, but to a large extent nevertheless this division of labour persists. Men still generally hold the most prized offices, leaving women to do the chores, although men and women start off equally equipped for all occupations.

Today we have entered a minefield of problems and controversy concerning the exploitation of women, women's rights and the sex war – matters to do with sex differences of any kind, regardless of nature or nurture. Possibly, we are too close to the shifting balance of power between the sexes to know for sure what is happening, to distinguish permanent changes from ephemeral ones, apparent changes from real, and ultimately beneficial effects from harmful. What is clear is that although most of the differences between men and women are not inborn, society thinks and acts as if they are and the sexual differences – innate or cultural, it hardly matters – are hard to modify.

THEORIES OF PSYCHOSEXUAL DEVELOPMENT

There are several theories that seek to explain how the sexual activities of infants and children develop. Such theories are not only of philosophical value; they are used in psychiatric practice to understand unusual behaviour in a child, its significance and its prognosis. They are used, too, as a basis for psychiatric treatment. Some psychiatrists stick firmly to one theory; others 'shop around' and employ whatever theory seems best to explain a particular aspect of a child's activity.

SOCIAL–LEARNING THEORY

Social-learning theory is part of behaviourism, a school of psychology that has found increasing favour in the past few decades. Behaviourists are determined always to be scientific and objective, basing their ideas not on what people think, nor on what investigators believe them to think, but on actual behaviour that can by fully observed in the laboratory or under laboratory conditions. For example, they see how rats in cages learn to solve simple problems. They then formulate principles to explain what happens, and apply these principles to explain all learning. Ingenious experiments have shown how to establish, maintain and modify complex patterns of behaviour, and have shown that these are learning patterns.

For example, in the classic experiments of B. F. Skinner, the founder of modern behaviourism, a rat is brought near to a lever in its cage by using a food reward. The rat soon learns to press the lever when it is hungry, and continues to press until it has had enough. But if from another lever the rat gets a small electric shock, it soon learns to distinguish between levers. That is, it learns by reward ('reinforcement' is the technical behaviourist term) and punishment. So do human beings: human behaviour can be established, controlled, shaped or stopped, and the two most important influences are 'reinforcers' and 'punishments'.

In addition to reinforcement, say the behaviourists, there is modelling on people of the same sex (which they call 'imitation'). Children pick up the habits, gestures and speech habits of adults they like or see as powerful. That may partly be through reinforcement and partly because they are natural mimics. However, such an explanation of psychosexual development assumes that boys model themselves only on men and girls only on women, whereas experiments with children who are given an opportunity to copy adults of either sex show that there is no consistent tendency to imitate same-sex adults. Research on personality features which are similar in parent and child does not show that children necessarily resemble one parent more than the other.

Reinforcement is clearly an important factor in psychosexual development, but biological factors, as we have seen, also seem to play a part. Moreover, there is no evidence that reinforcement is responsible for out-of-the-ordinary psychosexual patterns such as homosexuality or sado-masochism.

COGNITIVE-DEVELOPMENT THEORY

Cognitive-development theory concentrates on what a child thinks rather than (as in the social-learning theory) what a child does. Its main advocate has been Professor Lawrence Kohlberg of Chicago, and it is an extension of the work of Jean Piaget, the Swiss psychologist. Piaget showed how a child's ability to reason and to understand the world round about develops in predictable steps. Kohlberg maintains that psychosexual development is not the result of age-graded social learning but rather is part of the natural and gradual maturing of the thinking process. Children develop their unchangeable sexual identity, he says, at the same age as they perceive that physical objects remain the same. Preschool children, as we have seen, have a clear idea of gender; for them, boys have short hair and never wear skirts. Many pre-school children believe a girl could become a boy simply by cutting her hair and wearing trousers. That is the particular stage of thinking they have reached and no amount of reinforcement helps to advance it. Masculine and feminine values arise from children's need to maintain a coherent picture of themselves which includes being a 'proper' boy or girl. Then, and only then, is there imitation of same-sex models – in order to be masculine or feminine. The theory is that children 'socialize themselves'. Reinforcement and modelling themselves on others only furthers what is happening naturally.

There is much evidence that these processes do occur. However, as we have noted, sex-typed behaviour occurs *before* gender identity is established, and therefore cannot account for it. Like the social-learning theory, it does not account for out-of-the-ordinary psychosexual patterns.

BIOLOGICAL THEORY

The biological theory of Professor Milton Diamond of Hawaii argues that all sex differences, in physical appearance and behaviour, are attributable to biological causes. His theory is that sex differences are established in the brain very early in fetal life, under the influence of genetic and hormonal factors. Within four or five weeks of conception, certain parts of the brain begin to be organized along particular lines of development, and eventually become responsible for an individual's reproductive and sexual patterns. By sexual patterns, Professor Diamond means sex-typed behaviour – maleness denoting aggressiveness, assertiveness and large muscle activity, and femaleness denoting subtlety, passiveness, dependency, protectiveness and small muscle activity.

The theory holds that different sets of brain substance and intra-brain connections are responsible for sex-typed behaviour, gender identity, and sex mechanisms such as erections or orgasms. Males and females have both masculine and feminine sets of all these, but masculine sets are more dominant in the male, and females correspondingly have more developed feminine sets. Because of these inborn differences, even very young boys and girls respond differently to the same treatment. Usually, they are reinforced by society but they can exist independently of this reinforcement. Professor Diamond instances the almost universal tendency of boys to be physically aggressive and to engage in competitive

195

games, despite extreme differences in culture – culture only determines the particular game. He underlines this by pointing to prepubertal male monkeys who run, chase, wrestle and climb more than prepubertal females. He points out there is no actual evidence that society is responsible for the sex-stereotyping of children, and draws attention to the lack of any evidence of unusual upbringing either among transsexuals (who are mentally convinced they are of the opposite sex from what their body physically is) or homosexuals (who fall in love with people of their own sex). Diamond also notes the inability of treatment based on behaviour theory or psychoanalysis to change these people.

The importance of the biological factors on psychosexual development is unquestionable, especially the effect of hormones on the fetus. However, as we have seen earlier, culture plays a more major role than Professor Diamond ascribes to it.

PSYCHOANALYTIC THEORIES

Psychoanalytic theories are several and various. Freud himself added to his views and changed them several times after the publication of his *Three Essays on the Theory of Sexuality* in 1905. Some psychoanalysts have further elaborations, others have produced theories very different from anything Freud wrote. Freud's basic concept of psychosexual development postulated a sort of life force which is in all of us from birth: he called it libido, or sexual energy. When allowed to flow freely, it drives us towards procreation, but society rarely allows it to do so and it gets dammed up. When the libido is blocked like this, pressure increases and it diverts, like a river in flood, into other channels. Many of these channels of expression are approved by society and are necessary for its maintenance, but some are unwanted and unpleasant. At first, Freud used the word 'sexual' in its usual, everyday sense; later he extended it to body functions, for he had observed that adult sexual pleasure is often obtained in ways other than sexual intercourse. Freud noted that an infant gained pleasure – libidinous satisfaction, he called it – mainly from the three orifices: the mouth, the anus and the genitals. In normal development, he postulated, the infant's interest progressed from one centre of pleasure to another over the first five years of life. Advancing through these three main 'libidinous zones' was part of normal physical development, but how well the infant coped with them psychologically depended on society's influence – in particular on the way the infant's mother dealt with breast-feeding, weaning, bowel training, masturbation, and so on. In adulthood, the individual did not altogether give up the pleasures of any of the zones: an interest in the oral zone, for instance, was reflected in enjoyment of good food. But sometimes there was a 'blockage': one in the oral zone could show up as gluttony or a strong predilection for oral sex. In cases of less severe developmental disturbances, it was only when society was particularly frustrating that the libido was dammed back to an earlier stage.

According to Freud, the oral phase began at birth. A newborn infant could be seen making sucking movements before it was brought to its mother's breast for the first time. There were two stages. In the early – or passive – oral stage, pleasure was obtained by biting. Towards the end of the first year or so, as the oral phase moved from passive to active with the eruption of the front teeth, the anal phase began to take over. Just as the appearance of the active oral phase was regulated through physical development, so was the anal phase (the ability gained to control the opening and closing of the anal sphincter). The anal pleasure was obtained first by expelling and later by retaining. While it referred first and foremost to getting rid of and holding back bowel contents, it also referred to getting-rid-of and holding-back generally, to letting go of feelings and to the control of people, for instance.

The anal phase finished about the end of the third year, when the genital or phallic phase began. The genital phase was the same for boys and girls, surprising though this may seem. Separate male and female sexuality developed only at puberty. The source of pleasure during the genital phase was the phallus, whether it was the male phallus (the penis) or the female phallus (the clitoris). The pleasure was obtained by masturbation and day-dreaming. The genital phase ended when the child was about five. Thereafter, until puberty, there was the latent period. In that interval, there were no further sexual developments. Only when puberty arrived, bringing a resurgence of libido, did the individual resume development – this time into adult genital sexuality.

During the phallic phase, Freud maintained, certain things went on in the child's mind. A boy began to feel attraction towards his mother, accompanied by genital excitement. In addition, he became resentful and jealous of his father's apparent priority over his mother's affections. Wild fantasies went through his mind.

They concerned getting rid of his father and having his mother all to himself, like Oedipus in the Greek play, who killed his father and married his mother. Freud therefore called this sexual rivalry the 'Oedipal complex'. The little boy gradually became anxious, fearing his father would discover what was passing through his little mind and cut off his penis in retaliation. The boy would then be like the girls he knew, without a penis. That, said Freud, was 'castration anxiety' and it occurred in all boys during this phase. It compelled them to renounce both their illicit attraction towards their mother and their hatred of their father, or at least try to do so. They proceeded to want to be like father. Residual castration anxiety was covered up during the latency period but reappeared at puberty, when boys had another opportunity to sort it out. If a boy entered manhood with his Oedipal complex still unresolved, his castration anxiety was bound to give him trouble, disguised as some kind of neurotic illness. Unresolved Oedipal problems constituted the cause of all male sexual psychiatric disorders, Freud taught.

A girl's interest also became centred round her genitals during the phallic phase. Her undersized phallus compared badly with boys' penises she might have seen and so arose her 'penis envy'. Eventually she gave up hope of having a penis and came to the conclusion that she must have had one at one time but had since had it cut off. In other words, she too developed a 'castration complex'. On reconciling herself to this disaster, she began to feel an attraction towards her father, which was sometimes accompanied by genital pleasure. She became resentful and jealous of her mother, whom she saw as a rival, and wished she could be without her, like Electra in the Greek myth who killed her mother. Hence, Freud called this sexual rivalry towards the mother and the attachment to the father the 'Electra complex'.

Although it might seem just a female version of the Oedipal complex, the Electra complex was different. It worked the opposite way round. Whereas the boy had an Oedipal complex, fearing he might be punished, and so disentangled himself from his illicit feelings, the girl realized she had been punished and, as a consequence, developed her Electra complex. With girls, it was the result, not the cause, of castration thoughts.

The girl's acceptance that she had been castrated and could never be like a boy forced her on to new lines of thought, leading her to emulate her mother and to the development of her femininity. Her castration complex, in other words, led her to adopt feminine ways and feelings, including feelings of inferiority and passivity. Resolution of her Electra complex left her with a passive aim – namely, to be penetrated. To allow that development, the site of her genital pleasure shifted from the clitoris to the vagina. This emotional shift had to be accomplished before womanhood. If the Electra complex was still unresolved and sexual pleasure still centred on the clitoris, the immaturity would be manifest in one or other of the female sexual disorders, depending on the manner in which she weathered the libidinous phases. Male and female sexual disorders were different, Freud said, because the Electra and Oedipal complexes were different.

Those are the bare bones of the Freudian account of psychosexual development and of the genesis of sexual disturbances. It is the oldest theory currently held, and its high noon is past. Much of the psychoanalytic theory has serious defects in the light of modern studies. Parts of it, however, do still seem to provide an explanation for some aspects of human psychological development, and some of Freud's concepts which were harshly criticized when he introduced them – the idea that there is any sexuality in the normal child, for instance – are now fully accepted. But Freud's pioneering is given little credit.

There are some serious objections to Freud's ideas. His theory of libidinous energy – the concept of the libido being sometimes free-flowing, sometimes blocked and forced into side channels – is not a scientific theory, although Freud thought it was. It was in line with a 19th-century attempt to apply the principles of physics and chemistry to psychology, to make it a 'proper' science, and Freud's theory was an analogue of the law of the conservation of energy. It only looked scientific. A scientific theory, as Karl Popper has constantly reiterated, must be capable of being tested over and over again. The theory of the conservation of physical energy can be, and has been many times, in terms of units such as footpounds, but there is no unit of libidinous energy – if indeed it exists – and so the theory remains untested. Moreover, it was purely speculative and not derived by Freud from clinical observation. He altered it from time to time but he never abandoned it, and it is still used in psychoanalysis and in psychological therapies to interpret a patient's behaviour, thought and feeling. But it does not measure up against modern biological theory.

Take two simple examples of behaviour that cannot be explained in its terms. A baby stops crying on seeing its mother, but resumes soon after she goes away. This may be repeated several times. How can the stopping and starting of crying be related to the sudden blocking and release of energy flow? A bird builds a nest and stops building. If the nest is removed, it resumes building. Did it stop when it had spent all its building energy? If so, where did the energy for building the new nest come from? Freud's theory does not account for such activities, but they are readily explained in terms of signals arising from environmental changes.

To call the first year of life the oral phase, the second and third years the anal phase, and the fourth and fifth the genital phase is arbitrary. Other and probably more important activities are taking place. For example, studies over the past 25 years, especially those of Dr John Bowlby, have shown that the development of the mother–child attachment is the most important process in the first year, and observation of infant behaviour has shown that the complicated formation of this basic relationship does not arise directly from the infant's sucking at the breast.

There are many difficulties about the Oedipal and Electra complexes. Do five-year-old girls really have sexual desires for their father? We have to allow that their sexual desire cannot be adult, but do they have some kind of simple, naive, sexual desire? Freud maintained that such desires were entertained only deep in the little girl's mind, in her subconscious. He inferred their existence from women patients' accounts of how they had been raped by their fathers in childhood, rapes which, he established, had no factual foundation. They were, he concluded, figments of the imagination, false memories, stemming from hidden sexual wishes. Three questions arise. Was this an acceptable inference? If so, was it correct to generalize from a few cases? And were these patients really not molested by their fathers – that is, were their stories actually true? It has recently been claimed that Freud was deliberately twisting the evidence so as to advance his Electra complex theory. As for the other side of the Electra complex, there is no empirical evidence that all five-year-old girls hate their mothers and much evidence to the contrary. Some do appear to cool off around this age, but most remain warmly attached to their mothers throughout their childhood.

The same could be said against the claim that the castration problem hits every child at about the age of five. Some children do subscribe to the belief that girls have had a penis at one time:

a third of the children in one survey thought this, or that girls had either lost their penises or that their penises had shrunk. But even among this minority it was not necessarily a matter of anxiety. Nor is penis envy – when girls start to adopt a castration complex – common to all girls, or a matter of overriding concern for those who have a momentary wish that they could urinate with precision and to a metre or so (several feet) away, or that they could have genitals which they could see and manipulate easily. As for the idea that a girl adopts feminine behaviour *after* recognizing she is a girl, and *after* becoming aware, too, of the anatomical difference between girls and boys – Freud got it all the wrong way round. Sex-appropriate behaviour begins before gender identity dawns, and differentiating the sexes anatomically follows several years after that.

Freud stressed that only vaginal stimulation and 'vaginal orgasm' provide satisfaction for a sexually mature female. During the phallic phase, the clitoris was the dominant libidinous zone, but it had, he believed, to relinquish its sensitivity and importance in favour of the vagina if a girl was to progress to full sexual womanhood. But the Kinsey Report on female sexuality challenged this on the grounds that the vagina was insensitive to touch, and asserted that vaginal orgasms were a biological impossibility. Masters and Johnson continued this line of argument. Relying on their human experiments, they maintained that clitoral stimulation – either directly or by the thrusts of the man's pelvis – was always necessary for orgasm and, they concluded, there was only one kind of orgasm in the human female. It now transpires that it is more complicated than this, especially if emotional factors are considered, and the controversy over whether there is more than one kind of female orgasm continues. But Freud's idea that clitoral orgasm is immature has been discarded. There is no reason to regard a woman who is dependent on clitoral stimulation to achieve orgasm as 'immature' on that account.

Finally, there is no latency period as Freud supposed. The view held at the beginning of this century was that the sexual instinct began at puberty and that erections and masturbation in children were exceptional events, instances of precocity or even depravity. Freud contradicted this and asserted, against much protest, that sexual activities were common in the normal pre-school child. However, he failed to lift the lid right off and show that these activities continue to develop in the following five years, believing that sex abated during this period. Many studies have since shown that although there is usually increasing concealment, there is no such abatement.

DEVELOPMENT OF SEXUAL ACTIVITIES

Details of children's sexual activities and interests are found as far back as in Greek literature and art, well before the birth of Christ, and an open-minded attitude prevailed for centuries in many countries. Until comparatively recent historical times, children's sex games were treated as harmless and normal. But a negative attitude towards sexuality then began to develop, part of it involving the view of a child as a sexless innocent. The notion that masturbation, in childhood or adulthood, was unhealthy and sinful won almost universal acceptance in Western thought. The 'abnormal' and 'wicked' children who practised it were, it was said, likely to end up incurably insane and physically damaged. This denial of any sexual activity in normal childhood persisted for nearly 200 years, until challenged by Freud's *Three Essays on the Theory of Sexuality* in 1905. Yet in spite of the frankness that has slowly developed during this century, children's sexual activities are still often ignored or disapproved of. When they are acknowledged at all, it is usually only in terms of the future, when the child has become adult, and seldom as something valuable to the child itself.

Erections of the penis may be observed when a baby boy is still in the womb and immediately after he is born: there are usually not less than three and as many as 11 a day in the first few months. Because the baby girl has no outward indicator like a boy it is impossible to see genital activity before birth, and observation is still difficult as well as uncertain after. However, moisture in the vulva, first appearing within 24 hours of birth, suggests that girls too have early intimations of sexual activity.

The infants seem to enjoy their genital activity. If, when they are three or four months old, their genitals are stimulated, they smile and make cooing noises. Many babies engage in a simple form of genital play: in one survey, a third of the mothers of one-year-olds reported that they had observed this. It amounted to no more than touching and rubbing in most cases, although there was sometimes a kind of rhythmic activity. Pelvic thrusts accompanying this genital handling may be seen in babies of eight to 10 months.

These are the beginnings of masturbation. Kinsey, the greatest of the sex researchers, concluded that these infantile occurrences were unmistakably erotic and essentially similar to post-pubertal masturbation. (His gigantic survey showed that males masturbate at all ages, from infancy to old age, although the peak age is during puberty, when 95 per cent masturbate. Not all boys masturbate before puberty, but probably all touch their erect penises.) Not every pre-pubertal boy who masturbates reaches orgasm and there is no ejaculation at orgasm at this age, but it is noteworthy that up to 30 per cent of boys aged two to seven do masturbate, according to a recent study.

The pre-school boy who masturbates has little idea of sex – his masturbation is unconnected with it. His penis is for urinating. Even if he has sensible parents who have told him about the man putting his penis into a special hole between a woman's legs to make a baby, he does not connect this with his own erect penis or with masturbation. He may be eight before he learns, often from a friend at school, that his penis has anything to do with sex. He will be nine or 10 before he comes to know that adults have genital feelings and that these are to do with having babies.

Genital excitement, throughout childhood, is sparked off by all kinds of things which are not sexual in the ordinary sense of the word. This continues to be so even when a boy reaches puberty. Kinsey's Report in 1948 included a long list of genital stimulants in pre-adolescent boys – friction with clothing, taking a shower, punishment, riding in a lift, fast cycling, skiing and the movement in a car or bus are among the reported physical stimuli.

Fear of being late for school, being asked to go in front of the class, looking over the edge of a building, watching or playing exciting games and even hearing the National Anthem were among the emotional stimuli.

There is less information about girls' genital excitement but it would seem to be less frequent than in boys. Again, it is a matter of anatomical differences between boys and girls: whereas the boy's erect penis shows what is going on in infancy, to any observer and to the boy himself, and the wave of feeling inside him as an outward manifestation that is plain to see, a girl's genital excitation has no outward sign, even for herself. Her genitals are much less in evidence, and she can ignore them – which is what most parents encourage her to do.

This affects masturbation. A girl can stimulate herself without touching her genitals by crossing her thighs and rhythmically pressing them tightly together and not even appreciate what she is doing. She can easily bring herself to orgasm this way. Indeed, many grown women prefer this method. Girls can also bring themselves to orgasm by pressing on the corner of a cot, the leg of a chair or a door knob, for example. Boys can do this kind of thing, but not easily.

There are many girls who have never touched the clitoris – or rubbed it on furniture – or stimulated it cross-legged. Some may suddenly explode into orgasm while climbing a rope or pony-riding or cycling. It can be frightening or madly enjoyable. Next time, they may position themselves to get the excitement again, only vaguely conscious of what they are doing. They may go on experiencing orgasms for years like this, unaware that the pleasurable sensations have any sexual significance. For all these reasons, all depending on the anatomy, masturbation by girls is almost certainly under-reported by investigators and by the girls themselves.

Watching these anatomical differences between the sexes is the second commonest form of sex play in childhood. Children of three and four love examining one another's genitals. Boys show off their penises, girls can be persuaded to be on show. Touching these mysteries is a great pleasure for them, although opportunities for these early heterosexual exchanges may be infrequent and adults tend to be disapproving as if they themselves had never done such things. 'Doctors and nurses' games are a thin disguise for the true aim of outright exploration.

However, as with masturbation at this age, any connection with sex is tenuous. Bottoms and navels are almost as exciting, as is watching another child urinating. If the child has parents who allow penises and breasts to be as openly displayed as hands and arms, the genital organs lose much, though not all, of their mystery and forbidden quality.

As the child grows older, genital exhibition and exploration continue to hold pleasure and gain more sexual significance, but the opportunities to enjoy them become fewer. At puberty, boys may delight in a girl who obliges their interest in her genitals, but may have to settle for peeping – secretly watching nude or nearly nude children or adults. It is common among pre-school children, as is homosexual play, in the sense of genital play between those of the same sex, for sometimes the other sex is unavailable or the same sex is preferred. Like the sex play between boys and girls, play between children of the same sex is essentially for exploring and exhibiting. There is no end to the fascinating differences between one penis and another or one vulva and another.

Kinsey concluded that nearly all boys, and a fifth of all girls, had some sociosexual play before puberty, but with most of them it was sporadic or even a single event, for all the delight it provided. There is not the driving need of adult sexuality.

As puberty gradually draws on, there is a sexual quickening in both boys and girls; girls start a year or so earlier, at about the age of nine. Girls do not experience the insistent and sometimes bewildering yearning and upsurge of sexual drive which boys feel at the start of puberty and which reaches its zenith two or three years later, at about the age of 15 or 16. Girls experience a slow and steady increase of psychosexual arousal which does not reach its peak until the twenties or thirties.

Often, at this time of sexual development, boys get into conclaves for intensified same-sex genital exhibition and exploration of one another. Penises, now larger, and pubic hair are worth showing off. When ejaculations can be produced by masturbation they are compared in detail. Although this is often called the homosexual phase, there is no real connection with adult homosexuality. True, adult homosexuals usually recall this phase of their adolescence with fondness and regard it as significant for them: they tell how they proceeded to the stage of dating girls, but found that unrewarding, so sooner or later – years later sometimes – turned to same-sex gratification. But heterosexual men can recall this phase too, although perhaps with some embarrassment, as part of growing up and not particularly memorable. The sexual interest of boys is partly self-directed, partly heterosexual. The rapid and exciting physical changes they are experiencing bring boys together: they are narcissistic, interested in themselves and their development. Their sexual pleasure usually goes no further than masturbating themselves in one another's company or, occasionally, enjoying mutual masturbation. There are seldom any strong emotional ties. The boys assume that they will eventually have sex with females and they talk about girls, often on the basis of inaccurate and fragmentary knowledge. It is too soon to date girls – the boys are

still unsure about what to do and lack the emotional confidence
to do so. They may pretend to be women-haters to defend their
insecurity, but would be perplexed if they were thought to be men-
lovers.

The female sex drive is quite different. It increases slowly over
20 to 25 years and is seldom so insistent – fewer girls engage in
sex play with one another during the so-called homosexual phase
of puberty. Teenage girls do not so readily form gangs like the
boys, and seldom masturbate with one another. They tend to go
in pairs or in small groups, and if they indulge in some sex play,
usually do so by caressing in pairs. Sex arousal, even to orgasm,
might occur without them entirely realizing what is happening –
the sensation is pleasurable but vague and not confined to one
small area of the body. Nor do girls usually boast to their friends
about their latest sexual experience.

WOMEN'S SEXUALITY AND MEN'S SEXUALITY

Women's sexuality and men's sexuality are clearly different, but
the differences are not all radical, fundamental or black-and-white
so much as different in degree. Some are innate, many are cultural.
There are huge variations in women's sexual experience, and some
in men's, but this section aims at describing typical people. The
differences exist throughout sexual experience, from arousal to
orgasm.

A young woman's sexual arousal has to do with a particular
human relationship. That may be factual or it may be fanciful –
with a film star, the school gardener or the boy next door – but it
is with someone for whom she feels emotional attachment. A young
man's sexual arousal may also be connected with a particular
person – but often it is not. His sexual arousal often appears on
its own, unattached. Such undirected, unrelated arousal occurs
mostly, and at its strongest, in adolescence, urgently demanding
physical relief. By masturbating, a young man reaches orgasm
and the compelling excitement is over. It could be said that he has
little natural option because the physical urge is so strong, but a
young woman has no such compulsion and may never masturbate.
If she does, she may enjoy the pleasant physical feelings without
imagining any relationship, or she may recall some sexual
relationship she has actually had. That is in contrast with the
normal young man, who cannot masturbate with his mind blank.

He prefers fantasies to memories. His fantasies do not usually involve people he knows. Much more likely, it is an anonymous centre-spread nude in a magazine who is the obliging partner in his masturbatory fantasy. However, his sexual arousal does eventually become attached to a particular person for whom he has sexual feelings. But 'undifferentiated lust' continues to appear throughout manhood, although less often and less insistently as time passes.

A woman's sexual feeling may be experienced in many parts of her body, indeed throughout her whole body. For a man, all the excitement is in his penis. A few men, it is true, obtain pleasure elsewhere in the earlier stages of arousal, if the nipples are fondled for instance. But the penis soon gains a complete monopoly. However, a woman's sexual excitement is not confined to her clitoris or her vagina. Although the clitoris develops from the same embryonic tissue as the penis and although there are as many nerve endings on its small head as there are on the glans penis, not everything happens there.

Allied to this is the erotic pleasure which a woman derives from having her body fondled by her lover. Husbands know this, but often their perfunctory, orgasm-orientated lovemaking is far too much like giving a cold engine a little choke just to get it started. In this respect, lesbians can teach men a thing or two about how to arouse a woman – which is not surprising. The sexologists Masters and Johnson studied homosexual, lesbian and heterosexual couples and published their findings in 1979. The lesbians unhurriedly hold, kiss and caress the whole of their partner's body. Mutually, they savour it all. Only then do they turn to the lover's breasts, stimulating them manually and orally. When they move to genital play, they fondle the inner parts of the thighs, the mons veneris, the labia and the vaginal outlet before approaching the clitoris. By contrast, husbands with a get-on-with-the-job attitude rarely engage in body contact for more than 30 seconds to a minute. Half approach the clitoris directly and seldom ask their wives if their caresses are a turn-on, enjoyable and exciting.

Far from her feelings being focused into the genital area like a man's, a woman's sensation is diffused through her entire body as sexual arousal mounts and orgasm approaches. She feels differently all over, and there can be a floating or flying sensation. She may even be a little frightened and insecure about this body over which she senses she is losing control. More likely, though, she enjoys the piquant pleasure. There is great variation in women's body experiences and in their reactions to them.

Once a man is aroused, the ascent to orgasm is steep but straight ahead. His excitement mounts steadily until the peak is reached. There is the moment of ecstasy, and then it is all over. Distractions are ignored and the nearer he is to orgasm, the more he shuts out the environment. Of course it may not be always quite so straightforward – for instance homosexuals vary the pace, stop and start, allowing themselves to reach a high level of excitement, go back, reach the high level again and only after a while do they go on to orgasm. But for men it is basically uniform, in contrast to women, to whom surroundings matter a lot. The right place, the right time, the right things leading up to the sexual act, are all important. A woman is liable to be distracted. (Even rats show this sex distinction. Put a piece of cheese beside a pair of copulating rats and the female picks it up and eats it while the male ignores it.)

The laboratory investigations of Masters and Johnson showed how susceptible women are to distractions and psychological influences during intercourse. The course of the female ascent or orgasm is different, too. Instead of a steady rise, the sexual excitement rises, falls, rises again in waves, each wave tending to be a little higher than the last, until orgasm is attained. What homosexuals do after much practice, women do spontaneously.

The orgasm itself seems to involve the whole of the woman's body, floating and flying, expanded, distended and distorted, the distinctions between bodily parts all blurred, control lost. Some writers state that it is a momentary loss of consciousness. Judith Kestenberg (in *Children and Parents*, 1975) described orgasm as 'gradually ascending and descending waves of deep tension in the vagina which merge with spasms and sensation from all over the body, ending in dimming of consciousness.' But this is not universal. The remarkable Kinsey Report in 1953, the superbly researched findings which still hold good today, found only a few women who reported this to be so, an instance of how widely individual women differ in their orgasms in contrast to men.

Male and female orgasms differ in other ways. Men can have only one orgasm at a time. A few are sometimes able to have two close together, but they are exceptional. But many women – although not all – can have many consecutive orgasms. By contrast, another difference from men is that some women never reach orgasm during intercourse, and others only rarely. But orgasm is not so important for women, not the be-all-and-end-all, as it is for men. Nearly four women in ten, in their first year of marriage, were reaching orgasm always or nearly always during intercourse but a quarter never experienced it. Kinsey reported more than 35 years ago, when attitudes to sex, and therefore experience of sex, was radically different from today. But subsequent studies confirm this.

The Kinsey Reports, based on more than 11,000 confidential interviews, are still the most comprehensive source of information about sexual behaviour.

It may be surprising that people's sexual behaviour nowadays is not very different from what it was in the 1950s, except that now they start younger, even though 'the Swinging Sixties' and the so-called Sexual Revolution have intervened. The supposedly earth-shattering sexual life involving lots of intercourse recorded in some magazines for modern women, if not a myth, is not the norm. In Professor Seymour Fisher's *The Female Orgasm* (1973), New York University wives (who rated their own responsiveness as a little above average) were thus found to have intercourse 3.4 times a week on average, compared with three a week in Kinsey.

What distinguished these two groups, the high-orgasmic and the low-orgasmic? Kinsey found that the capacity to reach orgasm was greater among better-educated women. This is puzzling because one would imagine the opposite: the educated woman as a sexless blue-stocking. But the link between orgasm and education has since been found in many other studies, which have also shown that women from lower-class homes attain orgasm less consistently than those from the middle class. Educational level and social class are more closely related to a woman's 'orgasmic potential' than any factor – age, religious denomination, degree of devoutness, the partner's characteristics or the woman's position in her family give little or no clue.

Professor Fisher's study also added another interesting factor, the influence of fathers on their daughters' sexuality. Low-orgasmic women thought their fathers had been 'casual' towards them, whereas high-orgasmic women felt their fathers had been 'demanding'. That was how they tended to regard their fathers, although what they recalled and what their fathers were really like could have been very different.

Fisher also found that high-orgasmic women did not necessarily have more intercourse or enjoy sex more. Indeed, too much importance tends to be given to the female orgasm, as Kinsey admitted. 'It cannot be emphasized too often that orgasm cannot be taken as the sole criterion for determining the degree of satisfaction which a female may derive from sexual activity.'

A woman's sexual capacity develops until her thirties, sometimes into her forties, and then stays more or less unaltered for several decades, in sharp contrast to men, whose sex drive is at its peak in their teens, after which their sexual capacity slowly declines. By their 20th year of marriage, the number of women who regularly attained orgasm had increased from 39 per cent to 47 per cent, and low-orgasm women became fewer, down to only one in 10.

The ability to achieve orgasm, regularly by some and occasionally by others, thus took these women years to acquire. Could a physical factor be responsible for this, in the same way that the downward path of men's sexual capacities after adolescence probably has a hormonal basis? Or is the ability to attain orgasm psychologically acquired, learned from experience? It seems likely, and there is anthropological evidence to support it.

Margaret Mead studied the sexual attitudes and behaviour of women in three primitive societies in New Guinea. She found that whether or not a woman attained orgasm largely depended on which society she came from. Most women of one tribe had orgasms but those of another tribe mostly did not. In the first tribe, the women, like their men, were highly sexed, knew about orgasms and sought them with the same freedom as their partners. With the gentle women of the other tribe, orgasm was an unknown phenomenon. Margaret Mead argued that these extremes of female orgasmic experience were possible because whereas men have to reach orgasms and ejaculate to impregnate women, women do not need orgasms to reproduce, and for the tribe to continue.

All of women's sexuality has orgasmic potentiality, to be acquired and experienced to bounds silently laid down by society. For example, some Jewish women who have migrated to Israel from Iran have shifted their sexual responsiveness and the frequency of their intercourse in line with the higher Israeli levels. There have also been profound, similar changes in English middle-class women during the past century.

Here is an 'informed' mid-Victorian statement: 'I am ready to maintain that there are many females who never feel any sexual excitement whatever. Others, again, immediately after each period, do become, to a limited degree, capable of experiencing it; but this capacity is often temporary, and may entirely cease till the next menstrual period. Many of the best mothers, wives and managers of households know little of sexual indulgences. Love of home, children, or of domestic duties are the only passions they feel. As a general rule, a modest woman does not desire any sexual gratification for itself. She submits to her husband's embraces, but principally to gratify him; and, were it not for the desire of maternity, would far rather be relieved from his attentions. No nervous or feeble young man need, therefore, be deterred from marriage by any exaggerated notion of the arduous duties required of him.' William Acton, the author, was a meagerly qualified medical man who ended up in Harley Street with a flourishing practice treating sexual disorders. He recommended that marital sexual intercourse should take place no more often than once in ten days out of consideration for married women.

Acton was referring to middle-class women. Prostitutes, however, who sometimes outpaced their clients with their insatiable sexual demands, were highly responsive, as were most working-class wives. The same class-distinction existed in Austria, apparently, for the pioneering sexologist Krafft-Ebing wrote that a woman 'if physically and mentally normal, and properly educated has little sexual desire.' Acton and Krafft-Ebing could have been wrong, as they were about the 'devastating' effects of masturbation. But other contemporary evidence supports their observation, in particular *My Secret Life*, an anonymous but authentic million-word memoir of an upper-middle-class sexual adventurer. Moreover although the early feminists sought sexual equality, they gave no hint that they were having trouble with sexual feelings. Some sought the right of birth control by abstinence or coitus interruptus, and Mrs Pankhurst campaigned for moral purity (to end venereal disease), but only a handful of Suffragettes advocated free love.

Today, the educated middle-class woman has caught up with the working-class woman, largely thanks to improved contraception. Relatively safe and reliable methods of birth control have replaced the douches, sodomy and abortions which Victorian prostitutes and working-class women employed. Most women simply did not know what they were missing, and sexual frustration was not an identifiable problem. Culture influences man's sexuality too, and some societies require their men to be hot-blooded whereas others demand restraint, but there is a universally predictable and automatic element in men's sexual reaction – not potential, as with women, but actual. This explains, although nothing can justify, the ubiquity of prostitution in the 19th century. A considerate husband could not take advantage too often of his wife, who submitted only to please him, but his own sex drive was likely to have been insistent.

In this century, prostitutes have apparently lost much of their sexual responsiveness. Active and randy in Victorian times, they are more passive now. But not frigid: prostitutes do attain orgasm in their personal, 'non-commercial' sexual intercourse, and more often than other women. And many sometimes have orgasms with a client. Busy prostitutes tend to suffer from chronic blood congestion in their pelvic region, and orgasms once or more a day act as a physical relief. But there need be no psychological experience with each orgasm, so orgasms as such are not a good indicator of a prostitute's responsiveness. The prostitute's job has changed, and a reduction in her responsiveness is understandable. Today, her clients are often shut-in and lonely men, inadequate and unlovable sometimes, physically deformed occasionally, and often with grotesque or kinky requirements. Like her Victorian counterpart, money is the reason for her having chosen prostitution but, unlike her predecessors of a century ago, she seldom sees the healthy, normal man who is simply after straightforward sex he has been unable to get otherwise. The nearest to that category is the man with the Madonna complex, in which sex is irreconcilable with love and prevents him becoming aroused by his wife whom he loves, compelling him to seek paid, impersonal sex. But more than a mere change of clientele has been the transformation of society's attitudes.

Women's sexual responsiveness is greater than men's, and if women are less responsive it is only because of cultural restraints, according to Masters and Johnson. Not everyone agrees with them, as we shall see, but they have emphasized it repeatedly since their first book, *Human Sexual Response*, appeared in 1966. 'Women are incredibly similar to men, not different, in their facility to respond to effective stimuli.' This, together with her capacity to obtain many consecutive orgasms, means that 'a woman has the physiological potential to be a more responsive sexual entity than a man.'

Looking to the not too distant future, Masters and Johnson

forecast an early end to woman's submissive sexual role which has been the convention in our society, and an abeyance of the male's dominance. ' . . . Man's culturally experienced role as the sex expert, as the more facile sexual responder, or the most effective sexual performer will not be supported much longer.' But they warn women not to vaunt their sexual superiority, for that could damage heterosexual partnerships and increase lesbianism. Such forecasts of drastic sex role changes may be unrealistic. It is note-worthy that both the Kinsey Reports and the Masters and Johnson publications are also crusades for sexual liberation, and both, although unquestionably the two greatest contributions to sex research, are a little incautious at times, underestimating (for example) the potentially unhappy consequences of promiscuity.

The central finding of the Masters and Johnson research into women's sexual responses was that stimulation of the clitoris is always necessary for orgasm. It can be stimulated directly (by the woman or her sexual partner), or indirectly through the bodily contact and movement of sexual intercourse. Previously, it was held that there were two kinds of orgasm – vaginal and clitoral – but laboratory experiments by Masters and Johnson showed that there was only clitoral orgasm. The Kinsey team had pointed out that the vaginal wall was almost devoid of sensory nerve-endings and insensitive to touch, in contrast to the clitoris and the labia minora. That finding was happy news for the millions of women who needed to have the clitoris directly stimulated to attain orgasm. They are probably the majority, yet they had been made to feel inferior by the Freudian theory of clitoral-vaginal transfer. That notion is dead and buried for good.

The question has been raised whether the volunteers in the Masters and Johnson experiments who provided the data for their findings could be regarded as representing normal women. And could they genuinely respond to their partners in the 'sterile', 'scientific', laboratory just as they would at home? Uta West, in *If Love is the Answer, What is the Question?* (1977) expressed many people's doubts: 'The study *should* have been called "Human Sexual Behaviour Under Laboratory Conditions Using Subjects With Marked Exhibitionist Tendencies." Most people I know would not be able to function, let alone get off, surrounded by all those people and cameras and instruments.' All of the Masters and John-son women were multi-orgasmic. Yet only 14 per cent of the Kinsey women were regularly so. Perhaps some had not reached their potential, but not all of the remaining 86 per cent. And some women have a definite refractory period after orgasm, like a man. Furthermore, the few women who have had to have the clitoris removed for reasons of hormonal disturbance can still experience erotic sensation and even reach orgasm.

With Fisher, married women reported two very different types of sexual experience, clitoral and vaginal stimulation, often in the same woman. The women said that the clitoral stimulation resulted in 'ecstasy', 'tickle', 'electricity' and 'sharpness'; the vaginal stimulation produced 'depth', 'throbbingness', 'soothingness', 'comfort'. Also in 1973, Singer's *The Goals of Human Sexuality* speculated on two types of experience – a vulval experience accompanied by vaginal contractions, and a uterine experience without vaginal contractions but with breathlessness and strong emotional reactions, followed by a refractory period. The orgasms obtained in the Masters and Johnson experiments, he suggested, were vulval, mechanical and easy to produce. So, the evidence against the theory that there is only one type of orgasm continues to accumulate.

Women's sexuality, then, may be more complex than Masters and Johnson thought. Inborn characteristics as well as the cultural traditions and society's conventions may influence the differences between male and female sexuality. Women have steadily become more like men in many ways in this century, especially during the past twenty years, but there are still marked differences – and no sign of the dominance-submission crisis about which the researchers warned. Women still have more fantasies about submission than men, they still expect men to be the pursuers, to make the advances, and many still regard it improper for the woman to initiate lovemaking, even in marriage.

Two other matters should be covered. First, masturbation, which is not quite the same in men and women, and not only because of the anatomical differences. Secondly – and unconnected with masturbation except that they both culminate in orgasm – are activities such as fetishism (when a person is aroused only by a shoe for instance, or some other item of clothing), transvestism (when a person has to dress up in the other sex's clothing to get an orgasm), and other 'kinky' ways of getting sexual pleasure – some involving a victim. There is a striking difference between the sexes here: they are primarily men-only activities.

Men's masturbation does not vary much, for their sexual arousal is penis-centred and orgasm-orientated, uniform and predictable for the most part. They rub their penis, genital excitement steadily mounts, orgasm is reached, ejaculation occurs and then there is the refractory period of inertia and fatigue.

By contrast, women's masturbation varies greatly in technique. The tempo continually changes from fast to slow and there is stopping and starting. Some women reach orgasm, some have multiple orgasms, some prefer not to attain orgasm. Women usually stimulate the clitoris. Sometimes they also insert something into the vagina, but relying on that alone is unusual. Some cross their legs and rhythmically squeeze their thighs together. They do not usually begin with the clitoris but first spend some time touching the breasts, abdomen, the inside of the thighs and the outer lips of the vulva. Some bring themselves to orgasm by moving to the inner lips, stroking and gently pulling them, but usually the woman's finger moves up to her clitoris and there it stays, at first on the glans and then, as the tension develops, on the shaft, although the clitoris needs more subtle treatment than the penis and there has to be variation in pressure and the rate of manipulation.

There are a few women who can reach orgasm without touching any part of their body and without it touching anything, simply by having sexual fantasies. Some bring on an orgasm simply by stimulating their breasts. There are women who regularly obtain sexual excitement for themselves without being more than vaguely aware of what they are doing, while horse-riding and cycling, for instance, with the vulva pressed against the saddle. Men imagine that women masturbate by pushing some homely object in and out of the vagina. In 1848, Dr William Moodie introduced a chastity belt designed 'to keep out everything – fingers, candles, artificial and natural generative organs, so that they cannot be put into the vagina, to cause pleasurable sensations by friction'. In Britain few women now use 'artificial generative organs', as he called them, or dildos. Some place an electric vibrator inside and stimulate the inner lips and clitoris at the same time. However, there are other cultures where dildos are used. The benwa, employed by Japanese women for many years, consists of two hollow balls, one empty, the other containing mercury, which are placed in the vagina. The woman sits in a rocking chair or lies in a hammock and rocks herself to orgasm, the vibrations from the balls spreading out to the labia minora and the clitoris.

Some women let a stream of warm water from the bath tap run onto their clitoris or use a hand shower. More bizarre methods, such as placing objects into the urethra and the rectum, are fortunately rare, for they can produce surgical problems. Men also have been know to push objects into the urethra and occasionally, disturbed men adopt dangerous, precarious stances while they masturbate.

Fantasy in masturbation is less imperative for women, and some masturbate over a period of years without any fantasies. Such fantasies as women have are likely to be connected with experiences they have enjoyed, or could have had, and there is usually love attached to the sex. Similarly, there is realism and love in the erotic literature which some women use as a 'turn-on' for masturbation. Men's imaginations, on the other hand, know no bounds. Typical 'turn-on' stories for men concern impossibly virile, well-endowed males who unexpectedly meet two unbelievably indulgent and provocative girls, always ambisexual although the man is always totally heterosexual, and no time is lost in beginning the endless round of loveless sex. But most men find pictures more exciting than words. Pornography is for masturbation; that is its use. But women obviously need it less for their masturbation – otherwise, there would be as many pornographic magazines for women as there are for men.

Such sexual deviations as fetishism, transvestism, exhibitionism, voyeurism, frotteurism, paedophilia, sadism, masochism (in real life), bestiality and rape are discussed, among other things, elsewhere in this book. Utterly different though they are, they are considered together here because they are all essentially male activities. Of course, if a close enough look is taken at the female population, some of those channels of sexual gratification are indeed employed by a few women. Even rape (or something akin to it, because legal definition is significant here) by women of men does occur on rare occasions. But women are hardly ever deviant, and there is no list of sexual subcultures and sexual offences peculiar to women. Kleptomania, or shoplifting, is commoner among women, and a few women do say they have an orgasm every time they steal. Even so, they do not go shoplifting for sexual kicks.

It is men who engage in diverse kinky practices, and they do so because they find them sexually exciting and immediately fulfilling. For these men, sex with a partner is unexciting and unfulfilling, totally or partly, always or sometimes, and not necessarily because they cannot find a partner. Some of the practices involve a victim, but none requires a partner. Thus, although man's sexuality is liable to go off the rails during his psychosexual development, there is no clear picture of how that happens or which facets of his sexuality are especially susceptible.

This section began by mentioning the episodes of undifferentiated lust which frequent the outset of any boy's adolescence. Normally these unattached, unrelated arousals become attached to a person, but they may, instead, become attached, and tenaciously stick, to objects and abnormal activities. There is often early intimation in childhood of a particular sexual practice, although it can be given undue significance with hindsight, but that does not explain why it is only men who have these hang-ups. We have also considered the compelling urgency which characterizes a young man's sexuality. The young woman is less troubled by this compulsion. She will always be able to tolerate sexual inactivity if circumstances require it, whereas young men may be drawn easily towards a diversion when the normal route is not immediately available. When the pretty girl next door is booked with a boyfriend already, the unattached young man might discover that he can peep from his bedroom into hers and watch her undress, or that he can surreptitiously rub against her as they travel to work in the crowded tube. These diversions may not only excite and even satisfy him but become his preferred or even sole form of gratification. The urgency inherent in a man's approach to orgasm is also relevant. The tension builds up and nothing will distract him as he approaches ejaculation, whereas a woman is easily distracted and tension then shuts her off. That modicum of tension for the male's orgasm (but only a modicum, for too much can shut him off also) is probably part of the pleasure of the deviant practice. The risk of being caught peeping or rubbing, for instance, may add to the thrill. The more we consider the characteristics of men's normal sexuality, the easier it becomes to understand why some men develop these unusual sexual practices, or deviations. They were once labelled perversions, a term no longer employed in that it implies a disapproving value-judgement on the morality of the practices.

It also becomes easier to understand why most men like to indulge at least a little in unusual sex, or occasionally wish they could. All men, said Freud, are 'potentially polymorphous perverts'; they all have the capacity for taking up any of several deviant sexual practices. There are degrees of deviancy. Whereas some men are possessed sexually by their particular practice, with others, including normal males, a 'kink' may only show up mildly and occasionally. Alex Comfort brought this out in *The Joy of Sex*. In his relaxed and reassuring style, refreshingly uninhibited, he persuades the reader that fetishes, dominance desires, and other little hang-ups may help to enhance a couple's sexual enjoyment. Perplexing, bizarre sexual inclinations can be transformed during sexual games into exciting, orgasmic aids for both partners. This assumes that the hang-ups are not overriding and that good communication and understanding flow freely between the partners. That understanding should include an awareness that there are differences between the sexuality of men, including their proclivities, and that of women.

DEVIATIONS FROM THE SEXUAL NORM

Dr Jack G. Weir

A deviation means, literally, a turning aside from the normal way – behaviour that is noticeably different from the average behaviour in our society. Some deviations are unquestionably wicked – rape, for instance – and these give the others a bad name. This happened to the term perversion, which also began life meaning any turning aside from the common use, but has had to be discarded as a general holdall because it acquired a strongly pejorative connotation. Deviation may soon suffer the same fate, but there is no other term to cover all these sexual behaviours. By sexual deviations we mean particular out-of-the-ordinary patterns of sexual behaviour in which some people habitually find their sexual gratification. Usually they are compulsive, giving the individual little or no choice. Most of them, however, are often enjoyed in small amounts as condiments to a normal, successful sex life. Most of them are essentially men-only activities, even though there is always a small minority of women who indulge in them – though never compulsively. This chapter is not exhaustive. It does not include necrophilia (sexual intercourse with a corpse), necrosadism (sexual gratification from mutilation of a corpse), or pyromania (sexual excitement from incendiarism), for instance, but the commoner sexual deviations are here.

BESTIALITY

Bestiality is obtaining sexual gratification by intercourse with an animal. Boys in their early teens sometimes experiment with dogs, out of curiosity or as a prank, not for sexual excitement – that

219

does not count as bestiality. It is variously practised by the man inserting his penis into the vagina, anus or mouth of the animal, or – in rare cases – by putting the animal's penis into his mouth or anus. Dogs, horses, cows, pigs and sheep have all been used. The practice occurs almost entirely in rural areas, as might be expected. Young men who work on lonely, isolated farms are most likely to try it because the animals are there and human partners are not. The absence of girls is the key – the youths do not use animals from preference. The appearance of the animal never arouses them: bestiality is a make-do, a form of masturbation, for the country lad, a teenage activity which he will almost certainly soon leave behind. However, in rare instances a man continues the practice, sometimes because he cannot make satisfactory relations with women, sometimes because he actually prefers it. In this very uncommon sexual pursuit there is occasionally a sadistic component, the animal undergoing some kind of torture.

Like almost all sexual deviations, bestiality is a pursuit for men only. On the rare occasions in which women engage in it, it is for men's gratification and the women themselves get no sexual pleasure. Some years ago, a young woman appeared in Danish pornography having sexual intercourse with a dog, a stallion and other animals, and in 1952 an English court heard how a young wife was twice compelled to have a dog's penis inserted into her vagina, her husband having excited the dog. Such instances are very rare. It is only in myths, such as that of Leda producing the beautiful Helen with the help of a swan, that the woman enjoys it.

The law against bestiality has always been severe. Under the English Sexual Offences Act, 1956, the maximum sentence is life imprisonment. Even an attempt (that is, when vaginal penetration has not been achieved) renders an offender liable to ten years' imprisonment. It is strange that men seek sexual pleasure with animals, but society's intolerance is stranger still. It stretches back thousands of years, to times when all non-procreative sex was condemned by warlike tribes who needed as many males as the women could reproduce. The ancient Jews fiercely condemned bestiality. 'If a man lie with a beast he shall surely be put to death', the Levitical law stated, and 'if a woman approach unto a beast, and lie down thereto' she should be killed also. St Thomas Aquinas, the thirteenth-century theologian, whose writings deeply influence Roman Catholic thought, codified bestiality as a sin

220

against nature. Others were intercourse in unnatural positions (all except the missionary position), masturbation and homosexuality. The Church is silent about unnatural positions now, and generally quiet about masturbation. There is some softening of its condemnation of homosexuality. But the intolerance of bestiality remains unmodified.

COPROLALIA

Coprolalia is the sexual excitement obtained from saying sexual words or talking about sexual matters. Not uncommonly during foreplay a man may use certain earthy words he does not normally use. Perhaps they lend a piquancy to his love-song. 'Vulgar' words are defined as 'used by those who have no wish to be thought either polite or educated', but polite and educated men occasionally produce them in their lovemaking. Some polite and educated women are turned on when an unlikely four-letter word reaches their ears, and some are known to chatter a string of them as orgasm approaches. Some women are turned off.

Any enhancer is an optional extra and best used sparingly. But – whether it be bondage, discipline, scoptophilia or coprolalia – it can be the sum total of an individual's sexual world. Coprolalia is sometimes compulsively pursued in preference to normal heterosexual relations, but more often it acts as a substitute to young males unable or afraid to commit themselves. Making obscene telephone calls is a common activity. These telephone calls are motivated, like rape, by aggression and by a need to humiliate and hurt an unsuspecting woman. The victim is nearly always chosen at random from the telephone directory. The success of the call depends on the consternation registered by the outraged woman. The caller masturbates. If he enjoys the woman's reaction, he will want to phone her again another day. The obscene caller is nearly always a male and nearly always a stranger – but not always.

A woman is probably more likely to be a victim of this deviation than of any other, judging by the frequency of obscene telephone calls. At best they are a nuisance, but they may produce anxiety and fear. The ideal response is to hang up, quietly. Slamming the phone down will suggest to the caller that he has been able to cause distress, and he may be encouraged to try again. Engaging in conversation or, worse, attempting to return his abuse is the

221

response he wants and finds sexually exciting. It is best to say nothing or, if the recipient is up to it, advise him with a quiet, unruffled voice to find a good psychiatrist for himself.

Obscene calls are crimes and they should be reported to the police. The telephone authorities are sympathetic towards victims who contact them and they will help the police by trying to trace the calls, but the criminal law is for the police to enforce. It helps the police if full notes are kept, with details about the voice – whether it was male or female, young or old, with an accent, resembling that of someone known, the time, and what was said.

There are some precautions which women should take against receiving obscene calls. Their entry in the telephone directory should consist of simply surname and initials. The 'Ms Mary Smith' kind of entry invites attention from the discerning obscene caller. To say 'Hallo' is less warm and welcoming than to say 'Hallo, this is Mary Smith', but safer. When a stranger asks 'What number are you?' it is prudent to ask 'What number do you want?' These precautions are also precautions against rape.

Short obscene telephone calls persistently made account for most coprolalia, but not all. A recent medical journal report describes unusual obscene calls which occurred in New Jersey. It could have happened only in America, where people are used to answering lengthy questionnaires over the telephone. The caller, having selected names from the directory, introduced himself as a doctor or a health employee carrying out a survey. He had two question-naires, one about anatomy and the other about social behaviour. Both began with innocuous questions, but they progressed to size of breasts, for example, and sexual behaviour. He was 34 and had begun making obscene telephone calls when he was 15. In his mid-twenties he was caught by the police, and spent five months in a psychiatric hospital. He had no motivation to change his ways, however, and the psychotherapy he was given there was ineffec-tive. He was still without any desire to change after he had been again traced by the police.

A much less significant coprolalia problem came to the notice of this writer recently. An unprepossessing undergraduate had found a formula which allowed him to talk at length about sexual mat-ters to selected women students he had met at church. His ploy was to approach one of these kind women, start off about being distressed about himself, and gradually move into sex, particularly sado-masochism, which was his main interest. It was so helpful to be able to talk about it, he would say, and add that it was part of his hang-up that he couldn't bring himself to confide in a man. When the women compared notes eventually the undergraduate was pressed into seeing the writer and it soon became clear that he did not want professional help.

Coprolalia may, in some instances, be completely involuntary. There is a very rare and distressing condition, pleasingly called Gilles de la Tourette's syndrome. The patient suffers from twitching of the muscles of the face and jerking movements of the body, he repeats words used by others, and he shouts obscenities. Although the condition may fluctuate in severity, it tends to be progressive.

Treating coprolalia means treating the underlying condition, and this varies greatly. For a long time there was no treatment for the Gilles de la Tourette syndrome, but it has been found in recent years that Haloperidol, a major tranquillizer, reduces the movements of the face and body and sometimes overcomes the obscene verbal outbursts. It is not a cure, but while it is taken the symptoms are diminished. At the other end of the scale, having been caught out may be sufficient to end an adolescent's obscene telephone calling. In severer and long-standing cases, a major mental illness is occasionally identified. In many cases, however, there is no evidence of major illness, and psychotherapy or behaviour therapy has to be considered. For therapy to be successful substantial motivation on the part of the offender is required.

EXHIBITIONISM

Exhibitionism is exposing the genitals to strangers in order to obtain sexual gratification. The victim is a young woman or a girl and more often than not she is around the age of puberty. She encounters an exhibitionist in some unpopulated spot, on a heath or in a lane. He has strategically positioned himself and suddenly he displays his erect penis. She is startled and shocked, and nervously she moves on. This thrills and excites him, and he completes the act by masturbating. If he is to be gratified, it is necessary for her to look startled and impressed. The apocryphal French lady who remarked 'You'll catch cold, monsieur' was a dead loss. He may try another girl if the first one has been unresponsive, and another, until he gets the required reaction. However, the

223

exhibitionist – or flasher as he is often called – does not lay a hand on his victim or pursue her: he is not a rapist.

Exhibitionism is a sexual pursuit pursued by men only. Although genital exhibition plays a role of varying significance in love-play, no woman attains ultimate sexual delight through exposing herself. A strip-tease artist does not take up that occupation because she is proud of her genitals and wants the opportunity to show them off. Strippers recall their profound embarrassment when they started. They move into the work for the same reason that most people move into work – to earn money. (And this can be substantial. Successful strippers in Soho, London, do their five-minute turn in five or six nearby clubs. With six shows a day in each club they can, at £6 a turn, earn over £1,000 per week, so it is not altogether surprising that amongst them there are university graduates who have forsaken their chosen profession.) The good stripper titillates by not quite revealing her genitalia throughout her act until a final quick pubic flash. The stripper who does not know how to tease and has everything off too soon is less sought after. A stripper obtains satisfaction in showing off the rest of her body, and in retaining her audience's attention. There is a sense of domination sometimes. But there is no sexual arousal, and no enjoyment from seeing the gazing eyes fixed on her genital region.

Perhaps there is an element of exhibitionism in all men, left over from boyhood. The Freudian explanation is that women have come to terms with having no penis, but men continue to experience a degree of anxiety about castration and have to reassure themselves they still have a penis. Why a man relieves his castration anxiety by exhibitionism (rather than by, say, fetishism), the explanation runs, is because of his mother's excessive attention to his body and his genitals. However, there are serious criticisms of the Freudian theory about the universality of castration anxiety.

It is understandable, although reprehensible, that the exhibitionist should choose innocent young victims, for they are going to be more impressed by what he has to show them than mature and experience women would be. An increasing number of exhibitionists arrested by the police are young themselves; now more than a quarter are under the age of 21. There is a cluster of emotions which the exhibitionist wants to evoke in his victim. Affront, horror and disgust are more desired than curiosity, admiration and excitement, but he would like her to feel them all.

Only a mentally subnormal exhibitionist puts his genitals on show purely as a way of sexual approach. Male apes and monkeys use genital display in order to affront. Female primates do so much less frequently.

Dr F. G. Rooth published a series of clinical studies on exhibitionism in the 1970s. The exhibitionist, he said, obtained above all a feeling of dominance and mastery when he displayed himself to a young, sensitive female. Normally they were anything but dominant and masterful, being usually timid and unassertive with women. They were under-achievers, unduly sensitive to minor upsets and easily hurt. They looked young for their years. The married ones invariably had wives who looked older and who had adopted a maternal role. They were harmless, apart from the unpleasantness their abnormal behaviour produced. There was, however, a small minority of exhibitionists (they could perhaps be more properly called paedophiles) who consistently chose children as their victims, and some of them progressed to having physical contact.

Many women recall having been confronted by a flasher sometime in their lives. In a group of nurses, 44 per cent had seen an exhibitionist in action, usually in their early teens. It was very unpleasant for most of them, but lasting effects were unusual. Occasionally, a woman will blame an unfortunate encounter with an exhibitionist for her psychiatric condition, a chronic anxiety, for instance, or frigidity. But other determinants emerge when she unfolds her story. It is well to warn girls entering puberty about these men who haven't grown up, who are harmless, but who should be given a wide berth.

Some exhibitionists rarely expose themselves, and do so only after some social or sexual trauma, for example when there has been a domestic quarrel or their wife is pregnant and will not engage in sexual intercourse. Others do it habitually, preferring it to normal sex, and their masturbatory fantasies are about exhibiting themselves. The latter group is difficult to treat, on those occasions when a court recommends treatment. Group therapy conducted by highly experienced psychoanalysts has been moderately successful, but such treatment is rarely available. Individual counselling of these offenders encourages them to adjust towards a fuller life which will not need exhibitionism to satisfy it. The very requirement of having to report regularly to the counsellor may help to keep him on the rails. Offenders who regularly choose

225

the same spot to expose themselves may be asked whenever they find themselves on the road leading to the spot – even though exhibiting themselves has not crossed their mind – to stop at the telephone kiosk and phone the counsellor. There are other similar controls. However, all these treatments require the offender's co-operation, and sometimes there is none. Hormones and neuroleptics reduce their sex drive, but it is hard to ensure prolonged administration because these drugs have unpleasant side-effects.

One-third of all sexual offenders are exhibitionists. There are two interesting findings about the 2,000 to 3,000 exhibitionists who are caught by the English police every year. Most of them respond to the shock of their court appearance, and whether fined or imprisoned do not land in trouble again. But a sizeable number go on flashing and being caught. (The re-conviction rate was found to be 18.6 per cent over four years, in one important study, and 40 per cent of these occurred within the first year.) The second interesting finding is that although many exhibitionists take pains that they are not caught, some appear almost as if they were taking pains that they are. An ingredient in their excitement appears to be the risk of being caught.

FETISHISM

Fetishism is the need – almost always in men – to use a particular object, usually clothing, or a part of the female body such as the foot, to achieve sexual gratification. The man who obtains sexual pleasure from a shoe, and only from a shoe, has a classic fetishism. No woman, however alluring – not even the owner of the shoe – could arouse the sexual excitement that it produces for him. This is real fetishism. However, the term is used more widely to cover the small, individual 'turn-ons' which most men have – for instance, when a man's partner wears a particular item of clothing which he finds especially exciting. In such cases, the fetish is not a substitute for normal sex but enhances it.

Fetishism almost always affects men: hardly any women are 'turned on' by shoes or other objects. For some men, the fetish may be essential for potency. It can be a simple matter – and his partner may derive additional pleasure for herself in helping him indulge his fetish – or it can be complicated and intrusive and turn her off as decisively as it turns him on. In such cases, he may find he can have successful sex only when he pays a prostitute to join his act. In other cases, the fetish is not essential for potency. Many fetishists enjoy both normal sexual relationships with their regular partners and, on occasions, sexual excitement centred round their fetish. This may be with their regular partner, with someone else, or through masturbation.

Usually, a fetish is part of the body, probably some part not customarily seen – a woman's leg above the knee, for example. A glimpse of bare leg is attractive to most men, but to the fetishist it can be totally and irresistibly enchanting, to the exclusion of the rest of the anatomy and, indeed, of the woman herself. There need be nothing particularly beautiful about it and it is not essentially different from his own leg, but the sight of it remains his supreme delight. As times change, the parts of the body that modesty dictates should be covered also change. A century ago, hand and foot fetishes were common. The sexologist Krafft-Ebing had an otherwise totally impotent patient who could be stirred sexually only by the sight of a hand of a beautiful young lady with her glove removed, especially when she wore rings. Freud recalled a man who was 'quite indifferent to the genitals' but who could be 'plunged into irresistible sexual excitement by a foot of a particular shape wearing a shoe.'

The fetish may become a truly deviant obsession or fixation. For some men it may run as far as admiring their partner's vulva (see SCOPTOPHILIA (page 282) or the pleasure of watching or hearing a woman urinating (see UROLAGNIA page 296). Then either their love-making goes no further and they are impotent when they try, or they only perfunctorily complete the sexual act.

There are deformity fetishes when men are excited only by women with physical defects – hunchbacks or amputees, for instance. Normally, often, a small asymmetry of the face, or an exaggerated feature, or a slight squint perhaps, may lend an extra sexual attractiveness to a woman, and deformity fetishes perhaps derive from this.

Fetishes may also be articles of clothing, usually pants and brassieres – not fancy, frilly ones but those for regular use which – and this is essential – a woman who is not a relative or sexual partner, has worn. A transvestite, a man aroused by dressing in women's clothes, does not have these stipulations – new clothes, his wife's clothes, anyone's clothes will suffice.

The materials fetishists favour have also changed over the years. In Krafft-Ebing's time they were fur, silk and velvet; today they

227

are rubber, plastic and leather. In a 1979 study rubber fetishists contacted through 'rubber' societies and sex shops were found to be little different in most respects from other men with similar scores in neuroticism, introversion and masculinity and similar family and domestic histories. But they were more impersonal and prudish. They all indulged in conventional sex as well as their rubber fetish.

We do not know what causes fetishism, why some men become fetishists, why one fetishist needs a used brassiere, another a rubber coat. Freud saw fetishism as a way of combatting castration anxiety, but had to admit that it was not always possible to explain how fetishes were determined.

There are probably a number of factors contributing to the production of a fetish. Many young men indulge in a kind of embryonic fetishism when their sexual drive is barred from normal expression: 'Get me a kerchief from the breast, A garter that her knee has pressed' – a quotation from Goethe's *Faust* that was cited by Freud. Real fetishism develops when the kerchief or the garter is preferred to normal sex. The development of the fetish seems to be the result of a 'learning process', a conditioning, rather than a childhood fixation as Freud came to maintain. This was borne out in the survey of rubber fetishism, for it showed that nine per cent of the fetishists were more than 20 years of age when they first experienced rubber as a sexually attractive material. It was also borne out by investigators who showed that erection may be conditioned to various unusual stimuli (in the same way that Pavlov's dogs were conditioned to salivate on hearing a bell ring). Presumably the few who prefer garters to sexual intercourse have been hindered in progressing to intercourse by external circumstances or anxiety, and have reinforced the connexion between the garter and their sexual pleasure through masturbation.

Fetishists seldom seek treatment. Those who come the way of a psychiatrist have been directed by the law (which they have offended by stealing lingerie from clotheslines or from inside a house), or pressed by their wives (because their fetish has been getting in the way of marital sex). But the unfortunate fetishist himself must have come round to thinking that his particular fetishism is a liability and something he would dearly like to discard. Otherwise treatment is ethically wrong and therapeutically hopeless. Behaviour therapy has largely usurped psychotherapy in the treatment of fetishism. It is usually quicker and more effective. The early form of behaviour therapy was by aversion. While imagining his fetish, the fetishist was given electric shocks or drugs producing nausea, and any pleasure obtained from the fetish was systematically dispelled – or such was the aim. There is now a positive approach. The fetishist masturbates, fantasizing about his fetish. Just as he reaches orgasm he switches to a fantasy of normal sex. Gradually he switches over earlier and earlier. Devising a series of masturbatory fantasies with an increasing amount of normal sex and a decreasing amount of fetishism in them is a modification of this. This treatment has been developed by John Bancroft and the reader is recommended to consult his *Human Sexuality and its Problems* (1983) for more details about this – and, incidentally, about most of the other matters in this chapter; it is a mine of information. There are certain cases, however, where some form of psychotherapy or 'talking treatment' is indicated from the start. For instance, when a wife starts complaining about the intrusion of her husband's fetishism into their sex life – after she has gone along with it quite happily for several years – it may well be a sign of marital discord. When the real cause of the disharmony is uncovered and corrected, there may be no more complaint about the fetishism. And there are other cases where the simple, mechanistic approach would not apply – lift the lid and underneath is a shut-in personality, afraid to venture into ordinary sex, for instance, or a sadist, or a transvestite. But it is surprising how often it is effective.

FROTTEURISM

Frotteurism, or frottage, is obtaining sexual excitement by having contact, through clothes, with some part of a woman's body. It happens mostly in crowds and is mostly confined to men. All men are 'potential polymorphous perverts', to quote Freud, or polysexual as they say nowadays, and many men have had a passing frotteuristic delight – when travelling in a densely packed train, for instance, and being pressed against an attractive woman. The woman feels no delight, it need hardly be said. She feels revulsion if she senses that the man is not being pressed against her entirely involuntarily, although it may be difficult for her to disengage and embarrassing to protest except silently. It is mostly confined to men, but not entirely. A handsome Pakistani cricketer recently complained publicly about being pawed by Australian women.

229

Frotteurism is always reprehensible, but it becomes a serious problem when a man develops a compelling need for this kind of sexual excitement, driving him to use lifts and trains for which he has no need but which may afford him opportunity to press and rub his penis against young buttocks. He is sexually stimulated, later masturbates, and then feels guilty about his behaviour. Or a victim becomes aware of what he is doing, protests – if only with a look of disgust – and he feels guilty. But the compelling need wells up again, driving him to further activity. Frotteurism in this compulsive form is not only distasteful for the women to whom the frotteur attaches, but is also – although it will not appear so to the women – a matter of great unhappiness for him.

In some men the compulsion takes the form of incessantly patting bottoms or stroking breasts. This does not occur in crowds, but when a man is alone with a woman. Because the woman knows who the man is, this is more dangerous than frotteurism in an anonymous crowd. He is usually in a position of respect – a minister of religion, a doctor or a professor, say – so he partly reassures himself that his pats will be taken to be innocent, friendly, playful, avuncular gestures. Even if she should complain, he tells himself reassuringly, her allegations will be discounted by all who know him to be a man of God, happily married, a family man, a pillar of society. It is much easier for women to dispose of the attentions of a rubber or toucher who is in a position of less standing. Without fear of serious repercussion they can say 'No', and if 'No' should be taken to mean 'Yes' they may complain – to their employer, personnel officer or shop steward as the case may be. More than likely, the man in high standing's partiality for bottoms or breasts is taken as an unfortunate foible by those women with whom he works, and they simply learn to take precautions to minimise opportunity. Nevertheless, he is taking risks. Today women are encouraged to protest against uninvited and unwelcome sexual attentions of any kind. They are told to take action, even though it may mean facing disbelief, being labelled a troublemaker, losing respect or even losing promotion. They are advised, if they face sexual harassment at work, not meekly to find another job, but to compile notes of incidents of harassment and work in concert with colleagues also subject to the man's harassment. More charges of indecent assault arising from sexual harassment by frotteurs seem to be reaching the courts.

Most frotteurs will desist after a showdown like this. For those men who have a highly compulsive form of frotteurism which they cannot keep in check, there are good prospects from behaviour therapy.

HOMOSEXUALITY

Homosexuals are those who are erotically attracted to their own sex. The Greek *homo* means same and *hetero* means other. The slang term for a male homosexual used to be 'queer' (it has been superseded by 'gay'), but there is nothing odd or queer, nothing out of the ordinary, other than the homosexual's sexual attraction. Sexual attraction to one sex or the other is referred to as gender preference or gender orientation. The latter term is the better one, because preference implies choice and generally the homosexual has no choice. Liking it or not, the homosexual is landed with his or her homosexuality. It is part of the personality, not something consciously assumed. Gender orientation is the only way, basically, in which homosexuals differ from the general population, although myths and misconceptions about homosexuality abound.

Other differences exist which are social consequences of this basic difference. Homosexuals tend toward being unmarried and childless. Some do get married, usually vaguely or fully conscious of their homosexual inclinations, though they do not tell their future partners. They get married for several reasons: a fondness for their intended spouse, a desire for a stable and socially acceptable relationship – which they can't hope to expect from living with a homosexual friend – a need to conceal their gender orientation from relatives, friends and business colleagues, a yearning for a 'cure', or a wish to have children. But their marriages with a few exceptions are unhappy and shortlived. Several American investigations bear this out, though – random samples being unattainable – their results must be treated with caution. They indicate that about 20 per cent of homosexual men and about 30 per cent of homosexual women have been married sometime or other, but that their marriages almost always end within three years and often much sooner. Thus, though a surprisingly large number enter marriage, few of the marriages last. Occasionally there is a child, more often when the wife is the homosexual partner.

Homosexuals have a tendency to become depressed. Young homosexuals can scarcely avoid becoming depressed on gradually becoming aware of their sexual inclinations. It is unacceptable to them and it may well be unacceptable (at least at first) to their parents, brothers, sisters, ministers and friends – almost everyone from whom they want love and approval. Eventually they find a compromise or a solution for living with their homosexuality – only in rare cases for rejoicing in it – but they continue to live in a rejecting, discriminating society. Insurance companies have for long regarded homosexuals as being more prone to suicide than heterosexuals and several recent large-scale investigations have confirmed a tendency towards depression. What irony that 'gay' should have become the term favoured by those who want to acknowledge themselves to be homosexual.

The human race is not divided sharply into heterosexuals and homosexuals. There are people who are exclusively heterosexual, it is true, and they would abhor the thought of engaging in a homosexual relation. There are those who are totally homosexu- ally orientated, who would be equally averse to the idea of any heterosexual contact. But there are many people who are bisexual, who practise – or have practised – both ways. Some of them may be almost exclusively one or the other. A young, attractive, hetero- sexual prisoner, for instance, may accept the homosexual advances of a high-status prisoner who is capable of making life easier for him, or he may submit in fear. Or a wife, who enjoys a secret, active homosexual relationship, may dutifully submit to matri- monial intercourse when required. On the other hand, there are bisexuals who engage in an equal mixture – ambisexuals, Masters and Johnson call them – who seek overt sexual experience with members of both sexes and respond with equal ease and pleasure. Sexual orientations are immensely varied.

It is difficult to know where to draw the line between what is homosexual practice and what is not, and who is homosexual and who is not. The young attractive prisoner just mentioned could only uncertainly be called bisexual, let alone homosexual.

Kinsey offered a way out of the muddle by providing a seven- point heterosexual-homosexual scale. It is based on the assumption that all gender orientations lie along one continuum. Each rating is carefully defined in the Kinsey Reports and the following is only a summary:

0 Entirely heterosexual

1 Largely heterosexual, but with incidental homosexual history

2 Largely heterosexual, but with distinct homosexual history

3 Equally heterosexual and homosexual

4 Largely homosexual, but with distinct heterosexual history

5 Largely homosexual, but with incidental heterosexual history

6 Entirely homosexual

This simple scale continues to be widely employed in surveys and discussions on homosexuality. However, there are several matters that it does not encompass – at least not without unwieldy modification – and these have to be mentioned. A person's sexual behaviour may be orientated in a different direction from his or her feelings and although sexual behaviour is easier for the research worker to elicit and categorize, it is sometimes a poor indicator of the direction of the person's sexual desire. For instance, if our heterosexually-orientated prisoner who practises homosexuality because of his circumstances becomes an inveterate recidivist spending most of his days in prison, his sexual behaviour rating on the scale would be 4, whereas theoretically his inner orientaton would be 0. This is a far-fetched example, but some discrepancy between feelings and behaviour is not rare. Secondly, there may be an alteration of a person's orientation over the years, both in behaviour and feeling: in addition to the usual pubertal homosexual-to-heterosexual change, there is occasionally a heterosexual-to-homosexual change – usually because of acceptance of hitherto unconscious feelings. Lastly, the Kinsey scale implies that bisexuality is always a watered-down mixture, the more of one, the less of the other, whereas some people may have energetic homosexual lives and equally energetic heterosexual ones.

The most shattering part of the Kinsey male report of 1948 was its estimation of the incidence of homosexuals. People had had no idea that there were so many. He obtained his figures by rating the 5,300 subjects of his sample of white males on his seven-point heterosexual-homosexual scale. 'Thirty-seven per cent of the total population has at least some overt homosexual experience to the point of orgasm between adolescence and old age.' This figure included many men who had no more than an ephemeral homosexual relationship during puberty – if homosexual it could always be styled. However, other substantial figures cannot be so easily passed over: '13 per cent of the population has more of the homo-

233

sexual than the heterosexual for at least three years between the ages 15 and 55' and 'four per cent of white males are exclusively homosexual throughout their lives after the onset of adolescence'.

The Kinsey interviewers were given extensive training to explore delicate topics. They were taught to uncover lying and suppression, especially through inter-related questions. They made external checks. When husband and wife were both interviewed, their answers were compared. Subjects were re-examined after a number of years. Much effort was made to get at the truth. It was hoped that by its vastness the sample would represent a cross-section of the white population of the USA. It was composed of volunteers, but one-quarter of them came from such groups as residents of hostels, student bodies, and church members. By dint of enormously zealous persuasion almost every one was interviewed.

Even with all their checks and counter-checks, however, the Kinsey interviewers may not have fully uncovered the whole extent of homosexuality. Though they were at pains to assure their subjects that all information given them was treated in confidence, and that they had an elaborate code for recording it so that if the papers fell into the wrong hands no one would be any the wiser, there may have been some people who were not fully convinced there was no risk of disclosure of their homosexuality. Considering how many sessions it may take an experienced psychotherapist to unfathom from his patient's shame the merest hint of unusual sexual practice, or fantasy even, it is amazing how much information they did obtain about such reprehensible and unlawful behaviour – as homosexuality was at that time. Thus four per cent may have been an underestimate of the incidence of exclusive homosexuals. On the other hand, the sample was not as representative as Kinsey believed; for one thing it contained a disproportionate number of criminals and this would make the figure too high. A re-analysis of a section of the cases, a smaller but more representative group of 2,900 young men, concluded that three per cent had exclusive homosexual histories.

Kinsey reported a lower incidence of female homosexuality. Nineteen per cent of the females, by the age of 40, had had sexual contact with other females. In any age group there were, compared with men, only a half to a third as many of the females who were primarily or exclusively homosexual. The interviewers were all males and it has been suggested that women might have been able to extract more homosexual confessions from women. Moreover, it must be kept in mind that these results refer to behaviour – as opposed to inner orientation or fantasy – and this may have had a bearing on the lower figures for women.

Obviously, to find the precise incidence of homosexual activity, or of homosexuals in our society, is impossible. But it is surely considerable. The Kinsey reports revealed that homosexuals are not rare freaks. The publication of the reports set in motion increased self-acceptance by individual homosexuals, greater social tolerance and modifications in the law. We live in the flux of these changes. While more and more homosexuals accept their own gender orientation and openly declare it, and while they protest against laws and discrimination, homosexuality becomes more noticeable – though there is no real evidence of an increase in the incidence of homosexuals.

These changes occur around us but our society's prejudice and disapproval have far from disappeared. Primitive societies often allow homosexual practice in some form. Some highly civilized societies, classical Greek and Roman particularly, not only accepted homosexuality but approved of it and regarded it as superior to heterosexuality. Platonic love – which has come to mean non-sexual heterosexual love – had to do with same-sex love, the only kind of love capable of reaching beyond purely physical love according to Plato. But in our society homosexuals have for long been seen in bad light, as up to no good. They comprise a minority group, and minority groups – blacks and Jews, for instance, or gypsies (and witches in their time) – are liable to create suspicion, fear, hatred and prejudice, which fuels more suspicion. The prejudices against homosexuals give rise to extraordinary, altogether unrepresentative, stereotypes: men who are effeminate, sensitive and artistic, irresponsible and weak, spiteful and ill-tempered, preoccupied with anal sex and constantly indulging in orgies of their odious pleasure, and given to molesting children; women who are dominating, insensitive, masculine and – it is usually presumed – sexless. In an American study made 15 years ago, three-quarters of the respondents thought homosexuals should not be clergymen, schoolteachers or judges, and two-thirds thought that they should not be doctors or in government service. This distrust does not seem to have lessened much.

Yet, as already mentioned, the homosexual population in general differs little from the adult population in general, except that the homosexual population tends to be disproportionately unmarried and childless, and there is a tendency towards depression. Early studies were made of homosexuals in prison or of psychiatrically ill homosexuals, and the results reflected the usual abnormalities of prisoners and psychiatric patients. The results of studies based on homosexuals recruited from gay-liberation clubs and organizations also have a bias. Evelyn Hooker, an American clinical psychologist, was the first to assess homosexuals who did not come from any of these classes. A likeable, stable young man whom she thought she knew well surprised her one day by telling her he was a homosexual. This prompted her first study in 1957. A group of his homosexual friends and a group of heterosexuals – 30 in each – were matched for age, intelligence and educational level and were given three well-known projective personality tests. Trained psychologists were given the results and asked to separate the homosexuals from the heterosexuals. They couldn't. Since that time numerous studies have concluded that homosexuality is not associated with any psychological abnormality.

As for their sex life, they are less active than heterosexuals. Because of circumstance and social sanctions, many homosexuals go for years without having any homosexual outlet. This is especially so among homosexual women. Those who have an active sexual life – and this includes the men who circulate in homosexual clubs, bars and parties, having many different partners – are less active than most young married heterosexuals. The Kinsey Report first brought this fact out into the light. As for their lovemaking, homosexuals use all the methods of sexual stimulation which heterosexual couples employ, except copulation of course. 'Except copulation' might sound like sex without sex, Hamlet without the Prince of Denmark. But this reflects the preoccupation with orgasm that besets most heterosexual lovemaking. Brief, perfunctory sex play to warm up the engine, and then into gear for a fast trip to the top. Masters and Johnson, for their *Homosexuality in Perspective* (1979), observed heterosexual couples and homosexual couples (male and female ones) making love and they were struck by the more relaxed attitude of the homosexuals, lingering at each step, enjoying each one for its own sake.

Male and female homosexual couples almost always begin their lovemaking by kissing and caressing one another – as heterosexual couples do, only the homosexuals do it for longer. This is as far as some homosexual couples go. Most, however, proceed to nipple or breast stimulation. Then comes genital play, in the same leisurely manner, without hastening toward orgasm. When excitement reaches a high level, the stimulation is withdrawn to allow a regression, and then the previous level is once again slowly attained. This slowing and speeding up is repeated many times if the couple are experienced. Orgasm is usually on a your-turn-my-turn basis, but there may be concurrent stimulation. The popular notion of the active and passive partner in a homosexual relation applies to a few couples only. Most homosexuals go no further than this form of prolonged mutual masturbation. However, mouth-genital stimulation is often part of the homosexual's repertoire, more so in America than in Britain. Hardly any female homosexual couples use a dildo, despite popular belief.

Not all male homosexuals, by any means, engage in anal intercourse. The stereotype of the male homosexual tirelessly and ceaselessly engaged in anal intercourse is well off the mark. Many have tried it, though the Acquired Immune Deficiency Syndrome (AIDS) now deters many from exploring the possible pleasures of this kind of lovemaking – as well as causing understandable anxiety in those who have. It was never the universal favourite. Male homosexual volunteers, interviewed for A. P. Bell and M. S. Weinberg's *Homosexualities* (1978), reported that oral sex – active and passive – was the most frequent method. Then, in order of frequency, came masturbation, anal intercourse and body contact. The active role was nearly always preferred by the anal intercourse devotees. Only six per cent liked the passive role better. Some heterosexual couples enjoy this form of sex, the reader may be reminded in passing. *The Joy of Sex*, by Alex Comfort, refers to it with considerable enthusiasm, pointing out that some women's feelings are more intense than those they obtain from vaginal sex. In the Masters and Johnson sample of homosexuals and heterosexuals, the females who engaged in anal intercourse experienced orgasm in 11 out of 14 occasions, whereas two males (out of 10 opportunities) reached orgasm and these two males were simultaneously masturbating themselves. But the centuries-old taboo on anal intercourse, sodomy, buggery – call it what you will – remains strong enough to deter most heterosexual couples from trying it. However, there are normally cautious writers who suggest that it is commoner (proportionately) among heterosexuals than among homosexuals.

There are a few men who restrict themselves to brief, anonymous homosexual sex. Attending a homosexual cinema and engaging in mutual masturbation with the man in the next seat is one way. It is all done in the dark, not a word spoken. The participants slip out separately and there is no more contact. Even more impersonal, and kinkier, is sex through a hole in the wall between cubicles in a public lavatory. The hole is large enough for the penis of the stranger next door to come through for rubbing or sucking. Certain lavatories become favoured because of their situation, infrequent legitimate use, and thin wooden partitions. The police get to know them and swoop occasionally. Plain clothes officers sometimes visit the gay cinemas. The danger of being caught adds to the excitement. Over the years the present writer has met some of these men, after they have been arrested. They have all been prosperous, well-respected professional and business men. They were either exclusive homosexuals who did not want to become involved in a personal relation because they believed that homosexuality was morally wrong, or to be seen in a club because their reputation could be damaged, or else they were middle-aged and happily married (though marital sex had petered out), wanting something more exciting than masturbation but without commitment. Their cinema or lavatory visits were extremely rare.

Only marginally less anonymous are those encounters which take place at well-known meeting spots in all large cities – in certain parks, heaths, pubs and lavatories. A glance or a nod is usually enough for one man to signify to another that he is ready and willing. They have stealthy, loveless sex there and then or else they move to somewhere safer. They might arrange to meet again for more, or they might not, but it is generally kept at an impersonal level.

Male homosexuals are prone to engage in transitory physical relations. Loving relations may grow out of them later. This does not apply to lesbians, however. In general, lesbian couples begin to have physical relations with one another only after years of strong emotional contact. Although male homosexuals tend to be promiscuous, lesbians seek continuing, faithful attachments. One reason given for this is the stronger social hostility and suspicion which male homosexuals suffer. Lesbians were never burnt, hanged or sent to prison for making love to one another. But among heterosexuals, men are more promiscuous than women and there may be an intrinsic biological fator which makes men promiscuous and which is compounded in man-with-man love. This

238

contrast between male and female homosexuals is, however, a generalization. There is a new breed of lesbians who quickly engage in physical relations and do not necessarily settle down into long, enduring relations. These are the loyal feminists, wanting no truck with men, who embrace lesbianism on intellectual grounds rather than being unable to escape it because of an unalterable gender orientation.

Even allowing for the promiscuity, it is strange how strongly opprobrious and disgusted many people are at the mere mention of homosexuality. Not all male homosexuals are promiscuous, lesbians are not as a rule promiscuous, and some heterosexuals are promiscuous. The appearance of the Acquired Immune Deficiency Syndrome (AIDS) has increased public condemnation, even though homosexual organizations acted promptly and responsibly when the problem first appeared. Those who regard homosexuality as loathsome – and there are many educated, thinking people among them – find it hard to account for their feeling. They might say that homosexuality is unnatural. If they mean that it is contrary to nature, they are faced with the difficulties that animals may engage in homosexual acts, and that shaving, regular bathing and even wearing clothes are not as nature intended. If they mean it is non-procreative, it needs to be pointed out that celibacy, which they would doubtless commend, is non-procreative.

Others appeal to the Bible to justify their opprobrium and loathing of homosexuality. However although it is generally accepted that the Bible regards homosexuality as sinful, during the past thirty years there has been a body of scholarship accumulating that challenges this. The seminal work was a modest book by Derrick Bailey, *Homosexuality and the Western Christian Tradition* (1955). Recent arguments favouring this new outlook were advanced in John Boswell's *Christianity, Social Tolerance and Homosexuality* (1980).

The main Biblical passage condemning homosexuality is generally said to be the story of Lot and the destruction of Sodom and Gomorrah, as told in *Genesis*, Chapter XIX. The standard reading of the passage is that when the Sodomites demanded to see the two men to whom Lot had given shelter it was because they wanted sex with them; and for this sin, on top of others which are unspecified, God destroyed them all. That reading is based upon translation of the Hebrew word *yadha* as 'to have sex with', a rendering strengthened by the reappearance of *yadha*, only three verses

239

later, unambiguously meaning 'to have sex with'. On the other hand, 'to become acquainted with' is the usual meaning of *yadha* in the Old Testament, 933 times out of 943 according to Bailey. His version is that Lot was a stickler for hospitality, risking his daughters' safety for the protection of his guests (not that daughters mattered much in his society); and because of his championship of hospitality he was not only spared the fate in store for the inhabitants of Sodom but his family line was perpetuated (and this was very important). The dissent against the orthodox interpretation cites the numerous references elsewhere in the Bible to Sodom, all regarding it as a wicked city with various faults specified – but never homosexuality; and Jesus implied that inhospitality was Sodom's final sin.

Modern scholars contend that it was during the first and second centuries, when the early church became deeply concerned about the sexual behaviour of its members, that the final sin of Sodom began to be regarded as homosexuality. Only in *Leviticus* is homosexual practice as such mentioned in the Old Testament, condemned along with hundreds more 'toevahs', all of which had to be avoided according to the Holiness Code. The code has no relevance to moral law in 20th century Western society. The specific reference in the New Testament is less easily dismissed. Saint Paul, towards the beginning of his letter to the Romans (Romans I, verses 26 and 27), had hard things to say about both men and women who forwent their heterosexuality for homosexual practice. As Boswell points out, however, he may have been referring to heterosexual men and women who were dabbling in homosexuality and not at all to those people with a permanent homosexual orientation, those at 6 or 5 on the Kinsey scale. These liberal interpretations appear to be gaining gradual acceptance within the Christian Church – Roman Catholics and conservative Protestants excepted – though the main body of opinion in all denominations still firmly condemns homosexuality. Though the power of the Church has greatly decreased during the past century, it continues to exercise immense influence on ethical thought, of its members and non-members, of believers and unbelievers.

Nevertheless, public opinion is slowly altering. This has been reflected during the past twenty-five years in many ways, including relaxation of legal restraints applying to male homosexual behaviour. (The law does not oppose female homosexual practice.) In France, Spain, Italy, Holland and Belgium homosexual acts between consenting adults have not been illegal since the beginning of the 19th century. These Catholic countries have had liberal laws because they derived from the French civil code adopted in 1804 and later named the Napoleonic code. The code, founded on the liberal principles behind the French Revolution, left moral choice to the individual citizen. The law in England and Wales was changed in 1967 to allow homosexuality between consenting adults. Certain states in the United States have also altered their laws accordingly, beginning with Illinois in 1962. It remains illegal for members of the armed forces of America and Britain, however. The laws in Finland, Norway and Austria were liberalized in the early 1970s. It is still legally forbidden in most of the United States, however, as well as in Australia, New Zealand and South Africa. Scots law has not been changed but adult homosexuals acting in private are never prosecuted. In those places where the law has been relaxed, however, the age of consent is generally 21 for homosexual sex, though 16 for heterosexual acts. There are various other discriminations against homosexuals, for instance in more restrictive definitions of privacy, importuning and procuring. But, overall, the law is slowly but surely changing.

Many reasons to account for homosexual orientation have been advanced, but it is still a mystery. Certain hormonal and genetic findings have prompted the search for physical determinants. Then fascinating environmental factors are discovered which switch interest onto psychological causes. During the past 40 years there has been a hunt for sex hormone differences. Earlier investigations showed no difference, but in the early 1970s there were several that seemed to show that exclusive or nearly exclusive homosexuals had low levels of testosterone in their urine and plasma. An American team led by R. C. Kolodny produced the best-known report in 1971. Although the testosterone was not sufficiently low to cause any noticeable difference in the size of genitals or pubic hair distribution, for example, or reduced sexual activity, they found these low levels were not found in matched heterosexuals and bisexuals nearer the middle of the Kinsey scale. However, when the surveys were repeated by other workers they did not always get the same results and faults in the experimental methods have been levelled against these investigations performed in the early 'seventies. For one thing, the men they employed for the tests were not only homosexuals, but also cannabis smokers apparently and cannabis lowers the testosterone level.

241

But there could be further, more refined, studies on this problem. What prompts this search are the experiments, already mentioned in the chapter on sex and gender, in which small doses of testosterone are given to female monkeys still in their mother's womb. It causes them to behave in masculine ways when they grow up, including mounting other monkeys. These experiments and others like them suggest that prenatal hormonal influence on the brain may possibly play a part in determining whether an individual human being is going to be heterosexual, bisexual or homosexual, although there is no knowing how big a part, or the kind of part.

A hereditary factor has long been suspected. Nowadays evidence of the hereditary transmission of any trait or disposition is usually sought through the study of identical and non-identical twins. Identical twins arise through the splitting of a single fertilized egg and so have the same genes. Non-identical twins are produced by the fertilization of two different eggs and so genetically they are like ordinary brothers and sisters. Thus identical and non-identical twins have the same environment, but only identical twins have the same inheritance. If a twin has some condition that is hereditary, then his twin is more likely to have it also if they are identical twins. In other words, the concordance rate, as it is called, is higher for identical than non-identical twins. F. J. Kallmann was the first to compare and contrast the two kinds of twins to see whether certain conditions were genetically determined. In 1952 he reported a 100 per cent concordance for homosexuality in identical twins and other twin studies which followed also found a high concordance rate for homosexuality in identical twins, though less than 100 per cent. However, there are two criticisms which might be levelled against these investigations. Firstly, the subjects were psychiatric patients – this is how they were traced – and this could have influenced the results. Secondly, non-identical twins, though they are brought up together, may have significantly different nurturings, while identical twins, looking so alike as to be almost indistinguishable by their parents, and of the same intelligence, are likely to have exactly the same upbringing. Thus the high concordance for homosexuality among identical twins could be because of identical rearing, not identical genes. Over the years pairs of identical twins, one homosexual, the other heterosexual, have been discovered. In some instances there has been striking evidence that they were treated differently by their mother – in one instance, for example, a twin had nearly died and was subsequently over-protected. This problem of nature versus nurture often arises in interpreting twin studies' results. The way out of the difficulty is to find a group of identical twins who have been separated early in life and had entirely disparate upbringings. However, very few pairs of twins such as these have been found. At least two pairs have been found, and in both instances the separated twins became homosexual. But had the propensity been laid down before they were separated? It is difficult to find cast-iron evidence.

The hypothesis that homosexuality is genetically transmitted receives philsophical backing from sociobiology. The scattering of homosexuals in a primitive society would have forced them to devote all their energies to hunting, food gathering and domestic occupations. Consequently their close relatives would have been free to have more children and to concentrate on their upbringing. Unless it has a useful sociological function, the homosexual trait would have evolved out by now. This may be an intellectually attractive theory, but surely in practice families in our societies have not seen any advantage in having a homosexual member? Many would say the reverse was so.

It need not be either-or, nature or nurture. If there is a genetic disposition towards homosexuality, it is surely not an inevitable, unavoidable, absolute determinant but a tendency. With environmental or psychosocial factors it will steer the individual towards a homosexual orientation. There has been much searching in order to identify these psychosocial factors.

Irving Bieber's investigation of 1962 is the most famous – or infamous, for the results are strongly resented by homosexuals and Bieber is a nasty word in the gay liberation movement. He concluded that male homosexuals had 'a close, binding, intimate relationship' with their mother. The objections levelled at Bieber's findings are almost as well-known as the findings themselves. Based on subjective impressions of patients having analysis, recorded by analysts with decided preconceptions, the information was bound to be biased. However, the same family constellation has appeared in surveys performed by workers without psychoanalytic leanings and in a number of the subsequent surveys the homosexuals interviewed were not patients of any kind but recruited from the community. Yet there is still much to explain. Since it is rare for there to be more than one homosexual son in a family, we have to assume that the mother didn't smother her

243

other sons and the father was friendlier and closer to them. Conceivably, the boy is born with a tendency to be homosexual and hidden qualities prompt his parents to adopt the attitudes they do. Homosexuals appear to exist in all societies, primitive and modern, and the neat, cosy Western picture with smothering mother and detached or absent father can hardly be universally applicable.

Homosexuals are often only sons or youngest sons. This fits in with Bieber's findings, for in such circumstances mothers would have more time to be close, binding and intimate with their young son and lack of playmates would make the boys seek their mother's company. The tendency is marked: in an English survey of 127 male homosexual volunteers from the community, 80 per cent of them had been reared either as only sons or as youngest sons. A Swedish survey yielded a similar result. As might be expected, the mothers (and fathers) of male homosexuals tend to be significantly older than normal. There have been no surveys of this kind concerning female homosexuals. Indeed, in general lesbianism has attracted much less attention from the researchers.

Seduction is not a cause. When an older person seems to have led a youngster into exclusive homosexuality, it only seems so, for it has been a matter of confirming an orientation and not a conversion. People do not choose to be homosexual. The choice is whether to accept one's orientation. Parents worry unnecessarily about their children patterning themselves on homosexual teachers and being seduced by them. This is presumably why many people object to homosexuals being employed as teachers. There is a much bigger risk of an adolescent girl being seduced by a male teacher. Indeed there is usually no clear distinction between seducer and seduced in homosexual relations when they begin. There is mutual consent.

Psychiatrists have altered their therapeutic role for treating homosexuals. Twenty-five years ago they invariably wanted to eliminate the homosexuality and change the person into a heterosexual. Nowadays they generally aim to help the homosexuals to accept and adjust to their homosexual orientation. The former approach was based on the traditional disease concept of homosexuality. It was psychologically unhealthy and therefore it had to be removed. The homosexuals for their part were keen to be 'cured', for they were filled with guilt, frustration and despair and acutely aware of the damage to their careers to which expression of their feelings could lead and even – in those days – the long prison sentence it could earn male homosexuals. But the 'talking cure' which psychiatrists and psychotherapists offered – tracing long-forgotten infantile experiences and fantasies and examining them in adult light – was ineffective. Even the few patients who were regarded as successes and entered holy matrimony were apt to have intermittent promiscuous lapses and heterosexual impotence if they were men and marital failure with bewildered upset children if they were men or women. On top of this, the gay liberation movement, which was born during this period, bitterly opposed what its members regarded as immoral and psychologically damaging interference. A homosexual orientation is the natural endowment of the privileged few, they claimed, and any attempt to revert or convert to heterosexuality should be firmly discouraged. Thus the days of treatment aimed at re-orientation are over – or almost over.

Occasionally, even now, homosexuals request help to change their orientation and sometimes there are grounds for attempting this. Frustration and guilt would not now be considered sufficient justification. Counselling them so that they could be reconciled to their sexual orientation would be regarded as more appropriate. Nor would there be any justification in attempting to make a heterosexual out of someone whose fantasies and inclinations have been consistently homosexual. But it could be otherwise for someone nearer the middle of the Kinsey scale, young and not too set in homosexual ways and thought, desperately keen to alter because of a career in the diplomatic service or enjoying an otherwise successful marriage. Traditional psychotherapy is still used, with a more direct approach though. However, behavioural therapy has largely superseded it for the treatment of sexual difficulties in general. It is much shorter and at least as effective – though this is not saying much, especially in terms of long-term results. The first behavioural therapy treatment for homosexuals was aversion therapy (electric shocks for the patient looking at photographs of same-sex nudes for example), but this has been followed by modification of masturbatory fantasies (switching from homosexual to heterosexual images at the point of orgasm, then slightly earlier, and earlier). Masters and Johnson have given the most optimistic reports of change. They treated 54 men and 13 women who wanted to convert or revert to heterosexuality, carefully chosen and highly motivated. Their treatment required an understanding partner of the opposite sex. It followed the same lines as their well-known, two-week rapid treatment technique for heterosexual couples with various sexual dysfunctions. On the follow-up after five years they estimated a one-third failure rate. Success and failure were not clearly defined by Masters and Johnson, but presumably they referred to ability or inability to perform as a heterosexual.

Mostly, however, troubled homosexuals are best helped by assisting their psychological and social adjustment to their homosexual orientation. Slowly and painfully they will have become aware of the direction of their sexual interests. They must be sick, immoral and wicked according to their social and moral standards, but their feelings persist, however unwelcome. They could be fortunate and happen to have a homosexual friend in whom to confide. The latter would know the transitory from the permanent and, having experienced the public hostility accorded homosexuals, would not encourage anyone to follow the same path unless there was no alternative. Otherwise they break the loneliness of their identity quest and make their problem known to someone who might understand, their minister or college counsellor for example. If rebuffed at this stage they might well plunge into a long, dreary reactive depression. Often enough a person with a homosexual identity problem comes to the psychiatrist with a depression. The homosexual difficulty is only unearthed later. On the other hand, patients over 30 and suffering from a primary depression may present themselves to a psychiatrist with an overwhelming concern about having turned into a homosexual. Patients with severe depressions often have delusions about being bankrupt, or being sent to prison, and such is the ignominy which many good-living, God-fearing people accord to homosexuals that they believe this is the fate which has befallen them while they are in their deep depression.

Sometimes patients in their thirties and suffering from an incipient paranoid schizophrenia visit a psychiatrist complaining that people are spreading rumours that they are homosexual. If the patient is still in adolescence the homosexual attraction may be no more than an enlarged and extended same-sex teenage relationship.

It takes years for a homosexual to come out. 'Coming out of the closet' was the code phrase among homosexuals to denote acknowledging one's homosexuality and letting it be generally known, but it has now become a hackneyed expression to denote disclosing anything. There are various approaches which psychiatrists and counsellors employ to help emerging homosexuals. In addition to traditional individual psychotherapy, there is group therapy with eight to 12 homosexual members and a therapist and this is now frequently employed in large centres. There are times when it is more telling for another member to point out a weakness, fear or excuse than when a therapist does it. Assertive training is sometimes given to those who are particularly anxious about telling friends and family; it takes the form of rehearsals, with the therapist playing the role of friend or parent. According to their inclinations, homosexuals may be advised about groups or clubs they might like to visit, the interdenominational Gay Christian Movement or the Jewish Homosexual Group for instance. Some may have drifted into marriage, but been unable to contain their homosexual inclinations, and the non-homosexual spouses may find counselling helpful. Some marriages have been able to continue with one member homosexual, Oscar Wilde's for instance. (Indeed, some marriages are able to continue with both members homosexual, that of Harold Nicolson and Vita Sackville-West for example.)

The parents of the coming-out homosexual have to come out, to acknowledge that their son or daughter is a homosexual. They, too, may require professional support when their son or daughter has broken the news. The latter should tell their parents, rather than lead a double life or leave them to find out for themselves. They should prepare for the occasion, carefully deciding what to say, restricting it to the central fact and keeping the small print for another day – or other days because there may be many discussions before they are reconciled, rehearsing the questions and answers with a friend or professional adviser. Even so, and even if it comes over in a calm, patient, loving way, the parents may take it badly at first. What have they done, upright and respectable citizens as they are, they may ask themselves? At such a time, temporary anger at whoever might be nailed as seducer and threats to break up relations are often followed by unwarranted but nevertheless powerful, wounding guilt and depression. Thus parents, who might demand that their child seeks psychiatric help, could well be in most need of it. Many parents are quickly in tune though and immensely helpful over the ensuing months. For those parents who are bewildered but hardly in need of treatment *A Family Matter: Parents' Guide to Homosexuality* by C. Silverstein

(1977) is a helpful book. For those who want to know more about homosexuality there is a choice between A. P. Bell & M. S. Weinberg's *Homosexualities* (1978), already mentioned, and D. J. West's *Homosexuality Re-examined* (1977).

INCEST

Incest is sexual intercourse between people who are closely related. Taboos prohibiting incest exist in all societies and have existed throughout history, but societies have differed in defining the precise closeness of the family relationship. So although it is well-nigh universal to debar sexual intercourse between brothers and sisters, some ancient cultures – in Egypt, Persia, Hawaii and Peru – encouraged or demanded the mating of brother and sister if they belonged to the royal households. At the other extreme, some societies regard sexual intercourse between cousins as incestuous.

The incest taboo is legally enforced in some countries, although not all the family relationships that might be regarded as incestuous are necessarily covered by the laws. For example, in England, it is a criminal offence for a man to have sexual intercourse with his daughter, grand-daughter, sister, half-sister, or mother, but not with his step-mother or daughter-in-law. That is distinct from laws concerning marriage, which do forbid a man to marry his step-mother or his daughter-in-law – and some other relatives too. There was no law against incest (except in Church law) in England and Wales until the beginning of this century, although in Scotland it had been a criminal offence since the sixteenth century. There is now pressure, from the National Council for Civil Liberties among others, to follow countries such as France and Holland where incest is not a crime and which rely on laws dealing generally with sexual offences against women and girls.

There is no simple explanation for the primeval prohibition of incest. Some say it is based on a need to avoid the dangers of inbreeding. However, primitive man would not have known the risks (although even he had incest taboos according to the experts). Anyway, inbreeding does not necessarily lead to weak or abnormal stock. It can lead to superior offspring, as every cattle breeder knows. The noble Incas suffered no disadvantage through 14 generations of brother-sister mating. Now there is a growing body of knowledge about chromosomal abnormalities, single-gene defects,

248

multifactorial disorders and genetic diseases. Our knowledge of these may buttress our incest taboo and has prompted medical bodies such as the Royal College of Psychiatrists and the British Medical Association to advocate retaining laws against incest. But primitive man knew nothing about genetics, so the taboo goes deeper than mere knowledge. Even though man did not consciously decide that the surest way of having healthy offspring was to outbreed, some brain mechanism may have evolved which inhibited close relatives from mating. Primates, too, usually avoid incestuous relations. Maurice Temerlin had a chimpanzee called Lucy which he brought up at home from infancy to maturity. In his book *My Daughter Lucy* (1975) he describes how she constantly treated him with affection, demonstrating it with lavish, wet kisses. However, when she started menstruation, she rejected him entirely. Temerlin concluded that this was the result of a biological taboo.

The main function of the incest taboo is not to prevent inbreeding but to preserve family structure and stabilize relationships within it. There is a social necessity to protect the family unit and prevent internal rivalry. If fathers, once their daughters had grown up, abandoned their wives and cohabited with their daughters – or if sons, once they felt strong enough to take on their fathers, threw them out and settled into their mothers' beds – the family unit would lose its structure and collapse.

Incest is mainly a male problem. It is generally men who take the initiative in breaking the taboo and leave their partners or victims with little or no choice, as the conviction figures show. In law, any female of 16 or more who has an incestuous relationship can be convicted, but in practice females are hardly ever charged. None has been in England and Wales for several years. Father—daughter and brother–sister are the common forms, but more cases of grandfather–granddaughter and mother–son incest have been heard in court. Brother–sister incest accounts for nearly a quarter of all incest convictions in England. But most incest is not reported to the police at all – nine cases out of ten are hushed up according to a recent American study – and probably the number of unreported brother–sister cases is particularly high, especially in poorer homes where shared beds or bedrooms are common. Father-–daughter incest poses the biggest problem – it accounts for three-quarters of all convictions; it is usually a long-term relationship lasting for a year or more (in contrast to brother–sister incest

249

which is usually a single, exceptional event) and offends the most profound part of the incest taboo; in other words it causes the greatest family disruption.

There seem to be three kinds of fathers who engage in sexual relations with their daughters: paedophiles, who have a predilection for sex with little children – other men's daughters usually but in these cases their own as well; indiscriminately promiscuous men, some of whom are heavy drinkers; and endogamic men, that is, men who confine themselves exclusively to their family, are likely to be restrained and moralistic, and perhaps devoutly religious. A quarter of the convictions for incest are to do with girls aged under 13. Nearly a half of the girls are aged 13 to 15, past their best as far as paedophiles are concerned, but nubile and vulnerable for promiscuous fathers and brothers. The figures drop sharply at 16, but tail into the thirties.

The most important question may not be what kind of man engages in sexual intercourse with his daughter, but in what kind of family does incest happen? Not uncommonly, the family has had problems before the incest begins, particularly in regard to sexual laxity and marital strife. In family therapy, which incest families need to have, faulty long-standing relationships between the members will be revealed and adjustments will be needed. All the members of the family need to participate in this treatment. If we restrict attention to the victim and her father, the disturbed family is likely to remain disturbed. During the therapy, it could well become apparent that the marriage is basically unsatisfactory and unsalvageable, and that the only solution is for father and mother to separate, with the support of family therapy to assist in rehabilitation.

Both the immediate and the long-term effects on daughters affected by incest are usually devastating. They feel profound guilt for acquiescing (as generally happens, although occasionally force is employed). Girls acquiesce because they are brought up to accede to their fathers' needs, to do what they are told and to be loving daughters – as is part of any father–daughter relation. But it is for not having followed their inner feelings that they feel the guilt, and feel depressed in consequence. Women may also suffer long-term effects when, in their early teens, they were involved for many months in an incestuous father–daughter relationship. A young woman may turn to prostitution, providing the use of her body for a reward, as she used to do with her father. In a recent

American study, three-quarters of the prostitutes interviewed said they had been in incestuous relationships. Other incest victims go on to break the law in various ways. It is easy to understand their lack of social conscience, for their fathers painstakingly taught them to ignore one of the most fundamental social laws of all. However, incest often takes place within families already at heavy odds against society, so more could be at work in moving these girls towards crime than their unfortunate incest experiences. At best, however, even those incest victims who have become good law-abiding citizens are likely to be frigid, finding sex distasteful or even frightening.

MASTURBATORY GUILT

Masturbation is sexual self-stimulation. In former days it was known as self-pollution and some dictionaries still define it as 'self-abuse', because it was regarded as reprehensible. Indeed, while moral advisers now reassure young people tht masturbation is not harmful, they still add provisos – 'in moderation' (whatever that may mean), 'for certain purposes' (to relieve tension but not for pleasure, for instance), 'without entertaining fantasies about people you know', 'without fantasies at all'. According to Roman Catholic doctrine, masturbation is a carnal sin. Although most priests play this aspect down, a minority sternly warn the young of its sinful nature. There is also concern about the sin of masturbation within the Protestant Churches. The Reverend Professor Jay Adams, a widely-read writer on pastoral counselling, inveighs against masturbation in several books. Masturbators, in his experience, often come in agony, begging for help to stop. They feel so guilty that they plead 'Do something for me; help me'. This appears in the section headed 'Masturbation is Sin' in *The Christian Counsellor's Manual*. The next section is 'Masturbation can be Cured' but it is clear that cure may be difficult. For a start, those 'trapped by this habit' and sinning at night, must have 'vigorous exercise' before retiring, whereas those sinning in the morning must have their alarm clock at the other side of the room so that they have to get out of bed to turn the alarm off!

Psychiatric patients still, occasionally, have masturbatory guilt but very rarely do they actually complain about it. The writer remembers a retired minister, a famous preacher of his day, who came to see him because of a craving to masturbate which brought awful remorse when he succumbed, because in his mind it was without a doubt sinful. Sometimes, too, patients with psychotic depressions may be anguishing about failing to obtain divine forgiveness for masturbating. Treatment for their depression soon washes away their guilt, but its existence suggests that society's disapproval of masturbation has not yet gone. However, masturbatory guilt usually comes to light only during psychotherapy and mainly among women. The writer recalls a missionary in her late thirties who had been flown back from the Far East with what was thought to be an acute thyroid disease. She had difficulty in swallowing and a fast pulse, had lost many pounds in weight, was very agitated and had several other symptoms. But investigations showed that her thyroid was normal. However, a little later she confessed that she had discovered masturbation a few years before. This she performed, in her lonely mission station, in a scalding hot bath or tied up naked in rough rope. She had wanted desperately to stop but, like the clergyman, sometimes found the forbidden fruit irresistible.

Masturbatory guilt does not usually appear so dramatically in psychotherapy. A woman may be only vaguely aware of masturbating and may also be subconsciously avoiding thinking about it. She may have read somewhere that it is a normal, healthy activity and may now be denying to herself that it worries her. Or she may think it is too disgusting to mention. It is surprising that such cases appear in this day and age, but they occasionally do. Philip Roth's *Portnoy's Complaint* is a portrait of a man suffering from masturbatory guilt. Portnoy's real tragedy was his failure to establish an enduring relationship with any of the three girls in his life, but he thought of himself as in bondage to masturbation.

There is still a hang-up about masturbation, a legacy of many centuries of condemnation. Prejudices do not change overnight, gut feelings resist logical argument; and one set of beliefs overlaps another. 'Humanity does not pass through phases as a train passes through stations,' C. S. Lewis wrote. 'Being alive, it has the privilege of always moving yet never leaving anything behind. Whatever we have been, in some sort we are still.' This is why we include the otherwise blameless activity of masturbation in this chapter. In addition, a look at the moral history of masturbation gives us a perspective from which to consider society's attitude of opprobrium towards other sexual activities, in particular homosexuality.

Masturbation was regarded as a serious sin for very many centuries. The Talmud, the Jewish code, which condemned all sexual acts which could not result in conception, even forbade a single man to hold his penis while urinating. Early Christianity followed on, prescribing harsh penalties for masturbators.

In the 13th century, St Thomas Aquinas produced a consolidated statement about sexual sins that has had a lasting and profound influence, especially in the Roman Catholic Church. Lust of all kinds was sinful, he said, for lust opposed reason, and the sins were either 'against one's neighbour and other people' or 'against nature'. So adultery, and even rape, which were among the former, were less serious than such acts as 'unnatural' intercourse (only the missionary position – face to face and man on top – was natural) and masturbation. Aquinas was a creature of his time and he was largely reflecting conventional thought. Later thinkers, such as Hume and Kant, also viewed non-procreative sexual acts as immoral, even though their independent minds completely changed the course of modern philosophy. Masturbation, homosexuality and bestiality, wrote Kant, 'make a man unworthy of his humanity. He no longer deserves to be a person'.

Nineteenth-century Protestants looked to the Bible for a ruling, and there masturbation seemed to be condemned on almost every page. The strongest evidence was in *Genesis*, in the story of Onan who, they decided, was destroyed by God for practising self-pollution or onanism, to use the term coined at the time. The fact is that Onan did not practise onanism (masturbation) but the withdrawal method of intercourse (coitus interruptus) as is perfectly clear in *Genesis*. No new Dead Sea scroll had to be studied, no new textual interpretation was required, to alter the 19th century interpretation to the 20th century one – only a change of public opinion. Public opinion influences moral teaching. In turn, moral teaching, chiefly by the Churches, consolidates public opinion and hinders it from changing. Even if we are undevout and unbelieving, we cannot totally escape absorbing, consciously or unconsciously, the prevailing moral attitudes.

During the 18th and 19th centuries, the religious condemnation of masturbation was augmented by medical condemnation (which shows how doctors, too, are largely governed by conventional attitudes). It came to be believed that masturbation caused, among other things, phimosis, priapism, impotence, gonorrhoea (more difficult to be cured than if caught during intercourse), fainting

253

fits, epilepsies, consumptions, vapours, and seminal emissions at night in men, and in women pallor, hysterical fits, consumptions and barrenness. Later came the notion of masturbatory insanity, which soon became part of accepted medical theory. The author of this idea, Dr S. A. D. Tissot, observed that in attaining orgasm by any means, energy is expended, and the degree of consequent fatigue suggested that this was considerable. Therefore, he reasoned, too many orgasms would lead to enfeeblement. The loss of even one drop of seminal fluid caused more damage than losing 40 drops of blood, he claimed. Moreover, because the self-polluter knew he was sinning, his brain was rendered more sensitive to damage. So the medical theory that masturbation was a major cause of illness, physical and mental, was now launched and it became generally accepted through the 19th century. Only a few medical men expressed their doubts. One was John Hunter, a contemporary of Tissot, who in his famous *Treatise on the venereal disease*, observed that as impotence was rare and masturbation common, there was probably no connection. When his brother-in-law, Sir Everard Home, surgeon to the King, brought out a third edition after Hunter's death, he omitted this from the book.

To prevent masturbation, instruments were devised to prevent young people indulging and there were even operations on masturbators. Chastity belts were really to prevent girls and young women masturbating, for chastity included the avoidance of masturbation as well as intercourse. Dr William Moodie's *A Medical Treatise* (1848) is mainly a description of a belt he had designed. 'It is chiefly for the purpose of preventing the young, and unmarried, from using artificial bodies in the vagina for exciting lascivious and licentious and pleasurable sensations, which are caused by friction, and pressure made on the sides of this highly sensitive and nervous canal or passage.' He thought a girl should have one when she became aged seven or eight, and that it could be replaced by larger ones as she grew older. 'It may be kept on until marriage, or until the girl has a command over her feelings, and has the moral courage to resist.' An ivory grate cushioned by leather or rubber was placed over the vulva. It was designed to allow the free flow of urine but prevented the insertion of even the tip of the finger or any instrument. It was kept in place by a broad belt or braces, the laces of which were fixed to a padlock. When the chastity belts failed, or if parents had been imprudent enough not to have their children so equipped, there was removal of the clitoris for diseases thought to have been induced by masturbation. Male anti-masturbation belts and devices included penile rings with spikes which would pierce the penis if it erected. Circumcision, and even castration, were employed in the treatment of male masturbatory illnesses.

Such nonsenses went out with the last century. But Freud, writing at the beginning of this one, did not rule out the harmful effects of masturbation altogether. Nor did some other early psychoanalysts. Their views too have now been discarded. However, there remains a sneaking fear that masturbation might be harmful in excess. In fact, a man's body has a built-in mechanism which prevents this. An ache in the scrotum and a pain in the penis discourage too many ejaculations. Repeated masturbation would create physical symptoms which would inhibit erection, so 'excessive' masturbation is impossible. One or two writers, not psychiatrists, refer to particular schizophrenics who masturbate excessively, ignoring the increasing physical symptoms and damaging their health – but these cases sound as if they belong to the masturbatory myth.

Extremely rarely, a man may suffer from an obsession to masturbate. Like any other obession, hand-washing for example, there is an overpowering desire to perform the act again and again. Although the sufferer decides to stop, the compulsion becomes overwhelming, he concedes to it, and then he feels guilty at having succumbed. But the fact that there exist these few cases of obsessional masturbation is not a reflection on the practice of masturbation, any more than hand-washing obsessions, which are much commoner, indicate that we should never wash our hands, or be careful to control the number of times that we wash them. Some women who regularly masturbate by crossing their legs find it hard to reach orgasm in sexual intercourse, but that, too, is no reason to restrict masturbation or that method of doing it. The exhaustion which men and some women feel after masturbation is the same as they would feel after an orgasm in sexual intercourse. It is salutary after there has been pent-up tension, and it almost always goes after a few minutes.

Masturbation is more or less essential for adolescent boys and young men, and many women find it beneficial. It may be valuable when a couple are temporarily apart. Modern sex therapy employs it as an aid towards correcting many sexual disorders. All this is generally accepted now. Some authors recommend its regular employment because they claim that the sexual apparatus, like any other part of the body, needs toning up. Some women advocate it in preference to sexual intercourse with men which they regard as exploitation – Shere Hite of *The Hite Report*, for example, found 'so much to recommend it – easy and intense orgasms, an unending source of pleasure – but unfortunately we are all suffering in some degree from a culture that says people should not masturbate.' It is hard to take seriously, though, her apparent preference for masturbation, in its solitariness, to sexual intercourse as an expression of human love. It is a poor substitute, though not evil or unhealthy.

Of the men interviewed by the Kinsey team, 94 per cent said they had masturbated to orgasm sometime in their life, and perhaps some out of the remaining six per cent were unwilling to admit to what they regarded as a weakness or a sin. There is evidence that masturbation among women is on the increase. The Kinsey Report showed that although the frequency of intercourse had remained the same, female masturbation to orgasm had increased over a period of 40 years by 10 per cent among the younger generation to 40 per cent of all women. More recent studies suggest the rising trend has continued in the second half of the 20th century. Furthermore, these statistics are probably underestimates. This is not only because of the problem of persuading women to talk to interviewers about this embarrassing subject, but also because not all women who masturbate choose to go to orgasm. So it is sometimes difficult to know for sure whether a woman is masturbating or not and Kinsey chose orgasm as the indicator. How many women engage in non-orgasmic masturbation, or masturbate without being aware of what they are doing, remains unknown. It hardly matters.

Professor Jay Adams cannot find one reference in the Bible which condemns masturbation so he employs general arguments. For example, ' . . . if masturbation is normal then (presumably) Adam before the fall, and Christ, during His earthly life, masturbated. Does that statement startle you? If so, then you must not set norms by counting noses on sinful men!' It comes from his recent book *More than Redemption*. Perhaps masturbation was, indeed, one of the pleasures of Paradise.

NYMPHOMANIA

Nymphomania is excessive sexual activity by a woman in which she has an endless and unsatisfying chain of male partners. The sexual encounters are transitory, preventing the formation of lasting relations. There are several types of nymphomaniacs or nymphos, but in general they are sad, unsatisfied women despite all their activity. The parallel condition in men is satyriasis (see page 280).

Nymphomaniacs should not be confused with certain highly-sexed, multi-orgasmic women who restrict themselves to ephemeral sexual encounters either because they scorn the security and warmth of an enduring relationship and are conscious of the social restrictions it may entail or because they have not found a suitable partner and want to explore and develop their own sexuality. The advent of the Pill made this kind of lifestyle possible and a loosening of the social conscience made it more acceptable. It appears to be recommended less energetically nowadays, for a number of reasons. There is an increased awareness of sexually transmitted diseases. The Pill is not the perfect contraceptive after all, for there is the risk of various serious ill-effects after long-term use. Those feminists who advocated this way of life because they thought it would protect women from male exploitation later realized that it made everything easier and better for the sexual playboy. And there are some indications of a revived awareness of former moral values. But plenty of women still choose to live this way and are happy doing so. They are not propelled willy-nilly into an unpleasant, unfulfilling, unpredictable kind of promiscuity like the nymphomaniac.

There is no difficulty in distinguishing the two on paper but there sometimes is in practice, especially if the nymphomaniac is a single young woman. Her casual and immoderate sexual activity may take the guise of the other kind of promiscuity – which is discriminating and under control, though not limited by marriage or cohabitation. There is no problem in those instances when the nymphomaniac asks for professional help, which is not very unusual – in contrast to the satyr. The request is made because of her frustration and unhappiness with her uncontrollable cravings or because her embarrassed family or friends have persuaded her. Nymphomania is more likely to be detected if the woman is married – and may lead to marital discord or disruption – but it

257

may be disguised if her husband subscribes to wife-swopping, troil-ism and group sex.

Nymphomania arises in several ways not necessarily mutually exclusive. The woman may have a deep need to gain ascendency over men, by humiliating and abasing them sexually. This is akin to the satyr's insatiable need to conquer women by seducing them. The nymphomaniac scorns the men's potency and shows them up to be impotent. The point is reached when the men cannot further satisfy her enormous sexual capacity. This capacity could be real, that of a highly-sexed woman capable of 30 orgasms and more in an afternoon of lovemaking. More likely, there is some sexual fakery, to use Masters and Johnson's droll term, pretending to be strongly excited and orgasmic while deciding what to have for dinner, something women can do but men can't. These women, it often transpires, have had a childhood in which they hated the males around them for the preference they were always given and for their superior physical strength.

The nymphomaniac is not always a multi-orgasmic woman, but, on the contrary, may be an anorgasmic woman in search of an orgasm. She may be able to attain it by manual stimulation, but not through coitus, and in our orgasm-orientated culture she feels she is missing out. It is always just beyond her reach but, eternal optimist, she keeps up the search for the sexual partner who will help her to achieve it. Her anatomy may mitigate against success – a clitoris tucked too far out of the way – but she will be unaware of this. In other cases of nymphomania the impelling force, or the main one, is a general feeling of inferiority. The woman feels ordinary, dull and unattractive, but resolves to compensate by a willingness and enthusiasm for sex. Once the man is satiated, however, there is nothing else to offer and she is off looking for another man with whom she will employ the same method for her reassurance. Occasionally the nymphomaniac is denying a homosexual orientation, her upbringing making it totally unac-ceptable, and hence her endless search to find a man who will provide exciting heterosexual sex. Finally, there are nympho-maniacs whose quest is for the man that never was, an ideal mate they have built up in their dreams. There is often a mixture of these different factors impelling the nymphomaniac.

PAEDOPHILIA

Paedophilia – having sexual relations with children – is the most despised of all sexual practices. Paedophiles, like all sex deviants, are almost always men, though there have been occasional reports of adult women being charged with indecent assault for having sexual relations with a boy in his early teens. Women often stroke, cuddle and caress young children, with society's full approval. A man doing the same would earn its full disapproval. But these women are not seeking sexual gratification; and the man may well be.

Abhorrence of paedophilia knows no bounds. Experience has shown that paedophiles in prison have to be protected against attacks by fellow prisoners. The intensity of this near universal detestation is difficult to explain fully. It is understandable that the whole country should be angry when news appears of a little girl who has been abducted, taken to a deserted spot, raped and murdered. But this kind of tragedy is rare and such behaviour totally uncharacteristic of paedophiles. In general, they are shy, gentle men who are otherwise harmless.

The picture of the lustful, dirty old man, with bag of sweets, luring little children away for sexual intercourse, is also wide of the mark. Paedophiles may be any age, though the peak age is around the mid to late thirties. A man who does not begin making advances to children until he is 60 is probably suffering from arteriosclerosis or a disease of the brain, drunk, or unbearably lonely after the death of his wife. Generally, paedophiles have difficulty in forming easy relationships with adults, but most of them marry at some stage and they are more likely to be happily married than other sexual offenders. Their pursuit of sexual pleasure with children often co-exists with a satisfactory marital relation. Sometimes they marry mother-figures and the marriage is a child–parent relation, congenial enough but without sex. Others have normal sex in their marriage. Paedophiles are not usually strangers. They are more likely to be relatives, friends, neighbours, priests or youth leaders. Sexual play does not usually go further than viewing, showing, fondling or being fondled. Most commonly, the man fondles the child's genitals. Vaginal and anal intercourse is rare. The child often invites the physical relations and enjoys them. Some of the children benefit from a genuine loving relationship which may develop. However, these statistics, culled from British and American reports, in no way justify paedophilia.

So far we have referred to the object of the paedophile's desire simply as the child. Only a few paedophiles are bisexual, however, deriving sexual gratification from contact with both boys and girls. Most are drawn either to boys or to girls. They are usually referred to as homosexual and heterosexual paedophiles. But it has to be borne in mind that a homosexual paedophile rarely engages in adult homosexual relations as well, and that the detestation of paedophilia is probably nowhere more strongly felt than among adult homosexuals.

Men who are erotically drawn to boys tend to be younger, by five years on average, than those who are drawn to girls. The boys to whom they are attracted are mostly aged 11 to 15 years, the most popular age being 13. At this time of life, many boys in any case try same-sex sexual pleasure among themselves. The boys themselves, however, generally go no further than mutual genital admiration or perhaps masturbation, and it is purely physical, without emotional tie. In man–boy relations, the physical repertoire is often extended and some sort of romance may develop. The latter may be felt strongly by the man, who then concerns himself about the boy's general welfare and tries to steer him through the stormy waters of adolescence. This is the kind of relation advanced by Plato in *The Symposium*. (It is strange that Platonic love has come to mean something totally different, a purely spiritual love between a man and woman.)

Unlike the society in Classical Greece, our society strongly discourages man–boy love. No one knows why certain men need to have it so strongly that they defy society's proscription. Although it remains a mystery, there are one or two clues. Several studies have found that the boys who enter into these relations with men often come from unsatisfactory families – with neglectful, violent or drunken fathers, inadequate mothers, or broken homes – and have been seeking affection. The men themselves, these studies have also shown, have had unhappy, loveless boyhoods. There is a need in them, or so it seems, to give the boys the affection which they themselves missed, to be the generous parent they did not have. They are drawn to professions and leisure activities that provide them with opportunities to fulfil this need, becoming exceptionally good teachers, welfare officers, or youth leaders. At first they may be unaware of any desire for physical contact. Some may recognize it, or come to recognize it, but resolutely and painfully avoid fulfilling it. Others find the boys in their care irresistibly attractive. They find ethical arguments to reconcile their sexual relations – based on reports that show that boys engaged in them need not adopt a permanent homosexual orientation – and they take the risk of being caught, convicted and severely punished.

The girls whom paedophiles find attractive are younger than the boys. Most of them are 8 to 11 years of age, especially 10 to 11. Girls older than this are sexually attractive to men. As far as unlawful sexual intercourse is concerned, there are twelve times as many cases recorded by the police concerning girls aged 13 to 15 as there are cases concerning girls under 13. But the sexual partners of the older girls are not paedophiles but youths and young men – disregarding that their precocious partner is under 16. Surveys have shown that the prepubertal girls who become the victims of paedophiles are, like the boys, seeking affection. The men, more so than those attracted to boys, tend to be uneasy in adult company and are more comfortable when they are with little girls. Many of them have convinced themselves – or been convinced by experience – that they cannot win a woman's affection. Some of them have been married, more than once in a few cases, but they still find women frightening. The little girl, on the other hand, is unthreatening, undemanding, innocent and spontaneous in her affection. The paedophile may stop at this stage, enjoying the girl's company. But the girl's body, pure, undefiled, virgin, may be irresistible, so he carefully makes a plan to see and touch her genitals. Only rarely is it a sudden, impulsive move. Not infrequently, the man may show off his erect penis. The paedophile very rarely progresses to coitus, however. His plan will include impressing on the girl how they need to keep all their transactions secret. If he is a family friend and frequently about, he might take the precaution of subtly implying that the girl occasionally romances, fantasizes, strays from the truth a little bit. There is no knowing how often the girl chooses to tell her parents. Children are less likely to tell their parents when they have been actively involved in the sex play, or when they have freely consented to it. There is no knowing how often parents do not believe the girl, do not report the matter to the police so as to protect the girl from further upset, or do not report it because they hate losing an old friend. The number of cases which are reported to the police and followed up by them is probably only a small percentage of the whole.

A girl who has recently been the victim of a paedophile's attention is very likely to be upset. One-quarter of the women in Kinsey's sample reported having had some sort of sexual experience before they reached puberty with a post-pubertal male, and four-fifths of these women said they had been frightened or upset, although for most of them this amounted to no more than if they had seen a spider or an insect they did not like. Other reports, though, generally describe more pronounced immediate effects. Nightmares, bed-wetting, difficulty in falling asleep, fear of the dark, impaired concentration and poor performance at school, and even depression have all been reported. A minority seem unaffected, but it is possible that they have unconsciously blocked out the experience.

The effect the girl's parents have on her, when she comes and tells them or when they fathom the story, having noticed one or more of these symptoms appear, may be two-edged. They are shocked, and their shock which is much greater than hers greatly magnifies her shock, and their guilt compounds her guilt. On the other hand they can be supportive and understanding. The girl will recover more quickly if she has consistent love from her parents. She must feel that she is being believed, that being guilty for being too trusting is uncalled for, and that she may tell what she wants and when she wants.

It can be an agonizing problem for parents to decide whether or not to report the matter to the police. When a woman is raped it is important that she makes the decision herself, but in the case of a child, although she has to be given some say, her parents have to take the responsibility. They will be angry and want justice to be done, but the most important factor is the girl's welfare. Many of the problems confronting a woman who reports rape also crop up here. Even when the investigations are made sensitively, they may be traumatic for the girl. If the parents do report the matter, the police may decide not to proceed because of insufficient corroborative evidence or the emotional state of the girl. They caution more men and many more juveniles than they prosecute for having sexual intercourse with a girl under 16 years of age.

So much for immediate problems. As for long-term effects, few girls appear to suffer from long-standing symptoms. There have been numerous follow-up studies and that is the overall conclusion.

The studies included girls with inconsiderate and considerate parents, with dropped and pursued cases. An older girl, involved for some time in a sexual relation with a man, may be launched into an unhappy sexual precociousness. If the man has used violence, the girl may suffer from frigidity in her marriage. But cases of this nature are, according to the surveys, rare.

Even so, precautions should be taken to prevent children from falling prey to paedophiles. Obvious advice, such as to refuse gifts and car rides from strangers, is not enough, because the paedophile probably is not a stranger at all. Little children should be taught that their body is their own and that they should protest when a male, unknown or known to them, touches them or kisses them in a way that frightens or stimulates them, or asks them to take off their clothes. Ideally, schools should drill them into saying 'My body is mine', and teach them, unsensationally, about men taking liberties.

Society's detestation of paedophiles is reflected in the savage sentences meted out by the courts, and it is little wonder that most convicted paedophiles have no further relations with children. Yet a few of them do. The wonder is that these soft, gentle, fragile men, having survived a prison stretch, are caught with children again. Surely there ought to be some consideration of treatment apart from the demands for retribution. There are several therapeutic approaches. These men are often low in self-esteem. Psychotherapy may unfathom the causes and assist in building self-confidence. Counselling may help a paedophile to alter his lifestyle or change his work and thereby increase his self-respect. Many paedophiles are uneasy in adult company and might be helped by group psychotherapy or by 'social skills training'. This involves role-playing of relations with other adults. Through tape-recorders or video-machines the man hears and sees where he has been going wrong. With the help of the therapist he works out a new strategy of acting and interacting more effectively. In the early days of behaviour therapy, aversion treatment was widely and enthusiastically used for most sexual deviations. In the case of paedophiles, they were shown photographs of attractive children of the right sex and age, and at the same time they were given a low-voltage but painful electric shock in the arm. It continues to have a minor place. In those cases where there has been a number of convictions and the offender is not co-operative, hormone therapy – a kind of chemical castration – is attempted. Neuroleptic drugs are employed to dampen the sexual drive of the offender. However, there is the practical difficulty of ensuring that the unco-operative offender regularly takes the drug, especially in that both the hormones and the neuroleptic drugs have unpleasant side-effects.

RAPE

Rape is forced sexual intercourse without consent. It is almost always a man imposing sex on a woman, but there are exceptions. Homosexual rape does occur, nearly always in prison – perhaps not uncommonly among male prisoners although infrequently in women's prisons. A few controversial reports of women apparently raping men have appeared in the past few years. However, this section is about men forcing sexual intercourse on women, the usual meaning of the term rape.

Some authors widen the meaning of the term to include any form of sexual assault. Thus, a recent handbook issued by the London Rape Crisis Centre, *Sexual Violence* (1984), states on its first page: 'Rape is not confined to forcible penetration of a woman's vagina by a man's penis. It is all the sexual assaults, verbal and physical, that we all suffer in our daily contact with men. These range from being "touched up" or "chatted up" to being brutally sexually assaulted with objects.' Admittedly, restricting the term to forced vaginal penetration, and leaving out, for example, anal and oral sex, which is what some rapists demand, is somewhat artificial. But where to draw the line? And to include sexual innu-endos and jokes is stretching the term. Women are justified in objecting to these affronts, which they have silently borne in the past, but not in calling them rape. Finally, American authors often, and British authors occasionally, refer to forcible rape, which looks tautologous, but it is to distinguish true rape from statutory rape – which is not really rape but sexual intercourse with a consenting child.

Legally, the precise definition of rape varies from country to country and from state to state. Broadly speaking, wherever it happens, rape is sexual intercourse by a male with a female with-out her consent, either by means of force or when she is under the influence of drugs or drink. A husband, it is still universally allowed, may rape his wife as often as he likes, provided they are not legally separated or divorced. 'The husband cannot be guilty of rape committed by himself upon his lawful wife, for by their mutual matrimonial consent and contract, the wife has given up herself in this kind unto her husband which she cannot retract' is how the long-standing English law quaintly puts it. The law everywhere requires for rape some degree of penile penetration (right into the vagina in some countries, the slightest degree of entrance between the labia in others), but ejaculation by the offender is not necessary. Beyond these factors, it does depend on where the rape occurs. Some of the differences existing between English and Scots law are illustrative of the innumerable international variations. When a woman who has been drinking too freely is taken advantage of and raped, this is recognized as rape in English courts, but not in Scotland. There it is indecent assault and only when she has been 'plied with drink' may rape be considered. Boys from the age of eight upwards are deemed capable of the act of rape in Scotland, but if they live across the border they cannot be found guilty of rape before they are aged 14. When a man forces sex on a woman through threatening serious injury to her or her close relatives, this constitutes rape in England; but in Scotland, unless actual violence is used, it can be no more than indecent assault. (Indecent assault, it might be added, encompasses all indecent physical contact without the female's consent short of rape, from brutally forcing a hand, stick, or bottle into the vagina or anus to minor assaults such as 'touching up' breasts, buttocks or genitals. Sentences are shorter for indecent assault than for rape – the maximum sentence is two years and life respectively in Britain, and the average sentence six to 18 months and two to four years.)

Corroborative evidence is required from the rape victim before a charge is made. This is written into the law of some countries and some states, but whether it is or is not, the universal legal practice is to require it. It has always been so. The ancient Hebrews expected the woman to 'cry out'. It is all set out in *Deuteronomy*, Chapter XXII. Damsels who had sex forced upon them in the city were expected to cry out, or else they could be stoned to death along with the man. The rule did not apply when they were raped in the field because no one would hear them, and only the man was put to death. Corroboration may rest in statements from eye-witnesses or ear-witnesses (who have heard the woman's outcry), torn clothing, or medical evidence of injuries or the presence of sperm. This requirement is understandable. Incarcerating a man

265

for two to four years is a serious matter and it is vitally important to establish his guilt beyond all reasonable doubt. Paranoid and hysterical women may invent a story of having been raped. Rape may be fabricated by a girl afraid of parental wrath for coming home late, by an unfaithful wife caught in the act, or by a young woman discovered to be pregnant or suffering from a sexually transmitted disease.

The possibility that a woman's complaint of having been raped might be fabricated has always been kept in mind by both the police and the judiciary. Indeed – and this is the crying shame – they have held it to be a probability, almost a certainty. A myth has prevailed, and still prevails, that women are prone to concoct tall tales of being raped by innocent men. It is a sorry predicament for a rape victim, to find her word being constantly questioned. The judges in many of the states of America are obliged to read to the jury the Lord Hale Statement that rape 'is an accusation easily to be made and once made hard to be proved, and harder to be defended by the party accused, tho' never so innocent'. It comes from Matthew Hale's (1609–1676) address to the jury on the occasion this English lawyer successfully defended a 53-year-old man charged with raping a 14-year-old girl. English judges find their own words when they want to warn juries to beware of false complaints of rape. Judge Sutcliffe, summing up a rape trial in the Old Bailey in London in 1976, said 'It is well known that women in particular and small boys are liable to be untruthful and invent stories'. But long before her case is heard in court, when she first reports the crime to the police, a woman may find her complaint treated with scepticism and scorn. Here is advice for any English detective reading the *Police Review* for 28 November 1975: 'If a woman walks into a police station and complains of rape with no signs of violence she must be closely interrogated. It is always advisable if there is any doubt of the truthfulness of her allegations to call her an outright liar. It is very difficult for a person to put on genuine indignation who has been called a liar to her face ... Watch out for the girl who is pregnant or late getting home at night, such persons are notorious for alleging rape or indecent assault. Do not give her sympathy. If she is not lying, after the interrogator has upset her by accusing her of it, then at least the truth is verified and the genuine complaint made by her can be properly investigated.' Police attitudes have softened during the past ten years but, even so, English investigators have recently been claiming that between 50 and 70 per cent of all rape allegations are false. This gross exaggeration is through lumping together, as 'no crimes', fabricated accusations along with complaints having insufficient evidence for following up. With this high estimation of false allegations in mind, police officers have been apt to be insensitive, callous, impatient and insulting, requiring impressive corroborative evidence, and thereby contributing to a continuing high 'no crime' rate.

It is a myth that women are prone to make false allegations of rape against innocent men. False allegations of rape occur with the same frequency as false allegations of all other violent crimes: two per cent. The New York Police Force discovered this in the early 1970s. All rape complaints were investigated by a squad of women officers. They treated the rape victims sympathetically and began their interview with the assumption that the woman might be telling the truth. Previously, men had investigated rape complaints and decided that 18.2 per cent of cases were unfounded. The women officers came to the conclusion that three per cent of cases were unfounded. A similar finding was reached by a totally different type of investigation. Hursch and Selkin in 1974 found that in only 10 out of 545 cases of rape complaint had there been a false report.

She asked for it, the police have been inclined to say of many rape allegations, and they therefore drop the case. They mean that the woman was provocative – wore a 'Help Stamp Out Rape, Say Yes' sweater or an 'Incest, the Game the Whole Family Can Play' T-shirt – was flirtatious, or allowed genital foreplay without wanting coitus. This is known as victim precipitation. Some police forces routinely rule out rape if the man is an acquaintance, friend or someone she has dated, and so in practice they confine rape to strangers. If the woman is a prostitute or has a history of sexual promiscuity, her complaint of rape by even a complete stranger is likely to be thrown out, despite abundant evidence that she had been cruelly manhandled. In many instances, if the police investigated the case and made an arrest, it would fall down in court for the same reasons. Consent is the commonest defence offered in rape cases, and lawyers often with little or flimsy justification claim there has been consent. Injustice abounds. No female ever wants to be raped. She may have missed the last bus home and accepted an unexpected lift, or she may have gratefully offered a cup of coffee for some kindness rendered, but she was not asking to be raped. Girls, encouraged to look smart and attractive from their earliest years, are blamed for looking too smart and attractive when they get raped. Young men have no brakes for their highly powered sexuality, it is widely held, and young women have to be totally responsible for keeping within a safe speed.

Fortunately, police attitudes and procedure are changing for the better. On both sides of the Atlantic many police forces are providing courses on investigative techniques for sexual offences and delegating particular women officers to apply the new approach. Their interviews are conducted sympathetically and non-judgmentally. In some instances counselling and aftercare are provided for the victim and her husband or boyfriend. It is to be hoped that the momentum of this change continues. The San Francisco Police Force has a system whereby rape complaints that are weak on corroboration are not written off as 'no crime' but are kept on file for a two-year period. Even when no further evidence accrues that would prompt prosecution, the women are not left thinking that they were not believed by the police or that it was all their own fault, matters which add to the psychological trauma of the rape itself. Other police forces have been studying the system and it may soon have wider use.

Rape is more frequent than the number of rape convictions indicate. This follows from what has been said. Two-thirds of the recorded cases of rape in England and Wales do not reach the court, and one-third of those who are tried are acquitted. Thus, in 1980, out of 1,225 cases of complaint which the police investigated as possible rape, 421 men were found guilty. But how many cases were not investigated, and how many cases not reported, we do not know. 'Rape is probably the most unreported crime,' an FBI report commented in 1974. Rapes least likely to be reported seem to be among those on older women, children (because their parents want to protect them against the additional trauma of police investigation and court examination), and black women (particularly if the assailant is white). Those most likely to be reported are cases where there is a greater age difference between victim and assailant, the presence of witnesses, and an assailant who is a stranger. This comes from Menachem Amir's extensive survey of 646 rape cases in Philadelphia.

Rape is apparently commoner in America than in Britain. According to a report in 1969, American women were twelve times more likely to be raped than women in England and Wales, and three times more likely than Canadian women. Rape is probably more violent in America than in Britain. It appears to be becoming more frequent in both countries and growing faster than the other three crimes of violence – murder, assault and robbery. According to the United States Uniform Crime Reports of the FBI, more than 56,000 cases of rape were reported to the police in 1975, and this figure represented a 41 per cent increase from the figure for 1969. The number of reported cases in England and Wales was 869 in 1969, 1,170 in 1979, and 1,334 in 1984. Some of the increase, possibly, might reflect the changing attitude of the police and consequently less reluctance to report rape incidents, but there seems no way of denying that rape is markedly on the increase.

Rape occurs more frequently in the summer (when there is more social activity), at weekends (like most crimes), and at night. According to American figures, women living in big cities are three times more likely to be raped than women living in the suburbs, and four times more likely than women living in rural areas. In the same report, one-half of the rapists met their victim in the street (waiting for a bus or walking home) and one-quarter at their home. Other meeting places were bars, parks and the assailant's home. The rapes did not always take place at the meeting place, the rapist taking the victim to a more private setting, by duress or through a ploy, to her home or a car in most cases. British streets are still much safer, and her home is the likeliest place for a British woman to encounter her rapist. Some degree of violence occurs in about 80 per cent, and in 20 per cent it is substantial – although permanent disability is rare. Between one-quarter and one-half of American rapists threaten their victim with a weapon, but this probably occurs less frequently in Britain.

Any woman may be raped. No age group and no social class is immune. A sense of power, hatred of women, and camaraderie (in the case of paired and group rape) are more important ingredients of rape motivation than the sexual experience, and so a rape victim need not necessarily be a sexy, seductive young woman. Nearly one-half the victims in Britain are 13 to 17 years of age, and one-tenth are over 30. Although the high risk age in America is also 13 to 24, the victims are slightly older than the British ones, the age group 15 to 19 accounting for one-quarter of American rapes. Danish figures are in line with British. Adolescent girls are more likely to be the victims of gang rape (which accounts for 20 per cent of convicted rape in Britain and 40 per cent in America).

Victims of rape – and the rapists themselves – tend to belong to lower socio-economic groups. Black women are more vulnerable to rape attacks, according to all American reports. Half of the rapists are strangers, one-quarter are casual acquaintances, and one-quarter are friends and relatives, according to a recent English report.

Unmarried women are more vulnerable than those who are married, separated, divorced or widowed. This partly reflects the high-risk among young people, but not entirely. Victims belong to all professions and occupations, from nuns to prostitutes, as one survey puts it. (This is S. Katz and M. A. Mazur's *Understanding Rape Victims*, 1979, from which many of the statistics here have been taken.) Women in the caring professions are particularly at risk. It is generally recognized that rapists have often been drinking before the rape, but there is also some evidence that women who have been drinking (especially those who have been drinking heavily) are likely victims. According to one American study, some females of all ages tend to be sexually assaulted over and over again. This could be because they are rape-prone – showing lack of judgment or failing to recognize danger signals – or because they live in a rape environment. This has not been established. However, it needs to be repeated that any woman may be raped.

Women react in different ways to being raped. Not only the woman's personality but the manner in which she is raped affect her reaction. At one end of the scale (the end which does not appear in police statistics but is upsetting all the same) is the rapist who is the lover refusing to take no for an answer. At the other end there is the hooded intruder who terrorizes her into sexual submission, forces anal intercourse and fellatio as well, and urinates over her. She might put up a struggle and be badly beaten by the rapist. Usually, however, there is a profound 'primal terror', so that she submits for fear of death or being mutilated. At the time, the fear of death is greater than the fear of being sexually defiled. The different circumstances influence the reaction; but in all cases rape is a profoundly upsetting experience. At first, she may feel happy to be alive, but then reality hits her. The shock of the experience leaves the woman unnaturally calm and flat, or makes her inconsolably distressed, disgusted and tearful. She becomes understandably angry when she emerges from the shock. She may become illogically frightened that it is going to happen all over again to her, especially when she is in places and situations that remind her of the rape. She may be frightened to be left alone. Obsessional, frequent bathing or excessive house-cleaning are responses to the feeling that she is dirty and that her house is dirty. Given the most paltry excuse, she will feel guilty – for not having had a lock fitted to the door as she had meant to have, for not screaming, for not screaming loudly enough, for screaming and enraging the rapist, for accepting the lift. She may have sexual problems, either taking the form of frigidity with her husband, or profligacy, because she feels her body is defiled and worthless now and lasting relationships meaningless. She is likely to be depressed and sometimes severely so. The Rape Trauma Syndrome is distinct from, and more severe than, the reaction to other violent crimes, and it may linger on for months and years.

Friends and relatives of the rape victim will feel the same kind of effects – shock, distress, anger, guilt. Their reactions must not get in the way of their support of her. Above all, they must believe her. There is no need for them to rub salt in the wound if she was indiscreet or stupidly trusting, for she will be well aware of what she has done after the event. They too might feel guilty at not having fitted the new lock to the door, at having gone off for the weekend leaving her on her own, at having introduced her to her rapist; but airing their guilt or anger will only inflame her guilt and anger. The victim may be inert and painfully indecisive, and it is tempting for friends to take over and manage her, but they should patiently and gently encourage her to make her own decisions – about whether she should contact the police for instance – discussing the options and what they entail.

During the Bangladesh war in 1971, as many as 400,000 Bangladeshi women were raped by Pakistani soldiers. No good Muslim husband could take back a wife who had been soiled, no young man could choose a wife who had been defiled, and 80 per cent were Muslims. The Prime Minister officially declared the rape victims were national heroes, but this post-war campaign was unsuccessful and the women continued to be ostracized. In Christian countries, a husband's reaction to his wife having been raped is less severe. Nevertheless, husbands may feel a kind of primordial revulsion after their wife has been tampered with and occasionally be unable to continue the sexual relationship. They need counselling as well as the victim herself. A husband needs to be able to reassure his wife that he cares and loves, through physical contact but without rushing in with sexual demands that for the present she cannot fulfil. By insensitively pressing for sex

271

he will revive her rape fright and confirm her feeling that sex is what all men are ever after.

There is no cast-iron defence against rape, no foolproof technique to repel every rapist. Much advice is available, much of it sensible, in books such as *How to Say No to a Rapist – and Survive*, written by Frederick Storaska in 1975. But all the suggested precautions are expedients, not solutions. In so far as they separate women from men, they could be increasing the sexism that helps breed rape. Ultimately society must take steps through education and legal reform, to reduce the sexism and violence which already permeates it. The whole community needs to be educated afresh. Males are anatomically stronger than females, but from birth onwards the difference is fostered, manliness is equated with domination of women, the 'macho' mentality is encouraged. Educationists, teachers and parents have to be educated to bring up males to be less dominating and females to be more assertive, to obliterate the gap instead of enlarging it. Law reform is required to decrease violence – on the television screen for example – to facilitate rape reporting by victims, and to dispose of the convicted rapist more effectively for deterrence and reformation. In Britain a woman must herself report the crime to the police station nearest the scene of the crime – which may not be the one nearest her home – whereas in America a friend or relative may inform the police (in half of the cases they do and sometimes anonymously) and the police come to the victim. On the other hand, in America the victim goes to hospital to be examined – sometimes by an inexperienced resident physician, reluctantly, because he will have to lose time appearing in court and may encounter adverse cross-examination – and then she is billed for it, whereas in Britain she is examined by a police surgeon knowledgeable about rape, and a woman usually, without charge. Countries can learn from one another. Anonymous phone counselling, relaxation of corroboration requirements, and vetoes on prior sexual history being mentioned in court are matters which all countries need to explore. It must be made less distressing for the rape victim during police examination and in court. When a woman's house has been burgled, the end of the legal side is when she has reported the incident to the police. When a woman's body has been invaded and she reports it, she has to be prepared to stand trial herself.

Nothing has yet been said about the rapist, and there is not much to say about him. Despite a large number of studies about rapists, nothing very distinctive about the rapist's personality has emerged. Rapists are not usually psychiatrically ill. Peter Sutcliffe, the Yorkshire Ripper who raped and killed his victims during 1975 to 1980 and became the most notorious rapist in Britain, was clearly suffering from paranoid schizophrenia and under the command of hallucinatory voices. But he was exceptional. Only two per cent of rapists in prison in Britain receive any psychiatric treatment. The usual rapist is an unextraordinary violence-prone fellow, as Menachem Amir concluded in his Philadelphian study of 646 rape cases. They were a danger to the community, he said, not because they were compulsive sex fiends but because they were violent and aggressive. (It has been found, however, that rapists are more likely to be sexually aroused by sado-masochistic films and stories). Of Amir's rapists, 49 per cent had had a previous conviction, although not usually a sexual one. Often rapists are fuelled by excess drinking. Rapists are usually young. 40 per cent of convicted rapists in England were aged 17 to 20 and 19 per cent were 21 to 24, according to a recent Home Office study. Rapists come from lower socio-economic groups, often come from the same district as their victim, and usually belong to the same race as she does. About half are strangers – more if the victim is adult, less if she is an adolescent. About half of all convicted rapists were involved in pair or group rape – less than half in Britain, more in America.

A convicted rapist is almost always sent to prison, usually for years, occasionally for life. There is at present a strong demand for longer sentences. Retribution is sought by society in general as well as by the victim in particular. Thus there was public disquiet when Judge Bertrand Richards at Ipswich Crown Court in 1972 let a rapist off with a fine because, as he put it, the victim was guilty of 'contributory negligence' by accepting a hitch at night. 'Social control' is also served – putting the vicious rapist out of harm's way. Physical castration for the hardened rapist has been considered, and chemical castration by anti-androgen and oestrogen administration, but although these treatments might quieten the sex drive, the violent urge to attack women would not be altered. Prison sentences act as deterrents to others, although apparently not very effectively. Very long prison sentences probably do not greatly increase the deterrence, and they incline police and lawyers to require more corroborative evidence. Treatment is rarely considered in deliberations about the disposal of convicted rapists. Rapists are rarely suffering from a psychiatric illness. Like other criminals guilty of violent crime, it is their propensity towards violence which has to be altered. Psychiatrists specializing in the treatment of such men commonly maintain that they uncover a deprived childhood, with uncaring foster-parents or latch-key mothers, leading to a deep conviction that the world is a hard, unloving place. Often there has been violence and cruelty in the home. Highly skilled and dedicated psychotherapists are essential for building the bridges which were never built, and even so the outcome is uncertain in these difficult cases. Nevertheless, a minority advocates treatment of serious sex-offenders in special units within mental hospitals. For one thing, it is much cheaper, they say. Edward Brechner, an American advocate of this approach, has said it costs more to keep a man in maximum security than sending him to Harvard, and that sending him to a sex-offender unit would save $5,000 per year per man. But society's primordial need for vengeance is very strong.

SADO-MASOCHISM

Sadism is obtaining sexual gratification through inflicting pain, and masochism is achieving sexual excitement through receiving it. The two words are combined into one, sado-masochism, because a liking for the one is usually accompanied by some degree of liking for the other. A few people, the true sado-masochists, equally enjoy giving punishment and getting it. There are those whose great delight is simply in watching punishment taking place, recoiling at any prospect of meting it out or taking it. Some of these regularly identify with the punisher, some with the punished, but others with both. Homosexual couples who practise sado-masochism may always have the same relation, master and slave or schoolmaster and student – to use the jargon of the contact advertisements – but some work on a your-turn-my-turn basis. In general, however pronounced a person's sadism or masochism may be, there is usually a slight taste for the other in the background. The Marquis de Sade, imprisoned in the Bastille, dreamed dreams of flogging teenage girls, and occasionally of the girls flogging him. Sacher-Masoch, who spun sexually exciting fantasies of being whipped by powerful, dominating women, was not averse to inflicting cruelty himself.

Professor Krafft-Ebing, Europe's leading sexologist at the turn

274

of the century, coined the terms sadism and masochism from the names of these two pornographic novelists. The more famous and more widely read was Count Donatien-Alphonse-François de Sade, Marquis de Sade (1740–1814). He lived a licentious life and spent twenty years in prison for sexual offences, which included writing a pornographic tract, administering poison (the so-called aphrodisiac Spanish fly), and having a homosexual relationship with his male servant. Although in de Sade's real life sadism did not feature strongly, possibly not at all, it abounds in the novels he wrote in prison. Here is a striking illustration of the contrast between sadism in fantasy and reality, a matter which we shall later emphasize. The longer he was in prison, the more vile became the sadistic fantasies revealed in his writings. *Justine*, an early novel, confined its sadism for a good deal of the way to colourful descriptions of birching of beautiful, innocent, teenage girls. Eventually Justine had a toe cut off from both her feet, had fellatio and cunnilingus perpetrated on her, and was finally kept naked for five months while the monk who kept her captive repeatedly raped her. It was mild stuff compared to the depravity in *Juliette*, written six years later. That depicted people bitten to death and burned alive, young women dragged by the hair and suspended by it. When Minski, a Russian giant and cannibal, entertained Juliette, naked women on all fours were used for chairs and table, and the meal that was served had been made from Juliette's maid. It is six tedious volumes of rape, incest, tortures and executions.

The life of Chevalier Leopold von Sacher-Masoch, 1836–95, was very ordinary and his novels never progressed beyond depicting a man being whipped by a dominating woman dressed in furs – for Sacher-Masoch was a fur fetishist as well as a masochist. He and his novels would now be forgotten had not Krafft-Ebing perpetuated his name.

Masochism has always been a less popular subject in underground fiction than sadism. The predominant theme in Victorian pornography was sadism and in particular the trite, anonymous stories which inevitably led to the usual beating of cringing white female buttocks. There remains to this day a big demand for this kind of pornography, if we are to judge from the number of magazines on sale that specialize in spanking, caning, whipping and bondage. Kinsey pointed out that no other sexual deviation was so well catered for, and this still holds. The uninventive, predictable stories have changed very little.

Many people occasionally experience sado-masochistic fantasies spontaneously when they are sexually aroused, and some people regard such fantasies as old friends they use to initiate or to improve their sexual excitement. Although Masters and Johnson did not discuss these specific sadist and masochist fantasies in their study of sexual fantasy patterns, reported in *Homosexuality in Perspective* (1979), they pointed out that fantasies of forced sexual encounters were frequently entertained by both men and women. Gebhard and his colleagues, in their classical study *Sex Offenders* (1965), reported that an unusually large number of rapists had sadistic dreams and sadistic fantasies during masturbation. They also noted that a large proportion of them bit their partner during love-making. A recent study showed a marked tendency among rapists to respond sexually to films and stories about rape. Ordinary men who engage in mass rape under conditions of war have had their feelings of dominance and hostility developed.

Well-nigh universal are the games lovers play, getting the better of one another – the man of the woman, the woman of the man – in mock wrestling, pretending to be slaves and tying one another up, the playful slap of the bottom, pretending to kiss and then withdrawing, or love bites. These are often sexually stimulating and contain at least a kernel of sado-masochism. Men are twice as likely to be turned on by a love-bite than from reading a sado-masochistic story, and women four times as likely. Love-bites never progress to more overt sado-masochistic activity, whereas the other games may develop into bondage and discipline. These are still games, provided both partners enjoy them and provided it remains an occasional diversion.

The essence of bondage is in tantalizing a person, who is bound and immobilized, with the prospect of sexual gratification. There is a sophisticated game called Bondage which some couples include in their love-making repertoire. They decide which partner is to be bound, that partner is bound hand and foot (to the bedposts usually), and then brought – painfully slowly – to orgasm. For some men, however, bondage is their sexual be-all-and-end-all, not an occasional diversion but a deviation. Their favourite, or only, way of obtaining sexual gratification is through bondage, and they need to be bound, chained, handcuffed, suspended, put in stocks or tied to some apparatus, tantalized, mocked and usually given physical punishment by the prostitute they engage or by other devotees of the club they join. Rarely, very rarely, it is his wife who administers the chains and handcuffs and likes the game. A good deal of this bizarre kind of activity occurs only within the pages of bondage magazines and the individual content to pursue them in masturbatory fantasy. There are some sado-masochistic clubs, however.

Discipline, like bondage, is a game some people play now and again, and it is also a pursuit in which some people find all – or most – of their sexual gratification. Essentially, discipline is getting sexual excitement from physical pain and bondage from mental torment. Sometimes they are combined. Many more couples indulge in discipline than in bondage. Whether it amounts to mild, playful spanking or to something more organized, it acts as a turn-on, an aphrodisiac, for one or preferably both partners. Usually discipline is played in the guise of an offence having been committed and the appropriate punishment meted out, ritualistically and all according to a table of rules devised by the couple. Smacking buttocks, covered or naked, with bare hand or perhaps with a slipper or hairbrush, is generally all that is entailed. The spanker has no wish to hurt his or her partner more than the partner enjoys or at least accepts. Gosselin and Wilson, two research workers from the Maudsley Hospital, contacted a number of sadists and masochists, and discussed their interviews in their book *Sexual Variations* (1980). In one of their interviews they were told 'Of course, he doesn't *really* hurt me. I mean quite recently he tied me down ready to receive "punishment", then by mistake he kicked my heel with his toe, as he walked by. I gave a yelp, and he said, "Sorry, love – did I hurt you?"'

For some disciplined couples pain hardly comes into their act. Yet for others who receive marital spankings it is only the pain itself which is sexually exciting. Slappings with the bare hand may not be enough for them and a cane, tawse or birch is employed. They spin it out, the active partner gradually increasing the severity of the strokes until it reaches the point of maximum enjoyment or tolerance for the receiving partner. The latter may need a good deal of pain in order to obtain full satisfaction. 'I have to make her cry so that she can obtain an orgasm,' one husband told Gosselin and Wilson. He found dispensing the punishment pleasurable, so they were well-matched as far as sado-masochism was concerned.

This fortunate state of affairs, in which sadist meets masochist and they live happily ever after, must be extremely rare. Choice of partner is influenced by factors other than how much physical punishment he or she likes to give or to take. More than likely, there is an enthusiastic husband and a wife who acquiesces to a light spanking now and again, or perhaps a wife who likes to be spanked and a husband who goes along with it. The complaisant partners have come to know how to make their spouse passionate. But they may reach a point when they find the act so distasteful that they opt out. Wives may get the wind up when their partner reads the signs wrongly and goes a little too far. Sexual harmony requires free communication between partners, but it is required most of all when there lurks some sadistic need. It operates the other way round sometimes: a wife's refusal to participate in a discipline game, having gone along with it for years, may itself be a danger signal that something else has gone wrong in the marital relation.

These domestic upheavals constitute the likeliest reason for the sadist or the masochist to come to the psychiatrist, because ordinarily they like themselves as they are. Society is tolerant towards sado-masochism and applies no pressure to change. People shrug their shoulders and make little jokes, but there is none of the disgust and detestation which is accorded to paedophilia or even to homosexuality. When the real problem in the marriage has been fathomed, and a solution for it worked out, the wife may elect to have her husband remain as he is. On the other hand, a long-standing – but previously undeclared – disinclination to play in her husband's discipline game may have come fully into the open. It may not be possible to dispel her distaste. Her husband may wish to have treatment. Behaviour therapy, along the lines of the treatment for fetishism that we have mentioned – replacing new for old fantasies during masturbation – is quicker and surer of results than conventional psychotherapy.

Men stuck on punishment or bondage usually, however, have to look outside marriage for the fulfilment of their particular sexual pleasures. Some of them are content in the fantasy world of their specialist magazines. A few occasionally engage in flagellation or auto-bondage, not as ends in themselves but to foster fantasies – although flagellation was a practice in its own right encouraged within many monastries during the Middle Ages. Some join sado-masochism clubs, and through these they may participate in or watch group ritualistic punishments – victim bound to a frame and tormentor in jackboots and whip for instance. But many want a partner. Those of homosexual inclinations – male homosexuals and lesbians – may find a partner whose need complements their own through contact advertisements. There are prostitutes with a special understanding of bondage and discipline who have amassed a collection of items sufficient to satisfy the needs of most of their clients. Gosselin and Wilson contacted some of these women through the contact magazine *Superbitch*.

It is noteworthy, however, that some of the women they traced through this sado-masochist orientated magazine were not prostitutes. They simply wanted to torture and beat men because they found it sexually exciting. Moreover, those who charged frequently found it pleasurable. Thus sado-masochism is not a men-only deviation like fetishism, voyeurism, exhibitionism, bestiality or paedophilia. It is mostly men who are so inclined, but there are plenty of women who are sexually excited when given physical punishment or torture and some who like to give it.

Finally, there is a form of sadism as indefensible as rape, that exploits a victim as in rape: the obtaining of sexual excitement from giving physical punishment to children. It ought to have a section on its own, but it has no name. On the continent it is called the English disease, but it is nameless in Britain where once it thrived. Gone is the age when every classroom had its cane or tawse in daily use, but some readers will be old enough to remember it. Generally, teachers felt no pleasure – sexual or otherwise – and some distaste, at least until they became accustomed with the process. It was the traditional, unquestioned way of dealing with indiscipline. Generally, the children accepted the system as a necessary evil and suffered no lasting ill effects. It was an undesirable procedure in several ways but its greatest fault was in providing scope for sadistic schoolmasters. These men were uncommon. They betrayed themselves with their slow, ritualistic, thorough punishments for petty excuses, unable to conceal their pleasure, unconvincingly professing the beneficence of what they were regretfully having to do. This is written in the past tense, optimistically, in the belief that we have seen the end of sadistically-inclined teachers indulging their deviation. Those defending corporal punishment are always teachers, clinging to the old order. Those opposing it maintain that children who are caned or strapped are likely to become masochists or sadists when they become older. This assertion relies on a hoary, but widely held,

279

theory that schoolchildren are likely to be erotically stimulated when beaten, that some come to misbehave in order to be punished, and that in adulthood these people are likely to be masochists or sadists. It might be more sensible to argue that excessive and undeserved corporal punishment leaves unpleasant memories than generate, or help to generate, sado-masochistic desires. But it has to be said that there is no clear evidence of any connection.

SATYRIASIS

Satyriasis, a male deviation, is excessive sexual activity with many partners. It is sexual activity of a kind, for it is only seduction that the satyr is after, seduction of an endless chain of sexual partners, never staying with any of them long enough to develop a lasting relation. The satyr's many and frequent but always transitory encounters are conquests, proofs of his mastery over the other sex, and nothing more. Nymphomania is the parallel female condition.

Satyriasis should not be confused with high potency. Indeed, many a satyr is impotent when it comes to the crunch. It is paradoxical and the vanquished woman must be flabbergasted on finding her gallant, felicitous seducer to be a damp squib. Often enough the Don Juan overcomes the difficulty by not having sexual intercourse at all. Having charmed the lady into bed he produces some pretext and is gone. His pleasure has been fulfilled, so why wait. There are those who are potent, though, and adroit masters of the art sometimes. Only these same voluptuous fellows become impotent also if they linger with the same woman for more than a few days. They accredit their absence of form to the girl and pass on. Those who decide to have the joys of married life soon become impotent and they too blame their partner. Backed by their success rate over past years this looks feasible enough. The case of one such assiduous satyr in this plight might illustrate the whole problem of satyriasis.

He was a successful businessman in his early thirties, hoping to be a millionaire by the time he was 40. Previously, for a number of years, he travelled the world, working hard at selling a particular commodity and playing hard at seducing young women. He was as charming and effective at one as he was at the other. Brief details were recorded after each conquest. Every hundredth one he celebrated with a lavish dinner, the fêted girl unaware that she was no more than an important statistic. Then he changed to another line of business that did not require his travelling. He married his childhood sweetheart and teenage tennis partner. Her virginity at the altar accorded with his double standard, more widely and firmly held then than now. Alas, within a week he was impotent and he remained impotent so far as his wife was concerned. She was, he told himself reassuringly, naive and sexually ignorant. But his impotence became a bone of contention and before very long he moved out, into a flat on his own, but providing generously for his wife. His customary prowess re-appeared during occasional fleeting encounters and this added verisimilitude to the diagnosis he had already made of his marital impotence. A year or so later he was struck by a strong passion, much more than a passing fancy, for his young nubile secretary. She was adequately experienced and highly accomplished, he established, the girl for him this time, he told himself; and he invited her to move in with him. No sooner had she disposed of her own flat than he was impotent. There was no doubt in his mind now that he needed professional help. It soon became apparent from his story that he had been brought up in a world of authoritative, strict, stern, severe women; and he had built up a need to humble and abase all women. His father had deserted his mother before he was born, his mother had quickly dumped him with two aunts, and they had brought him up by adequate material standards but little else. This kind of background, which breeds the belief that women are domineering and hard, and a consequent need to humiliate them, is all too common among satyrs.

This is the classical form of satyriasis. Occasionally there are other forms, sometimes overlapping. The satyr may have homosexual inclinations which he dare not recognize, let alone follow, and he is on a fruitless quest for a woman who will provide him with heterosexual fulfilment. When it turns out to be dull and unexciting he blames this on the woman and continues on his way. On the other hand, he may be thoroughly heterosexual but overcoming feelings of inferiority, or proving his manliness to himself.

The satyr, impelled by some neurosis, wanting to prove that he can conquer women, that he is manly, that he is not inferior, is a different type from the highly potent, as yet unattached young man, with rather too much time on his hands, wildly chasing woman after woman. Nevertheless, in practice, it is not always easy to distinguish one from the other. Sometimes there may be a little of one in the other. Moreover, as in the case of any male sexual deviation, there is a little satyriasis, a delight in conquest for instance, in every young man's lovemaking.

SCOPTOPHILIA

Scoptophilia (or scopophilia) is an overriding pleasure in looking at a woman's vulva. It is not voyeurism, although many writers equate the two and they do have certain similarities.

There is nothing abnormal in a man exploring his partner's vulva in detail, with fingers and eyes. It is a common part of lovemaking. Men's sexuality is strongly dependent on visual arousal. Women's is not. If anything, it is tactile stimuli that specially arouse them. The cause of men's pleasure in looking could be some unidentified hormonal determinant occurring before birth, the natural concealment of girls' genitals, society's insistence on their complete concealment, or some mixture of these. The Freudian theory is that the man is searching for the woman's penis, to reassure himself she has not been castrated and in turn assuage his own castration anxiety. Whatever its cause, the difference is sometimes a puzzle to young lovers; to the female partner that he should linger on, gazing at this unbecoming part of her body; to the male partner that she should only momentarily look at the tip of his wonderful penis, cursorily feel his testicles and be done with her examination. This normal activity is abnormal only when it is the be-all-and-end-all of a man's sexual pleasure. The needle has stuck, he goes no further, or, if he does, it is perfunctorily. It becomes a fetish.

Walter, the anonymous Victorian author of *My Secret Life*, was a scoptophiliac. His life was largely spent pursuing sexual pleasures, and the greatest of these was admiring vulvas. He travelled widely and made copious notes of all he did and saw. From these he compiled his million-word work in his old age – not for the pornographic market, it might be mentioned, because only six copies were printed – but for his own excitement. He set out to prepare 'a plain narrative of facts and not a psychological analysis', but it is clear from *My Secret Life* where the main interest of this self-styled 'connoisseur of vaginas' lay. By candlelight, gas-jets and daylight, he stood, sat and lay, often for hours, gazing at, examining, classifying and reporting on them. It had been, at the least, boring for the owners, but he paid them well – a guinea, usually (which, incidentally, was the going rate for a physician's visit). Reading his descriptions of these hundreds of vulvas becomes boring. It was a pointless exercise, but the author was helplessly and endlessly propelled by his vulva fetish. After his customary full inspection, repeated when possible, he conceded to have intercourse. Even so, he was still essentially an observer and a reporter – of, for example, multiple orgasms a hundred years before Masters and Johnson – but not a sexual partner.

TRANSSEXUALISM

Transsexualism is the firm, abiding conviction which a few men and women possess that they are in a body of the opposite sex. The male transsexual believes himself to be a woman and desires to be accepted as a woman. Similarly, the female transsexual is convinced of being a man and strongly wants to be regarded as a man. They were born with normal, well-formed genital organs. There was no problem of pseudo-hermaphrodism, such as described in the chapter on the psychology of sex: the penis and scrotum, or the vulval slit, were unmistakeable at birth. The sex was correctly assigned. They were brought up accordingly as boy or girl. Yet, in spite of this, they developed their cross-gender identity. According to their own account in many instances, there were intimations of their paradoxical gender identity as far back as they can remember.

Some men recall thinking they were female when they were four or five years old and being angry for not being built that way. They grew up convinced of being female inside, although not outside. Others could not formulate their problem till they reached late adolescence or adulthood, but they wanted to play the games of the other sex, dress like them, look like them. Their parents in many instances took conscious steps to put them on the right rails, but to no avail.

Transsexualism has to be distinguished from transvestism. Transvestism is the compulsive desire to dress in the clothes of the other sex. Any transsexual man will understandably want to dress in women's clothes if circumstances permit and hence we could call him a transvestite – although he would maintain that he simply wants to dress in accordance to his real sex. The true transvestite, on the other hand, believes that he is a man but likes to dress and behave like a woman from time to time. There is a

283

body of opinion among the experts which claims that this is a half-way stage towards transsexualism, beyond which most transves-tites never proceed. But there are other experts who regard trans-vestism and transsexualism as two quite separate conditions.

Transsexualism has also to be distinguished from homosexu-ality. A homosexual man is erotically attracted to other men, but he knows he is a man and expects to be regarded as a man. Only a small minority of homosexuals – the queens, with their high-pitched voices and feminine gestures, and the tweedy, gruff butches – may in some instances have a gender identity problem. Most queens believe they are 100 per cent men and the butches do not usually doubt that they are women. But a few are mixed up. Some of them press for medical help to have their sex changed, and they may even be taken to be transsexuals for a start. One female-to-male transsexual (or so she regarded herself and was taken to be) attended the gender identity clinic at Charing Cross Hospital in London, was given hormones, grew a beard and body hair, and then decided she was a lesbian and not a transsexual after all.

It is easy enough to be confused about the orientation of trans-sexuals. If a man, fully convinced he is a woman, falls in love with another man, is he a homosexual or a heterosexual for instance? Little wonder that the transsexuals themselves sometimes become confused. Transsexuals become struck by the certainty that they are entrapped in the wrong kind of body at different ages. Men who are aware early on rarely get married. Some do, though, because they need someone to be close to and to love. They do not mind much whether the somebody is male or female, and some become involved in a homosexual relation.

Those who get married before their transsexualism fully dawns on them may enjoy a rich heterosexual relation, even though their marriage is unlikely to last long after the transsexual penny has dropped. When they have had sex re-assignment surgery, however, and feel comfortable in their female constructed body, all male-to-female transsexuals are likely to be heterosexual – that is to say, desiring sexual relations with a man. This was shown in an American study of 42 male-to-female transsexuals. Before surgery one-third were homosexual, one-third heterosexual, and one-third 'asexual' (without sexual experience, although one-half thought they were heterosexual). After surgery, almost all of them said they were heterosexual.

284

Unacceptable homosexual inclinations may influence young people in their early teens towards transsexualism, according to several authorities. In a study in the mid-1960s of 25 male-to-female transsexuals, it was found that they had held rigid views on sexual morality as boys and were regular church attenders. Dr Wardell Pomeroy who made the study seemed to feel that there had been an underlying but rejected homosexuality which moved these boys into transsexualism. A study in the mid-1970s of female-to-male transsexuals by Dr I. B. Pauly came to a similar conclusion. While they were young teenage girls, they had experienced the usual attraction towards other females which occurs at that stage of life. But it was morally wrong in their eyes to express same-sex love. Consequently they tried out sexual relations with boys. These turned out to be unsatisfactory. The girls had never been too sure of their gender and had always been interested in boys' interests, walked with a masculine gait, displayed masculine mannerisms, and so on. Thus it was possible for them to imagine themselves as boys (or so the author contended) and by taking this first step into transsexualism found a solution to their hitherto problematic attraction to girls.

This 'flight into heterosexuality' theory is one of a number which have been offered to explain transsexualism. The problem has attracted a vast interest out of all proportion to the number of transsexuals. Estimates range from one in 10,000 to one in 100,000, men and women being equally affected. Other psychosocial explanations and various physical theories have been advanced. Unusual parental attitudes have been held to be responsible for the transsexual's ultimate, persistent and immutable belief. Excessive maternal attention and physical contact; an absent or uninterested father; encouragement of delicacy, unaggressiveness, artistic sensibility, and other feminine attributes; and cross-dressing of the boy by his mother – these are the environmental factors which have been claimed to foster transsexualism in boys. Girls who become transsexual have been thought to have psychologically remote mothers – because of long-standing illness usually – and managing fathers who encourage masculine behaviour.

Others have held that transsexuals are suffering from a psychotic illness resembling paranoid schizophrenia or a severe depression with delusions of nihility. Their unshakeable belief, fanatically held, about belonging to the opposite sex despite the anatomical evidence, does resemble the delusions that some schizo-phrenics entertain about their bodies. On rare occasions psy-chiatrists do encounter a patient suffering from schizophrenia who expresses transsexual manifestations. However, comparatively large samples of transsexuals have been carefully examined with this in mind and no evidence of serious mental illness uncovered.

A number of physical factors have been thought to be the cause of transsexualism, particularly brain disorders and endocrine dis-turbances, and there has recently been an unusual immunological finding. Some sort of disorder of the temporal lobe of the brain has long been suspected. Electrical disturbances within this part of the brain are commonly discerned in transsexuals. As long ago as 1939 it was demonstrated that the temporal lobe normally func-tions in controlling sexual behaviour. But the transsexual effect may be a result of disturbance of some other function of the tem-poral lobe. Patients with an injury or a disease of the temporal lobe sometimes entertain curious delusions about an alteration of their body – about spots on their face which no one else can see, for instance, or about their nose having grown very large – and the transsexual 'delusion' might occur in the same way. Another part of the brain, the hypothalamus, has also been suspected of playing a part.

The most important finding has been unusual blood levels of the male hormone testosterone in transsexuals: it is abnormally low in male transsexuals and abnormally high in female transsexuals. The females report slightly abnormal menstruation, longer cycles and low blood loss for instance. It is thought that if there is an abnormality in this field which influences the development of transsexualism, it probably acts before birth. It is known that hormones play an important part not only in the development of the genital organs but also in sexual behaviour, according to experiments on lower animals.

A chance immunological finding five years ago has led research into a new field. It concerns the absence of H-Y antigen in transsex-uals, both male and female. Depending on the test method, this result may be found in more than 90 per cent of the cases. The H-Y antigen is normally found on the membrane of all male tissue cells and is vitally important in the development of the testis of the male embryo. If it is absent the undifferentiated genital area develops into ovary. The ramifications are highly complex and beyond the compass of this book. It is too early to know whether these early findings can be consistently repeated, but if they can this may be a highly significant discovery.

It may ultimately transpire that transsexualism is environmentally determined, but predisposed by a physical defect. The possibility of a physical predisposition is favoured by recent statistics which show that the abnormality is equally distributed between men and women – unlike the sexual deviations, which are exclusively male or almost so. Earlier figures implied more male than female transsexuals, but this was because more men than women sought professional help.

Most transsexuals actively desire a physical sex change operation. They become preoccupied with this need and leave no stone unturned to achieve it. They need to persist because gender identity clinics are justifiably reluctant to arrange surgery. Female-to-male operations are particularly difficult, prone to go badly wrong, and even when successful are limited in aim. Of the few surgeons prepared to perform sex change operations, most restrict themselves to male-to-female operations. They do not rush into these, but they agree when they are convinced that it is the only way to transform a permanently depressed and distraught person into someone who is relaxed and tranquil. They are in effect producing a neuter state and there is no going back. But with well-chosen cases, and successful surgery, the results are rewarding. Psychotherapy, behaviour therapy and drug therapy have been found to be singularly ineffective.

Gender identity clinics insist on at least two years' preparation and adaptation before surgery. The individual has to function in the new gender role over this time. The advantages and disadvantages will become clear and there is plenty of time to revert to the original role. The attitudes, mannerisms and gait are gradually acquired. Appropriate clothes are worn. Changing documents and certificates from Mr to Ms or Ms to Mr has to be done. Sex hormones are introduced. Oestrogens cause a man's breasts to enlarge and his buttocks to be rounder and larger; his hair softens and his voice rises in pitch. His facial hair is gradually removed by electrolysis. Testosterone given to a female induces growth of thicker hair, she develops a beard and her clitoris becomes larger. This long-term hormone therapy is not without risk. Men who are having oestrogens are more likely to develop deep vein thrombosis and the enlargement of the breasts can be very painful. Testosterone may produce mastitis in the breasts and there is a possibility of liver cancer. However, transsexuals are generally willing to accept these risks.

In some instances, this stage is far enough. The individuals, after all, are able to live in the gender they have chosen, looking as if they belonged to it, appropriately certificated and documented, full-time cross-dressers. Some settle for this. Some have to, because surgery is unavailable. Only rarely may problems arise: sudden admission to hospital, for instance. But others continue to press on, pursuing the elusive possibility of surgery – particularly the male-to-female operation, the end result of which is better, surer and easier to attain. The surgically-made vulva and vagina look and perform like those which nature has fashioned, but the man-made penis is a sexually useless and unconvincing ornament. Some surgeons construct a urethra within it so that at least it can be used for urinating, but this involves additional operations. Female-to-male surgery requires three to six operations – provided everything goes according to plan and there is no sloughing – but laying on a urethra inside the penis may increase the number of operations to 15. And the end product sometimes leaks along the shaft. It is their ultimate triumph, however, to be able to go into a public urinal to stand and urinate with the other men, and the female-to-male transsexual will go to no end of trouble and expense to achieve it. Male-to-female transsexuals usually do not have sexual partners during the period before their operation, but they are more likely to have one afterwards. If they are able to engage in sex like other women, this is surely the ultimate assurance for them that they are, in body and mind, female.

The first stage of the male-to-female operation is to remove the penis and the testes, but retaining the skin of the penis and the scrotum so as to fashion a vagina and external vulval folds. Half of those individuals who have the penis removed claim that they are still able to reach orgasm. Enough genital nerve endings may have been retained by the surgeon, or stimulation of other parts of the body may be responsible. An opening for the urethra is made on the skin surface. The breasts will have enlarged after daily oestrogen for two years or more, but to have generous, impressive breasts plastic implants are required. Minor plastic surgery may be employed to soften hard facial lines.

The first stage of the female-to-male surgical procedure is to remove breasts, ovaries and womb. The external vulval lips are sewn together to make a scrotum and two artificial testes are placed inside. The urethra has to be fashioned to open in front of this new scrotum. All this is fairly straightforward in the hands of an experienced surgeon. Making a penis, or phalloplasty, is the headache. One thing is certain: there is no possibility of ending up with a penis that is capable of penetrating a woman's vagina. The individual has to be content with a dildo even after successful sex-change surgery. The clitoris is freed from the inner vulval lips. A passageway may be made to allow the urethra to pass through it. This man-made penis can then be used for urinating, and it will be capable of erection, but not of ejaculation or penetration. However, even with individuals who start off with a large clitoris, and with subsequent testosterone enlargement, it is going to be a tiny penis, and penis size is always important to men. An alternative procedure is to make a penis out of skin flaps from the forearm, abdomen or the groin, with or without a urethra inside. Despite the limitations of phalloplasty and the things which often go wrong, transsexuals are usually pleased with the result. It does not come up to their expectation, but they are still pleased. They see their body to be in keeping with their true gender. They are able to live more contented lives.

TRANSVESTISM

Transvestism, transvestitism, or eonism is a compulsive desire to dress in the clothes of the other sex. In 'true' transvestism the individual feels a relief from inner tension, but not, usually, any sexual excitement. In certain other kinds of cross-dressing, however, there is strong sexual arousal. These include pseudo-transvestism and fetishistic-transvestism – which will be defined below.

Transvestism is not transsexualism, although the two terms are often confused. Transvestism is cross-dressing and transsexualism is cross-gender identity. Understandably, transsexuals indulge in transvestism. Just as a woman wears women's clothes, a man who believes that he is fundamentally a woman will want to wear women's clothes. A true transvestite, on the other hand, knows he is a man. Transvestism is common – it is thought that between one in 100 and one in 1,000 men practise it. Transsexualism is uncommon – about one man in 10,000 to 100,000 is affected.

Transvestism is sometimes confused with homosexuality. Most transvestites are not homosexuals but heterosexuals, and most homosexuals have no wish to cross-dress. There is a minority of homosexual men who occasionally dress up in women's clothes, but not for sexual excitement, nor to look like a woman, nor because they think they are essentially women. A homosexual dressed in women's clothes is more than likely to be going to a drag ball or a drag party, but he could be a male prostitute looking for a client. The dressing-up is a caricature or burlesque, probably at bottom a protest against society's restrictive rules about men not loving men, and there is no attempt to pass as a woman. Those homosexuals who dress in this manner are held in contempt by most homosexuals. Lastly among the misunderstandings is the assumption that transvestites are effeminate. One only needs to meet a few transvestites to realize that this is false.

Transvestism is almost entirely a matter for men only. It could be argued that society has made it so, because women may – and frequently do – dress in men's clothes without producing disgust and opprobrium and without risk of being arrested. However, they wear trousers because it is convenient or fashionable, not because they will become sexually excited. Female–male transsexuals feel a need to wear men's clothing, all day and every day if they can, but this fits in with their conviction that they are men.

Our society has long disapproved of men who practise transvestism. It is strange, for they are harmless – with the exception of the uncommon exhibitionist transvestite who finds enjoyment in startling strange women. But people are repulsed when they encounter a transvestite and close relationships are endangered. Marriages abruptly end when the wife chances to find her husband in her underclothes, for instance. In some American states there are specific laws against cross-dressing, energetically enforced in California and Texas. In some European countries, Denmark for instance, a transvestite is immune from arrest when he has a medical certificate to show the police. There is no law against it in Britain, but a transvestite may be charged with 'behaviour likely to cause a breach of the peace.' The sentence is light in those cases found guilty, amounting to a small fine at the most, but publicity from the court appearance can wreck a transvestite's career and his marriage. Male prostitutes found by the police in drag risk being charged with importuning. An attired transvestite with a full bladder has to decide whether he should retire to a women's toilet and risk being apprehended for breach of the peace, or to a men's toilet and risk being arrested for soliciting or importuning.

Only when there is a sexual purpose, however, does society disapprove of a man cross-dressing. The disapproval stems from the primeval condemnation of all non-procreative sexual pursuits, from homosexuality to masturbation. Ignorance led transvestism to be suspected as part of witchcraft or as a means of seducing young women. Cross-dressing done out of necessity or to create fun has never been condemned. Those episodes in Roman mythology when the heroes found it expedient to dress as a woman – for example, Hercules appearing as a handmaiden of the Queen of Lydia and Jupiter dressed as Diana – were acceptable, indeed praiseworthy. Shakespeare had to have all his heroines played by men because women were not allowed on the stage, and so he had seen a man dressed as a woman dress as a man in *As You Like It* and *The Merchant of Venice*. Plays staged in boys' schools continue this arrangement. The pantomime dame is traditionally a big, strapping man. He emphasizes his masculinity, which stresses the incongruity of his clothes, and reassures those inwardly sensitive about transvestism and transsexualism. The burlesque artist reassures in the opposite way, that he is not wanting to pass as a woman or to be a woman. He exaggerates feminine nuances beyond reality, into caricature and absurdity. Beyond that, many people become uneasy when they see serious acts of realistic impersonation. Logic does not readily overcome many centuries of suspicion and disapproval.

None of this, of course, refers to the excitement which lovers enjoy in their love-making by putting on something of their partner's, or by watching cross-dressing. Those who like it particularly, however, while they need have no fear of turning into transvestites, will get a whiff of the pleasure which transvestites have. It is like all the other sexual deviations: the embryonic form harmlessly enhances the excitement of love-making.

Chevalier d'Eon de Beaumont (1728–1810) is the archetypal transvestite. From his name Havelock Ellis coined the term eonism. The term has not caught on like sadism and masochism, but the fascinating Chevalier is being recalled by the British organization of transvestites, the Beaumont Society. He was a distinguished diplomat in the service of Louis XV who spent 49 years of his life as a man and 34 as a woman. He became an officer in the Dragoons and was an excellent swordsman. Having enjoyed dressing as a girl in childhood, and doing it well, his experience was put to the service of his country. The Russian court refused to have a French ambassador and d'Eon was sent to see what was going on, in the guise of his sister, as a lady-in-waiting to the Empress. For several months he shared a bedroom in the palace with another lady-in-waiting. One account has it that the Russians were tipped off but that the French court provided medical certificates stating that he was female. There was an improvement of diplomatic relations the following year, so he returned as a diplomat and no one seemed to associate him with the former lady-in-waiting. When he went to England to begin negotiations for the Peace of Paris on the King's behalf, widespread speculation about his sex began and huge wagers were made on both sides of the Channel. He was out of favour with the next King, Louis XVI, who ordered him 'to dress according to her sex.' On one occasion he was put in prison having been found in men's clothes. He made a living out of exhibition fencing matches. He did this, in his women's clothes, till he was 70. Following his death an examination of his body by a group of distinguished men established that he was a normal male. In his younger days, so it was reported, he had had affairs with Madame Pompadour, Madame du Barry, the Empress of Russia and Queen Charlotte.

The true transvestite believes himself to be a man and has no desire for sex change, but he likes to dress as a woman and practise feminine ways. It is a fantasy game. It is not a sexual turn-on, but a tension reducer. It is not unlike an obsession. A hand-washing obsessional, for instance, feels tension rising until he can stand it no longer. He gives in, washes his hands, and feels at peace with himself. Similarly, the transvestite obtains a delicious feeling of relaxation coming over him as he climbs into his female garb. He may live as a woman, as Chevalier did, assimilating feminine nuances of movement and speech, and being accepted as a woman. On the other hand, a transvestite may settle for wearing a pair of french knickers under his suit once or twice a month, changing out of them before he returns home. In between these two extremes, there are men who have accepting wives and who dress up as soon as they come home in the evening. Such a man might take his wife out in the evening and be greatly thrilled when they are taken to be sisters.

For most transvestites the joy of being in silky, feminine clothes is not enough and, additionally, they need social intercourse to provide opportunity for behaving and speaking like a woman. A transvestite may find a prostitute to visit, change in her house, and have a little hen party with her. More often, however, he will join a transvestite group. There are transvestite organizations in most Western countries which arrange for their members to forgather, cross-dressed of course, and engage in various social activities.

These transvestite organizations provide help about other matters, for instance shopping information and counselling of transvestites' wives. Women's shops with agreeable assistants and stocking large sizes are not easy to find and the transvestite usually likes to choose his clothes with care. The embryo transvestite may be satisfied with clothing belonging to his mother, sister or wife, but when he enjoys the sensation sufficiently he will want to buy his own. A few men obtain great delight from visiting ladies-wear shops, never the same shop twice, ostensibly to find a present for a female relative, handling the soft silky undies, discussing their merits with an innocent shop assistant. But this does not provide dresses and coats, wigs and shoes. There are shops that cater exclusively for the needs of transvestites and those sadists and masochists whose excitement needs cross-dressing. They carry large stocks of lingerie in male sizes. There are also ordinary shops which have someone on the staff, sympathetic and knowledgeable, who is summoned when a membership card of the society is produced.

Transvestites are generally heterosexual men with normal heterosexual inclinations, as likely to fall in love and to want to get married as other heterosexual men. Marriage may bring trouble, for not many women are at all content about their man cross-dressing. A few transvestites advertise for a partner in contact magazines, a few curious and adventurous women answer them, and occasionally it results in a marriage that accommodates the cross-dressing. Most brides of transvestites are blissfully ignorant of the groom's inclinations. The grooms believe married life will enable them to desist, or intend strictly to compartmentalize their transvestism. A few are late-starters and have not begun cross-dressing when they get married. Such a man may tell his wife later, in a moment when they are close and intimate, by way of confession but hoping she will allow him to dress up at home, if not introduce it into their love-making. But more likely he continues to dress up clandestinely, careful not to disturb their happy

293

marriage. Then one awful evening she returns home unexpectedly and discovers him at it. Or one awful morning she discovers undies that are not hers. Some women find it intolerable and walk out of the marriage; others come to accept and try to facilitate their husband's peculiar pleasure. Those wives who find the thought of their husband cross-dressing obnoxious may be helped to reconcile themselves in a loving, caring way, as other women learn to play along with their spouse's sadism or masochism. Those women who enter their marriage aware that their partner is a transvestite may also need a helping hand, particularly if he makes increasing and ultimately unbearable demands for his wife's participation. Obviously the most understanding and knowledgeable counsellors are likely to be those attached to the transvestite organization. On the other hand, those wives who go along with their husband's transvestism for 10 or 20 years and then protest strongly and threaten to leave are probably in reality protesting about some other additional, marital problem which has come to the boil.

True transvestites comprise the bulk of men who like cross-dressing, but there are other kinds. Transsexuals, homosexual transvestites and exhibitionist transvestites have already been mentioned, but in addition there are masochistic transvestites, fetishistic transvestites and pseudo-transvestites. These last three are sexually stimulated when they wear women's clothes, and it leads them to masturbation and powerful orgasm. Masochistic transvestites like to dress up in female clothing, in a gym slip say, and receive punishment. This may be spanking or caning, but some men's delight is a mock humiliation by scolding. Harry Benjamin, in *The Transsexual Phenomenon* (1966), referred to a man who dressed in servant girl's clothing and was ordered to scrub floors and clean the house. The man was a noted American cardiologist and this was the sum total of his sex life.

Fetishistic transvestism is not to be confused with fetishism. The fetishist who steals knickers from the clothesline – plain and well-used ones ideally – stares at them, feels them lovingly, smells them, but never wants to put them on. The fetishistic transvestite, in contrast, likes new, frilly, silky, feminine clothes, and likes to wear them. He wants to look like a woman. At the same time, the fetishistic transvestite is different from the true transvestite. The fetishistic transvestite's cross-dressing and his behaviour is exaggerated, showy, sexually evocative and patently artificial. His heels are so high he cannot quite straighten his legs, his cosmetics are garish and overgenerously applied, and his false eyelashes too long. It is a sexual act for him.

The pseudo-transvestite is not a transvestite at all, but typically a young explorer into the mystery of woman, an adolescent struck by his new, strong, obtrusive sexual feelings and wanting to know what a girl feels. Does the discomfort from being perched on high heels and squeezed into a tight dress affect her sexual feelings, he ponders, and is it connected with the sexual attraction she radiates? He gets into attire from his mother's wardrobe or his sister's and, imagining girls he knows tightly enclosed, is sexually excited. It is a transitory phase and so brief that many writers do not mention it. But a mother who surprises her teenage son wearing his sister's briefs may have agonizing fears that he is on the road to transsexualism or homosexuality nevertheless.

The cause of tranvestism remains a puzzle. The Freudians fall back on their old standby, the castration anxiety. All boys develop this on seeing that a girl's genitals lack a penis, the theory holds, and it continues to bother some men. The transvestite attempts to convince himself that women do possess a penis after all by representing himself as a woman with a penis under her clothes. The transvestite also tries, the Freudian theory goes, to accept that the clothes themselves represent the woman's penis. Recent research has made us less sure of the importance of castration anxiety in the development and maldevelopment of a man's sexuality. This apart, the explanation is unconvincing. Dressing as a woman and acting as one would surely threaten rather than bolster a man's masculinity. There is a growing body of opinion claiming that true transvestism is essentially a minor form of transsexualism. Indeed, following Harry Benjamin, it is maintained that the difference is only a matter of degree between pseudo-transvestism, fetishistic transvestism, true transvestism, and transsexualism. The arguments about the causes of transsexualism may therefore be relevant here.

Left to himself a transvestite does not seek psychiatric help. When he does ask for treatment it is occasionally at the behest of the law, but very often at the insistence of his wife. Most transvestites are married and have children – they are no different from the average man in these respects – but their cross-dressing often proves a stumbling-block to happy relations. So they come in the guise of contrition, hoping that their attendance will appease their wives and keep their marriage together, but not motivated to change. Little wonder psychoanalysis and psychotherapy have been found ineffective in the treatment of transvestism. In the 1960s, with the dawn of behaviour therapy, there was considerable enthusiasm for aversion treatment in various sexual problems, including transvestism. The idea behind it was simple. While the patient dressed up he was given something unpleasant, a drug which induced vomiting, or low voltage but painful electric shocks on his arm. The latter method was preferred because the timing of the administration in relation to the dressing could be more precise. Unfortunately, those who went through with this unpleasant treatment tended to revert back to their old ways after a year or two, sometimes much sooner. Others opted out of treatment. Aversion therapy has not been entirely discarded, but the main approach nowadays is exploring ways in which the transvestite can cross-dress in peace, if possible in congenial company, and ways in which his wife can be reconciled to his unusual need. There are branches of the Beaumont Society in most cities, and they offer experienced counselling, often by transvestites themselves or wives of transvestites.

UROLAGNIA

Urolagnia is sexual pleasure exclusively obtained from seeing a woman urinating, preferably when standing. There is no end to the pleasures that take men's fancy and many men have enjoyed this sight in fantasy if not in reality. Urolagnia may be construed as an extension to scoptophilia, which is the pleasure obtained from examining a woman's vulva: urolagnia is examining it in action. When it becomes the be-all-and-end-all of a man's sexual pleasure it is an over-riding fetish.

Urolaginists have justified and glorified their unusual source of sexual pleasure, regarding it as more exciting than the normal sex of normal people, and waxing lyrical when opportunity presented itself. Henry Havelock Ellis liked it and was eulogistic about it. He was an exact contemporary of Freud, less famous, but a diligent researcher (which Freud was not) and, mainly through his seven-volume *Studies in the Psychology of Sex*, he became the central figure in the advent of modern sexual thought. He was impotent almost all his life – with his wife and his several extramarital friends – and he relied on urolagnia for his sexual pleasure. He wrote in *My Life* (which was published the year after his death) that he 'was surprised how often women responded to it sympathetically'. His mother did it in his presence while they were visiting the zoo when he was 12 and once again a little later. He thought this is how it arose.

Also in his autobiography, he described one of his women friends responding sympathetically. The language used by this normally restrained researcher is reminiscent of the ecstatic descriptions of vulvas in *My Secret Life*. HD's 'tall form languidly arose and stood erect, taut and massive it seemed now with the length of those straight adolescent legs still more ravishing in their unyielding pride, and the form before me seemed to become some Olympian vase, and a large stream gushed afar in the glistening liquid arch, endlessly, it seemed to my wondering eyes, as I contemplated with enthralled gaze this prototypal statue of the Fountain of Life, curved by the hands of some daring and divine architect, out of marble-like flesh.'

Is it strange that this shy, moral, social scientist and reformer should have had this strange fetish? It illustrates that fetishists are usually ordinary people, not at all socially dangerous. The opprobrium would have been far too outrageous if he had made public his kinky pleasure when he was alive. But fortunately he enjoyed his urolagnia so much that he disclosed it in his posthumous autobiography.

This particular delight of Havelock Ellis was most peculiar. But he should not have been so surprised at the women who indulged him, he of all people. Many a woman will break clear of convention to accommodate the needs of the man she loves, provided she is not enslaved to a fiercely Puritanical upbringing. However, it is not so odd nowadays. Surprisingly, urolagnia is not mentioned in *The Joy of Sex*, for many modern couples apparently include it in their repertoire. Usually the wife stands urinating over her husband when they are having a bath together. The wife enjoys it, if only as a declaration of her liberation from society's restrictions and a return to infantile freedom. The man enjoys it. Urine is sterile, and the game of 'golden showers' or 'watersports' as it is called is harmless.

The trouble occurs when it becomes a man's only source of sexual pleasure. So it was with Havelock Ellis, who was impotent with his wife and with these obliging girlfriends. If he could come now seeking treatment for his urolagnia he would be given instruction about switching fantasies while masturbating – in the manner described in the treatment of fetishism. In addition, the various aspects of his impotence would be explored and treated in conjunction with his wife.

Urophilia, a degree farther off course, is the fetish of the man who is aroused and potent only if his partner urinates on him and into his mouth. Some men have strange sexual needs and some women are strangely indulgent! No rhapsodic account of urophilia can be found in serious literature, but at least it can be stated that urine is sterile in healthy, normal people. Morarji Desai, a prime minister of India, drank some of his own urine each morning for medical purposes – or so it is claimed.

VOYEURISM

Voyeurism usually means obtaining sexual gratification by surreptitiously watching a woman undressing or undressed. 'Surreptitiously' is important: it has to be surreptitious, clandestine, done by stealth, to be exciting. The woman is unaware of being watched and would heartily disapprove if she knew. This is the basic requirement of the voyeur or Peeping Tom – the name of the furtive Coventry tailor in the story of Lady Godiva. His wife or girlfriend undressing before him is dull stuff compared to the more distant view of the unsuspecting stranger taking off her clothes. It need hardly be said that such a sight would arrest any man's attention. It becomes voyeurism when he wanders through dark streets in different residential neighbourhoods each night, surveying houses for bedrooms with curtains undrawn, and when he prefers peeping to normal sex. It occurs only in men, and it is one example, among many sexual abnormalities, of the importance of visual stimuli for men.

Voyeurism is, less commonly, used to denote a rather different kind of peeping – spying on loving couples engaged in sexual activity. The likely hunting ground for this kind of voyeurism is a public park, common or heath. A development of this kind of voyeurism, observing couples in sexual activity – but openly, without the spying – is a widespread new cult. It accommodates voyeurs, those who like to be watched, and many who like it both ways. Advertisements in one recent issue of a contact magazine illustrate the preferences: 'Couple would like to watch and be watched', 'Attractive young male wants sexy couple who will let him watch their fun', 'Male voyeur wants to watch two gay females at play', and 'Couple seeks singles, couples, voyeurs for interesting evenings'. The boundary-line of any deviation is uncertain and always shifting.

The terms voyeurism and scoptophilia are regarded as synonymous by some writers – especially those from this side of the Atlantic – but it seems desirable to retain a distinction. Scoptophilia should refer to the dependency on looking at the woman's genitalia for sexual excitement. It is not surreptitious.

Peering through bedroom windows is the commonest, but not the only, activity of voyeurs. They may strategically station themselves within a house or building. Rarely, they are able to make an inconspicuous peep-hole in the wall between two rooms. It is interesting to note – if only to remind ourselves that voyeurism is nothing new – that the Victorian author of *My Secret Life* always packed a gimlet when he was going abroad, although he often found his hotel room already equipped with spy-holes. The present writer recalls his first voyeur patient, a young professional man who spied on his wife's lodger through a small periscope in the ceiling of her room. Occasionally men hide themselves in ladies' public lavatories to watch women. The risk of being caught is high, but this seems to be an important element in their excitement. One case on record is of a man who had nine convictions, all for public lavatory offences in London. Such men verge on urolagnia, and those who intrude themselves simply to hear lavatorial sounds from the women more so.

Voyeurs are generally shy with women. They are less likely to be married than any other type of sexual offender. Lovers like to look at one another – men more than women – but the looking is preliminary to uniting their bodies. The voyeur enjoys the looking, but at a distance, and furtively. Some of those who are married still prefer their sex at a distance because of indelible voyeuristic patterns already laid down, a continuing difficulty in relating, or a disturbance in the marital relationship. Voyeurs are generally harmless. The exceptions are among those peepers – not true-blue by our definition – who intimate their presence by, for instance, tapping on a window. They may progress to sexual assault of some kind.

Unlike exhibitionism, voyeurism is not a criminal offence in the United Kingdom. Those Peeping Toms who are caught by the police are generally bound over to be of good behaviour or to keep the peace. Of course those who break and enter private property, or public lavatories, commit criminal offences.

SEXUALITY IN THE SOCIAL CONTEXT

Dr Peter Dally

In itself sex is nothing more or less than the means by which our species is perpetuated. But in our efforts to control this force of nature, we try and bend it to our own needs and purposes, not always with success. This has been the case as far back as our knowledge of human societies extends. Quite apart from studying the effect of sex on past generations, our observation of animals has greatly contributed to our misconceptions and insights about it.

Most people would agree with Jung's analysis that sex and power have equal influence on human behaviour. It can also be said of individuals that their sexual attractiveness is power, and that success, power and wealth are aphrodisiacs – which complicates the picture when trying to define the mainsprings of our sexuality.

Sexual appetite is always relative, subordinated to the greater human needs of sleep, water and food, freedom from fear, pain and illness. Only when these basic requirements have been met do we experience the urge to copulate.

Conditioning and habit also play their part. The child who grows up in a large family, with brothers and sisters close to him or her in age, discovers his own and his siblings' sexual proclivities naturally. And, depending on parental attitudes to these discoveries, the child may then experiment openly or furtively. If parents and those about them are demonstratively affectionate to each other and constantly fondling the children, the latter are likely to grow up spontaneously and naturally seeking sexual intercourse with those to whom they are attracted. On the other hand, only children who live without the intimate and continuous company of other children, perhaps looked after by nannies and other mother-substitutes, not seeing much of their parents, often lack that sexual spontaneity.

We know of the sexual deprivations and frustrations suffered by those in unusual circumstances, like monks and nuns living in convents and monasteries. But from all accounts, after the initial period of enforced or voluntary celibacy, depending upon the individual's sex drive, there comes a time when they no longer have the same urges and desires as someone leading a more normal life.

Havelock Ellis believed that sex was an essential part of a sane and balanced life, and needed to be removed from taboos and guilt feelings. But he was the last to deny the importance of love with sex. At times today it seems as though love has become a mere appendage of sex. Certainly, when people talk of sex they all too often ignore the element of love. It can perhaps be argued that this is a development that in certain cases leads to healthier, less fraught, relationships. But in the long term it diminishes what is possible in a good sexual relationship.

Still, the gains of the sexual revolution of recent years are enormous. Women have attained sexual freedom and are virtually on the same footing as men, able to pick and choose at will. Men and women can cohabit without fear of unwanted pregnancy, and without incurring strong social disapproval. Diseases associated with sex, apart from AIDS, have lost much of their terror thanks to both the efficacy of antibiotics and co-ordinated efforts of health authorities. No one need be trapped in a loveless marriage any more, for divorce is readily available to either sex.

A SATISFACTORY RELATIONSHIP

Today many people choose to live together outside marriage, preferring not to commit themselves fully, to keep their options open for as long as their partner is of the same mind, or until a desire to have children stirs. Marriage is usually sought as an affirmation of the relationship when children are desired, for the family unit is still the basic fabric of our society.

Homosexuality is accepted in a way unthinkable even 20 years ago – although he is a brave (or perhaps imprudent) homosexual man who, intent on a professional career perhaps, proclaims openly his proclivities – and two homosexuals of either gender can live together without exciting much comment. Transvestites may now publicly indulge their fancies, even perhaps to the extent of going to work dressed in drag. And transsexuals, with surgical assistance, can change their sex and be accepted in their new role with scarcely an inquisitive stare.

Surely then, with such apparent social tolerance, with men and women sexually liberated and comparatively free to do as they choose, there should be a much wider sense of contentment and well-being. Yet the discontent and the mental and physical disorders that arise from unsatisfactory sex lives do not seem to lessen. On the contrary, from the point of view of a doctor, they seem to be on the increase. For although the extreme prudery and sexual repression associated with the Victorian era have largely vanished, the essential problems inherent in any sexual relationship are no different. Expectations of sex vary. What satisfies one person may be anathema to another. What is marvellous one day may be boring or irritating the next.

Of course some people can ignore sex with impunity. Celibacy as a chosen way of life never caused anyone physical harm, and it is reasonable to assume that sexual energies can be displaced into non-sexual channels; ambition for power and success in work, for instance. Not everyone can achieve this, however. Perhaps it is only possible for those people whose sex drive is comparatively low and who rarely experience lust.

SEXUAL NEEDS

Sex creates wide-ranging needs. Sexual desire and extreme hunger for food have much in common. Hungry and lusty individuals

303

are restless, urgently searching for the means of gratification, preoccupied with thoughts of food or sex. Once satisfied, everything is relieved and 'back to normal'.

The greater the desire, the less discriminating an individual becomes in his or her choice of sex object. Just as a ravenously hungry person often eats food that may well be found repellent at other times, so lust can transform some previously unattractive being into a desirable one. Of course, sex has a great advantage over food in that imagination can be some substitute for reality – a hungry man simply has to find food sooner or later, or starve. A lustful one can create his own diversions, so to speak. The solitary masturbator can conjure up any situation he desires, peopled by whom he will, and stimulate himself until he reaches orgasm. Hungry people can, as we all know from experience, allay some of their hunger for a time by fantasies of food, but unlike sexual fantasies food fantasies cannot replace the real thing.

Like hunger, sex is there from the beginning. The sensual pleasure that children derive from their bodies, and the intense interest they take in exploring and investigating those of others, in part at least stems from it. It was one of Freud's greater achievements to point to the sexuality of children. Sex does not suddenly appear with a bang at puberty. It develops from birth, and steadily diffuses through what Freud called 'erotic zones' until it comes to centre around the genital areas. Sex supplies the drive for sensual pleasure, especially from erotic (erogenous) zones of the body before puberty. At puberty and afterwards sensuality flows into genital sexual pleasure and orgasm. The earlier sensual pleasures are not entirely lost and replaced by genital sex. They remain and are a source of delight, and should be a prelude to orgasmic sex. Indeed, for some men and women, they may be more important than genital sex. Slow massage of the whole body, or particular areas, can lead to such an intense accumulation of feeling that at times it overflows into actual orgasm.

All the feelings and fantasies of a growing infant and child that accompany every event – satisfaction and frustrations, pains or discomfort, rage and helplessness, comfort or rejection, being held and fed, excretion, playing with a favourite toy, the pleasure of being bathed – they all affect sensual, and subsequently sexual, development.

To go back to the beginning again, first of all there is our self and what pleases or displeases us. And we learn to recognize that it is the living beings outside us who provide or withhold our pleasures and dissatisfactions. So we come to love those living beings because we need them. They sustain and protect us, and show us the world. They are the prototypes of the lovers, heroes and teachers whom we love in later life. Generally it is a mother, father or an elder sibling who fills such a role most consistently from the start, but it can as easily be a grandparent or another close relative, even a family friend.

Sometimes, however, children may feel deprived of love and become unsure of themselves, so that their emotional development suffers. Are they so unattractive and unlovable, their subconscious worries, that their parents cannot give them affection? What can they do to gain love? It may be that the parents really are unable or unwilling to give love. Or perhaps, because of some inherent abnormality, the child's perception of the love received is impaired. Whatever the cause the child, and later adult, feels empty and is forever seeking love, for reassurance that he or she is indeed good and lovable. Such a neurotic need for love can rarely be satisfied, and it must be contrasted with real, adult love, in which another person is loved for his or her own sake, not just for the emotional response.

A young woman had the reputation among her friends of being a nymphomaniac. She went from man to man, craving sexual relief. She experienced multiple orgasms, and yet was never satiated. Sex for her was an endless search to prove that she was lovable and wanted by others. She was driven not by lust but by her appetite, the nature of which (it is to be supposed) had been influenced by her deprived and affectionless early life, and steadily reinforced by the stream of rejections and the unsatisfactory nature of her affairs. Eventually, in despair, she married, hoping that children would supply the love that had always eluded her. She killed herself when she learned that she was infertile as a result of earlier pelvic infections.

For the average healthy young man or woman relaxed and on holiday, three or four orgasms a day is usually more than enough to keep sexual desire satisfied. Neurotic love, on the other hand, can be almost insatiable. An insecure, anxious individual may continue to masturbate or make love throughout much of the day and night, even though sexual pleasure is minimal and orgasm is no longer possible. He or she thus strives to overcome insecurity through sexual activity, thereby obtaining emotional comfort and warmth, just as some people eat for comfort. Masturbation may become unsatisfactory and fail to alleviate the anxiety underlying the need. At that stage, only a satisfying sexual relationship is likely to bring about lasting tranquillity. But sexual relationships require growth, and that may not be within an insecure individual's power. It is when such a relationship begins to fail, and the emotions that accompany that person's sexuality are no longer met, that he or she is driven towards non-sexual outlets and ways to relieve anxiety, such as shoplifting, gambling or alcoholism.

OBJECTS OF ATTRACTION

It is important to recognize three other aspects of sexuality: drive, gender and sex object. Drive has already been mentioned, particularly the huge discrepancies that exist between one man or woman and another. The strength of an individual's drive depends partly on constitutional factors, genetic and intra-uterine influences, and partly on psychological events after birth, together with the emotional forces that become linked to sexual appetite and its satisfaction. A strong sexual appetite obviously goes with a strong drive; a man with a low sex drive behaves very differently from one who possesses a strong appetite.

Gender describes our awareness of being male or female. Most of us have few doubts, in spite of the ambiguity of clothing and hairstyle that exists among young people today – although the turbulent changes of puberty, particularly in males, occasionally gives rise to vague transitory fears about gender. Only those rare beings, transsexuals, are convinced they are not what they seem, that a woman is imprisoned within the male carapace, or vice versa. Gender has little or no link with homosexuality or transvestism. The vast majority of male homosexuals are of male gender, and react indignantly to any suggestion that they are not. Similarly, lesbians have no doubt about their femaleness. What is concerned here is not gender but sex object.

This somewhat daunting term refers to anything or anyone we are drawn to sexually. Most of us are sexually attracted to people of the opposite sex, but the number and variation of the qualities which go to make a person attractive to someone else are almost infinite.

Good looks attract attention initially, but do not necessarily arouse sexual interest. A man who is particularly attractive to one woman, or to a homosexual male, may make no impact whatever on another. Another man is aroused only by young women with beautiful figures and long blonde hair; their deeper attraction for him may lie in the envious looks they evoke from other people and the sense of power he derives from this when he is with them. Indeed, power is a great aphrodisiac, and a tycoon, however ugly his appearance, is never likely to be at a loss for sexual partners. Some women are attracted only by strength of character, by men who appear outwardly to be strong and reliable. Woe betide a man if such a woman discovers the qualities that initially drew her to him are illusory. For her, a sexual relationship can come into being only when she feels 'protected' by a strong partner. Others are attracted by inadequacy or inferiority of some kind – people of lower social class, education or intelligence – by those who look up to them and pose no threat to a dominant–subservient type of relationship. It is sometimes the gratification of power that compels a man or woman to seduce the spouse of a close friend or relative, or the secretary to engage in an affair with her boss. The sense of triumph is short-lasting and illusory, for if the powerful individual is overcome, surely he or she cannot in fact have been all that powerful; anxiety and sexual dissatisfaction quickly set in.

Sometimes the sexual object may be inanimate, or a specific feature of an individual, in which case it is known as a fetish. Some fetishists – they tend to be predominantly male – are drawn to a woman's feet, slanting eyes or long hair. No matter how she looks or behaves as a person, her attraction to the fetishist resides almost entirely in the fetish. Others are aroused by inanimate objects; rubber or plastic mats and aprons are the most common. How such compelling attractions are formed is largely a matter of conjecture. What is certain, though, is that they begin in childhood and continue throughout life.

Thus are we driven by our particular predilections, often helpless to resist, which influence our choice of partner and behaviour. Most people are not entirely restricted in their choice of sexual partner. A range of attractive sex objects exists for them, although with variable degrees of attraction. One can in fact construct a hierarchy of attraction for a specific person, which often remains fairly static throughout his or her life. But it is not unusual for an 'object' to change position on the scale of attraction, becoming more or less compelling with age. A heterosexual man or woman can pass through a bisexual phase and eventually end up being predominantly homosexual. Neither gender nor drive changes in such an individual, only the 'object'. For the fetishist, the fetish rarely loses its compelling top attraction. Sexual pleasure is intense whenever the fetish is involved, either during solitary masturbation or with a partner. Particularly when the partner is co-operative and enters enthusiastically into the 'game', the partner in the fetishist's eyes takes on some of the attractive qualities of the fetish. The fetishist can certainly be attracted to other people – the majority of fetishists are, after all, married, often with families – but the strength of attraction for such people is way below that of the fetish, unless they become linked with it.

For those people of both sexes who enjoy bondage – tying or being tied up, beating or being beaten – partners can only be seen as strongly sexually attractive if they become associated with such activity. But whereas it is a comparatively simple matter for the fetishists to link his fetish with his wife or mistress, provided she agrees, it is not always easy for those who need to indulge in bondage to do so with someone they love.

LOVE, SEX AND PROMISCUITY

Love is hard to define, yet most people recognize the feelings associated with it; there is affection and liking, a desire to share and participate in at least some aspect of the loved one's life, and above all, mental propinquity. People's views on love invariably differ in minor degree, for they are coloured by what they have seen and experienced of love in childhood. Influential, for instance, are how reliable and consistent the love of parents was, not only towards their children but also for one another; the course and nature of important friendships; even perhaps what is seen on television and in films.

Sexual love is all this with the addition of sex, although this is an oversimplified definition. Sex requires physical attraction and compatibility. It is particularly in this last respect that problems may arise, for although there may be physical compatibility when two people first meet, the development of love between them can actually negate this.

Sexual love in Western society today is heavily weighted on the side of sex. Love is not ignored, but the emphasis in any sexual relationship is largely on physical gratification. A passionate affair is tempestuous and emotionally overwhelming. Each partner is the centre of the other's world, almost blind to other people, and certainly deaf to criticism. Love may be present, but not necessarily so, and the couple may have to wait for passion to fade before they can be certain of this. Marriage at the height of passion is a risky business, for a relationship based only on sex is almost certainly doomed in the long term. On the other hand, in a marriage of convenience, or an arranged one, sex and love, provided they germinate, are likely to grow slowly and perhaps more harmoniously together.

Good and lasting sexual love requires sex and love both to endure. The predominance of one or the other inevitably fluctuates with time and circumstances, but the essential interactions of sex and love, so necessary for the growth of both, continue. Yet although – as we have said – a relationship built on sex alone cannot exist for long, a relationship that has largely lost its sexual component and is finally based simply on love alone has a better chance of survival. It is liable to be an irascible relationship, however, lacking as it does the safety valves and satisfactions ordinarily provided by sex.

Some people cannot equate love with sex. They can enjoy sex, and they can love, but they cannot incorporate the two into a unity.

What is it that makes love and sex incompatible in this way for such people? A casual affair is no problem for them. They can allow themselves to have intercourse or to masturbate, but never in the presence of love. Sex gives transitory satisfaction, but in the long term serves only to highlight their sense of loneliness, their inability to find a lasting partner whom they can love and who can love them. Sex for them is blemished, its manifestations only possible in the absence of love. The convoluted feelings behind this arise from concepts in childhood that love is only for 'good' people, and that sex is 'bad'; the essential dichotomy between good and bad is thus 'translated' as a comparison between love and sex. It is totally illogical when looked at from an adult viewpoint (as is so much adult sexual behaviour). But it is not unreasonable when viewed through a child's eyes.

Sometimes compromise is possible, as time and development lessen the intensity of the internal conflict, and some kind of sex life becomes possible with someone who can be loved. Once begun with an understanding partner, it can grow. But sex under such circumstances is liable to be dull. The man or woman affected may feel compelled to have outside affairs, exciting although not always pleasing, with someone who is 'forbidden' and therefore unlovable. Or they may rely on masturbation and its fantasies. Occasionally it is possible to introduce some variation, such as sex *à trois*. A 'wicked' outsider is then brought in to share their sex, which temporarily imbues the partner with badness and therefore attraction. This calls for a partner who is not only understanding but sufficiently secure both to cope with the conflicting emotions that are liable to result, and to derive pleasure from the encounter.

Homosexuals in particular seem liable to experience difficulties of this nature with sexual love. For many, sex fades when love appears. It is one of the reasons, among others such as loneliness, that so many homosexuals, especially male, tend to be promiscuous.

But promiscuity has also increased among heterosexuals, male and female, in recent years, due to contraception and the availability of legal abortion, both of which have changed social standards, and the rapid efficacy of antibiotics in treating syphilis and gonorrhoea. However, the spread of genital herpes and better information about its possible consequences, and more recently the danger of AIDS, seem to be bringing about an overall reduction in promiscuity.

A generation or so ago, the mere thought of venereal disease (VD) – let alone actual infection – caused many people to experience shame and guilt. Today, most of the people who attend VD clinics show little or no fear (apart from those at risk from AIDS) and are rarely ashamed of their condition. Guilt is only prominent among VD-clinic attenders when they have good reasons for feeling so; they have been unfaithful to a long-term partner, seduced a friend's lover, or perhaps are pathologically depressed. However, fear of AIDS has caused many formerly promiscuous homosexual men – and women with a penchant for bisexual men – to considerably modify their behaviour. Some have restricted themselves, where psychologically possible, to a single partner; others have abandoned anal sex and fellatio and limited their sexual activities to mutual masturbation and body rubbing, duller but safer.

Not so long ago, preachers would have proclaimed that AIDS, like syphilis in its heyday, had been sent by an angry God to punish the wicked for their sexual misdeeds. No one maintains this today because no one believes it. In place of superstitious fear based on ignorance we have understandable fear tempered by knowledge and recognition of the disease, how it may be transmitted and how it may be avoided. Logical and responsible behaviour is thereby encouraged.

SEX AND THE ADOLESCENT

It is sometimes claimed that sexual guilt is most likely to develop in Christian societies. But in fact sexual conflicts and difficulties are probably just as common and troublesome in other cultures. The suggestion by Freud that the more urbanized and controlled a society is, the greater its sexual problems, does not stand examination. It is now clear that neurotic problems of sexual origin are not at all uncommon in primitive societies.

The family forms the basis of virtually every known society. Attempts to abolish the family have invariably met with failure and caused more problems than they set out to remove.

Every society and family directly or indirectly shapes the sexual *mores* and behaviour of its members. Sex is never freely allowed to find its own pathway. Societies have always recognized that sex can be a powerful and potentially destructive force. Their members have usually agreed to moderate its force by imposing certain restrictions upon its indulgence.

Children learn and absorb the attitudes of their families and culture towards sex from an early age. They may misbehave in the course of sexual exploration of themselves and their friends, but in no way can such behaviour be seen as rejection of family standards. It is only when adolescence is reached that the standard of true rebellion is liable to be raised.

Adolescence is a time of exploration and self-assertion. The adolescent boy or girl is set to discover new dimensions and new values in the course of self-fulfilment. Every new generation challenges the ideals and customs of their time. Since World War II, American and European societies have done more than any others in the past to encourage the next generation to go their own way. It has not been difficult to give them this freedom; so many of the older generation have lost faith in their institutions, and question the values they live by. Particularly in the sexual field, adolescents have achieved a degree of sexual freedom hardly dreamed of a generation ago. Such freedom has drawbacks, however, for there are far fewer parental standards than in former times to follow or rebel against, and all too often the adolescent may become lost. For a majority of male teenagers physical sex is all-important; love is often seen as unnecessary and restricting. Young female teenagers, on the other hand, look first for love; sex is more often than not a means of attracting and retaining a partner rather than a source of genuine enjoyment. With time and the growth of self confidence, an adolescent can usually begin to permit sex and love to intermingle.

Some adolescents react badly to pressures from their peers to begin sex as soon as they meet a potential partner. If they refuse, on the reasonable grounds that they want to know the partner better before they go all the way, they all too often feel left out of their group, and come to see themselves as social outcasts. Many young women in particular, and not a few middle-aged ones, cannot take sex lightly. Just as a century ago a kiss stirred up strong emotions and fears, so today intercourse, or the thought of it, can cause even stronger tremors, and not just among the children of parents who hold strong views on chastity and extra-marital sex. Some teenagers deal with this dilemma by concentrating on work and academic success, ostentatiously looking down on those who apparently waste their time and talents on sex. Others search for strength through religion, especially the evangelical kind. Yet others go to the opposite extreme and become promiscuous, jumping from bed to bed, almost at times it seems with closed eyes, thereby ensuring that no steady relationship develops.

Our society today is multiracial, and it is difficult for young Asiatic women in particular to cope easily with their sexuality. Many are brought up in traditional ways, expected to be virgins for what may be an arranged marriage. Yet on all sides their white friends are sexually active, and the world they inhabit away from the family is both tempting and forbidden. They find themselves trapped between what the rest of society might think of as a Victorian way of life and the permissive society. It is small wonder that some of them temporarily resolve their conflicts through psychosomatic and hysterical illness.

Some adolescents fail to achieve a measure of self-confidence and remain emotionally tied to their families. They stay at home out of timidity rather than for convenience, discontented, moody and difficult. Not infrequently such immature behaviour is inadvertently encouraged by one or both parents, reluctant to contemplate life without the presence of their child. The more sophisticated parents may encourage their child to marry another 'child', someone they can control. They buy the young couple a house. They possess a key to the front door. They call, or expect their son or daughter to visit them, every day. Nothing must be withheld from them.

It is hard for such an immature couple to develop and grow into adulthood, impeded at every turn by such protective parents. They may continue, outwardly undisturbed, for many years until the parents die and then, perhaps suddenly, they break up. Often, one of the partners – usually the woman – becomes more and more dissatisfied. She may try in various ways to provoke her partner into noticing the emptiness of their life together, usually to no avail. She may be alarmed by the strength of her growing resentment and try to control her feelings, for instance by starving herself. Anorexia nervosa, beginning at or shortly after marriage, or while the couple are setting up together, very often stems from such a situation. As the woman loses weight, she withdraws from her husband, even to the extent of refusing to share meals with him. Eventually nothing is shared other than habits and indirectly expressed resentment. Yet only rarely is one partner confident enough to make a break. Most of these couples continue to soldier on, too frightened to abandon the familiar for the unknown, prepared to hide behind sickness rather than show their real feelings and needs.

MARRIAGE AND DIVORCE

Many couples today choose to live together before contemplating marriage, to ensure that they are sexually compatible, reasonably tolerant and adaptable together, and capable of functioning as a social unit with mutual friends. Each continues to work and maintain a reassuring sense of independence, not simply financial, irrespective of how close the couple feel when together. The danger of overdependence is reduced and each partner grows in confidence. Regular sex has a strong bonding effect. After a year or more, such a couple may be ready to accept the increased responsibility of marriage without such formalization having any adverse effect on their satisfying sex life.

Marriage still carries a sense of permanence and security which an affair, however long-lasting, somehow lacks. It is less painful to end an affair than to divorce, and there is far less sense of failure and shame. Most young people who marry today do so largely because they want children in the near future. Commitment to one another is greater in marriage. Marriage implies that each partner trusts the other without reservations. A child both reinforces and enhances this trust.

But marriage does not always follow such ideal lines. Some people feel trapped by marriage. Although they may have lived in apparent contentment for several years with the partner who is now their wife or husband, marriage changes the relationship. Sex declines and may cease altogether.

Divorce today is a comparatively simple and common procedure. For some this is good. But sadly, divorce at the present time sometimes brings almost as much misery as it is intended to relieve, especially when young children are concerned. Many couples who divorce have a sense of guilt and failure that can persist for years. But whereas in general society deplores divorces that break up families with young children, there is no actual stigma attached to being divorced today.

LOVE AND SEX WHILE GETTING OLDER

The middle-aged have been strongly disturbed by social and sexual changes. Parents who led comparatively chaste lives before they married, worked hard to give their children the maximum opportunities to achieve success and what they themselves perhaps missed – a place at university followed by a professional career, for instance – are at first upset, then later envious at what they see as the sexual freedom of their adolescent children, especially daughters. Sex and success are for these parents incompatible. Sex is the very abnegation of the self-control they believe is necessary for success in life. Their children's behaviour is all too often seen, initially at any rate, simply in terms of promiscuity, self-indulgence and irresponsibility. Parents may only begin to recognize later that their 19-year-old daughter's affair with a fellow undergraduate has consistency and depth, contains some degree of love, and may not necessarily be irresponsible or abandoned. They may even come to see the intimacy and pleasure of the youngsters in stark contrast to the state of their own marriage. Suddenly they may become aware that they have missed something, that they have never experienced 'good sex'. And in consequence they may jettison their lifelong inhibitions and behave like anxious teenagers, searching for some missing part of their identity, for essential experiences that they may soon be too old to have. A kind of madness grips one or both of a couple, which may bring transitory excitement, but is all too often succeeded by loss of self-respect and depression. Ideally, if it is not too late, a phoenix can emerge from the ashes of their marriage, but this requires understanding and determination, and for a couple to discuss with honesty their mutual failings and feelings. More often than not, such a couple have to separate, unable to cope with their resentments and misery. A warning notice, 'Always look at yourself before castigating your teenage children,' should be hung in every parent's bedroom, for it is in such teenage behaviour that parents may see, if they are prepared to look, many of their own problems.

Men and women are capable of being sexually active in middle and old age. Some people are happy, sometimes relieved, to switch off and close that page of their lives. But most older people enjoy sex, often with more time and opportunity than in earlier years, and have if anything a greater need for closeness. Of course, like love, closeness is a relative term and does not necessarily always depend on maintaining a good sexual relationship. A couple can be held by their mutual interests and work. In such instances, though, one partner is always seen as 'stronger' and liable to be idealized by the other. By and large, a relationship is liable to be emotionally lukewarm if sex is lacking, although a couple can make up for that by fanatically embracing some ideal. Not everyone can campaign continuously for nuclear disarmament, or for the abolition of blood sports, however, and without a reasonably good sex life 60-year-old couples on their own are liable to become touchy and tense. Plenty of long-standing marriages continue to exist without sex, for habit is strong. But it is not rare for 70-year-olds to break up and divorce.

GREAT EXPECTATIONS: CHOOSING A MATE

Sex can be marvellous for two people who live together for a short period. Passion for a time magically converts black into white, or at least makes obvious drawbacks seem unimportant. But passion always fades and ultimately dies unless accompanied by a sustaining force of love. Robert Browning held the romantic belief that 'marriage was made in heaven', that there existed one person alone ideally suited to another, and that if those two people failed

315

to recognize this when they met, or for whatever reason failed to seize the opportunity, they would never be truly happy. They might instead marry a second-best, but the emotional intensity experienced could never match what could have been possible with the ideal.

Browning's own marriage to Elizabeth Barrett can perhaps be cited to back up his point, but few of us would accept his view without strong reservations. It may be less contentious to claim that the moulding of sexual relationships occurs within the family rather than in heaven – although some people may equate the two! A first wife or husband almost inevitably steps into the shoes of his or her parent-in-law. Expressed in a more homespun although oversimplified form, a man expects his wife to have the qualities of a *loving* mother. But of course in fact his mother may have been far from loving, and in any case no one can be consistently so. If his mother spoiled and fussed excessively over him, he is liable to choose a woman who will mother and spoil him in similar style. If she was of a hysterical disposition, screaming and raging one moment, warmly embracing him the next, he may well take a wife of similar character – marital rows and uproars will then only serve to reassure him that his wife loves him. Similarly, a wife looks for a copy of what she admired in her own father, or perhaps instead for the opposite of a father who was frequently drunk and brutal and caused much unhappiness at home. These early patterns of parental interaction often seem to leave indelible traces in the nervous system. Every child sees his or her parents at some time in ideal fantasy shapes, at variance with reality, and when a partner is eventually chosen expectations and hopes may be so unrealistic that conflicts rapidly ensue.

Consider two sisters. The elder married a gentle, unassertive man, the very opposite of her father in character. The younger chose a man who was aggressive, a womanizer, someone who constantly kept his wife at arm's length and railed against what he called her over-possessiveness. Neither marriage was successful.

It is a common occurrence to encounter men and women who seem to be engaged in an endless search for an ideal father or mother figure, and who in the process always choose people who fail conspicuously to match their ideal. The inadequate man looks for a woman who can take care of him, but at the same time not 'possess' him. He expects her to be loving and caring, yet he continually pushes her away, even while criticizing her for not concerning herself enough with him. Some people appear incapable of learning through their experiences, and their destructively immature behaviour never changes. In extreme instances an individual may repeat the same mistakes over and over again, marrying and separating from almost identical partners.

The choice of a mate depends on several factors, of course, not just needs that emanate from childhood. Good looks may start the ball rolling, but are not usually the clinching factor. For the most part there have to be interests in common, a similar sense of humour, and the ability to surprise and excite. Perhaps most important in reinforcing feelings of attraction is the interest shown by a potential mate, the ability to listen and draw someone out, the power to make the other person feel special and thereby raise their self-esteem.

Most people choose to marry or live with someone whose age approximates to their own. Not only are interests and friends more likely to be shared, but the prospect of bringing up children, and living together in old age, seems less daunting. Yet partners of wide age-difference can and do have extremely good, steady sex relationships. Sexual excitement and pleasure can be as intense – at times perhaps even more so – between a 24-year-old and a 54-year-old as between couples of similar age. The disparity is usually between a younger woman and an older man, but the reverse is not unusual. It is perhaps platitudinous to refer to the older partner as a father or mother figure. There may be childhood associations, but such relationships are frequently stable and satisfying to both, not in any way static.

Those relationships between couples of disparate age which break down quickly, do so for different reasons. Middle-age despair and fear over the passage of time, loss of youth and potency, or fecundity, is temporarily alleviated by an attractive young sex symbol. The symbol itself, male or female, may be flattered at first, especially if the older person has power, fame or money, but love is unlikely to flourish in such a climate. The relationship turns sour, depression re-emerges in the older person, and not infrequently the search for perpetual youth resumes.

SEX DIFFICULTIES

It is obvious that a good sexual relationship, whether heterosexual or homosexual, requires the partners to be sexually compatible.

317

Sexual compatibility on the simplest level merely implies that intercourse is possible. Compatibility varies enormously between couples. For a man there has to be physical attraction of some degree. Desire for sex by one partner may outstrip that of the other; compatibility should include tolerance. It is nearly always possible for a really compatible couple to reach a reasonable compromise.

Only rarely is intercourse impossible because of frigidity, muscle spasm and extreme pain on the woman's part. On the other hand, male impotence as a temporary or lasting problem is not at all uncommon.

Impotence is the inability of a man to maintain a full erection or to maintain one long enough for reasonable penetration, which for most women or homosexual partners is at least a few minutes. One of the most common complaints of a woman is that her man loses his erection soon after penetration, sometimes before ejaculation. A parallel male complaint is that he ejaculates prematurely, sometimes even before he enters, and this may occur with every partner or only with his wife. Clearly the former signifies a deeper-seated sexual problem. The vast majority of difficulties of this kind have a psychological cause. If impotence or relative impotence develops with one woman only, it is usually possible to discover why and perhaps correct it. A vital step in successful treatment is to enable the couple to see that the fault lies not with one or other partner but in the relationship itself. What is there between them to cause a man to see his partner as too frightening or forbidding for sex? For it is fear that distorts the neuronal impulses from the brain which are responsible for erection in a healthy man, and causes him to 'switch off'.

Dread of sexual failure or an inability to acknowledge and express anger or resentment are common characteristics of an impotent man. These are often reinforced by his partner's reactions and expectations. His wife sighs and turns aside immediately making no attempt to lessen his sense of failure, leaving him unhappy and resentful. Both partners in a relationship of this kind are likely to be sexually inexperienced and immature, ignorance or unrealistic expectations preventing either from helping the other. The man feels hopelessly inadequate and becomes increasingly reluctant to make sexual overtures. His wife sees herself as unattractive and unwanted. She is confused and angered by her husband's insistent reiterations that he loves and wants her, when all the time he seems by his inability not to. The result is sexual stalemate and bitterness.

Many men experience failure when they first start to make love, but unless their partner's reactions are so outrageous – anger and abuse, or laughter and ridicule – that they suffer a mortal blow to sexual confidence, anxiety rapidly fades and potency returns. A woman would have to be very insensitive and out of step with her lover to behave like this. In any reasonably good relationship each partner should have the ability to recognize the other's fears and uncertainties and to try to help in any way possible.

Impotence may sometimes develop when sex begins to diminish and love to become stronger. That love is antagonistic to sex for some people has been discussed earlier, and accounts for an initially satisfying sex life slowly fading into nothing.

Impotence can develop at any stage of a relationship. Often it reflects tensions and dissatisfactions, perhaps unexpressed and sometimes not even consciously sensed, between the partners. A wife may have devoted too much time to the children or her job, and her husband has become bored with her and sexually uninterested; he has perhaps begun an affair by way of compensation. Similar feelings could have arisen in the woman and she may no longer be physically attracted to her husband, no longer trying to arouse him. Impotence should indicate to a couple that it is time to examine the quality of their lives including the nature of their relationship, and to make changes. Sex is, or should be, a continuous reaffirmation of love, and an awareness of each other's needs.

Can a healthy couple have an acceptable relationship relatively free of tension without sex? Some couples do subsist sexually on tactile and oral stimulation alone. But more often than not the sense of incompleteness, felt especially by heterosexual women, after this kind of sex, only ends in aversion. Sexual desire may then be appeased in both partners by solitary masturbation, at least for a time. Sometimes sex can be switched into intellectual intercourse and shared activities; similarly, the drive of sex may be transformed by some into an urge to reform or change a system in some way.

It is a different matter when one or both of a couple is so disabled that normal everyday sexual activity becomes difficult or impossible. However disabled an individual is, sex of some kind is nearly always possible; it is often essential if a relationship is to survive, certainly if it is to grow.

319

Sex can help a paralysed man or woman to adapt to the disability and rebuild self-confidence. But it is far from easy for a husband or wife to adjust to physical changes in the spouse. All too often the couple retreat emotionally from one another, and although the healthy partner may hide this behind a flurry of helping hands, the core of their relationship is liable to be eroded eventually. Sex helps to preserve their deeper feelings and prevents the healthy partner indulging in pity. It lessens the risk that the disabled person might become childlike and overdependent.

An injury or illness often becomes the excuse for abandoning sex altogether, and this is especially likely when resentments have long been present. A heart attack in a man is sometimes followed by cessation of sex, although no real physical reason to stop exists. He rationalizes this on the grounds that the exertion of intercourse may cause his death. Alternatively, his wife may maintain that her husband is at risk and insist on his remaining celibate.

It is less usual for sex to stop after the wife suffers a heart attack. More commonly, women abandon sex after hysterectomy or after a mastectomy. Most women take some time to adjust to losing a breast, but some never do, and refuse sex for fear their husbands will see or feel the scar. The heart attack, mastectomy, or whatever the disability, has become a focus around which underlying tensions and resentments have surfaced and suppressed sex. Until the couple can readjust to one another and develop their relationship in such a way that sex can return, the situation will never improve; one partner will forever remain something of an invalid. Only when sex is resumed – and this requires considerable understanding and patience on the part of the husband – can the woman begin to recover a sense of wholeness and restore her self-esteem.

PORNOGRAPHY AND SEX

We are bombarded with sex literature and scenes on film and television which only a few years ago would have been proscribed or resulted in prosecution. Today it seems that only strongly sadistic pornography is illegal. Yet there is no convincing evidence that porn has undesirable consequences for society or the individual, despite the warnings of the Mrs Grundys of the world. Most of us are interested in the sexual antics of others, if only momentarily, and exhibit some degree of voyeurism. Straightforward copulation scenes do not hold attention for long, unless they are read or watched as a prelude to sex itself. But aberrant sexual practices frequently cause intense interest – an indication, perhaps, that some aspects of sex can still arouse shame and guilt in many of us. With time, shame of this kind is certain to decline in our society unless the sexual climate again becomes more restrictive. The sexual revolution has undoubtedly helped many people to accept their sexual inclinations as 'normal'. Oral and anal sex are no longer generally viewed as abnormal (although sodomy is still a legal offence in many countries), but the appearance of AIDS has put something of a damper on the practice among homosexuals. In pre-contraceptive days they were for some a useful form of contraception. Not everyone finds such activities enjoyable, however. Some feel that they are dirty and abnormal; others simply do not like such forms of sex. It is always most desirable for partners to talk openly to each other about what sexual behaviour most appeals to them and what they find unacceptable. Good sex requires understanding and compromise at times.

Aids to sexual excitement and arousal, such as pornographic videos and stories, are now widely available and used, and are especially helpful to couples whose taboos are still strong. Once the initial reserves are overcome, which is not difficult when *both* partners are in accord, such a couple can gain immense pleasure from, and understanding of, one another. Porn used in this way can be a sex enhancer. Its effects are bad only if it is allowed to dominate sex. It is then liable to demean a relationship.

MYTHS ABOUT SEX

Myths about sex abound in every age and society, reflecting people's anxieties and inadequacies. Ours is no exception. We constantly read about orgasm, its importance, the difference between clitoral and vaginal, between male and female, the number of orgasms possible in the space of 30 minutes, and so on. An orgasm occurs at the climax of sex, coincident with the sudden release of sexual tension. Its intensity and duration vary enormously, not only from person to person but in the same individual; one day it may last so long and so vividly as almost to have the quality of a mystical experience; on another occasion, with the same partner, orgasm compares to the *phut* of a damp squib. In both sexes orgasm is followed by satiety. Desire is appeased for a time, but this also

321

is extremely variable. A kind of sub-orgasm is experienced by some people, women especially, which can occur repeatedly. It has given rise to the myth of the insatiable woman – a concept that causes the less confident male to quail.

Another myth is that orgasm always occurs at the end of sex. With uninhibited and pent-up passion this is so. But with established partners, able to have sex when they will and who love one another, orgasm is by no means essential. There is enormous pleasure in making love for its own sake, in the physical contact, in the sense of intimacy or communication, silent or spoken. It is, to misquote Wordsworth, orgasm in tranquility. It is difficult for those who fear they are sexually inadequate to experience non-orgasmic sex. The man who continues intercourse, robot-like, until his wife has an orgasm and only then lets himself come, reveals a lack of self-confidence, an uncertainty of acceptance by his wife. He feels that if he does not please her by giving her an orgasm, she is certain to be displeased. He does not realize that such an attitude diminishes sex as an expression of love and closeness. Ideally, a couple who have lived together for a year or more should, if they are honest and open with one another about their sexual needs and fantasies, have no problems over when or whether to reach orgasm.

It is a common myth that with good sex both partners climax together. They may do, but more often than not one climaxes before the other. If the man ejaculates long before his partner is ready (in the vernacular 'is inconsiderate'), and if his wife wants an orgasm, he should then consider using other methods, manual or oral. Some men are embarrassed at first, or see such behaviour as undignified, a reflection of what they feel to be their inadequate potency. But many women cannot reach orgasm by vaginal intercourse alone. Penetration is pleasurable and necessary for their satisfaction, but for the most part they need oral sex or masturbation finally for a really satisfying orgasm. It is vital for a good sex relationship for both partners to understand and accept this as normal, and not to see it as a sign of any inadequacy on either side. Men, too, may have difficulties in reaching orgasm within the vagina. Often they continue to thrust out of insistent pride that they can and will climax, grinding away without pleasure and causing their partner discomfort and irritation.

A male myth, which stretches back through centuries, is that a man may not be able to satisfy a woman because his penis is too small. The fact that a flaccid penis is small is no bar to an adequate erection on which intercourse depends. A fully erect penis of whatever size is perfectly adequate for satisfying intercourse because with sexual excitement the vagina contracts around the penis, unless the woman is unable to respond.

GOOD, BAD, AND FUTURE SEX

Good sex is followed by a sense of well-being, an upsurge of exuberance and zest, a conviction that almost anything in life is possible. This is not simply the release of tension that follows orgasm for it is rare, for instance, after solitary masturbation or a casual affair. It is very much related to sex in a loving relationship, and to the sense of having shared an exalting experience.

Good sex is always a renewal of belief in oneself, a reaffirmation of goodness. It brings back childhood sensual pleasures, marvellous scenes and experiences, memories of things only half glimpsed and perhaps forbidden at the time. Past and present come together in lovemaking. For each of us, therefore, sex is unique and cannot be fully understood by or communicated to a partner, however close. Sex is both shared and solitary, both a communal and individual activity. But these intense experiences during sex do not occur every day. They reflect the nature of a relationship and what is happening within it. Most sexual encounters can be described as enjoyable and relaxing, nothing more or less – and occasionally, dull.

At the other end of the scale, sex can become disastrous or nonexistent as two people grow apart from each other and for whatever reason cease to communicate. Resentment, despair and loneliness build up. Sex, if it continues, becomes mechanical and separated from affection. Sooner or later such a couple is likely to split up.

The sexual revolution is unfinished. Sexual standards continue to change; differences in male and female sexual roles have become less; marriage is no longer a necessity, although still sought by people wanting children. Today it is accepted that we can change partners through divorce or mutual consent without stigma. Society no longer seriously constrains or instructs us to do one thing or another. Yet there is something in human nature which wants to make a perfect and lasting one-to-one relationship. This is at variance with a perhaps equally strong urge to seek the refreshment and inspiration of change.

Obviously, one ideal of sexual fulfilment on that basis would be the love affair or marriage that could incorporate all these aspects – a couple, for instance, whose passionate and trusting relationship was stimulated by other people's minds and bodies being part of their union. Most of us are unlikely to achieve such an ideal at present.

Many seek a Tristan-and-Isolde type of relationship, longing to express and experience their sexual love to the full, however short-lived the relationship might be. Those who have known such passionate love can be grateful – but aspiring lovers should remember that those legendary ones paid a hefty price for their experience, and those around them were all but destroyed in the process.

It is this two-sided nature of sex, both constructive and yet potentially destructive, which makes it such an unpredictable force, both for individuals and for society. What course the sexual revolution will take from here on is anybody's guess.

GLOSSARY

*Many words freely used by doctors
are confusing to some people and
if used in a different context mean
something quite different. It is for
this reason that a glossary has been
included in this book.*

Abortion Medical word meaning
the surgical, medical or natural
termination of the pregnancy
before the embryo or fetus can
live independently of its mother.

Adhesion Medical name for scar
tissue that binds tissues
together. This always occurs
internally, to some degree,
following an operation.

Adolescence The time of
physical and mental
development occurring between
the onset of puberty and
adulthood.

Adrenal glands Two endocrine
glands, one on top of each
kidney, which produce hormones
such as adrenaline,
noradrenaline, cortisol and
aldosterone, and small amounts
of male and female hormones.

Allergen *See* Allergy.

Allergy Unusual sensitivity of
the body towards a specific
substance or substances,
generally causing the localized
release in the body of histamine,
which results in the common
symptoms of skin rashes, watery
eyes or a running nose.
Substances that provoke an
allergic reaction are called
allergens.

Anaemia Condition of the blood
in which there is insufficient
haemoglobin, the oxygen-
carrying constituent of red blood
cells.

Androgen A male hormone.

Anorexia nervosa
Psychological disorder in which
a person starves obsessively. It is
most common in young women
but also occasionally occurs in
men and older women. The
condition requires skilled
psychiatric treatment.

Ante- Before, prior to.

Anterior Before, at the front.

Anti- Against, in order to
counteract, to prevent.

Antibiotics Group of drugs
prescribed to treat bacterial
infections; there are many types.

Antigen Foreign substances in
the body that provoke the
formation of antibodies.

Anus The orifice at the lower end
of the alimentary canal normally
held closed by the anal sphincter;
the opening from the rectum.

Arousal Sexually, the initial
reaction of the body to sexual
stimuli, generally involving
deeper breathing, heightened
sensation, the erection of erectile
tissue, and so on.

Arteriosclerosis Hardening of
the arteries. *See* atherosclerosis.

325

Artificial insemination The fertilization of an egg using artificial technology, either by the introduction of sperm into the cervix or in the laboratory (*in vitro*).

Atherosclerosis Hardening and thickening of the arteries.

Bacteria Microscopic, single-celled organisms.

Bartholin's glands A pair of lubricating glands situated at the back of the entrance to the vagina.

Behaviourism Form of psychology based on the observation of human or animal behaviour.

Behaviour therapy Form of psychiatric treatment in which behaviour is modified or altered by appropriate rewards or punishments.

Bestiality Sexual intercourse between human and animal.

Birth control *See* Contraception.

Bisexual Able to derive sexual pleasure with a person of either sex; or one who is an hermaphrodite.

Blastocyst The very early stage in the development of the fertilized egg when it is a fluid-containing ball of cells.

Blood pressure Measure of the effectiveness of the heart as a pump of blood round the body, taken as a ratio between the pressure of the beat (systole, when the blood is being forcibly pumped) and the subsequent rest (diastole).

Bronchodilator Drug which causes the air passages to the lungs to expand and thus take in more air to ease breathing.

Cap A female barrier method of contraception using a rubber ring to cover the cervix (neck of the womb) and upper end of the vagina.

Cardiovascular disease Disease of the heart and the blood vessels.

Castration Removal or destruction of the testes or ovaries.

Catheter Flexible tube made of rubber or plastic used to duct fluids into or out of a body cavity.

Cautery, Cauterization Destruction of tissue by heat, electricity, acid or, sometimes, laser, in order to remove such things as warts, stop persistent nosebleeds or to prevent infection in the tissues such as the cervix.

Cell A basic, microscopic, enclosed structure that may survive on its own or be the minute part of a much larger organism.

Cervical smear (test) Test to detect cancer cells in the cervix of the womb by painlessly removing a few cells and studying them under a microscope.

Cervix Literally 'neck', but referring almost exclusively in this book to the neck of the womb, the connection between uterus and vagina.

Change of life In a woman the time around the cessation of menstruation (menopause) with its accompanying physical and psychological changes. It is also called the climacteric.

Chromosome A string of thousands of genes in the nucleus of a cell. In a human cell there are 23 pairs of chromosomes, each pair spiralled together, but in the sperm and ova there are only 23 single chromosomes.

Chronic Lasting for a considerable time; the opposite of acute.

Claudication Cramp in a muscle (particularly in the calf) during exercise; literally means lameness.

Climax The moment of greatest sexual excitement, commonly called the orgasm.

Coeliac disease Disorder of the cells lining the small intestine.

Coil *See* Intra-uterine device.

Coitus Medical word for sexual intercourse.

Coitus interruptus Sexual intercourse between a man and a woman in which the man withdraws the penis from the vagina just prior to ejaculation.

Conception The moment when the male sperm penetrates and fertilizes the egg. The male chromosomes combine with the female chromosomes to produce the nucleus of a new cell. *See* Fertilization.

Condom *See* Sheath.

Congenital At and from birth. Usually used to refer to any condition or abnormality found at birth.

Contraception Methods by which conception may be avoided.

Contra-indications Reasons for a doctor not prescribing a particular form of treatment that might otherwise have been prescribed.

Corpus luteum The cells that remain on the ovary after the egg has left the Graafian follicle. It produces the hormone progesterone.

Cowper's glands A pair of glands, adjacent to the prostate gland, which help in the nutrition of sperm.

Crabs An infestation of lice that live in the pubic hair.

Cunnilingus Oral stimulation by mouth and tongue of a woman's clitoris and vagina.

Cyst Fluid-filled swelling in body tissues.

Cystitis Bladder infection, generally leading to painful and increased frequency of urination.

Cystocele Swelling of the bladder, akin to a hernia, into the front wall of the vagina, as part of a prolapse of the uterus.

Debility Weakness, lethargy.

Depression A change in mood in which there are feelings of hopelessness and fatigue, lack of enthusiasm, lowering of sexual drive and interest, lack of initiative, and loss of normal ability to make judgments; and, in severer forms of depression, suicidal thoughts or even the development of true psychotic illness with sensations of persecution, hallucinations, etc.

Deep-vein thrombosis *See* Thrombosis.

Diaphragm Female contraceptive method known

327

also as the Cap and Dutch cap. *See* Cap.

Dildo An artificial, erect penis, used for sexual stimulation.

Dutch cap *See* Cap.

Dysmenorrhoea Painful menstrual periods.

Ectopic pregnancy Implantation of a fertilized ovum outside the womb, usually in a fallopian tube.

Ejaculation Involuntary reflex action of the penis and associated sex organs to emit semen at orgasm, generally in a few short bursts.

Embryo The earliest stage in the development of a human baby, from the moment the ovum is fertilized (conception) to the end of the third month of pregnancy. Thereafter until birth it is called a fetus.

Endocrine gland Sometimes called a ductless gland, it produces and secretes hormones into the blood circulation to reach the tissues in other parts of the body that will respond to the hormone. An example of this is the way in which the anterior pituitary gland stimulates the ovaries or testes.

Endometriosis A condition in which parts of the womb's lining (endometrium) are found in unusual situations such as on the ovary or within the muscles of the womb. It may cause pain and heavy menstruation.

Endometrium Membrane that lines the interior surface of the womb, which thickens during the menstrual cycle and then is shed during menstruation.

Endoscopy The use of an instrument – now generally a fibre-optic one – passed through a body orifice or artificial opening to examine internal cavities or passages.

Enzyme A chemical which, in minute amounts, helps to break down complex chemical substances without being affected itself.

Epididymis Part of the testis in which sperm mature before passing into the sperm duct (vas deferens).

Erectile Able to stiffen, to become hard, as of the penis or clitoris through the infusion of blood following sexual arousal.

Erogenous zones Areas of the body, which vary from person to person, that are specially sensitive to sexual stimulation.

Erosion The breaking down of the surface of body tissues from causes such as bacterial invasion or old age.

Fallopian tube One of two tubes attached to the womb.

Fellatio Oral stimulation of a man's penis.

Fertilization Penetration of an ovum by a sperm to form a single 46-chromosome cell. *See* Conception.

Fetish Originally this referred to an object thought to possess magical powers so it was regarded with particular love or fear. Today, it is an object that has sexual significance and may be used as a help in normal sexual stimulation; occasionally, it is the only thing which gives sexual satisfaction.

Fetus (or Foetus) The stage of development of a human baby in the womb from the end of the third month of pregnancy until birth. *See* Embryo.

Fibre-optic Made of flexible glass or plastic fibres which conduct light and can therefore convey an image from one end of their length to the other. *See* Endoscopy.

Fibroid Benign growth of fibrous tissue in the uterus or vagina.

Follicle-stimulating hormone Hormone produced by the anterior pituitary gland that stimulates the production of oestrogen by the ovary and of testosterone by the testis.

French letter *See* Sheath.

Frigidity The loss of normal sexual response. It is most commonly experienced in women and in extreme form may produce vaginismus.

Frotterurism Derivation of sexual gratification by rubbing against another person, often a complete stranger.

Gay bowel syndrome A medical term used to describe a number of intestinal infections caused by anus-oriented sexual practices.

Gender The sex of an individual – male or female.

Gene One of the many thousand components of a chromosome. Each gene carries particular 'instructions' for a certain characteristic, such as a blood group or eye colour.

Genitalia Reproductive organs, that may be external, such as the penis and vulva; or internal, such as the prostate or uterus.

Gestation The length of time from the moment of conception to childbirth. This is about 280 days in humans.

Gonad Term used for an ovary or a testis.

Graafian follicle The egg breaks out of a small cyst, the Graafian follicle, that develops in the middle of each month on one of the ovaries. It also produces the hormone oestrogen.

Gynaecologist Specialist in the disorders of women.

Gynaecomastia Increased breast growth in either sex.

Haemodialysis Purifying the blood by filtration through a membrane in a dialysis machine.

Hallucination False awareness by sight, sound or feeling of something that does not exist.

Heartburn Burning sensation in the oesophagus caused by the rising of acids from the stomach, generally through indigestion or overeating.

Hermaphrodite Individual who has both testes and ovaries. Hermaphrodites are rare.

Heterosexual A person who is sexually attracted to someone of the opposite sex.

Hodgkin's disease A form of cancer that affects the lymph glands. It is commonest in young adults.

Homosexual A person who is sexually attracted to another of his or her own sex; the term is commonly used of men rather than women. *See* Lesbian.

Hormones Chemical substances

produced by the cells of one organ or gland to regulate or stimulate the activity of other cells or organs elsewhere in the body. Some hormones, such as those in the intestinal tract, may act on adjacent structures while others, such as those produced by endocrine glands, affect more distant parts.

Hot flush Wave of warmth felt across the face and upper body; it is a common symptom of the menopause and sometimes accompanied by sweating.

Hymen Fold of membranous tissue round the vaginal entrance of a girl. The hymen will stretch or tear naturally during sexual intercourse and with the use of internal tampons.

Hypogonadism Condition in which physical and sexual development has been retarded due to reduction or lack of production of sex hormones.

Hypothalamus Part of the brain responsible for instinctual drives like hunger, thirst and sex, and for body temperature regulation.

Hysterectomy Surgical removal of the womb.

Immune system The body's natural mechanism for defence against invasion by disease.

Implantation When the fertilized ovum attaches itself to the inner lining of the uterus, the endometrium.

Impotence In a man, the inability to produce an erection. It is not the same as sterility.

Infection Disease caused by bacteria, viruses, fungi or various tiny organisms.

Infertility Inability to achieve pregnancy when normal sexual intercourse has taken place over a period of time.

Inflammation Localized body tissue reaction to injury or disease or heat, chemicals or allergens, generally resulting in swelling, superficial redness and warmth, and pain.

Injectable Form of contraceptive, a spermicide, that can be 'injected' by syringe into the vagina.

Interstitial The space between body cells.

Intra-uterine device Contraceptive method known as the coil or by the initials IUD or IUCD, comprising a piece of plastic or metal that is inserted through the cervix into the womb.

In vitro In a test-tube, glass container, or other artificial environment. In contrast to *in vivo* – in the living body.

IUD and IUCD *See* Intra-uterine device.

Lactation The presence and the yielding of milk in a suckling mother's breasts.

Laparoscopy Examination of the inside of the abdomen by means of an instrument called a laparoscope. *See* Endoscopy.

Latent Hidden; potentially available but not apparent.

Lesbian A woman who is sexually attracted to another woman.

Libido Term describing

conscious or subconscious sexual drive and desire.

Ligament Band of fibrous tissue that supports and confines a joint or an organ.

Loop *See* Intra-uterine contraceptive device.

Luteinizing hormone Hormone, produced by the anterior pituitary gland, that helps initiate ovulation in conjunction with the follicle-stimulating hormone and maintains the production of oestrogen.

Mastectomy Surgical removal of all or part of a woman's breast.

Masturbation Manual stimulation of one's own or anothers genitals.

Menarche A girl's first menstruation.

Menopause The cessation of monthly menstruation. *See* Change of Life.

Menstrual cycle Time between the first day of one period and the first day of the next. Varies in length but in most women is about 28 days.

Menstruation Natural bloody discharge, lasting from three to seven days, from the uterus about every 28 days or so in a woman of child-bearing age who is not pregnant.

Mini-Pill Form of the contraceptive pill containing the hormone progesterone (and not the hormone oestrogen).

Miscarriage Common term for a spontaneous abortion.

Mons Veneris Sometimes called 'Mount of Venus', the soft tissue (and pubic hair) covering the front part of the pelvic bone in

women. It is called the mons pubis in both sexes.

Mucus Slimy secretion of the body's mucous membranes; it acts both to lubricate and to protect.

Obesity Condition of overweight (at least 15 per cent above the average for age and height) that may result directly or indirectly in the need for medical treatment.

Obstetrician Specialist in the care of women during pregnancy, labour, childbirth and the period just following childbirth. *See* Gynaecologist.

Oestrogen A female sex hormone, several of which are normally present in a woman's body, and to a minor extent in men, and are important to the menstrual cycle and the maintenance of other secondary sexual characteristics. Synthetic oestrogens are used in the Pill and in other forms of treatment including cancer of the prostate in men. *See* Progesterone.

Oophorectomy Surgical removal of an ovary.

Oral sex Stimulation of the sexual partner's genitals, possibly to orgasm, by mouth.

Orgasm Sexual climax.

Ovulation The release by an ovary of an ovum (or egg).

Ovum A female sex cell (or egg) which contains 23 chromosomes. *See* Conception, Sperm.

Pap smear *See* Cervical smear.

Peer group A group of people to which an individual is attracted and tries to imitate. This behaviour may be socially constructive, or, in some instances, anti-social and delinquent.

Pessary Medical preparation, similar to a suppository, which dissolves at body temperature, that is inserted into the vagina and contains a drug or chemical for use as a contraceptive or to treat infection.

Phallus The penis.

Pharmacopoeia Reference book containing information on drugs, their preparation and composition, their effects and side-effects, and any legal requirements for those who prescribe or dispense them.

Phlegm Mucus in or from the air passages of the head or lungs.

Phobia Extreme fear or dread, eg, claustrophobia, the fear of being shut in a confined space.

Pill Oral contraceptive in the form of pills taken by women.

Pituitary gland Extension of the brain responsible for the secretion of a number of hormones some of which control other hormonal secretions around the body. It consists of two parts, the anterior and posterior glands.

Polyp Small growth – normally benign – on a short stalk upon one of the body's mucous membranes, common in the nose, the uterine cervix and the colon.

Post-coital Immediately following sexual intercourse.

Posterior To the rear, at the back; behind.

Premature ejaculation Ejaculation before vaginal or anal penetration or the partner has reached full arousal.

Pre-menstrual tension Physical and psychological changes that may occur in the week or so before menstruation. Common symptoms are breast tenderness, headache, weight gain (due to fluid retention), anxiety and depression.

Prepuce The anatomical name for the foreskin.

Procreation The generating of children.

Progesterone Female sex hormone important in the second half of the menstrual cycle as the main cause of the monthly preparation of the uterine lining for a fertilized ovum. *See* Oestrogen.

Progestogen A synthesized form of progesterone, commonly used in the contraceptive pill.

Prolactin Hormone responsible for stimulating the supply of milk in the breasts of a mother after childbirth.

Prolapse Downward displacement of an internal body organ.

Promiscuity A term describing having – or the freedom to have – a number of sexual partners.

Prostate gland Gland beneath a man's bladder responsible for secretions that sustain the sperm before ejaculation.

Psychoanalytical Of the system for treating mental disorders originally defined by Sigmund Freud.

Psychosexual Of the way a person thinks of and about sex;

of the effect that mental imagery and associations have on sexual performance.

Psychosomatic Of the effect that the mind – its convictions and desires, conscious and unconscious – has on the condition of the body.

Puberty The physical changes that take place between the onset of sexual development and its completion. *See* Adolescence.

Rape The forcible use by one person of another's body for sexual gratification. Whether this involves vaginal, anal or oral penetration is a matter of legal definition.

Rectum The final part of the colon (from where faeces are passed through the anus); the back passage.

Refractory period Stage in a course of treatment at which the condition apparently remains static, fails to improve.

Retrograde Going backwards, reverting; worse.

Sado-masochism Sexual gratification gained by inflicting (sadism), or the endurance of, (masochism) pain.

Salpingitis Inflammation of a fallopian tube.

Scrotum Wrinkled sac behind the penis which maintains the enclosed testes at a slightly lower temperature than the rest of the body.

Semen Fluid ejaculated from the penis at orgasm containing sperm and secretions from the prostate gland and seminal vesicles.

Sex stereotyping Apportioning different roles to males and females.

Sexually-transmitted diseases Diseases contracted through sexual intercourse or through sexual practices.

Sheath Contraceptive also known as a French letter or condom, comprising a thin rubber or plastic sheath progressively rolled on to a man's erect penis before intercourse in order to contain semen on ejaculation.

Smegma Sebaceous secretion of the glans penis.

Sodomy Term commonly used for anal intercourse. It can refer also to bestiality and oral intercourse.

Spastic Medically this usually means remaining in a rigid or cramplike condition.

Sperm Male sex cell containing 23 chromosomes. *See* Ovum.

Spermatocele A cyst of the epididymis.

Spermicide Form of contraceptive comprising a jelly, foam, pessary or liquid preparation that can be syringed or placed high in the vagina to kill sperm.

STD Abbreviation for sexually-transmitted disease.

Sterility In a sexual sense, the inability to have children. *See* Impotence, Infertility.

Sterilization Surgery or natural event in the body that prevents a man or woman from having children. In a man, the surgical operation is called a vasectomy and halts the passage of sperm; in women, the fallopian tubes are either tied or removed, so that no ovum reaches the womb.

Temporal lobe In the brain, the outer, lower side of each hemisphere.

Testis (or testicle) One of two ovoid organs in a man's scrotum. Each testis is the site of sperm production and the hormone, testosterone.

Testosterone Male sex hormone produced in the testes, responsible for the development and maintenance of male secondary sexual characteristics.

Thrombosis The formation of a blood clot (thrombus) in an artery or a vein. Deep-vein thrombosis is thrombosis in a vein that is not visible on the surface.

Transsexual A person who by conviction, temperament and disposition is sure that he or she has somehow been born in a body of the inappropriate sex.

Transvestite A person who dresses in the clothing of the opposite sex.

Trauma Damage or injury to the body or psychological shock.

Ultrasound High-frequency sound waves focused into a beam and used by a specialist for diagnosis or therapy.

Urethra Tube that ducts urine from the bladder to the outside world, considerably longer in men than in women.

Vaginismus Extreme form of frigidity in women in which the muscles surrounding the entrance to the vagina go into spasm, thus preventing sexual intercourse.

Vas deferens The sperm duct between the testis in the scrotum and the seminal vesicles in the groin by the bladder.

Vasectomy *See* Sterilization.

Venereal Of sexual intercourse, sexually-transmitted. (Literally 'of Venus'.) Venereal diseases are legally classified in most countries.

Venereophobia Excessive fear of sexually transmitted disease that can sometimes produce symptoms of a geniune disease.

Vesicle In the tissues, a container of fluid; thus either a bladder (such as the gall bladder) or a fluid-filled blister (as in shingles).

Voyeur One who derives sexual gratification by watching (from a secure hiding-place) others in a state of undress.

Vulva The external urogenital area of the female body.

INDEX

Index

Index

Index

Popper, Karl, 199
pornography, 320–1
  sadistic, 275
post-coital contraception, 43
  use after rape, 43
post-coital test for male infertility, 53
posthitis, 160
pox *see* syphilis
pre-menstrual tension (PMT), 28
pregnancy, 14
  ectopic, 18, 38, 39, 42
  fear of, 33
  herpes infection during, 154
  infection during, as cause of
    congenital abnormality in baby,
    151
  in older women, 50
  significance of fitness in, 14
  termination of, 43, 49
  transmission of syphilis to foetus
    during, 178
priapism, 87, 168
proctalgia fugax, 168
proctitis, 168–9
progesterone, 17, 20, 40
progestogen, 39, 41, 42
prolactin, 62, 79
prolapse, 87
promiscuity, 112, 113
  among teenagers, 312
  associated with syphilis, 175
  associated with trichomoniasis, 180
  increase in, 310
  and male homosexuals, 238–9
  and nymphomania, 257
  and risk of herpes infection, 154
  and sexual liberation, 213
prostate gland, 23, 181
  cancer of the, 169
  enlargement of the, 169
  removal *see* prostatectomy
prostatectomy, 88, 169
prostatitis, 165, 169, 183
prostatomegaly, benign, in increasing
  age, 169
prostitutes,
  and incestuous relationships, 250–1
  and sado-masochistic practices, 279
  in the twentieth century, 212
  in Victorian times, 211, 212
pruritis *see* itching
pseudo-hermaphrodite, 188
psoriasis, 170

psychoanalytic theory, 196–202
Psychology of Sex Differences, The, 192
psychosexual development, theories of,
  biological, 195–6
  cognitive-development, 194–5
  psychoanalytic, 196–202
  social-learning, 193–4
puberty, 25–9, 205–6
  development of secondary sexual
    characteristics, 15, 25

rape, 264–74
  the Bible and, 265
  fantasies about paternal, 200
  legal definition, 264–5
  need for education and legal reform to
    prevent, 272
  police attitudes to claims of, 266–8
  religious attitudes to, 271
  reported incidence of, 268–9
  victim's reactions to, 270–1
Rape Trauma Syndrome, 271
rashes in genital region, 170, 181
rectum, inflammation of the, 168
  associated with STD, 168
Reiter's disease, 165, 169, 171–2
religious attitudes,
  Christian, 240, 271, 311
  Hindu, 32, 48
  Muslim, 32, 34, 48, 271
  Protestant, 32, 251, 253
  Roman Catholic, 32, 44, 49, 220, 251,
    253
  Sikh, 32
Rooth, Dr F G, 225

sado-masochism, 274–80
  bondage in, 276
  discipline in, 277–8
  fantasies in, 276
safe period, 44
  Billing's method, 44, 183
  calendar method, 44
  temperature guide, 44
safer sex, 122, 128
salmonellosis, 172
salpingitis, 58, 166, 172
Sarrel & Sarrel, 102
satyriasis, 280–2
scabies, 172–3
schizophrenia, 89
scoptophilia, 227, 282, 296, 299
scrotum, 22, 77, 161, 181

abnormal swelling within, 162
goose skin appearance of, 160
infection of hair follicles surrounding,
   161
lesions from scabies, 172
varicose veins in, 162
sebaceous cysts in genitalia, 162, 177
self-esteem, 66, 81
semen, 24, 182
analysis, 53, 54
serum hepatitis *see* hepatitis B
sex assignment, 188, 189
sex change operation, 189, 287
sex differences, 191–3
aggressiveness and, 192, 195
anatomical factors in childhood, 203,
   204
cultural influences and, 190–1
psychological factors in, 192
see also gender identity
Sex Offenders, 276
sex, psychology of, 187–218
sex therapist, 81
sexual anatomy and physiology, 11–30
sexual arousal *see* sexual response
sexual attraction, 306–8
sexual desire, altered,
in mental illness, 89
in thyroid hormone disturbance, 90
sexual desire, loss of, 76, 80, 83, 88, 89
sexual deviations, 216, 217, 218, 219–98
sexual functioning,
alcohol and impaired, 92
drugs and impairment of, 66, 79, 89
drugs to improve, 89
effect of prescribed drugs on, 94
effects of physical disease on, 70
sexual harassment at work, 230
sexual hygiene, 107–8
sexual intercourse,
after episiotomy, 75
angina during, 68
excuses for abstaining from, 320
pain during, 166
physical loving without, 103, 105
positions, 68, 70, 82, 83, 107
and recurrence of herpes, 153
substitutes for, 67
and transmission of HIV, 121
sexual liberation, 141, 213, 257, 303
Sexual Offences Act (1956), 220
sexual orientation, 231, 232

counselling homosexuals to adjust to,
   244–7
genetic disposition as determinant of,
   243
hormonal balance as determinant in,
   241
and nymphomania, 258
sexual problems,
after hysterectomy, 80
after menopause, 71
caused by arthritis, 68–9
caused by depression, 89
caused by diseases of the digestive
   system, 72
caused by epilepsy, 74
caused by excessive alcohol, 92
caused by heroin addiction, 93
caused by hypertension, 79
caused by incompatibility, 318
caused by kidney failure, 82
caused by loss of limb, 81–2
caused by multiple sclerosis, 83
caused by ostomies, 84
caused by thyroid hormone
   disturbance, 90
as consequence of heart attacks, 76–7
in women, 75
sexual response, 99
cultural determinants in female,
   210–11
female, 21, 206–7
in lesbians, 207
male, 24–5, 206–8
physical changes during, 29–30
sexual revolution, 114, 209, 321, 323
sexual skills, 100
sexual stimulant,
alcohol as, 92
amyl nitrite used as, 92, 116
cannabis as, 93
see also fetishism
sexual stimulation,
by means of body massagers, 107, 109
by means of erotic literature, 107,
   109, 216
by means of erotic videos, 74, 107, 109
by means of pornography, 216
by means of vibrators, 69, 76, 91, 109,
   169, 215
pornographic aids in, 321
of self *see* masturbation
in women, 214
Sexual Turning Points, 102

343

Index

JANE R. HIRSCHMANN
CAROL H. MUNTER

Overcoming Overeating

Lose weight naturally. Enjoy the food you most desire.
Forget your preoccupation with eating and weight. Discover the freedom of no restraints. Give up dieting forever.

Overcoming Overeating makes this all possible, for the
authors have returned eating to its natural place in life,
so that food becomes something to be enjoyed rather than
feared.

Concentrating on the normal physiological hunger that
we all experience Jane R. Hirschmann and Carol H.
Munter help you to break out of the lonely cycle of diet,
binge, recrimination and self-loathing. Both practical and
reassuring, they offer radical, realistic guidance on how
to conquer an obsession and restore the compulsive eater's
self-esteem.

'This is the best book on dealing with compulsive eating
that I've read. The authors themselves are veterans of
"mouth hunger" as opposed to "stomach hunger", and the
compassion and understanding with which they address
you, the reader, magically motivate you to join them in
becoming a noncompulsive eater.' Penelope Russianoff,
author, *When Am I Going To Be Happy?*

DAVID LEWIS

Helping Your Anxious Child

'Anxiety is a curse which can cast a damaging spell over your child's life. But there is a cure. It is to be found in this book – and in your hands.'

Is anxiety making your child's life a misery – causing problems at school, difficulties in making friends or facing new experiences, even affecting physical health?

Chronic anxiety is a serious problem which may be general, may be a specific anxiety about taking exams or doing sums, or a phobia about anything from trains or spiders to eating in public or going to the toilet. It can, however, be treated successfully, and David Lewis offers practical guidelines to parents of anxious children.

By being 'positive, patient, persistent and prudent', you can transform your child into a happy, confident member of society.

ALICE KING

Winewise

How many times have you wished you knew what wine to order in a restaurant, or which bottle to buy from the numerous shelves in the supermarket?

Written in a lively, amusing and utterly unpompous way. *Winewise* dispels all the snobbery and myths about wine.

To be Winewise, you need to know the basic tricks of the trade: which wines to look out for and when, which to use as a benchmark on a restaurant wine list, which cheap wines to go for and which to avoid. You need to know how you can deduce the contents of a bottle by its shape; what type of wine glasses to choose; when to use decanters and when not; how to read a label; how to taste and what goes best with the food you're eating. And you will also discover here all the important wine-growing regions, their characteristics and their best bargains.

Winewise will give encouragement and confidence to anyone who buys wine, would like to know more about it, but who believes, above all, that wine-drinking is fun.

Alice King is Britain's youngest nationally read wine writer.

GILLIAN PEARKES

Complete Home Winemaking

If you think home winemaking is a complicated and messy process with an inferior end-product, then this book will show you that it is not. It is a fascinating and relatively simple pursuit, inexpensive to engage in with richly rewarding results.

This new edition has been completely revised, and embellished with attractive and informative drawings, to include new recipes and all the most modern scientific techniques, while still concentrating on making wines naturally and with natural products.

So for those who already enjoy the art of home winemaking, there are many new and exciting recipes for all kinds of wine: fresh-fruit wine, dried-fruit wine, flower wine, cereal wine, vegetable wine, and also cider, mead, perry and liqueurs. And for those who are making their first cautious step into home winemaking, this book will guide you through to the most ambitious wines.

HUGO CORNWALL

Datatheft

Datatheft: the undetectable crime that grows wherever new opportunities exist. The typical computer criminal is not the genius programmer or hacker, but the middle-ranking, apparently loyal employee with inside knowledge. Computer fraud is a problem that goes to the heart of management responsibility. Read this book – you may never know what you're missing.

The bestselling author of the controversial *Hacker's Handbook*, Hugo Cornwall, a computer security consultant, is uniquely qualified to describe the nature of the crime that has no discernible parameters. Even in law it is an area of lightest grey.

'Required reading in every computer department in every company in the country.' *PC Week*

SIMON FRITH

Facing the Music

What frustrates the rock fans and critics of today is the
tenet held by so many of their contemporaries that current
music should be measured in terms of what it meant
twenty years ago. Now that the 45 r.p.m. record – the
symbol of that notion – looks set to go the same way as
the 78, the music which so persistently seeks novelty,
sensation and change deserves some critical redefinition.

Simon Frith's invigorating anthology fills the void.

Jon Savage suggests that youth, the core market of rock,
has won the battle to define its counterculture whilst
assimilating itself just as surely into shopcounter
commercialism. . .

Mary Harron expounds the idea of pop as a commodity,
that hype is not simply the peripheral patter to good
music but the crucial vernacular that identifies it. . .

Simon Frith himself assesses the implications of techno-
logical and cross-media developments without succumb-
ing to the simplistic lament for lost innocence and
authenticity. . .

Further contributions include support for the black cross-
over into white sound, and a history and rationale of
rock's fundamental institution – the radio. Original and
thought-provoking, these essays challenge the accepted
constructs of rock ideology.

'Required reading for every music fan who complains that
the universe of rock & roll has been reduced to one never-
ending jeans commercial.'

Metroland

A Selected List of Non-Fiction Available from Mandarin Books

While every effort is made to keep prices low, it is sometimes necessary to increase prices at short notice. Mandarin Paperbacks reserves the right to show new retail prices on covers which may differ from those previously advertised in the text or elsewhere.

The prices shown below were correct at the time of going to press.

☐	7493 0109 0	**The Warrior Queens**	Antonia Fraser	£4.99
☐	7493 0108 2	**Mary Queen of Scots**	Antonia Fraser	£5.99
☐	7493 0010 8	**Cromwell**	Antonia Fraser	£7.50
☐	7493 0106 6	**The Weaker Vessel**	Antonia Fraser	£5.99
☐	7493 0013 2	**The Crash**	Mihir Bose	£4.99
☐	7493 0014 0	**The Demon Drink**	Jancis Robinson	£4.99
☐	7493 0015 9	**The Health Scandal**	Vernon Coleman	£4.99
☐	7493 0016 7	**Vietnam – The 10,000 Day War**	Michael Maclear	£3.99
☐	7493 0022 1	**The Super Saleswoman**	Janet Macdonald	£4.99
☐	7493 0023 X	**What's Wrong With Your Rights?**	Cook/Tate	£4.99
☐	7493 0196 1	**Afganistan**	George Arney	£3.99
☐	7493 0061 2	**Voyager**	Yeager/Rutan	£3.99
☐	7493 0113 9	**Peggy Ashcroft**	Michael Billington	£3.99
☐	7493 0027 2	**Journey Without End**	David Bolton	£3.99
☐	7493 0177 5	**The Troubles**	Mick O'Connor	£4.99

All these books are available at your bookshop or newsagent, or can be ordered direct from the publisher. Just tick the titles you want and fill in the form below.

Mandarin Paperbacks, Cash Sales Department, PO Box 11, Falmouth, Cornwall TR10 9EN.

Please send cheque or postal order, no currency, for purchase price quoted and allow the following for postage and packing:

UK
55p for the first book, 22p for the second book and 14p for each additional book ordered to a maximum charge of £1.75.

BFPO and Eire
55p for the first book, 22p for the second book and 14p for each of the next seven books, thereafter 8p per book.

Overseas Customers
£1.00 for the first book plus 25p per copy for each additional book.

NAME (Block letters) ....

ADDRESS ....

....